The 'Ukulele

The 'Ukulele

A HISTORY

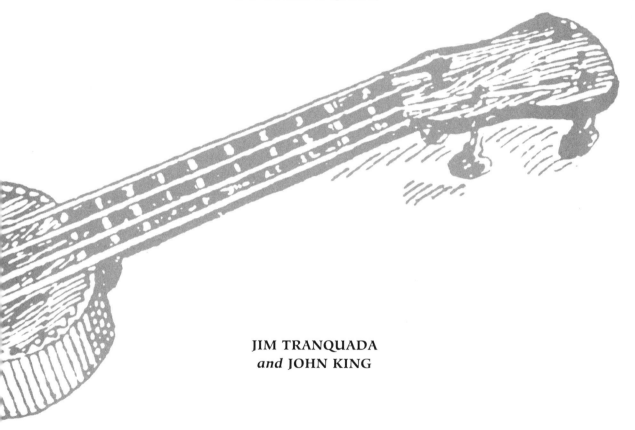

JIM TRANQUADA
and JOHN KING

A Latitude 20 Book

University *of* Hawai'i Press
HONOLULU

17 16 15 14 13 12   6 5 4 3 2 1

Library of Congress Cataloging-in-Publication Data
Tranquada, Jim.
    The ʻukulele : a history / Jim Tranquada and John King.
        p.   cm.
    "A latitude 20 book."
    Includes bibliographical references and index.
    ISBN 978-0-8248-3544-6 (hardcover : alk. paper)—ISBN 978-0-8248-3634-4 (pbk. : alk. paper)
    1. Ukulele.   2. Ukulele—Hawaii—History.   I. King, John.   II. Title.
    ML1015.U5T73 2012
    787.8'91909—dc23
                                                                                2011052157

Unless otherwise identified, images are from the authors' collections.

Designed by Mardee Melton
Printed by Sheridan Books, Inc.

CONTENTS

Acknowledgments   ◆   vii

Introduction   ◆   1

CHAPTER 1. These Little Instruments, of Which They Are So Fond   ◆   5

CHAPTER 2. The Sound of Pa, Ko, Li   ◆   20

CHAPTER 3. The National Instrument of Hawaii   ◆   37

CHAPTER 4. Have You Seen the Bouncing Flea?   ◆   55

CHAPTER 5. A Landscape Set to Music   ◆   74

CHAPTER 6. A Craze of the Frisco Exposition   ◆   92

CHAPTER 7. The Height of Its Popularity   ◆   114

CHAPTER 8. Made of a New Gleaming Plastic Material   ◆   136

CHAPTER 9. The Growing Underground Movement   ◆   153

Appendix A: Chronological List of Early Hawaiian Luthiers   ◆   167

Appendix B: Annotated Checklist of Selected 'Ukulele Methods and
   Songbooks, 1894–1920   ◆   173

Notes   ◆   179

Bibliography   ◆   253

Index   ◆   271

ACKNOWLEDGMENTS

> I could never understand how two men can write a book together; to me that's like three people getting together to have a baby.
>
> —Evelyn Waugh

In seven years' work, we have incurred numerous debts to a large group of friends, scholars, family, and members of the 'ukulele community. We have built on the work of pioneers, including George Kanahele and his collaborators, whose monumental 1979 volume, *Hawaiian Music and Musicians,* remains an indispensable resource for anyone exploring this field; Bob Krauss of the old *Honolulu Advertiser,* who applied his considerable reportorial skills to a thicket of conflicting claims with admirable results; and Jim Beloff, who wrote the first history of the 'ukulele and whose energy and vision have played such a central role in the latest 'ukulele revival. We are grateful to Jim and to Lyle Ritz and Ian Whitcomb for their willingness to be interviewed about their historical and musical roles in the modern life of the 'ukulele. It has been our privilege to work with the descendants of a number of important historical figures who have been generous with their knowledge: Vicki DeLeo of the Kia/Nahaolelua family; Andrea Low, a great-granddaughter of Ernest Kaai; Rick Cunha, grandson of "Sonny" Cunha; Eleanor Rente, granddaughter of Leonardo Nunes; and Ronnie French, a great-granddaughter of Jose do Espirito Santo.

As independent scholars, we owe a great debt to Dr. Amy K. Stillman of the University of Michigan and Dr. Noenoe K. Silva of the University of Hawaii at Manoa for their willingness to share their expertise with two amateurs in the groves of academe. In the same way, we are grateful to fellow independent scholar Malcolm Rockwell, author of the encyclopedic *Hawaiian & Hawaiian Guitar Records 1891–1960;* Doris Naumu of the Portuguese Genealogical Society of Hawaii; Warren Nishimoto and Michi Kodama-Nishimoto of the University of Hawaii's Center for Oral History; and Michael Simmons and Jason Verlinde of the *Ukulele Occasional* and the *Fretboard Journal* for their contributions to this book.

Like all researchers, our work depends on the skill, knowledge, and professionalism of librarians, whose role grows greater, not lesser, in this digital age.

We are grateful to the many librarians and staff members at Cal State Northridge, Eckerd College, the National Library of Australia, Occidental College, Princeton, Stanford, SUNY Buffalo, UCLA, UC Davis, UC San Diego, University of Hawaii at Manoa, University of Iowa, University of South Florida, Yale, the central branch of the Los Angeles Public Library, the Hawaii State Archives, Hawaii State Library, Bishop Museum, Hawaiian Mission Children's Society, Photographia Museu "Vicentes," and the Arquivo Regional da Madeira whose assistance made this book possible. We are particularly grateful to Dick Boak of the C.F. Martin & Co. Archives, to the late Lydia Guzman of Honolulu, and Luis de Sousa Mello and Ana Isabel Spranger of Funchal, Madeira, for their help in ransacking the archives.

In keeping with the long tradition of collectors in many fields whose passion has informed scholarship, we have benefited from the generosity of collectors of 'ukulele and Hawaiiana, including Jack Ford, Cyril LeFebvre, Greg Miner, Andy Roth, Steve Soest, Terry "Toebone" Tucker, and Damian Vitale. Jeff Carr and Jeff Turner were particularly helpful with the book's illustrations. Dealers who also have been generous with their time and expertise include Don and Michelle Stewart and William D. Voiers. We are grateful, too, for the support and encouragement of family, friends, and colleagues who sustained us during the long gestation of this project: Sue Bober, Ted Bosley, Tony and Margaret Coleman, David Dial, Michael De Silva, Gabrielle Foreman, James Hill, Paul and Joan King, Richard and Mary Long, Tim Mullins, Karl Neuenfeldt, Paul Oldack, Gary Peare, Simeon Pillich, Pepe Romero, Mark Switzer, Bob and Jan Tranquada, Robert Wheeler, and Byron Yasui. We owe special thanks to Manuel Morais of Lisbon, the musician and scholar who has done so much to illuminate and revive the musical practices of nineteenth-century Madeira, from which the 'ukulele comes, and to Tom and Nuni Walsh for their friendship, support, and willingness to share from their own impressive body of knowledge and their important personal 'ukulele collection and archive. We are thankful to Tom and Nuni and to Jim Beloff for their careful reading of the entire manuscript. We also are grateful to the anonymous readers of the manuscript, whose thoughtful comments spurred us to rethink our approach to several important issues and to the ways in which we had structured our narrative. (Of course, we remain solely responsible for any errors in this work.) Masako Ikeda, our editor at the University of Hawaii Press, was a model of calm patience and encouragement as we struggled to deal with the constraints of having to earn a living, as well as what John Evelyn (1620–1706) ruefully called "that which abortives the perfection of the most glorious and useful undertakings: the insatiable coveting to exhaust all that could or should be said upon every head."

For inspiration, we are indebted to Dolores King, John's mother, who introduced him to the 'ukulele in Hawaii as a child, and to Elma Cabral, Jim's great-aunt who died at the age of 101 just before the publication of this book, a talented writer, teacher, and working mother who showed the way by being among the first to try and distinguish ʻukulele fact from ʻukulele fiction. To our families—Debi, Katie, Emma, and Amy King, and Kristin and Alex Tranquada—we owe our greatest debt. It was they who lived through the seemingly endless research and writing of this book and whose love, encouragement, and tolerance for our mutual obsession made possible its completion. This book is dedicated to Kristin and Debi.

Finally, I have to acknowledge the loss of my friend and colleague, John King, who died in 2009 at the age of fifty-five before this book was completed. His remarkable musical talent, tireless initiative, insatiable curiosity, hard work, and demanding standard of scholarship and musicianship set a very high bar for all those who follow him. I have done my best to honor his example.

> *Hoa aloha wale iaia*
> *He aloha ia la-e*
> *Aloha aku au a pau kea ho.*

Introduction

Traditions, indeed, are abundant; but traditions are a mass of rubbish, from which it is always difficult to extricate truth.

—Rev. Sheldon Dibble, *History and General Views of the Sandwich Islands Mission*

The ukulele is a toy guitar and not worth a second thought.

—Hart Stilwell, *Esquire*, October 1940

When seventy-nine-year-old Manuel Nunes died in July 1922, the brief obituaries of the "inventor of the 'ukulele" that appeared in Honolulu were quickly picked up by wire services and reprinted in newspapers nationwide. The ubiquity of the 'ukulele, which had swept the mainland during the previous decade, ensured that news editors in Los Angeles, New York, Boston, and Philadelphia would find space for two or three paragraphs about the elderly musical entrepreneur who had arrived in Hawaii aboard an emigrant ship more than forty years before. While usually a brief item consigned to an inside page and quickly forgotten, the report of Nunes' death provides a fascinating glimpse of the complex and often conflicted role this diminutive four-stringed guitar has played in popular culture in Hawaii, the United States, and abroad. The story reported as fact the myth that the 'ukulele was invented in Hawaii, even as it sought to debunk the popular misconception that it was an instrument of Native Hawaiian origin. Headlines in several newspapers emphasized that a white man had invented the 'ukulele, a reflection not only of an era that witnessed the national rise of the Ku Klux Klan but also of old mainland stereotypes of Hawaiians as ne'er-do-well, childlike savages. This crisis of authenticity also tapped into a widespread dislike of the 'ukulele as a noisy nuisance, a reaction to its overwhelming, faddish popularity, its adoption by convention-defying youth, and its reputation—assiduously cultivated by music retailers—that it was the instrument anyone could play, a strategy that simultaneously increased sales and undercut its standing as a legitimate musical instrument.

Today, the 'ukulele is enjoying what is often referred to as a third wave of popularity—the first being the Roaring Twenties, which made Manuel Nunes' death a news item, and the second coming during the early fifties, when Arthur Godfrey's lifelong enthusiasm for the 'ukulele combined with the power of the new medium of television and the miracle of postwar plastics to sell millions more. Still, for all the 'ukulele's new visibility—festivals around the world, concert performances by such artists as Paul McCartney, tens of thousands of YouTube videos, record prices on the collectibles market, and an international surge of media coverage—for most people outside Hawaii it remains, as one headline recently put it, "the Dangerfield of instruments." According to the *Cleveland Plain Dealer*, "The ukulele's unhipness seems to be one of the pillars on which our modern civilization is built." In the modern musical cosmos, the *Boston Globe* asserts, the 'ukulele "ranks in most people's minds somewhere between asteroid dust and space junk." The 'ukulele has been described as "a tiny four-stringed thingamajig" (*Worcester* [Mass.] *Telegram & Gazette*), "a comical little has-been guitar-wannabe" (*Los Angeles Times*), and "just plain silly" (*USA Today*). "Hard as it is to believe, there are people who take the ukulele seriously, or at least seriously enough to play it for other people," Jon Pareles, the pop music critic for the *New York Times,* wrote not too long ago.

For modern audiences (and many journalists), the 'ukulele conjures up images of Tiny Tim warbling "The Good Ship Lollipop" on *Laugh-In,* or George Formby singing "Leaning on a Lampost," and there the story ends. As we hope to demonstrate in this book, there is a far more interesting—and meaningful—story to be told. Since the 'ukulele's introduction to Hawaii by Madeiran contract workers in 1879, it has functioned simultaneously on a number of different levels—musical, cultural, economic, and even political. As an instantly recognizable symbol of Hawaii, the 'ukulele has been many things over the past 130 years: a promise of an island paradise; a tool of political protest; an instrument central to a rich and celebrated musical culture; a musical joke; a symbol of youthful rebellion; a highly sought-after collectible; a cheap airport souvenir; a lucrative industry; an early adapter to new technologies; and the product of a remarkable synthesis of Western and Pacific cultures. These multiple levels parallel what in Hawaii is known as *kaona*—the ability of the Hawaiian language to simultaneously convey both a literal meaning and an underlying layer of metaphor and allusion with an entirely different thrust. Consider, for example, the century-old tradition of playing Sousa marches on the 'ukulele, a practice popularized by Jesse Kalima, who once confided to a Chicago newspaper reporter his ambition to be the best 'ukulele player in the world. On the most basic level, this is an expression of the continuing tradition of adapting a challenging repertoire to demonstrate the 'ukulele's musical legitimacy. Yet this also is an instance of a Native Hawaiian artist performing music that epitomized U.S. imperial ambitions that led to the loss of Hawaiian sovereignty—music written by the son of a Madeiran father and played on an instrument originally from Madeira that in less than a decade became a symbol of Hawaiian patriotism. The Madeiran immigrants who first manufactured 'ukuleles relied on the patronage of the royal family to ensure its popularity, yet they quickly signed oaths of allegiance to the new revolutionary government after the overthrow of the monarchy in 1893.

This book, then, has the temerity to take the 'ukulele seriously and examine some of its hidden meanings. Because the 'ukulele was introduced to Hawaii in the modern era, it is possible to trace its development in contemporary records in a way that is impossible for many other older instruments. Yet over the years most historical accounts of the 'ukulele have relied heavily on tradition, a few widely circulated and often repeated secondary accounts, and occasionally rank speculation. This book approaches its subject with a different agenda: We wanted to place the 'ukulele in a broader historical and cultural context, relying whenever possible on contemporary sources. We wanted to know why and how: Why did Madeiran immigrants come to Hawaii in the first place? How did the machete become transformed into the 'ukulele, the national instrument of Hawaii, in less than a decade? Why did 'ukulele become explosively popular after the Pan-Pacific International Exposition in 1915? Why did it become a cliché of the mainland youth culture of the 1920s? Why, despite a renewed wave of popularity in the 1950s, was the 'ukulele regarded as nothing more than a toy? In attempting to answer these and other questions, we cast a wide net for source material: books, newspapers, magazines, city directories; court, church, tax, immigration, passport, and census records; oral histories, business records, catalogs and brochures, sheet music, songbooks, copyright registrations, auction records, novels and short stories, and movies and newsreels. In particular, we took advantage of the digitization of newspapers in the United States and overseas to trace the career of the 'ukulele—and Hawaiian music generally—not only in Honolulu, San Francisco, Los Angeles, Chicago, and New York, but in Anaconda, Montana; Duluth, Minnesota; Fort Worth, Texas; Valparaiso, Indiana; Pawtucket, Rhode Island; Winnipeg, Canada; Sydney, Australia; and Manchester, England.

It is a story that draws on such familiar figures as Queen Liliuokalani, Arthur Godfrey, and Tiny Tim, as well as Lewis Carroll, Rudyard Kipling, Malcolm Lowry, P. G. Wodehouse, Jack London, Al Jolson, Bing Crosby, George Gershwin, Irving Berlin, Aaron Copland, Jimmie Rodgers, Neil Young, the YMCA, Sears, SpongeBob Squarepants, and a host of remarkable Hawaiian artists rescued from obscurity: George Kia Nahaolelua, Nulhama "William" Aeko, Samuel K. Kamakaia, James Shaw, John Edwards, and Henry A. Peelua Bishaw, to name but a few. It is a story played out on an international stage, one that begins on the island of Madeira, a small dot off the coast of Morocco, travels halfway around the world to Hawaii, then recrosses the Pacific once more to the United States and Canada to the east, Australia, Java, and Japan to the west, and ultimately to Europe. We think it is a story worth telling.

A Note on the Text

In our own text, we use Hawaiian diacritical marks only in the word "'ukulele." In all quoted sources, we follow the authors' original usage. All other Hawaiian words and names appear without diacritical marks.

CHAPTER 1

These Little Instruments, of Which They Are So Fond

On Summer eve to see the festive dance,
I'd take thee when the golden sun had set;
Methinks more soft would grow thy blue-eyed glance
While list'ning to the little dear machete.

THE DREAMER: A POEM (1848), OSSIAN MACPHERSON

In the summer of 1923, the newly formed Hawaiian Legends and Folklore Commission brought anthropologist Helen Roberts to Hawaii to collect and publish the ancient songs and chants of the Islands. Over the following year, she visited the islands of Hawaii, Maui, Oahu, and Kauai, seeking out practitioners of the "old culture" and recording hundreds of *mele* and *oli* on wax cylinders. Yet one of the first local reports on her work had little to do with traditional music. Instead, it was her conclusion that the 'ukulele "which one associates with Hawaiians and which has been carried far by tourists under the impression that it is an instrument of native invention, or if not that, an instrument invented in the islands," had been introduced to Hawaii in 1879 by Portuguese immigrants from the island of Madeira.[1]

Today it seems surprising that Roberts' comments about the little four-string guitar should have eclipsed the rest of her groundbreaking, four-hundred-page report. But in 1924, the 'ukulele had been an international, multimedia phenomenon for almost a decade. Mainland sales had reached an estimated four million instruments, and dozens of styles were available in big city department stores and mail-order catalogs for as little as two dollars each.[2] Hawaiian trios, quartets, quintets, and orchestras were playing across the United States, Canada, Europe, and Australia in vaudeville, chautauqua, tent shows, restaurants, and nightclubs. Mainstream artists such as Frank Crumit (whose recording of "Say It with a Ukulele" was released that year) and Johnny Marvin (soon to be known as the "Ukulele Ace") accompanied themselves on the 'ukulele as they sang popular hits in the recording studio and on the explosively popular new medium of radio.[3]

It was in 1924 that George and Ira Gershwin made their Broadway debut with the musical *Lady Be Good,* starring Fred and Adele Astaire and Cliff Edwards. Known professionally as "Ukulele Ike," Edwards and his 'ukulele teamed up with the Astaires to introduce the Gershwins' "Fascinating Rhythm" to the nation.[4] It also was the year singer Wendell Hall began using his nickname—"The Red Head"—to market an eponymous line of 'ukuleles with scarlet pegheads. Sales of Hall's 'ukulele-driven recording of "It Ain't Gonna Rain No Mo'" reportedly reached two million copies that year, prompting one newspaper to report "a virulent epidemic of ukelele has broken out. . . . Efforts to check it have proven unsuccessful and physicians say that it will probably run its course far into the winter or at least until 'It Ain't Goin' to Rain No More.'"[5]

By 1924, touring companies of Richard Walton Tully's Hawaiian potboiler *The Bird of Paradise*—each with its own troupe of Hawaiian musicians strumming 'ukuleles and guitars—had earned more than $1 million in profits in the United States, Canada, England, and Australia, inspiring a host of Hollywood imitations. More than three dozen films set in the South Seas—what some slightingly called "ukulele dramas"—had been produced by the mid-1920s, featuring such stars as Mary Pickford, Tyrone Power, and a young Boris Karloff.[6] European royalty also had been smitten: the *New York Times* reported that summer that Edward, Prince of Wales (who as Edward VIII would abdicate the throne in 1936 to marry an American divorcee), had "expressed a desire to learn to play the Hawaiian instrument."[7]

Although he was likely unaware of the fact, Prince Edward was only the latest in a long line of Englishmen and women to fall prey to the charms of the unassuming little guitar. Half a world away from Hawaii, Madeiran musicians had offered lessons on the instrument they knew as the machete to tourists for more than a century, including another royal, Elizabeth of Bavaria, empress of Austria, who visited in 1860–1861.[8]

Largely unknown to each other until the last quarter of the nineteenth century, Hawaii and Madeira shared a number of striking similarities: Both were volcanic archipelagoes with tropical climates and spectacular scenery that delighted tourists (one Honolulu visitor noted that "the Sandwich Islands have been styled by Californians the Madeira of the Pacific"); both were dependent on a single cash crop, wine in Madeira and sugar in Hawaii; and both were dominated economically by foreign powers, England in Madeira and the United States in Hawaii, who regarded the natives with disdain.[9] It was a single dramatic point of difference that ultimately led to the introduction of the machete to Hawaii: While Hawaii's native population was plummeting, leading to repeated predictions of inevitable extinction, Madeira was overcrowded—sometimes to the point of starvation. Demography defied geography to bring the machete to the Islands.

Lying more than 500 miles southwest of Lisbon and 360 miles off the Moroccan coast, Madeira was uninhabited and covered with thick forests—*madeira*

1 - Helene Taxis (1834 – 1891) irmã mais velha da Imperatriz
2 - Imperatriz Elizabeth Amalie Eugenie - "Sissi" (1837 – 1898)
3 - Lily Hunyady
4 - Matilde Windischgrätz

Austrian Empress Elizabeth of Bavaria, one of Madeira's most famous tourists, poses with a machete and her ladies-in-waiting during an 1860–1861 visit to the island. Courtesy of Photographia Museu "Vicentes," Funchal.

means wood in Portuguese—when it was claimed by Portugal in the early 1420s. Superstitious seamen believed the dark mass of clouds that perpetually obscured the island masked the mouth of hell, and they were reluctant to venture near it.[10] The small, steep island of 286 square miles quickly flourished as Europe's first center of sugar production, a role reflected in the coat of arms of the capital city of

Funchal, which bears five *pao de acuças,* or sugar loaves.[11] By 1500, Madeira had become the world's largest sugar producer, and Funchal was a major international port, thanks to the use of slave labor and a cosmopolitan mix of entrepreneurs from Portugal, France, Flanders, Florence, and Genoa.[12] It was in Madeira that the viability of slavery in commercial agriculture was tragically demonstrated to the rest of the world—a model later transplanted to Brazil, the Caribbean, and England's American colonies.[13]

Eventually eclipsed by cheaper and higher-quality sugar from Brazil and the West Indies, the Madeiran sugar industry withered in the last half of the sixteenth century, to be replaced by vineyards that produced the famous Madeira wines: *sercial,* malmsey, *boal,* and *verdelho.*[14] Unlike wines from the European mainland, Madeiran varieties not only are heat resistant but actually improve in hot weather and with rough handling—unique qualities that made Madeiran wine a staple commodity in the New World and later in India.[15] Madeira was a favorite of the North American elite, with George Washington, Thomas Jefferson, and Alexander Hamilton going to considerable trouble and expense to buy what Jefferson called "good and genuine Madeiran wine." In 1783, John Adams assured the Portuguese envoy at The Hague that in America, "Madeira was esteemed above all other wine."[16]

Thanks to Portugal's desperate need after 1640 for English support to preserve her newly recovered independence from Spain, British merchants dominated the Portuguese wine industry. A series of treaties between the two countries allowed Madeiran wine to be imported directly into British overseas possessions but gave the British the upper hand economically.[17] By 1755, Portuguese prime minister the Marquis of Pombal lamented that the British had "conquered [us] without the inconvenience of a conquest. . . . England has become mistress of the entire commerce of Portugal."[18] Nowhere was this dominance more obvious than in Madeira. Garrisoned by British troops from 1807 to 1814 during the Napoleonic Wars, Funchal was home to a prominent colony of resident English merchants who ran more than twenty houses or firms and patronized their own club, schools, reading room, church, cemetery, and physicians. English and other foreign currency, not Portuguese, was the medium of exchange; even carpenters and cabinetmakers used English feet and inches to measure their work.[19] "It is almost certainly anglicized to a greater degree than any other island that does not wear the British flag," one visitor wrote in 1909.[20]

It was the English who first broadcast the lush and balmy glories of Madeira, which by the early nineteenth century had become a popular haven for tourists and invalids. "O Madeira, Madeira, O thou gem of the ocean, thou paradise of the Atlantic," Henry Nelson Coleridge, nephew of the poet, rhapsodized in 1826 after fleeing a cold, rainy English January. "Here I found what I used to suppose peculiar to the Garden of Eden."[21] By midcentury, English visitors could choose from among half a dozen island guidebooks and a score of other volumes, some lavishly illustrated, on its history, flora and fauna, climate, geology, and scenery.[22] The reaction of Isabella Hurst de França, who visited in 1853, was typical: She called the island "the most beautiful sight which it may perhaps ever fall to my lot to see." Her first glimpse at dawn from off Funchal revealed "the beautiful island of Madeira, looking perfectly unlike anything that I had ever seen or imagined. . . . Within the bay, lay the city of Funchal, looking beautifully clean from the sea, with its white houses, and green gardens, now flowering with oleander, heliotrope, blue hydrangia, the white blossom of the coffee tree, and a thousand other flowers new to an English eye, and more brilliant in colour than can be described."[23]

Exotic flora, a warm climate, and "a most majestic landscape . . . [to which] I am sure no artist has ever done justice" were the chief attractions for tourists, all of whom were headquartered in Funchal, Madeira's capital, chief port, and only city.[24] Surprised by the steepness of its narrow, pebble-paved streets and by the lack of wheeled vehicles—*carros de bois,* or ox-drawn sledges, were the rule—visitors were less impressed by Funchal's architecture, whether of the fifteenth-century cathedral or the city's whitewashed stone buildings. "I never was in the town of 20,000 inhabitants so well built, so cleanly and prosperous, and so well situated, in which architecture as an aesthetic art had been so entirely ignored," one visitor complained.[25]

The showy display of Madeiran gardens and the island's dramatic volcanic scenery often overshadowed the Madeirans themselves in the accounts of nineteenth-century visitors. While universally commended for their polite manners and sober, good-tempered behavior, the Madeirans were often described as lazy, ignorant, and superstitious—traits Protestant English and American observers attributed to the islanders' Catholic faith and the balmy island climate.[26] As early as 1772, Johann Reinhold Forster declared that "the heat of the climate; the easy way of getting a great price for the wine, which costs them but very little trouble; the little encouragement farmers meet with, if they even were willing to make any improvements; the few wants they are under against cold and the inclemencies of weather in a mild climate; the method of watching the vineyards leading a great number of hands towards a constant idleness and many more articles contribute towards confirming the people in laziness and indolence."[27] Islanders' belief in *feiticeiras*—witches—struck outsiders as medieval, and their resistance to modern innovations made them the butt of frequent jokes.[28] Visitors who parroted such stereotypes often contradicted themselves, accusing islanders of ignorance while reporting that English-speaking servants were easy to find. Nevertheless, illiteracy was widespread. Despite a program of compulsory public education mandated in 1844, few islanders could read or write; according to one estimate made in 1856, less than 4 percent of the island's 17,900 children were attending school regularly. More than half a century later, 80 percent of the population of Funchal were still unable to read or write.[29]

While books were few, visitors to the island heard music everywhere: in the streets of Funchal, outside peasants' homes in the evening, while being carried in *redes* (a kind of portable hammock), at parish festivals and other public holidays, and in the drawing rooms of the Madeiran elite. The fact that most windows in Funchal were without glass no doubt made it more difficult to avoid hearing music.[30] While the peasantry often sang while out of doors, the wealthy enjoyed balls and concerts in their city homes and quintas, or country villas. During a stop at Madeira in 1788, Maria Riddell attended several soirees at the homes of upper-class English and Portuguese residents, including that of the island's governor, whose wife entertained "with an elegant ball and concert." Riddell also described the "lower class of people" as being "very musical, and extremely gallant. You seldom pass a night at Madeira without hearing a serenade of guitars and mandolins in some part of the street."[31]

Although the pianoforte dominated the European and American musical landscape in the mid-nineteenth century, it was the sound of stringed instruments that filled the air in Funchal, including the Spanish guitar (*viola françesa*) and the *guitarra,* described as an "old English guitar, with six double wires."[32] These instruments, as well as the violin (*rebeca*) and cello, received their due in the guidebooks of the day, but by all accounts the chief ornament of Madeiran music making was the machete, "a small guitar, with four strings."[33] Some Madeirans regarded the machete as an island invention, but on an island that had served as an international entrepot since the fifteenth century, it seems more likely that it was introduced—possibly

The first (and somewhat fanciful) depiction of the machete appeared in William Combe's 1821 pictorial volume, *A History of Madeira.*

by immigrants from northern Portugal, from which two-thirds of the island's early settlers had come.[34]

The earliest known reference to the instrument, dated 1716, appears in Raphael Bluteau's *Vocabulario Portuguez e Latino:* "Machete. Viola pequeña" (Small guitar). Bluteau notes that the alternate term *machinho* "tambem he viola pequeña" (is also a small guitar).[35] Four- and five-string *machinhos* were included in the 1719 *Regimento para o oficio de violeiros* (Regulations for the luthiers guild) from the city of Guimaraes in the northern Portuguese province of Minho.[36] Some scholars believe the Minhotan *machinho,* the Madeiran machete, and the *cavaquinho* found elsewhere in mainland Portugal are among the many descendants of the small, four-course guitar of Renaissance Europe.[37]

Because the term "guitar" often was applied generically during the eighteenth and nineteenth centuries to a family rather than a specific instrument, the first vague references to guitars in eighteenth-century Madeira suggest the instruments referred to could have included machetes as well as violas.[38] In his account of Capt. James Cook's 1772 visit to Madeira, George Forster described how peasants each evening "assemble from different cottages, to dance to the drowsy music of a guittar."[39] British tourist Fanny Anne Wood, née Burney, was the first to record the name of the little guitar that was heard so frequently in Madeira. As the great-granddaughter of musician and music historian Dr. Charles Burney and a member of a family celebrated for its literary and scientific achievements, it's not surprising Wood paid attention to music in Madeira. "Most of the Portuguese," she wrote, "can play the 'Machete' (a little instrument peculiar, I believe, to Madeira) by ear. In the evening they often amuse themselves with their Guitars (Violas) and Machettes, upon which they frequently perform well. On such days as this—Festas—the countrymen go about in parties, dancing, singing, and playing to the music of these little instruments, of which they are so fond."[40]

Country playing and singing—that is, by farmworkers or *vilãos* outside Funchal—left most island visitors unimpressed. Holding their fingers loosely and striking the strings with their fingernails, peasants "never make any tune, but produce three or four notes, which they repeat over and over again for hours," de França complained. Others compared Madeiran singing to "snatches of a funeral dirge very dolefully rendered" or "the howling of a dog in the moonlight" and described voices with "a nasal twang most distressing to anyone unaccustomed to such sounds."[41] Singers in Madeira, declared John Dix, a future American general, diplomat, and New York governor who visited with his ailing wife in 1843, "are almost invariably harsh and discordant. It is said to be a characteristic of the islanders; and from what we have seen, there is no reason to doubt it. There is singing enough in the streets, but not a particle of music in it. Nothing can be more grating to the ear."[42] Even today, country people continue the tradition of *desafio* or *despique,* an improvisational form of singing in which one or more performers trade rhymed insults or recount local gossip to the accompaniment of the machete and frequent bursts of laughter from those listening.[43] *Desafio* could be heard while peasants were at work in the vineyards, walking to or from town, or during religious processions and other public occasions. "The morning was delightful, and the groups of peasantry, coming into the market, which we met along the roads, made it quite enchanting," wrote William Wilde in 1837. "Each little party was preceded by its guitar player. . . . At times the performer accompanied it with his voice, and the whole group joined in the chorus."[44]

In Funchal, string music also was the rule—the heavy duty placed on imported pianos made them scarce—but the musical technique found there was more to the liking of well-to-do visitors. "The generality of their island music is merely a succession of very simple chords; but [the machete] is said to boast of much higher capabilities when played by a masterly hand, and the most brilliant waltzes and mazurkas of the best German composers may be skillfully rendered on this toy-like instrument," one visitor noted in 1854.[45] In February of that same year, de França attended a soiree at the home of Dr. Antonio Luz Pitta, a prominent physician and president of the Funchal city council, or *camara*. "After tea some national music was provided for our entertainment; a machete exquisitely played, a viola, or large guitar, and a cavaquinho, a machete with six strings, instead of four, peculiar to Oporto. Their instruments were all well played, and harmonized well together, in the music peculiarly their own. I was much pleased with it."[46] John Dix was less than diplomatic, calling its music "thin and meagre" and predicting that "It is not

Andrew Picken's 1840 lithograph "Funchal from the East" shows an event often described by nineteenth-century visitors to Madeira: a peasant procession led by machete players.

probable that the machete will ever emigrate from Madeira. It is the most common instrument here; but I doubt much whether it would be, if this were not its birth-place."[47] Even Dix grudgingly admitted that there were "two or three performers in Funchal who have attained a wonderful proficiency in playing on it; their execution is astonishing." Still, he hastened to add, he could not help thinking "with how much more effect their skill would be expended on the guitar, which is in all respects a finer instrument."[48]

Among the Madeirans whose execution might have astonished Dix was Candido Drumond de Vasconcelos, a descendant of a Scottish merchant who had arrived in Madeira in the fifteenth century. As early as 1841, Drumond offered a concert of virtuoso machete music for the Sociedade Philharmonica that was enthusiastically applauded, according to the Funchal newspaper *O Defensor*. The style and scope of Drumond's repertoire only recently has come to light with

The "Rita Polka" is one of forty-one compositions included in Candido Drumond de Vasconcelos' *First Collection of Different Pieces of Music,* arranged for machete and guitar by Manuel Joaquim Monteiro Cabral ca. 1846. Courtesy of Manuel Morais.

the publication of his *Primeiro Colecção de differentes Peças de Muzica* of 1846, a manuscript collection of forty-one waltzes, marches, polkas, and other drawing room dances, as well as themes with variations written for the machete with guitar accompaniment—music undoubtedly similar to that which delighted Dix and de França.[49]

Despite tourists' complaints about the quality of Madeiran music, island teachers found them willing pupils for machete lessons. "English visitors sometimes attempt [playing the machete]," noted Sir Richard Burton in 1863, "but as they expect to be perfect after a dozen lessons—it takes about five years—they rarely succeed."[50] White and Johnson's 1860 guidebook advised that "skillful instructors on the guitar and machete may be easily found"—a group of professionals that included Joaquim Monteiro Cabral, a teacher, composer, and performer who wrote a primer for the instrument, *Estudos para machete*. Cabral's manuscript contains not only traditional Madeiran dances but arrangements of "Rule Britannia" and "God Save the Queen!" as well as exercises, scales, and cadences in eighteen major and minor keys.[51] The author of an 1860 phrasebook included a section on a machete lesson, with such helpful phrases as "Take the machete so" (*Pégue no machête assím*) and "Now play—not so—this way" (*Agóra toque—assím não—é assím*).[52] The machete's small size, novelty, and portability also made it an attractive souvenir. The earliest known photographs of the machete were taken in England by Lewis Carroll, among them an 1858 portrait of Alice Liddell—the inspiration for Carroll's *Alice in Wonderland*—and her two sisters decked out in Madeiran lace and cradling machetes.[53] Unusual fish-, leaf-, and pear-shaped machetes with ten, eleven, and twelve strings in the Stearns collection at the University of Michigan suggest that more elaborate designs were created specifically for the tourist trade.[54]

Demand was enough to support at least half a dozen instrument makers on an island long known for the quality of its woodworking. Timber was a notoriously scarce resource in fifteenth-century Portugal, and chroniclers note that Madeiran lumber made it possible for the first time for the mainland Portuguese to routinely erect buildings more than one story high.[55] Not surprisingly in a place dominated by the wine industry, "the coopers of Funchal are known to be excellent workmen and the pipes [barrels] made are very much admired for their perfect construction," one observer wrote.[56] Madeiran furniture, made of what became known as Madeiran mahogany (*Persea indica*, or *vinhatico* to the Madeirans), was one of the island's early exports. *Vinhatico* is "of a fine grain and brown like mahogeny, from which it is difficult to distinguish it," botanist Joseph Banks observed in 1768, citing as an example a bookcase made for an English resident that combined the two woods.[57] One nineteenth-century visitor reported that local cabinetmakers had "entirely superseded the importation of foreign furniture."[58] Furniture shops were plentiful in Funchal in 1889, according to guidebook author Ellen M. Taylor, and in some, "excellent wardrobes, chairs, and tables may be found of Til, or Vinhatico, walnut, or plane."[59] Twenty years later, a British resident described how "good old English

Lorina Liddell, sister of Alice, was photographed dressed in Madeiran lace and holding a machete by *Alice in Wonderland* author Lewis Carroll in 1860. Carroll's photographs of Lorina and Alice are believed to be the earliest photographs of a machete. Courtesy of Princeton University Library.

furniture" could be found in many houses in Funchal, some of it local copies. "And as the Madeira cabinetmakers have always been masters of their craft, the latter not to be despised," he added—a reputation that lingers to this day.[60]

Taylor listed two shops where machetes, "both large and small," could be purchased: from Rufino Telles in the rua da Carreira and from Vicente de Menezes in the calcada de Santa El. Prices ranged from 3,000 to 5,000 reis, or roughly $3 to $5. There were also at least four other *fabricantes* or *artistas de instrumentos de corda* active in Funchal in the nineteenth century, including Octaviano João Nunes da Paixão (1812–1870) on the rua de São Paulo; his son, João Augusto (also known as João Augusto Diabinho, 1850–1927); Augusto M. da Costa (1840–1915) on the rua de Joao Tavira (who made several of the instruments in the Stearns collection); and Antonio dos Reis Quintal on the rua do Tanoeiros.[61]

An 1897 array of instruments made by Funchal luthier Augusto da Costa, including a five-stringed *rajão* (center), a machete (second from right), and a fish-shaped machete. Courtesy of Photographia Museu "Vicentes," Funchal.

British and American visitors viewed Madeirans' love for music with a sense of complacent satisfaction, regarding it as a demonstration of "a high degree of chearfulness, and contentment," as Johann Forster put it in 1772. Madeiran music "is pleasing to the stranger chiefly because it indicates a cheerful, contented spirit," agreed S. G. W. Benjamin in 1878.[62] But the air of cheerful contentment tourists chose to see ignored an increasingly troubled island economy and chronic social problems. In the early part of the nineteenth century, Madeira and its wine trade prospered. "The increased demand for the wines of this island has so far advanced the prosperity of its inhabitants as to cause a total change in their mode of life, manners, and exterior appearance, both as to their persons and their dwellings," an English observer wrote in 1821.[63] By the next decade, however, prosperity evaporated when recession hit North America, the West Indies, and England, a downturn aggravated by the abolition of slavery in the British West Indies and throughout the British colonies in 1834. By 1842, Dix found Madeira's commerce "exceedingly depressed. . . . Such a season of inactivity in business has never before been known. But for the influx of invalids, who come here to pass the winter months, and who expend, at the lowest calculation, $150,000 in Funchal, the suffering would be still greater."[64] This also was a period of great political instability in Portugal, a half-century of Napoleonic invasions, revolution, and civil strife between liberals and monarchists that did not end until 1851 and saddled Portugal, already one of the poorest countries in Europe, with crippling debts.[65]

At the same time, what one historian has called "the pervasive tyranny of the island's geography" began to be acutely felt. Only one-third of the mountainous island is inhabitable, and most farmland, in narrow *poios* or terraces that literally had to be carved out of its steep flanks, was devoted to vineyards. As a result, the island had never been able to grow more than half of the food it needed to sustain its growing population, which by the 1840s was believed to be approaching 120,000. Food shortages—and even famine—had been a regular feature of life throughout the island's history.[66] International recession, overpopulation, a British-dominated system of monocultural agriculture, and chronic political instability created a pervasive poverty that tourists often complained obscured the sublime scenery. "You no sooner put your foot on the stone stairs [at the landing in Funchal] than your winding way of ascent is beset by innumerable lazzaroni most offensive in habit and appearance, whose rabid importunities for alms will not permit you to say them nay," J. W. Spalding complained in 1855.[67] Aggressive beggars—men, women, and children—were "the great plague of Madeira," de França lamented. "Before a child can utter any other word, its Mother teaches it to hold up its little hands and make a sound intended for 'Dez reisinhos'—a little halfpenny—on the approach of a stranger."[68]

Poverty and famine triggered a massive wave of emigration in the 1830s and 1840s, despite the best attempts of the authorities to stop it. A trickle of emigrants to Trinidad in 1834 and to British Guiana (then known as Demerara) in 1835 became a steady stream in the 1840s as British sugar planters eagerly sought new sources of cheap labor in the wake of the abolition of slavery.[69] *O Defensor* noted in January 1842 that the previous year had been "noteworthy for the large emigration to Demerara as a consequence of the invitation that would not have been accepted [by many] if their hunger and misery, necessary consequences of the stagnation of the economy, had not obliged them to."[70] Painfully aware of the transformation of Madeirans from onetime slave owners to a cheap substitute for slave labor, government officials denounced emigration agents as "white slavers" and imposed fines and jail sentences in an attempt to stop the flow.[71]

But the failure in 1846 of the potato crop—the chief source of food for most islanders since its introduction in the 1820s—raised the specter of real famine. That winter, while civil war raged on the mainland, food was so scarce that many Madeirans were reduced to eating sugar cane while the governor and British merchants scrambled to organize an international relief campaign.[72] Although the worst of the food shortages were over by the following year, the crisis drove thousands of islanders overseas. So great was the exodus that in 1847, known as *"o ano de fome,"* or the year of hunger, the Portuguese navy stationed ships off the island, and a shore patrol armed with bayonets was posted on the Funchal shoreline in a vain attempt to stem the tide of *clandestinos*—illegal emigrants—seeking to evade the heavy passport duty imposed by Lisbon.[73] Although no reliable figures exist, Governor Jose Silvestre Ribeiro estimated that as many as forty thousand islanders fled between 1840 and 1850—as much as one-third of the island's entire population.[74]

As they fled, Madeirans took their machetes with them. "Fond of music, [Madeiran emigrants] enlivened their homes with the guitar, accompanied by the voice," wrote Henry G. Dalton in his 1855 history of British Guiana. "A small kind of guitar, called by them 'michette,' is a very favourite instrument, with which, playing the most pleasing airs, they often perambulated the street."[75] By the end of the century, several Madeiran instrument makers were exporting machetes to emigrants in British Guiana, Trinidad, and other Caribbean islands. Rudyard Kipling also found machetes in Gloucester, Massachusetts, in early 1896 when he was researching the cod fishery as the setting for his next novel, *Captains Courageous.*[76]

The 1846 famine presaged a tragic catalog of natural disasters visited on Madeira during the last half of the nineteenth century, each prompting new waves of emigration. By 1849, although the immediate crisis had passed, one English visitor wrote that he had "nowhere seen, not even in the worst part of Ireland, more intense misery than among the people of this island. A stranger is assaulted, wherever he appears near these destitute and overpopulated districts, with crowds of mendicants, whose emaciated and diseased appearance shows too plainly that their food is insufficient and unwholesome."[77] In 1852, the *Oidium Tuckeri* fungus (known to the Madeirans as *mangra*) devastated the vineyards. "No one can form an adequate idea of the blasted appearance of the vines who has not seen them," wrote the Reverend John O. Choules, a visitor in 1853. "They look as if they have been scorched by fire."[78] Wine production plummeted; by 1855, only fifteen of seventy shipping firms were still in business, and the island was again threatened with food shortages. The following year, an army regiment from Lisbon brought cholera to the island, triggering an epidemic that caused the deaths of an estimated seven thousand people. "The destitute condition of the island population cannot, however, be too strongly stated," one visitor wrote that same year. "The truth is, the population of the island is disproportionate to the demand for labor. . . . Wages are insufficient to bare existence, and threaten to become lower."[79]

Efforts to rebuild the wine industry by introducing American grape stocks resistant to *Oidium* inadvertently resulted in another agricultural disaster—the introduction of phylloxera, a tiny aphid that once again devastated the vineyards. Production plummeted for a second time, from 16,000 pipes of wine annually to 3,500.[80] By the spring of 1883, a *New York Times* correspondent reported, "Here the poverty has deepened into downright beggary. All the men you meet look limp and nerveless; all the women stunted, bowed, prematurely aged. Even among the children a rosy face or a well-knit frame is as rare as snow in July."[81] British consul George H. Hayward reported to London that the island "is not in a prosperous condition" and that without major changes in government policy, "it is useless to hope for any permanent improvement."[82]

By the late 1870s, many Madeirans likely would have agreed with Hayward's pessimistic assessment of the island's future. Forty years earlier, poverty-stricken Madeirans had left the island for Demerara "with nothing but a shirt, and trousers, and a *carapuça* [pointed cap] on their heads, but no shoes on their feet, and returned in satin waistcoats and gold chains, beaver hats and polished boots."[83] As had tens of thousands of islanders before them, many were looking for a way out—even if it meant taking a chance on a previously unknown destination called the Sandwich Islands, a tiny Pacific kingdom at the end of a six-month voyage.

CHAPTER 2

The Sound of Pa, Ko, Li

Hear a good deal of opera singing in this town—& pianos.
—TWAIN, *MARK TWAIN'S LETTERS FROM HAWAII*

W hen Frank Vincent Jr. sailed into Honolulu in 1870, he was surprised—and not a little disappointed—by what he saw: an American-looking city, with brick and stone warehouses, long lines of drays, crowds of newly arrived immigrants, and, through a half-open door, a glimpse of the inviting interior of a saloon. "We were dumbfounded," he later wrote. "We had dreamed of groves of cocoa-palms made picturesque by half-naked Undines and houris, and we found billiard-tables, bowling alleys, sangarees, and sample rooms."[1] For many nineteenth-century visitors to Hawaii, as remarkable as the tropical scenery or the volcanoes was the dramatic transformation of what was regarded by westerners as a backward nation of half-naked savages into a country with a written language, Western-style laws and government, churches, schools, commerce—and music.[2] "Behold what the missionaries have wrought!" Mark Twain wrote from Honolulu in 1866.[3] Yet intertwined with the astonishment at the changes that had come about in less than half a century was a sense of disappointment that the primitive and provocative South Seas society they had hoped to find was a paradise lost to billiard parlors and streetcars. Twenty years after Vincent's visit, Henry Adams' vision of hula girls draping leis around his neck on the verdant slope of a volcano turned out "quite different," he wrote to a friend. "One drives everywhere over hard roads, and can go most places about Honolulu by horse-car or railroad. . . . [It is] about as thoroughly Americanized as Newport."[4]

This openness to billiard tables and horse cars, Western harmony and hymns, minstrel shows and melodeons made it possible for the Madeiran machete to be regarded as more than just a foreign novelty after its arrival in the Islands. The new instrument arrived at a time of great change, as a new mix of Western melody and instrumentation combined with Hawaiian poetry, rhythms, and a unique cultural sensibility to create a new kind of music. That music ultimately would be harnessed to address Western visitors' deep-seated desire for tropical exoticism, providing a soundtrack for the paradise they sought despite the macadamized roads and bottled beer.

Honolulu's transformation into an American-style metropolis could be said to have begun in 1820 with the arrival of the first party of seventeen Protestant missionaries dispatched by the American Board of Commissioners for Foreign Missions (ABCFM).[5] Through what they regarded as a stroke of divine providence, they arrived just after Liholiho, the son and successor to the late Kamehameha I, abolished the traditional system of *kapu* and declared the old gods dead. But unlike the explorers of the previous century who viewed the Hawaiians and other Pacific peoples as happy examples of Edenic innocence, the missionaries could not seem to find sufficient adjectives to describe what they regarded as the sinful state of the natives. "We find them destitute, ignorant, wild, beastly, and degraded—inconceivably so," the Reverend Sheldon Dibble wrote in 1839. "The longer we live among the heathen, the more fully does [the missionary] realize the ignorance, the vileness, and the abominations of the horrible pit in which they are sunk."[6] Like the Madeirans, Hawaiians were regarded as lazy, ignorant, and superstitious—victims of a theory of geographical causation dating back to Hippocrates that insisted such characteristics were the inevitable result of a warm climate.[7] Hawaiians' color—the southerner Twain called them "almost as dark as negroes"—made them seem even more exotic, emphasizing their otherness. The missionaries' first glimpse of "the chattering, almost naked savages . . . was appalling," the Reverend Hiram Bingham recalled. "Some of our number, with gushing tears, turned away. . . . Others with firmer nerve continued their gaze, but were ready to exclaim, 'Can these be human beings!'"[8]

While the missionaries may have been appalled at their first glimpse of Hawaii, merchants and traders eagerly took advantage of this strategic way station—the only place in the vast North Pacific where their ships could put in for repairs, buy needed supplies, recruit new sailors, or transship cargoes. By 1820, Hawaii had become a central pivot for the trade between the United States, California, the Hudson's Bay Company on the northwest coast, Russian Alaska, and China.[9] Traders had established themselves in Hawaii several years before the arrival of the missionaries; as early as 1812, a commercial agent had set up shop in Honolulu to coordinate the operations of several ships and to handle business in the Islands. Ships bound for China with furs from the Oregon Country added cargoes of fragrant sandalwood, a commodity monopolized in Hawaii by Kamehameha I until his death in 1819.[10] That same year the first American whaling ships arrived in Hawaii, spurred by the discovery of the sperm-whale grounds of the South Pacific the year before. Honolulu, Lahaina, and other Hawaiian ports quickly became the principal rendezvous, supply, and recruiting points for the whaling fleet: Between 1826 and 1840, more than 140 ships visited the Islands every year—almost all of them American.[11] Many ship captains and crews were vociferous critics of the missionaries, whose growing influence with the royal family and the *alii* led to repeated attempts to ban liquor, halt prostitution, and impose curfews—all of which led to a series of sailor-incited riots.[12]

By the time Twain arrived as a correspondent for the *Sacramento Union* shortly after the end of the Civil War, Hawaii had been transformed from an isolated, traditional society based on subsistence agriculture into a constitutional monarchy fully integrated into the global economy—a nation with enough of the trappings of civilization to surprise visitors expecting a vision out of Melville's *Typee*.[13] "In no corner of the world can a half-century show such marvelous change," another American newspaper correspondent marveled.[14] The American takeover of California in 1846 and its rapid development in the wake of the discovery of gold in 1848 had only served to increase American interests in the Islands. Just as the British dominated Madeira, the Americans dominated Hawaii—and were not shy about proclaiming that fact. "The great bulk of the wealth, the commerce, the enterprise, and the spirit of progress in the Sandwich Islands centers in the Americans," Twain reported to his California readers. "Americans own the whaling fleet; they own the great sugar plantations; they own the cattle ranches; they own their share of the mercantile depots and the lines of packet ships. Whatever of commercial and agricultural greatness the country can boast it owes to them."[15] Even American money had been adopted as the Islands' standard currency; Hawaii had no coinage of its own until 1884.[16] The fruits of the missionaries' labor included an extensive network of public schools, a high rate of literacy, a system of written laws and property ownership, a burgeoning system of commercial agriculture—and a pervasive contempt for Hawaiians. "Though inferior in every respect to their European or American brethren, [the natives] are not to be . . . wholly despised," Henry Whitney, a son of missionaries, editorialized in the *Pacific Commercial Advertiser* in 1857. "In proportion as they come in contact with the foreigner, and acquire correct habits, skill and industry, in that proportion do they rise in our estimation."[17] Many Americans found the idea of an independent monarchy in the Islands a laughable idea. "In our country, children play 'keep house'; and in the same high-sounding but miniature way the grown folk here, with the poor little material of slender territory and meager population, play 'empire,'" Twain wrote, calling Hawaii "a playhouse 'kingdom.'"[18] A series of international crises in the 1830s and 1840s demonstrated how fragile Hawaiian sovereignty was: A single European warship anchored in Honolulu harbor could, and did, dictate terms to the Hawaiian government.[19]

One dramatic illustration of the impact of what Whitney called "contact with the foreigner" was the spread of Western-style music in Hawaii. Protestant hymns—or *himeni*—in the New England tradition were one of the first and most lasting influences on modern Hawaiian music.[20] Like almost all aspects of Hawaiian culture, indigenous music was dismissed by the missionaries, whose cultural rigidity extended to the belief that bonnets made better headgear than the native wreaths.[21] "There is none who ever make any difference of sound between mi and fa and la and fa—all is the same to native ears and native voices. No one knows when he sings right and when he is wrong," lamented Asa Thurston in 1834.[22] The missionaries' characterization of Hawaiian chant was remarkably similar to British and American tourists' condescending descriptions of Madeiran music. The Reverend Lowell Smith, for example, described the native singing he heard on Molokai as "howlings and intonations, apparently unearthly and inhuman."[23] But the chief objection to Hawaiian *mele* was that these "filthy" and "vile" songs so inescapably associated with hula were "connected with idolatry and licentiousness, and wholly incompatible with Christianity."[24] More accurately defined as poetry that is chanted, rather than music, *mele* were central to the meaning of traditional hula: As Adrienne Kaeppler has put it, "Dance without poetry did not exist."[25] Although condemnations of filthy songs were aimed specifically at the *hula mai* that honored the genitals and procreative power of an *alii,* all *mele* were tarred with the same indiscriminate brush.[26]

Music was the missionaries' companion from the first. Two days after their arrival in 1820, Liholiho heard the missionaries sing hymns in a service held on the quarterdeck of the *Thaddeus,* accompanied by George Kaumualii on the bass viol.[27] Kaumualii again accompanied the singing on the missionaries' first Sunday in Honolulu two weeks later, which Bingham believed "appeared attractive to native ears."[28] Congregational singing had always been an essential part of public worship in the Puritan tradition; as early as 1647, the Reverend John Cotton of Massachusetts affirmed that the "singing of Psalmes with a lively voyce, is a holy duty of God's Worship."[29] Hiram Bingham is believed to have made the first effort to teach Western-style singing in June 1820 by setting up an evening singing school in Honolulu. Despite missionary complaints about the lack of Hawaiian musical skills, they proved apt and eager pupils: By the following year, Sabbath school pupils in Honolulu were able to perform a rude translation of "Come, Holy Spirit, Heavenly Dove."[30] Enthusiastic Hawaiians in 1824 "succeeded beyond our expectations in imitating the sounds and gave us much encouragement," Levi Chamberlain wrote of a Honolulu singing school.[31] The popularity of singing schools quickly spread to Maui, Molokai, and the Big Island, where in 1847 the Reverend Lorenzo Lyon reported "the excitement was perfectly astonishing. Wherever I went, wherever I spent the day or night, nothing saluted my ear so frequently as the sound of pa, ko, li (fa, so, la)."[32] For Lydia Kamakaeha Paki (1838–1917), crowned in 1891 as Queen Liliuokalani, this aptitude was not surprising. "The Hawaiian people have been from time immemorial lovers of poetry and music," she wrote.[33] Just as the first book printed in New England, *The Whole Booke of Psalmes,* was dedicated to music, so too was the first book printed in Hawaii in March 1824: *Na Himeni Hawaii.*[34] The reception was enthusiastic. When a shipment arrived in Lahaina, "our houses were thronged with eager applicants for them," wrote C. S. Stewart, who at the time was training native teachers in reading, writing, and singing three days a week. "The richest treasure could scarce be received with greater enthusiasm than these 'himeni paiia'—stamped hymns, as they are called."[35] The Reverend Lowell Smith, who began a singing school in Kaluaaha, Molokai, in 1833, continued his efforts after his transfer to Honolulu; early in 1838, he despaired over his inability to handle the hundreds of boys and girls who wanted to learn to sing.[36]

Although often criticized for their harsh and unbending Calvinistic theology, the missionaries were progressives when it came to their belief in the importance of musical education. Music did not become part of the public school curriculum anywhere on the mainland until Boston adopted it after much lobbying in 1838.[37] In some cases, the missionaries appear to have been motivated as much by a genuine love of music as by religious concerns. Bingham and Smith, for example, were both described as being "sweet singers" and well-trained musicians; Gerrit P. Judd was the nephew of Thomas Hastings, the well-known hymnodist and author of "Rock of Ages," with whom he corresponded and with whom he and Princes Alexander Liholiho and Lot Kamehameha visited in 1849.[38] Nor were they lacking institutional models: Dr. Samuel Worcester, a founder of the ABCFM and its first corresponding secretary, was the compiler of a popular collection of hymns known as "Watts and Select."[39]

As a result of the missionaries' efforts, traditional Hawaiian music began to fade. Just seven years after the missionaries' arrival, British naval captain F. W. Beechey was invited to a hula performance in Honolulu by Liholiho and noted that "it was difficult to procure performers of any celebrity, and both bards and dancers were sent for from a considerable distance." His appreciation of the hula and a sham fight with short spears was heightened by his realization that "in a short time, no doubt, both they and the dances will cease to be exhibited."[40] In 1863, when the ABCFM's Rufus Anderson toured the four major islands, he was met by choirs and Western-style musical performances everywhere he went. "The music was conducted entirely by natives, and was as good as I remember in my early days in New England," he said of his visit to Wailuku, Hawaii.[41]

Music was also an important feature at the schools established for the education of missionary children. Singing lessons were part of the original curriculum at Punahou School, which opened in 1842. The school's headmaster, the Reverend Daniel Dole, being "fond of music, and wishing to introduce it as far as possible made every effort to secure instruments, above all a piano."[42] Pianos, much sought after by missionaries and foreigners as a symbol of cultivated taste and civilization, initially were very expensive.[43] There were a few in Honolulu by the early 1840s, including one at the Royal School established in 1839 and run by New England teachers Amos and Juliette Cook. It was the Royal School's instrument that American Chester Lyman heard with delight during an 1846 visit. The young chiefs "sing excellently, and some of the young ladies are fine performers on the piano. I had not heard that instrument before since leaving the United States, and the associations it awakened were highly pleasing."[44] By 1849, writing home to Albany, New York, Catherine Lee boasted that "scarcely a house in Honolulu is destitute of a Piano."[45] The piano and violin were the chief instrumental accompaniment at the monthly meetings of the Musical Society, organized by foreigners in Honolulu in the 1850s. At first, the society "hardly ever ventured any choral singing beyond English and American glees, with above all an abundance of parlor ballads," Mrs. Charles de Varigny wrote in 1855, noting approvingly that "in it the puritan element was less dominant, which made it possible more often to prolong the party with a few waltzes."[46] Eugene Hasslocher, a German who taught at Punahou, put the thirty-member, coed society on a schedule of regular rehearsals in 1860, with the result that its music became much more ambitious, with a performance of the Haydn oratorio *The Creation* at Fort Street Church and selections from Italian opera (in English) at a musical party at High Chiefess Bernice Pauahi Bishop's. "Who would have thought of hearing first-rate music in the heart of the Pacific, some of the most attractive performers being Hawaiian, a race which fifty years ago was in the very lowest depths of savage life!" marveled English visitor Sophia Cracroft in 1861.[47]

Ships' bands, a regular feature of life in Honolulu during the first half of the nineteenth century, were another early source of Western-style music. American, British, and French warships all carried bands, which when in port played at royal funerals, annual school examinations, balls, and other public occasions. After the arrival of the British frigate *Blonde* in May 1825, C. S. Stewart "listened with satisfaction to her band of music, which I could distinctly hear, and which lost none of its charms by being a little distance on the water."[48] Such bands were the inspiration for what became the Royal Hawaiian Band, whose first incarnation as the King's Band appeared in the 1830s.[49] The band aboard the frigate *United States* created a sensation when it played in Hilo in 1843. "So great was the enthusiasm excited by the band, that Mr. Coan opened his big church, and the Commodore [Catesby Jones] came on shore with his musicians and treated the assembled population to the first concert ever given by a complete orchestra in Hawaii," Henry Lyman remembered.[50] However, not all ship's bands were created equal: On a visit that same year, the U.S. Sloop-of-War *Cyane* mustered what gunner William Meyers sarcastically called a "magnificent orchestra" consisting of two fiddles, a clarinet, and a trombone.[51] Whether the bands were large or small, by midcentury Honolulu society heard them often: Clerk James Gleason attended at least seven balls during a nine-month period in 1843, and American consul David Lawrence Gregg recorded thirty dances held by the royal family, members of the local community, or by naval commanders between 1854 and 1857.[52]

As a busy international port and home to many of the resident foreigners in Hawaii, Honolulu inevitably heard popular music from the United States and Europe. Brief glimpses in contemporary records from the first half of the nineteenth century suggest that such music was common: In 1831, the government barred "some of the Sabbath Day amusements of the foreigners, such as fiddling, dancing, and carousing"; ten years later, Honolulu merchant Stephen Reynolds complained that a curfew had been imposed, with no music after 9 p.m. and no dancing in private houses; and an 1842 ship captain's hotel bill included a $1.50 charge for "fiddler's pay."[53] Minstrel troupes, which made their first appearance in the Islands as early as 1849, were regular visitors among the musical performers who stopped in Hawaii on their way to or from Australia. David Gregg recorded a visit of the Boston Minstrels of San Francisco in 1855 and of a troupe from the USS *John Adams* in 1856.[54] Other entertainment was more eclectic: One 1854 concert at the Honolulu courthouse combined popular songs of the day and Mozart; another featured the vocal talents of Miss Catherine Hays singing selections from Handel, Rossini, Donizetti, and "Home Sweet Home," which encored twice. This "thrilling melody" also had been featured at a concert at the Varieties Theater a few months earlier. The following year, a courthouse concert offered a mix of "pleasing Polkas, Waltzes, and Quadrilles," and such songs as "The Last Rose of Summer."[55] Hawaiian-language newspapers published inspirational lyrics urging Hawaiians to farm and go to school to be sung to such tunes as "Oh Susannah" and "Billy Boy."[56] Even missionaries were not immune to the charms of the sentimental ballads of the day. Laura Fish Judd recalled how the piano at newspaper editor James Jackson Jarves' house was a major attraction—"You would laugh to see us all hang around [Mrs. Jarves] as she plays and sings, 'Woodman, Spare That Tree.'"[57] In 1866, Mark Twain complained that

> The popular-song nuisance follows us here. In San Francisco it used to be "Just Before the Battle Mother" every night and all night long. Then it was "When Johnny Comes Marching Home." After that it was "Wearin' of the Green." And last and most dreadful of all, came that calamity of "When We Were Marching Through Georgia." It was the last thing I heard when the ship sailed, and it gratified me to think I should hear it no more for months. And now, here in the dead of night, at the very outpost and fag-end of the world, on a little rock in the middle of a limitless ocean, a pack of dark-skinned savages are tramping down the street singing it with a vim and energy that makes my hair rise!—singing it in their own barbarous tongue! They have got the tune to perfection.[58]

Five years later, while boasting of American influence in Hawaii (and the inevitability of annexation by the United States) Henry Pierce, the U.S. minister at Honolulu, claimed that Hawaiians' "favorite songs and airs are American. Sherman's 'Marching Through Georgia' and 'John Brown's Soul Is Marching On' are daily heard in the streets and in their schoolrooms."[59] Even in the leper colony at Kalaupapa, Molokai, one inmate in the early 1870s described how, when sitting on the beach or riding a horse in the hills, he sometimes sang his favorite songs— "Annie Laurie," "Home, Sweet Home," and "What Are the Wild Waves Saying?"[60]

Western-style music required Western instruments, but the expense and difficulty of shipping them to the Islands meant that initially most were small and portable. Missionaries eventually succeeded in obtaining organs and melodeons for their churches to accompany choirs, but most other instruments mentioned in accounts of popular music prior to 1875 are less bulky: violins, flutes, fifes, clarinets, and accordions.[61] In Hilo, the Reverend David Lyman and his wife started a flute orchestra among the students at their boarding school because they were the least expensive instruments available.[62] Such instruments had become widespread by 1870, when one Honolulu newspaper noted "a tendency . . . among the Hawaiians to learn to play on musical instruments, and to club together for the purposes of musical amusement. . . . Instruments and music have been furnished, so that already, in several country places, bands have been organized which have attained to considerable skill in their performances."[63]

Remarkably, there are relatively few early references to the guitar, which was to play such an important role in modern Hawaiian music. Over the years, there has been much speculation as to how it was introduced to the Islands. According to one of the most common accounts, it was introduced by the *paniolos,* or Mexican vaqueros, who had been brought to Hawaii by 1830 to manage herds of wild cattle descended from the original stock introduced by Vancouver.[64] Guitars were found in California as early as 1792, and many well-to-do Californios played the guitar and violin—albeit without any formal training.[65] With the exception of drums and trumpets at Monterey, Richard Henry Dana said of his 1835 visit to California that the guitar and the violin were the only instruments he saw.[66] When Edwards Perkins visited the Islands in 1849–1850, he reported finding "a guitar in Honolulu, that had made its way there from the Spanish Main."[67] However, it is also possible that the guitar was introduced by one of the thousands of Hawaiian sailors who served on foreign ships around the world, by American merchants who stocked an astonishing range of goods in Honolulu in the 1820s, or some other source.[68] As American historian Philip Gura has pointed out, the guitar and its music spread rapidly in America during the first three decades of the nineteenth century because of its reasonable cost, portability, ease of tuning and maintenance (as compared to the piano), and because, as an 1838 guitar method proclaimed, "from no other instrument can be produced so much music in so short a time."[69]

The earliest evidence of guitars in Hawaii is an advertisement in the June 6, 1840, edition of the *Polynesian* inserted by Henry Paty & Company of Honolulu for merchandise that includes bass viol, violin, and guitar strings.[70] The first known reference to a guitar performance is an account by U.S. Navy chaplain Walter Colton of a visit to the Royal School in Honolulu in 1846, in which he "adjourned with the scholars to the parlor, where Mrs. Cook[e] placed one of the misses at the piano, while another took the guitar, and they all struck into a melody that might have gratified a more fastidious taste than ours."[71] Four musicians from the USS *Mississippi* offered lessons on a variety of instruments in 1855, including the guitar.[72] Charles Derby, manager and proprietor of the Hawaiian Theater, was offering piano and guitar lessons in 1867.[73] The following year, when the Girls' Seminary in Makawao, Maui, burned to the ground, among the losses were "one piano, two melodeons, two guitars, and all our music."[74] When George F. Wells opened a new music store on Honolulu's Fort Street in 1878, he boasted of an inventory that included "Guitars, Violins, Accordeons, Concertinas, Banjos, Harmonicas, Tambourines, &c. &c."[75] By the mid-1880s, the guitar was a familiar presence throughout the Islands. The San Francisco correspondent of one Honolulu newspaper was unimpressed with the Spanish Students, a guitar-playing sensation of the early 1880s, contending that "I have heard [guitar-playing] as well done by native boys in Honolulu serenading for a 'hapalua' [half dollar]."[76] Guitars were advertised regularly by Honolulu retailers (W. G. Wood of one such firm, Lycan & Co., had "a very costly" guitar stolen from his house), and lessons were available from H. H. Babcock of West, Dow & Co.[77] Guitars also were a feature of performances throughout the Islands: at a concert at the Hawaiian Hotel; at a housewarming on King Street; at a building fund benefit at Kaumakapili Church and a concert at an assembly of Sunday schools at Kawaiahao Church; at a dance in Waimea and a nighttime serenade in Waipio Valley, both on the Big Island; and a dance aboard a schooner anchored off Maui.[78] The music Hawaiian performers produced with their guitars even inspired a local poet:

> An island song the native sings, while the guitar he fingers,
> "Aloha oe, we'll meet again," still the stranger lingers
> For the delicious strains charm the listening ear
> As the kanaka with song welcomes the bright New Year.[79]

All of these disparate musical influences—*himeni,* pianos, opera, the popular song nuisance, and guitars—came together at the Royal School, where two of the four siblings known as Na Lani Eha, the Heavenly Four, received their earliest training. Through their social and political influence, David Kalakaua (1836–1891) and Liliuokalani (who attended the school) and Miriam Likelike (1851–1887) and William Pitt Leleiohoku (1854–1877) (who did not) helped to create and popularize a new musical idiom that synthesized traditional Hawaiian poetry with New England–style hymnody. As ethnomusicologist Helen Roberts explained, the royal composers and the songs they wrote "represent a period in which the foreign art, stamped with a fresh viewpoint, was being adopted by the Hawaiians, and being made to assume distinctive features at their hands."[80]

Kalakaua and Liliuokalani received their musical training at the Royal School.[81] "We encourage their finding amusement in music as it prevents idleness and gives a task for rational pleasures," an 1844 entry in the school's journal notes. "They [the students] have all a decided taste for music. Several play on the accordion and piano; all sing."[82] Amid the political turmoil of the 1840s, Laura Fish Judd found

King David Kalakaua and Queen Liliuokalani, seen here as a princess in an 1887 portrait taken in London, played key roles in shaping and popularizing a new kind of music that blended Hawaiian *mele* with Western musical forms. Courtesy of Hawaii State Archives.

"one of the bright sides of the picture . . . is the Sunday evening service held in the palace drawing-room. The pupils of the Royal School attend, and constitute a choir, as they have fine singing voices."[83] The school and its students were frequently put on display for distinguished visitors, including U.S. Navy lieutenant Charles Wilkes, who proclaimed himself "delighted with the order and cleanliness of the whole establishment" after his 1840 visit. The children "were hardly to be distinguished from well-bred children of our own country; were equally well-dressed, and are nearly as light in color," he noted approvingly.[84] Sir George Simpson, governor-in-chief of the Hudson's Bay Company, was equally impressed in 1842 by the children's fluency in English and good behavior, "although some of the young ladies did occasionally raise the skirts of their frocks in order to scratch their ankles or, perhaps, the calves of their legs." Despite this unladylike behavior, Simpson counted his visit as "perhaps, the most interesting hour that we spent in Honolulu."[85] The year of Simpson's visit was also the year four-year-old Liliuokalani was enrolled at the school. By her own description "a studious girl," Liliuokalani demonstrated an early aptitude for music, including the ability to sight read or "sing by note" as it was then known. "After leaving school, my musical education was continued from time to time as opportunity offered, but I scarcely remember the days when it would not have been possible for me to write either the words or the music for any occasion on which poetry or song was needed," she recalled. "To compose was as natural to me as to breathe."[86]

The royal family had a long history of interest in Western music. Kamehameha III and his sister, Princess Nahienaena, had what were described as "excellent voices," which Nahienaena put to use leading the choir at Kawaiahao Church.[87] Both Kamehameha IV and Queen Emma were educated at the Royal School and were patrons of and participants in the Honolulu Musical Society; on his 1849–1850 tour of America and Europe, Liholiho attended opera performances in London, Paris, and Washington, D.C.[88] Lunalilo, whose anthem "E Ola ka Moi i ke Akua" ("God Save the King") was published in a Honolulu newspaper in 1862, was serenaded with several songs of his own composition on his first royal visit to Hilo.[89] Princess Victoria Kamamalu, another Royal School alumna, "was an accomplished pianist and vocalist" who served as the organist and choral director at Kawaiahao Church before her death in 1866.[90]

But it was Liliuokalani and her siblings who enjoyed an international reputation for being "excellent musicians."[91] Liliuokalani, Leleiohoku, Likelike, and Kalakaua all maintained what she described as "separate clubs or musical circles" made up of

Singing clubs organized by Princess Miriam Kekauluohi Likelike and Prince William Pitt Leleiohoku were at the center of the new Hawaiian music during the last half of the nineteenth century. Courtesy of Hawaii State Archives.

friends and admirers "engaged in friendly rivalry to outdo each other in poetry and song. . . . Our poems and musical compositions were repeated from one to another, were sung by our friends in sweetest rivalry, and their respective merits extolled: but candor compels me to acknowledge that those of Prince Leleiohoku were really in advance of those of his two sisters. . . . [His] singing club was far superior to any that we could organize; it consisted in a large degree of the very purest and sweetest voices to be found among the native Hawaiians."[92] Lorrin Thurston agreed: "Leleiohoku . . . was the most devoted member of the family to the development of Hawaiian music," he wrote. "He was credited with having written the words of many songs, and with composing the music of a number of others."[93] Perhaps one of the earliest accounts of one of these royal clubs comes from Mark Twain, who in an April 1866 letter described how after enjoying an elaborate five-course dinner with Kalakaua, "they called in the 'singing girls' & we had some beautiful music, sung in the native tongue."[94]

Kalakaua and Liliuokalani learned to play the piano and sing while at the Royal School; Sophia Cracroft was crestfallen in May 1861 to learn that after she and her husband left a royal dance early they had missed the music and singing that followed, including "the Queen accompanying Kalakaua and his sister, who has a beautiful voice."[95] Contemporary accounts show that Kalakaua, Leleiohoku, and Liliuokalani also played the guitar. In a notebook dated 1860, Kalakaua recorded a song—presumably one of his own—that describes its sound: "Hone ana i ku'u Dreamings, / ka leo o ke guitar, / me ka sweet voice nahenahe . . ."[96] In 1874, during his first visit to Hilo as king, Kalakaua held an evening reception at the planters' house where he was staying. "After more singing by the crowd, the king brought out his guitar and sang a mele of his own composing, accompanied by the queen [Kapiolani] and his sister the princess Lydia [Liliuokalani], who is a fine singer and a good performer on several musical instruments."[97] The following year, Leleiohoku and his entourage visited the village of Laie on the windward coast of O'ahu. "Supper out of the way, we, with a number of our native friends who had gathered in, spent the evening in social conversation, singing, playing on musical instruments, &c., in all of which he took an active part," an observer wrote. "He is an expert on the guitar, his party bringing one with them, besides other instruments."[98] John Cameron, master on several interisland vessels in the 1880s, heard Kalakaua sing on board on a number of occasions and remembered how the king's retinue "listened to the king's sallies on almost any subject, serious or ludicrous, or to his songs, for he was an excellent conversationalist, a good musician, and no mean composer."[99]

While all four wrote songs that became staples of the Hawaiian repertoire—"Adios ke Aloha" and "Moani ke Ala" (Leleiohoku); "Nani Wale Kuu Home o Ainahau" and "Kuu Ipo i ka Hee Pue One" (Likelike); "Sweet Lei Lehua" and the Hawaiian national anthem "Hawaii Ponoi" (Kalakaua)—Liliuokalani was by far the most prolific and the best known as author of "Aloha Oe," "Ka Mele Lahui Hawaii," the first Hawaiian national anthem, and scores of others, which by her own estimate numbered in the hundreds.[100] While Liliuokalani's music was more heavily influenced by hymnody, Leleiohoku's has been described as more secular and incorporating a greater interest in foreign music.[101] The common thread that runs through the work of all four royal composers is the influence of Henry Berger, the Prussian military musician originally lent to Kamehameha V in 1872 for four years to reorganize what was to become known as the Royal Hawaiian Band. Berger, who became a naturalized Hawaiian citizen in 1879 and headed the band until his retirement in 1915, had an enormous influence on modern Hawaiian music.[102] "It was he who was responsible for directing the development of Hawaiian music toward the end of the transition period from himeni to the secular form of modern Hawaiian music," Donald Billam-Walker has explained.[103] Berger worked closely with the royal four, providing music for their lyrics (as in the case of "Hawaii Ponoi" and "Sweet Lei Lehua") or arranging their music for performance and publication ("Aloha Oe"). Berger's compositional skills spurred Hawaiian composers to write lyrics specifically to fit his melodies, a dramatic departure from the traditional Hawaiian emphasis on words and meter in composing *mele*.[104]

Berger's musical influence extended far beyond the Heavenly Four: He organized and conducted the Reform School Band; taught music at the Kamehameha School, the Kawaiahao Girls' Seminary, and the former Territorial Normal School; alternated with Liliuokalani as organist at Kawaiahao Church; regularly assisted with amateur musical performances; and published more than a dozen songs he wrote or arranged known collectively as *Mele Hawaii* in the mid-1880s.[105] Through the literally thousands of concerts he and the Royal Hawaiian Band presented beginning less than two weeks after his arrival, Berger helped introduce the works of such European composers as Bach, Chopin, Brahms, Wagner, Verdi, Rossini, Bizet, and Weber to Hawaiian audiences.

"The band, under the efficient leadership of Herr Berger, is an institution of which Honolulu is justly proud," the *New York Times* reported in 1875. "It is an invariable surprise to visitors to hear in this remote little city, and from these native boys, the finest music of the best composers rendered in truly artistic style. On Saturday afternoon they play in Emma Square . . . and there are few who willingly miss these weekly concerts."[106]

As capital and principal metropolis of the kingdom, Honolulu dominated Hawaii's economic, social, and political life. By the late 1870s, the population of Honolulu numbered about twenty thousand—smaller than the Madeiran city of Funchal. Only a tiny fraction of the shipping in the crowded harbor brought any tourists to the Islands. Served by a single government-funded hotel "affording all the conveniences of a first-class hotel in any part of the world," only a handful of visitors made the 2,500-mile, weeklong trip from San Francisco each year. Undaunted, in 1875 Henry Whitney optimistically published *The Hawaiian Guide Book for Travelers*—the first of its kind.[107] With the North Pacific whaling fleet a

Henry Berger and the Royal Hawaiian Band, shown here on the steps of Iolani Palace in Honolulu ca. 1889. At various times, the band included some of the Islands' most talented musicians, including David Nape and Mekia Kealakai. Courtesy of Hawaii State Archives.

fading memory, commercial agriculture had become the mainstay of the Hawaiian economy, revolutionized in 1876 by the signing of a long-sought Reciprocity Treaty with the United States that allowed Hawaiian sugar to be shipped to the mainland duty free. In 1874, Hawaiian planters shipped almost twenty-five million tons of sugar to the United States; by 1879, the total had almost doubled to forty-nine million tons. As the *Pacific Commercial Advertiser* observed that year, "sugar is king."[108]

However, the sugar boom only underlined the grim reality that had plagued the Islands from the days of Kamehameha I: the seemingly inevitable decline of the Hawaiian people. By the official count, there were more than 130,000 people in the Islands in 1832; by 1878, their numbers had dwindled to fewer than 58,000.[109] Twenty years earlier, Charles de Varigny, chief secretary of the French legation in Honolulu, found that "all about me people were predicting the inevitable, and by no means remote, decline of the native race, ending in their absorption by the United States."[110] After ascending to the throne in 1874, Kalakaua made his priorities clear in his opening speech to the Legislative Assembly: "The subject, however, that awakens my greatest solicitude is to increase my people, and to this point I desire to direct your earnest attention."[111] The steady decline of population not only created an acute labor shortage in the wake of the signing of the Reciprocity Treaty but raised real fears that the kingdom's independence was in jeopardy.[112] Immigration, not just of laborers but entire families, seemed the only answer—one the government recognized in 1850, when the use of contract labor was legalized and the newly organized Royal Hawaiian Agricultural Society appointed a committee "to devise means for procuring more labor."[113]

The first Chinese laborers arrived in 1852 to work for $3 per month, and they continued to arrive in fits and starts until large numbers began to arrive regularly in the late 1870s.[114] A small group of Japanese arrived in 1868, but none followed for almost two decades.[115] Desperate for plantation labor, Hawaiian planters looked to Dutch Malaysia, British India, and other Pacific islands for potential workers— a search that would last for almost a century and over the years lead to Germany, Norway, Sweden, Spain, Italy, Russia, Korea, the Philippines, Puerto Rico, Louisiana, Tennessee, Alabama, and Texas.[116] Eventually, fears of numerical domination by the "unassimilable" Chinese, regarded as a reliable, relatively inexpensive source of labor but resented for their success as urban entrepreneurs, led the Board of Immigration in late 1876 to turn its attention to Madeira and the Azores.[117]

The key figure in the effort to recruit Portuguese labor was William Hillebrand (1821–1886), a German physician, entrepreneur, and botanist who first came to Hawaii in 1850, became a Hawaiian citizen, and in 1865 traveled to south Asia with a commission from the Hawaiian government to find a new source of contract workers.[118] In 1876–1877, Hillebrand was in Madeira with his invalid wife Anna and wrote to the Hawaiian minister of the interior promoting the idea of recruiting there.

> In my opinion your islands could not possibly get a more desirable class of Immigrants than the population of the Madeira and Azore Islands. Sober, honest, industrious and peaceable, they combine all the qualities of a good settler and with all this, they are inured to your climate. Their education and ideas of comfort and social requirements are just low enough to make them contented with the lot of an isolated settler and its attendant privations, while on the other hand their mental capabilities and habits of work will ensure them a much higher status in the next generation, as the means of improvement grow up around them.[119]

Appointed Hawaiian commissioner of immigration for Madeira and the Azores, Hillebrand printed an anonymous twenty-two-page pamphlet, *Breve Noticia Àcerca das Ilhas de Sandwich,* that painted an alluring picture of Hawaii's salubrious climate, its flat, fertile, and largely uncultivated soil, high wages, and low cost of living.

Hawaii, the pamphlet shrewdly promised, was not only a country where emigrants could prosper and make a fortune but recapture some of Portugal's former

BREVE NOTICIA

ÁCERCA DAS ILHAS DE SANDWICH

E das vantagens que ellas offerecem
á emigração que as procure.

Dr.LR

FUNCHAL.
TYPOGRAPHIA LIBERAL
26—RUA DAS QUEIMADAS DE BAIXO—26
—·—
1878

William Hillebrand's *Breve Noticia* was written to help recruit the first Madeiran emigrants to Hawaii—even though most nineteenth-century Madeirans were illiterate. Courtesy of Arquivo Regional da Madeira.

imperial glory. Through "the gradual multiplication of their number," the Portuguese could eventually dominate the islands, the pamphlet claimed. "There is no reason why this cannot happen. . . . This will represent, in fact, a peaceful conquest of new territory, in the enlightened sense of modern times, that to a certain extent can compensate Portugal for the loss of its ancient prestige."[120]

Prestige or no, Hillebrand apparently had little trouble in finding Madeirans willing to take a chance on a new life in Hawaii by signing a three-year contract to work in the fields at wages of $10 per month for men and $6 to $8 for women, with food, housing, and medical care provided.[121] The idea of contract labor was not new to the Madeirans, as previous generations had served as indentured workers in British Guiana and Brazil.[122] What set these laborers apart is that while Hillebrand was careful to refer to them as *colonos*—those who left Portugal in furtherance of a national enterprise—they were in fact emigrants, leaving for personal reasons and unlikely ever to return.[123] The first group of 123 men, women, and children arrived in Honolulu in September 1878 aboard the *Priscilla*. It was the start of a movement that would eventually bring more than twenty-five thousand Portuguese to the Islands—including thousands of Madeirans who brought their beloved machete with them.[124]

CHAPTER 3

The National Instrument of Hawaii

A musical instrument is more than wood, wires and glue; the essence
of the object lies in the meanings the culture has assigned to it.

—KAREN LINN, *THAT HALF-BARBARIC TWANG: THE BANJO IN AMERICAN
POPULAR CULTURE*

On a warm August Saturday in 1879, a British bark out of Liverpool
slipped into Honolulu Harbor, carrying the second shipload of Madeiran contract workers brought to the Islands. It had been a grueling four-
month voyage of twelve thousand miles, during which the 427 passengers aboard
the *Ravenscrag* endured eight straight days of winter gales off Cape Horn and the
deaths of three small children. As the relieved emigrants piled their luggage on the
ship's deck, João Fernandes, a happy-go-lucky twenty-five-year-old plumber from
Funchal, borrowed a machete from a bashful bachelor, João Gomes da Silva, and
left his baby daughter with his wife Carolina as he sang and played in celebration of
the ship's safe arrival. This was the moment, it is widely believed, when the Islands
were introduced to what within less than a decade would become known as the
'ukulele, the national instrument of Hawaii.[1]

Although small numbers of Portuguese—primarily from the Azores—had
been present in Hawaii for generations, no evidence has come to light that they
had introduced the machete prior to 1879.[2] Impromptu musical celebrations like
Fernandes' had been seen elsewhere: In 1841, Madeiran emigrants landing in what
is now Guyana "were so delighted to have reached the 'El Dorado' of their dreams
that they danced and sang and embraced the sailors on their arrival."[3] But Fernandes was not the only musician aboard the *Ravenscrag,* nor was his borrowed
machete unique. Less than two weeks later, a reporter for the *Hawaiian Gazette*
spotted the new arrivals on the streets of Honolulu:

> During the past week a band of Portuguese musicians, composed of Madeira
> Islanders recently arrived here, have been delighting the people with nightly street

concerts. The musicians are fine performers on their strange instruments, which are a kind of cross between a guitar and banjo, but which produce very sweet music in the hands of the Portuguese minstrels. We confess to having enjoyed the music ourselves and hope to hear more of it. "Music hath charms to sooth the savage breast," it is said, and although not savage ourselves, we plead guilty to the soothing influences of the Portuguese music.[4]

Among the *Ravenscrag*'s passengers were three men who would play central roles in the development of the 'ukulele: cabinetmakers Manuel Nunes (1843–1922), Jose do Espirito Santo (1850–1905), and Augusto Dias (1842–1915).[5]

Like most of the men aboard, Nunes, Santo, and Dias had signed contracts as plantation workers and were officially listed as *trabalhadores,* or laborers.[6] But they and more than half of their traveling companions were natives of the city of Funchal and likely had never worked on a farm in their lives.[7] Although charged with bringing plantation labor to the Islands, the Hawaiian Board of Immigration appears to have sought to recruit a wider range of skills. In its recruiting pamphlet *Breve Noticia,* the board claimed that "craftsmen like cabinetmakers, carpenters, blacksmiths, tilelayers, etc. never receive less than 1,500 *reis* per day, and can sometimes earn 2,500 *reis* or more"—several times the average wage for skilled workers in Funchal.[8] Little more than a month after the *Ravenscrag*'s arrival, the *Pacific Commercial Advertiser* reported that word was circulating of a new shipment of Azorean immigrants "said to be agriculturalists almost exclusively, and therefore

Within six years of their arrival in Hawaii, Manuel Nunes, Jose do Espirito Santo, and Augusto Dias all had set up shop in Honolulu as cabinetmakers and guitar makers—the first 'ukulele makers in the Islands. Santo portrait courtesy of Ronnie French.

more to be desired than the mixed lot of mechanics—cobblers, tinkers, and all sorts—who came by the Ravenscrag."[9]

Regardless of their actual professions, most of the passengers on the *Ravenscrag* were shipped off to the plantations—Nunes to the island of Hawaii, Santo to Maui, and Dias to Hawaii and then to Kauai. Where Fernandes lived during his first years in the Islands is unclear.[10] Like many other Portuguese contract workers, Nunes, Santo, and Dias left the plantations as soon as their contracts expired. They naturally gravitated to Honolulu, which as the kingdom's largest city and commercial center promised the best opportunities for pursuing their trade. Honolulu's first professional cabinetmaker, Louis Morstein, had opened his doors half a century before; by the mid-1880s, the city's growing population supported a flourishing furniture trade, with twelve manufacturers listed in the 1884 city directory.[11] Several elaborately inlaid tables of the period, including one owned by King David Kalakaua, have been attributed to Nunes and Santo, both of whom are believed to have worked for C. E. Williams, proprietor of the Pioneer Furniture House, Hawaii's oldest and largest furniture store.[12]

Dias also appears in the 1884 directory—the first of the 'ukulele pioneers to appear in Honolulu as a luthier.[13] Augusto Dias, guitar and furniture maker, was listed as living and working at 11 King Street near the bridge over Nuuanu Stream, in Honolulu's crowded and jerry-built Chinatown, regarded as Honolulu's worst slum.[14] His neighbors on the street packed with two-story wooden storefronts were Chinese poi makers, laundries, a baker, a fruit stand, and across the street, the office of building contractor Henry Mead—a far cry from the carriage-trade blocks farther east on Fort, Merchant, and King Streets, where the haole elite shopped.[15] By the following year, Nunes—who years later called himself "the inventor of the ukulele"—had opened a rival "cabinetmaker's shop of string instruments, guitars and machetes" on the edge of Chinatown three blocks away at 77 Nuuanu Street, and Santo had similarly taken out a newspaper ad to announce that he was "prepared to undertake any job in connection with his Profession of Guitar and Cabinet Maker" at 72 Nuuanu.[16]

Whether Nunes, Santo, and Dias made instruments in Madeira before emigrating to Hawaii isn't clear. J. A. Gonsalves, a fellow *Ravenscrag* passenger, reported that the three men had been partners in Funchal in the making of musical instruments, but no evidence has surfaced to confirm his account.[17] They are not among those known to have built stringed instruments in Funchal during the last half of the nineteenth century, including Octaviano João Nunes and his son João Augusto Nunes. Whether Octaviano was a relative of Manuel's also is not clear.[18] Dias, Nunes, and Santo are all identified as *marceneiros,* or cabinetmakers, in their emigration files, rather than as *violeiros,* or makers of stringed instruments.[19] However, their knowledge of the specialized techniques needed to build machetes and guitars suggests that they were not novices. Given the numerous examples of nineteenth-century European and American cabinetmakers who also turned their hands to instrument making, it's possible that Santo, Nunes, and Dias began building instruments on the side while working in one of Honolulu's furniture firms.[20]

It was a less than auspicious time for immigrant entrepreneurs to launch new businesses in an untried market. A 25 percent drop in the price of sugar combined with the brash overconfidence and free-spending habits of planters led to a serious business depression in 1884, one that led planters to watch the market "with feverish anxiety," the American minister in Honolulu reported that May.[21] Just as economic conditions were beginning to improve, fire broke out in Chinatown on the afternoon of April 18, 1886. It quickly burned out of control among the shoulder-to-shoulder stores, offices, and tenements in the neighborhood, wiping out thirty-seven acres from Bethel Street east to the Nuuanu Stream. All of King Street, including Dias' shop and living quarters, was reduced to "a black waste of smoking debris."[22] This may explain why Dias was in Santo's shop that July, when *O Luso Hawaiiano* reported "a more than disgraceful" unprovoked attack by the displaced guitar maker on a fellow immigrant that resulted in a broken window and numerous cuts to the victim.[23] Santo and Dias were working as partners early in 1887 when their Nuuanu Street music store was burglarized by boys from the Industrial and Reformatory School in Palama.[24] To make a living, Dias, Nunes, and Santo not only advertised the manufacture and repair of stringed instruments but likely seized whatever opportunities presented themselves—buying, selling, and trading guitars and other instruments, selling strings, pegs, and bridges, and even offering lessons.[25] The burglars' spoils in 1887 and in two similar incidents at Santo's "ukulele and guitar shop" in 1904, which included 'ukulele, taro-patch fiddles, mandolins, guitars, and a banjo, give some sense of the inventory they carried.[26]

Instrument repair was prominently featured in Santo's half-page display ad in the 1888–1889 Honolulu directory—the first directory in which all three musical entrepreneurs were listed as guitar makers.[27] "Jose do Esp'to Sante, Guitar Maker And Repairer, located on Nuuanu Street near Beretania," announced that "I make a specialty of repairing all Musical String Instruments, and solicit orders from all the Islands. Any work sent in will be attended to immediately. I guarantee first-class work in all respects. Special orders taken to make Guitars of all sizes."[28]

Santo's phrase "guitars of all sizes" underscores the difficulty of tracing the earliest evolution of the 'ukulele.[29] For example, the taro patch fiddle, or simply taro patch, has been generally understood since World War I to be a large 'ukulele with four courses, double or less commonly single—the instrument described in early method books as a "Hawaiian mandolin" that has "about three times the volume of its smaller brother."[30] But "taro patch" was the term applied to both the machete and *rajão* in the first years after their arrival. In November 1885, for example, the *Daily Honolulu Press* complained that "the melodious Hawaiian night-warblers are making the taro-patch fiddle a little too lively."[31] In 1892, an Ohio tourist described the taro patch fiddle as "a diminutive guitar of four strings," and as late as 1918, in describing the 'ukulele, Albert A. Stanley could confidently state that "'taro-patch fiddle' is a name frequently applied to the instrument."[32] It wasn't until almost a decade after the *Ravenscrag*'s arrival that the first reference to the 'ukulele appeared in print, in an account of a church concert in Lihue, Kauai.[33] Thus it is not clear which instrument the nocturnal Honolulu serenaders were playing or the family of novelist and poet Robert Louis Stevenson took with them at the start of their 1889 voyage from Honolulu to Samoa, which his wife Fanny described as "a native instrument something like a banjo, called a taropatch fiddle."[34]

However, there are numerous contemporary references that make clear that there was a clearly understood difference between the 'ukulele and the taro patch. An 1893 newspaper correspondent described "the ukalele, which is sort of a baby guitar, with only four strings all the same size and instead of plucking the strings the[y] are strummed; [and] the taro patch, a stringed instrument a little larger than the ukalele, but with five strings, as the guitar."[35] Both Nathaniel Emerson in his *Unwritten Literature of Hawaii* and ethnomusicologist Helen Roberts used the same definition. "The taro-patch fiddle in its original home [Madeira] had five strings, as it has here [in Hawaii], and was known as the 'rajao'; while the ukulele with four strings had its Portuguese representative in the 'braga,'" Roberts wrote in 1924.[36]

The Madeiran tuning for the five-string *rajão* was reentrant—that is, D-G-C-E-A, the lowest note being the third string, C.[37] The earliest published tuning for the 'ukulele, in Edward Holstein's pioneering 1894 publication, *Chords of the Taro-Patch Guitar,* is the standard, reentrant, my-dog-has-fleas G-C-E-A tuning known today—as Holstein makes clear, "the tuning of which is the same as the Taro-Patch deprived of the fifth string."[38]

However, this tuning differs substantially from that described for the machete in nineteenth-century Madeira: intervals of thirds and a fourth in descending order, or D-G-B-D.[39] Twenty years after Holstein published his method, Angeline Nunes, a daughter-in-law of Manuel Nunes, coauthored a brief primer unique in its insistence on tuning a 'ukulele like a Madeiran machete: D-G-B-D. "The original way of tuning the Ukulele has not been put into print, consequently it is unknown to most people," Nunes and coauthor A. A. Santos wrote. "There are several methods in circulation which are adapted to the taro patch instead of the Ukulele. In fact, it is the taro patch method which has been applied to the Ukulele."[40]

In her account of a visit to Hawaii in 1890, tourist Helen Mather described a high tea in Honolulu where "native musicians, on the guitar, violin, *taropatch,* and *ukelele,* were rendering delightful music."[41] This is one of the earliest known references in print to 'ukulele on the mainland; the origins of the name have been the subject of endless speculation. The word "'ukulele" was not coined in response to the introduction of the machete but appeared decades earlier to describe another European import—the cat flea. Defined in Lorrin Andrews' 1865 Hawaiian dictionary as simply "a flea," 'ukulele appears in earlier accounts of life in the Islands. Missionary Hiram Bingham described an overnight stay on Oahu while traveling

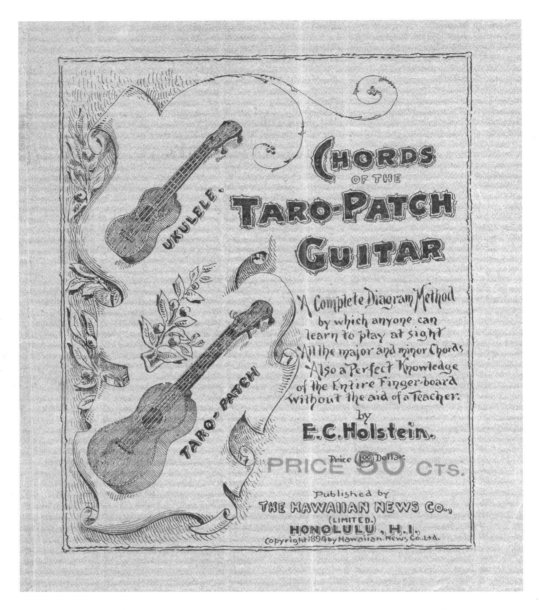

Edward Holstein's *Chords of the Taro-Patch Guitar*, published in Honolulu in 1894, was the first in a long line of teach-yourself 'ukulele publications. Courtesy of Hawaii State Archives.

with Kamehameha III in 1823 in a house "the occupancy of every inch of which was stoutly disputed by the uku-lele."[42]

By the turn of the century, "'ukulele" was commonly understood to mean "leaping" or "jumping flea"—a definition first seen in print in 1892.[43] Novelist Jack London, who spent several months in Hawaii in 1907, wrote in *The Cruise of the*

Snark that ʻukulele "is the Hawaiian for jumping flea as it is also the Hawaiian for a certain musical instrument that may be likened to a young guitar."[44] Instrumental virtuoso, composer, teacher, and musical impresario Ernest Kaai provided the first extant rationale for the name in his 1906 method book: "The Hawaiians have a way of playing all over the strings at the same time, strumming and skipping their fingers from one side of the instrument to the other, hence the name, Ukulele (a bouncing flea)."[45]

One of the most frequently cited accounts of how the ʻukulele got its name focuses on Edward William Purvis (1857–1888), born in Sumatra into a large and well-traveled Scottish family. The former English army officer arrived in Hawaii to join his family in 1879 and subsequently served four years as vice-chamberlain to King Kalakaua.[46] Because Purvis was "slight of stature, agile, and light on his feet, . . . rather a contrast to the large-bodied and slow-moving Hawaiians," he was reportedly tagged with the nickname "ʻukulele."[47] Provided with one of the newly introduced machetes by his siblings in the fall of 1882, shortly after he began work at the palace, he became a proficient and is said to have taught Kalakaua how to play. This close and highly visible association with the new instrument is supposed to be how the vice-chamberlain's nickname was adopted as its name.[48] However, the circumstances surrounding Purvis' departure from royal service raise some questions about this account. He resigned on August 31, 1886, the day after Chamberlain Charles H. Judd was abruptly dismissed for "improper conduct." Both Judd and Purvis were suspected of feeding derogatory information about the government to the *Hawaiian Gazette.*[49] Three months later, Purvis published *The Grand Duke of Gynbergdrinkenstein,* a notorious political satire of Kalakaua and his ministers.[50] It seems unlikely that the nickname of a man who sought to undermine the king in the politically charged atmosphere prior to the imposition of the Bayonet Constitution of 1887—which severely curtailed the power of the monarchy—would have been applied to an instrument favored by Native Hawaiians. This seems even more unlikely given that just twelve months prior to Purvis' resignation, Nunes and Dias were advertising "machets" for sale and that the earliest known musical use of the word "ʻukulele" did not appear in print until December 1888, four months after Purvis' death in Colorado.[51]

The first Hawaiian name applied to the machete has been reported to be *pila liilii,* or little fiddle.[52] A Santo business card (ca. 1898) suggests that this name may actually have referred to an instrument larger than the ʻukulele. The card identifies Santo as a manufacturer of large guitars, small guitars, and ʻukuleles—"*Mea hana i na Pila Gita Nunui Pila Gita Lii Lii a me na Pila Ukulele*"—consistent with his previously advertised readiness to build guitars of all sizes.[53]

In an 1895 newspaper ad, Santo identified himself as a guitar maker, offering "Taro-Patch and Ukulele Guitars . . . [at] reasonable prices."[54] The name "taro patch fiddle" has traditionally been attributed to the instrument's use by Hawaiians during breaks while working in their taro patches. However, contemporary sources

JOSE de ESPIRITO SANTOS

Kihi o na Alanui Moi me Alakea, Honolulu.

❋—MEA HANA I NA—❋

Pila Gita Nunui 🎻 Pila Gita Liilii

A ME NA PILA UKULELE.

HOOIAIA KA HANA A ME NA MEA HANA.

O KA HOOMAEMAE KA HANA OI LOA.

Jose do Espirito Santo's ca. 1898 business card underscores the importance of *kanaka maoli* customers to the earliest 'ukulele makers. Courtesy of William Voiers.

suggest that another possibility is that the name was intended to be a derogatory one, coined by haoles and tied to Western stereotypes that routinely painted the *kanaka maoli* as lazy and ignorant. Mark Twain used the term that way in 1866 in describing the deliberations of the Hawaiian legislature: "Cow-county members— or perhaps I should say taro-patch members—lay the sides of their faces on the desks, encircle them with their arms, and go to sleep for a few moments at a time."[55] During an 1888 legislative debate over proposed changes to school attendance requirements, Noble H. S. Townsend urged that the Board of Education "ought to have the power to revoke any excuse from attendance at school which they find is only adding one to the number of loafers and taro patch fiddle players." Representative A. P. Paehaole agreed, arguing that if the bill passed, "the height of ambition with some will be to get out of school and get a taro patch fiddle."[56]

As its name varied, so too did the design of the first 'ukulele. The earliest surviving examples from the 1880s retain the elongated shape and extended seventeen-fret fingerboard of the Madeiran machete and sometimes boast elaborate rosettes and bindings.[57] Peghead shapes varied dramatically, from the traditional figure eight ("oito") and designs similar to *kapu* sticks to elaborate scrolled shapes that appear to have been borrowed from banjos.[58] By the 1890s, fingerboards had shrunken to twelve frets that ended flush with the edge of the top bout, and button bridges had been replaced with simple slotted versions—changes that could be attributed to pressures of meeting growing demand "at reasonable prices." It wasn't until the turn of the century that the familiar crown peghead appears to have made its first appearance.[59] Regardless of the design, by the turn of the century the name "'ukulele" had taken firm hold—as had the instrument itself on the musical culture of the Islands.

Hawaii's rapid adoption of and identification with the 'ukulele is nothing short of astonishing. In the spring of 1884, less than five years after the arrival of the *Ravenscrag*, a Honolulu newspaper reported a complaint about the city's mounted police, specifically "their musical fiend who plays on a 'taro-patch fiddle' for 27 hours out of the 24."[60] On the island of Hawaii, a visitor described seeing the proprietor of a Hilo beer shop "keeping time on a 'taro patch fiddle' to the quick step of three hula girls."[61] In 1886, Honolulu newspaper editor and amateur musician Augustus Marques commented in the *Hawaiian Almanac and Annual* that Hawaiians "of late have taken to the banjo and to that hideous small Portuguese instrument now called the 'taro-patch fiddle.'"[62] A few months later, another Honolulu newspaper called a military drumbeat "as ordinary a sound as the strains of the taro-patch fiddle."[63] The 'ukulele's ubiquity was such that a visitor who took a trip aboard the interisland steamer *Kinau* in 1888 described how the Native Hawaiians camped out on deck sleeping, smoking, and "playing the taropatch fiddle—the national instrument of Hawaii."[64] *Chords of the Taro-Patch Guitar* was published by the Hawaiian News Co. in 1894—a sixteen-page pamphlet aimed at tourists who bought the instruments as souvenirs at the Merchant Street publisher, bookseller, and music dealer. "These musical instruments are very popular amongst the natives of the Hawaiian Islands and almost all of their homes contain one or more of them, which they use on all occasions for singing and dancing," author Edward C. Holstein wrote.[65] During the winter of 1896–1897, while in Washington, D.C., Queen Liliuokalani described how the daughter of California congressman Samuel Hilborn sang some of the queen's songs to the accompaniment of "our instrument, the ukulele, [and] gave me that joy, so sadly sweet, of listening to the sounds of home in foreign lands."[66]

Just as quickly, the 'ukulele became an indispensable element of island iconography. Among the hundreds of photos taken by amateur photographer Alfred Mitchell during an 1886 visit is a portrait of an unidentified Hawaiian woman dressed in a *holoku* and posing with a 'ukulele.[67] By 1892, commercial studio photographs of a trio of hula dancers in grass skirts posing with a 'ukulele, a guitar, and a taro patch were on sale in Honolulu—an archetypal and widely circulated image that as a postcard sold for decades.[68]

On his 1897–1898 trip to Hawaii, artist Hubert Vos painted "Kolomona: Hawaiian Troubadour," a Honolulu stevedore "in the act of playing an ukulele . . . the adopted native musical instrument of these modern days."[69] The 'ukulele was even incorporated into the design of a souvenir spoon created in the 1890s by prominent Honolulu jeweler Wichman & Sons.[70] Contemporary photographs

In a widely distributed studio portrait by Honolulu photographer J. J. Williams, taken ca. 1890, hula dancers pose with (left to right) a 'ukulele, a guitar (note the price tag still attached), and a taro patch. Courtesy of Hawaii State Archives.

also provide evidence that the 'ukulele had become fashionable among Honolulu society and haole families. An 1888 photo taken on the front lawn of Old Plantation, the Ward family estate on what was then the outskirts of Honolulu, shows several young ladies cradling a variety of stringed instruments, including a banjo, a 'ukulele, and a five-string taro patch.[71] The first documented appearance of a 'ukulele on the mainland was in the hands of James Wilder, a member of one of the Islands' most powerful merchant families, at an April 1890 concert by Harvard's freshman glee and banjo clubs, singing "a Hawaiian love song, with ukulele accompaniment."[72] Possibly the first appearance of the 'ukulele/taro patch in England was in the hands of the sons of Theophilus H. Davies, prominent English businessman and longtime Honolulu resident, who upon his return in 1890 from a two-year trip abroad said that "one of his greatest enjoyments in England was to hear his boys play their taro patch fiddles and sing the songs of Hawaii."[73]

Why did the 'ukulele become so popular so quickly and become fixed in the public imagination so firmly as a uniquely Hawaiian instrument?[74] Clearly, some of its popularity was due to its being small, portable, and with just four strings, easy to tune and to play. Just as musical entrepreneurs on the mainland had touted the guitar half a century earlier as offering such "peculiar facilities," the 'ukulele was equally attractive. It was played by both men and women, although most professional musicians of the period were men. Its price tag was smaller than that of most guitars, although the purchase of a 'ukulele still represented a major investment during an era when the vast majority of workers were employed in unskilled or semiskilled jobs. Plantation laborers on average were earning less than $18 per month, and house servants and gardeners made even less—$8 to $12 a month.[75] In 1894, 'ukuleles and taro patches in Honolulu were priced from $5 to $20 each, "according to finish"—anywhere from a third to an entire month's salary.[76] Yet "the music of the taro-patch fiddle has power to move the Hawaiian dollar," a Honolulu newspaper reported in October 1885.[77]

Not surprisingly, Nunes, Dias, and Santo turned first to their fellow immigrants as customers. In 1889, Santo sought to broaden his appeal by advertising his "guitar factory" (Fabrica de Violas) on Nuuanu Street as capable of producing twelve-string guitars just like those made on the island of São Miguel in the Azores.[78] But the Azoreans, Madeirans, and other Portuguese, who made up about 12 percent of the kingdom's population in 1884, represented a relatively small portion of the market. As their contracts expired throughout the 1880s and 1890s, they left the plantations—and often Hawaii altogether—for California, where their hunger to own land could be satisfied.[79] "I venture to say that 25 percent of the Portuguese have left this country within the last 18 months," Maui plantation manager C. B. Wells said in May 1893. "Many more would leave the country if they had the means."[80] Immigrant Chinese and Japanese, who made up something less than a quarter of the population in 1884, were unlikely to be customers because of language and cultural barriers. Haoles—Americans, British, and Germans—made up less than 10 percent of the population. The single largest market for 'ukuleles was the Native Hawaiians, the *kanaka maoli,* who in 1884 still constituted a clear majority of the population and had enthusiastically embraced the guitar.[81]

The patronage of King David Kalakaua, leader of the late-nineteenth-century revival of traditional Hawaiian culture, played perhaps the most visible role in popularizing the 'ukulele, in fostering its new identity as a native instrument, and building a market for the early makers. The earliest direct evidence of its use in the royal circle can be seen in an 1889 photograph of the king with Robert Louis Stevenson: Behind them are ranged the King's Singing Boys, one of whom is playing a 'ukulele.[82]

The Singing Boys were "that little group that played for him at our suppers and private parties," wrote Stevenson's stepdaughter, Isobel Strong, who as the wife of painter Joseph Strong lived in Honolulu for seven years (1883–1889) and became a frequent guest at Iolani Palace. "There were five of them, the best singers and performers on the ukulele and guitar in the whole islands."[83] At an all-night Waikiki party in 1893, two years after Kalakaua's death, it was the King's Singing Boys—"all

The King's Singing Boys, accompanied by ʻukulele, entertain King David Kalakaua and guest Robert Louis Stevenson, ca. 1889. Courtesy of Hawaii State Archives.

uniformed in white and wearing leis"—who provided the entertainment. "They played upon a very sweet-toned native instrument somewhat like a mandolin, and not only played for the dancers, but sang," wrote newly arrived Chicago reporter Mary Krout, describing what was likely the ʻukulele.[84] Kalakaua himself learned how to play and occasionally performed during late supper parties at Iolani Palace, according to Strong. "He would occasionally pick up a ukulele or guitar and sing his favorite Hawaiian song, Sweet Lei-lei-hua, and once he electrified us by bursting into

> Hoky poky winkum wum
> How do you like your taters done?
> Boiled or with their jackets on?
> Sang the King of the Sandwich Islands."[85]

João Fernandes reported that he, Dias, and fellow Madeiran João Luis Correa often played for Kalakaua in the king's bungalow on the palace grounds: "Lots of people came. Plenty kanakas. Much music, much hula, much kaukau [food], much drink. All time plenty drink. And King Kalakaua, he pay for all!"[86]

Christina Dias Gilliland, the oldest of Dias' nine children, recounted that Kalakaua was a frequent visitor to her father's King Street shop and asked him to build a five-string taro patch based on his own royal design. Dias enjoyed "being part of the scene at King Kalakaua's court," Gilliland remembered.[87] Liliuokalani also played the 'ukulele, although she appears to have favored the autoharp and guitar.[88]

Princess Victoria Kaiulani, Kalakaua's and Liliuokalani's niece and the queen's official heir, also played the 'ukulele. When English captain James C. Dewar held a party for Honolulu's social elite aboard his yacht *Nyanza* on January 25, 1889, the princess, her half-sister Annie Cleghorn, and one of the daughters of Judge Hermann A. Widemann played a 'ukulele trio as part of the evening's entertainment.[89] Cleghorn can be seen holding a 'ukulele in a photograph with Kaiulani and another unidentified young lady taken on the grounds of the Cleghorn estate, Ainahau, prior to thirteen-year-old Kaiulani's departure for England in May 1889.[90]

Princess Kaiulani (right, in kimono with parasol) and an unidentified woman (left) pose with Annie Cleghorn (center), who holds a taro patch, ca. 1884. Kaiulani reportedly took a 'ukulele with her to England. Courtesy of Hawaii State Archives.

A 1956 contest to find the oldest 'ukulele in Honolulu identified a Dias instrument dated 1884 that allegedly accompanied Kaiulani to England.[91] Elizabeth Kahanu, wife of Prince Jonah Kuhio Kalanianaole, also played; one turn-of-the-century visitor to their Waikiki bungalow noted that in addition to the koa piano, "mandolins, guitars, and the Hawaiian ukuleles and taropatches lie about."[92] After her husband was elected territorial delegate to Congress, it was reported that "the native instrument of Hawaii, a variety of guitar which lends itself readily to Kanaka folk music, is frequently heard in the drawing room of the fine residence in Massachusetts avenue maintained by the Kalanianaoles."[93]

Kalakaua's most public endorsement of this new musical innovation was likely during the celebrations surrounding his coronation in 1883. The coronation is believed to mark the first public performance of *hula kui*—literally a blend of old and new musical and dance styles accompanied by various combinations of guitar, 'ukulele, taro patch, banjo, violin, or piano, rather than by the traditional *ipu* (calabash drums).[94] As Amy Stillman has shown, *hula kui* was a departure from the *himeni*-style songs that characterized earlier Hawaiian music, a genre that reflected the new nationalist consciousness.[95] A photograph of a hula performance believed to have been taken at Kalakaua's 1886 Birthday Jubilee shows five dancers posed, arms akimbo, two kneeling chanters, and behind them a violinist and 'ukulele player.[96] An account of a poker party at Healani, Kalakaua's Honolulu boathouse, from the same period described the musical accompaniment as "a troupe of men with guitars . . . who began to play and sing a slow, melancholy ode."[97] Claims of royal patronage—either implied by the use of the royal Hawaiian coat of arms on 'ukulele headstocks, used by many makers after 1915, or stated directly in advertising—testify to the commercial importance of the royal seal of approval.[98]

However, there was more to Kalakaua's patronage than personal preference. His seventeen-year reign, during which the 'ukulele was introduced and rose to ubiquity, was a period of convulsive political conflict that pitted Native Hawaiians against the Islands' powerful haole elite.[99] At stake was nothing less than the fate of the monarchy and Hawaiian independence. Fueled by the explosive growth of the sugar industry, haole economic clout was joined with a contempt for Hawaiians and Hawaiian culture, a firm conviction in the inevitability of annexation by the United States, and the belief that as an inferior race Hawaiians were doomed to extinction—an opinion shared by Charles Darwin himself.[100]

Under the 1876 Reciprocity Treaty, profits continued to soar as sugar production rose from less than 25 million pounds in 1874 to 242 million pounds in 1889. By 1890, 99 percent of Hawaiian exports were shipped to the mainland; sugar was America's single largest import.[101] The result was to bind Hawaii ever more tightly to the United States. As the *New York Times* noted in 1892, the reciprocity treaty "tended to make Hawaii socially and commercially an American colony," or what U.S. Secretary of State James Blaine called "an outlying district of the state of California."[102] At the same time, the population of Native Hawaiians continued its catastrophic decline, shrinking by 16 percent over the same period to less than 41,000. "The native population [of Hawaii] need not give us much concern, not more surely than our own savage wards, whom we have caged for the most part in reservations, all that are left of them," California historian Hubert Howe Bancroft wrote in 1899. "Native nations when not wanted have an amiable way of disappearing before a superior race."[103] Talk of annexation to the United States—a regular topic of private conversation among planters for more than forty years—moved into the open.[104]

Despite the Hawaiian kingdom's rapid transformation during the preceding decades, by the end of the nineteenth century most Americans and other foreigners still regarded Native Hawaiians as taro patch–strumming savages—lazy, indolent, and childlike, lacking in the kind of intelligence or force of character needed for effective self-government and still loyal to the old gods despite a deceptive veneer of Christianity.[105] Even leading American anti-imperialists took this view. "It is a well-known fact that the great mass of people in those regions, in a state of freedom, labor just enough to satisfy their immediate wants; and these are very limited in a climate of perpetual summer," Carl Schurz wrote in 1893. "As . . . the high temperature discourages every strenuous and steady exertion, it is but natural that wherever in such climate labor is left to itself it should run into shiftlessness."[106] As the conflict between the Native Hawaiians and the planters grew, the monarchy and the cultural revival it fostered became the chief symbols of that struggle.

Kalakaua, whose election as king in 1874 triggered riots in Honolulu, was the first *moi* or king who was not a direct descendant of Kamehameha I and did not enjoy unanimous support among the *kanaka maoli*. As Jonathan K. K. Osorio has shown, it was vital that he demonstrate his high rank and fitness for the throne according to traditional Hawaiian standards.[107] All the symbols of Kalakaua's own legitimacy and more generally of Hawaiian national sovereignty—his coronation, construction of Iolani Palace, creation of a Board of Genealogy by the Legislature, the public revival of traditional hula and other Hawaiian arts—were regarded by the haole elite as compelling evidence of a retrograde barbarism and immorality. Under Kalakaua, "efforts to revive heathenism were now redoubled under the pretense of cultivating 'national' feeling," charged W. D. Alexander.[108] "Laws were passed at the King's nod, appropriating vast sums for such revels and indecencies as his lewd and extravagant tastes suggested; while orgies, debauchery, hulas, and 'sounds of revelry by night' made the neighborhood of the royal palace offensive to all but the royal debauchees," Volney Ashford sneered in 1893.[109] What white critics denounced as "frippery and nonsense," Osorio points out, were "highly assertive of the glory and vitality of Hawaiian traditions and affirmed the cultural distinctions between natives and foreigners." Unable to summon any meaningful support among Native Hawaiians for annexation, the haole elite presented their case as Christian civilization fighting against a rising tide of heathenism and immorality.[110]

The machete's adoption by the *kanaka maoli* and its rapid emergence as the 'ukulele and new identity as a uniquely Hawaiian instrument were inextricably bound up with the revival and politicization of Hawaiian culture—particularly the new music, or *hula kui,* for which it increasingly provided the accompaniment. Songs of the period were often a form of political discourse. Liliuokalani's first known composition, "Onipaa" ("Stand Firm," 1864), urged support for the new constitution promulgated by Kamehameha V.[111] Sometimes overtly, more often relying on *kaona,* or the hidden, layered meanings of Hawaiian, *mele*—published in newspapers, books, in sheet music, and presented in public performances—enabled Hawaiians to communicate, to comment, to protest, to build a sense of national solidarity, and to foster a sense of pride in Hawaiian language and culture.[112] When Liliuokalani was imprisoned by the provisional government in 1895 after a failed royalist counterrevolution, it was through *mele* published in the Hawaiian-language newspaper *Ka Makaainana* that she was able to convey a message of hope and resistance to Native Hawaiians.[113] *Ka Buke Mele Lahui (The Book of National Songs),* published in 1895, is full of political metaphors and more explicit language.[114] The first song in this collection is the famous "Kaulana na Pua o Hawaii," ("Famous Are the Flowers"), written in 1893 to celebrate the refusal of the members of the Royal Hawaiian Band to sign a loyalty oath to the new revolutionary government.[115] This was one of the songs that the King's Singing Boys performed on March 22, 1893, at an open-air concert of vocal and instrumental music at the Hawaiian Hotel before a crowd estimated at four to five thousand people—the triumphant first appearance of the new Hawaiian National Band.[116] "It was ostensibly musical, but in reality political," newspaper correspondent Mary Krout reported of the event held just after news arrived that President Grover Cleveland had refused to proceed with immediate annexation of the Islands. "At the conclusion of the last number, which was a vocal selection in Hawaiian . . . there was another outburst. The song proved to be written in Hawaiian for the occasion, in which the missionaries and the provisional government were soundly rated. Its reception was unmistakably warm."[117]

Counterrevolutionary songs like "Kaulana na Pua" were part of what Bernice Piilani Irwin called "a great wave of patriotism" that followed the overthrow of the monarchy. "The streets were filled with men wearing hatbands inscribed *Aloha 'Aina* (Love of Country)," Irwin wrote. "Hawaiian women busied themselves making flag-patterned bed quilts while men fashioned shields of koa wood, painting them with the Hawaiian coat of arms surmounted by crossed Hawaiian flags in order to keep their beloved emblem constantly before their eyes."[118] Koa (*Acacia koa*), a large evergreen hardwood unique to Hawaii, long had a special significance for Native Hawaiians—a role that in this highly politicized environment was an important factor in the 'ukulele's rapid popularity. Originally used primarily for canoes, it quickly became a mainstay of Island furniture makers upon the arrival of the missionaries, its commercial potential noted as early as 1793.[119] In the last half of the nineteenth century, samples of koa and other Hawaiian woods were a staple

Hawaiian exhibit at international exhibitions in the hope of developing a significant export market.[120] "Koa is perhaps the most valuable tree of the islands," William Hillebrand wrote in his pioneering 1888 Hawaiian flora. "For cabinet-work there are few woods to excel it. Being capable of receiving a high polish, under which its wavy lines appear to great advantage, it is much employed for veneers."[121]

But koa and other native woods were never in a position to compete with the imported lumber that flooded the Islands. Beginning in 1829, when the Hudson's Bay Company shipped its first cargo of timber to Honolulu from the Columbia River, foreign lumber dominated Hawaiian markets.[122] Small, undercapitalized logging concerns on the islands of Hawaii and Maui, handicapped by poor transportation and old-fashioned methods, couldn't compete with mainland firms like the Puget Mill Co. that shipped more than 1 million board feet to Hawaii in 1857 alone to meet urban and plantation demand.[123] As a result, from a very early date imported lumber was cheaper than native wood, a price gap that only widened when the reciprocity treaty admitted mainland lumber duty-free.[124] By 1890, Oregon pine cost less than 3 cents per foot, while koa sold for 14 cents per foot, a price that reflected not only backward production methods but a growing scarcity due to the depredations of livestock, clear cutting, and other environmental damage to upland forests.[125] The following year, the *Hawaiian Gazette* reported that "koa wood is becoming every year more scarce, and will soon be extinct unless measures are taken to preserve the forests."[126]

Despite its high cost, koa furniture found a ready market among Native Hawaiians as a symbol of *aloha aina*. Koa was intimately associated with Hawaiian royalty in the nineteenth century, literally from the cradle to the grave. The first royal throne, commissioned for Kamehameha III in 1847, was made of koa; the cradle for the heir of Kamehameha IV was made of koa; Hawaiian royalty slept in koa bedsteads and were buried in koa coffins.[127] Koa trees grew on the old palace grounds, and koa was used for the main staircase and other woodwork in Iolani Palace.[128] Liliuokalani's pew in Kawaiahao Church was made of koa; just months before the 1893 revolution, she was presented with a custom-made koa grand piano for which logs had been shipped to New York.[129] These facts could not have been lost on the Madeiran instrument makers, who had already worked with Hawaiian woods while building furniture.[130] Trained in European techniques, they used spruce or pine for the tops of their earliest Hawaiian-made instruments—softer woods they knew would produce a more traditional sound.[131] Yet they quickly began to make all-koa instruments—the single most important innovation in the transformation of the machete into the 'ukulele. Despite the greater cost and unconventional sound, koa appealed to the ardent patriotism of the *kanaka maoli* in the same way flag quilts or *aloha aina* hatbands did. This was one of the reasons why both Santo and Dias advertised instruments "made out of Hawaiian wood."[132] But royal patronage and a patriotic Hawaiian market did not make the 'ukulele makers royalists themselves. In one of the many ironies of Hawaiian history, like many Portuguese immigrants both Dias and Santo pledged their loyalty to the new Republic of Hawaii in 1894, swearing they would not "either directly or indirectly, encourage or assist in the restoration or establishment of a Monarchical form of Government in the Hawaiian Islands."[133]

Although the political dimension of much of the new Hawaiian music was often lost on the haole elite, the commercial possibilities of what one visitor called "the soft minor strains of the Kanaka minstrels steal[ing] outward on the air with a pulsing voluptuous sound" was not.[134] This was a far cry from the missionaries' complaints of unearthly howling by a people with no conception of Western harmony. Now, Hawaiians were described as natural musicians, passionate about music and "wonderfully pleasing" singers.[135] "To the novice, their music is delightful, it is so low, dreamy, and gentle, reminding one continually of the voices of birds," is how one tourist described it in 1892.[136] Hawaiian music as a commodity had arrived—one destined not only to play a defining role in the Islands' tourist industry but to become the latest Hawaiian export to the mainland.

CHAPTER 4

Have You Seen the Bouncing Flea?

Some would call the Ukulele an insignificant instrument, and yet we have all
there is necessary to make and cover an accompaniment for the most difficult
opera written.

—ERNEST KAAI, 1906

As the nineteenth century drew to a close, few people had a better sense of
the commercial potential of Hawaiian music—or were in a better position to exploit it—than Lorrin Thurston. Born in Hawaii to missionary
parents, classmate of Theodore Roosevelt at Columbia Law School, politician,
entrepreneur, and former minister of the interior, Thurston worked to promote
the Islands' fledgling tourist industry while simultaneously (and surreptitiously)
seeking the overthrow of the monarchy.[1] Appointed by Queen Liliuokalani in 1891
as a commissioner to help organize a Hawaiian exhibit for the upcoming World's
Columbian Exposition in Chicago, Thurston pursued both business and revolution as he sought a concession for his Kilauea Volcano cyclorama, as well as a better sense of the Harrison administration's attitude toward annexation.[2] When the
exposition and its gleaming white buildings opened on May 1, 1893, Liliuokalani
had been deposed, a haole-dominated provisional government had been installed
in Honolulu, and the privately funded Kilauea panorama stood ready for business
on the fair's mile-long Midway Plaisance—the only exhibit from Hawaii at the fair.[3]

To compete with such popular successes as the Ferris Wheel and the "Street
in Cairo," featuring the infamous belly dancer Little Egypt, Thurston relied on the
Volcano Singers. Posted in the elaborate bandstand that stood in front of the octagonal cyclorama building topped with Hawaiian flags and fronted with a towering
plaster statue of the goddess Pele, the quartet—Keoui Maipinepine, Keoui Elemeni,
A. O. East Kamualualii, and Nulhama "William" Aeko—played guitar, 'ukulele, and
taro patch, "singing in their native language the sunset songs of Hawaii."[4] As James
Revell Carr points out, this wasn't the first commercial or public performance of

Hawaiian music on the mainland: Four Native Hawaiian sailors gave a concert "in the native Sandwich Island language" in Portland, Maine, in 1838.[5] The Volcano Singers did, however, offer something new: the earliest-known professional performance in the new *hula kui* style accompanied by ʻukulele and taro patch.[6]

The Volcano Singers, who also played at international concerts presented in the exposition's Festival Hall, received some favorable notices, including one from a *Chicago Daily Tribune* critic who found the quartet "unique and interesting":

> The Hawaiians accompanied their numbers upon two guitars, a taro patch, and a ukelele. The latter instruments, on the guitar order, are respectively five and four stringed. The voices of the quartet are sweet, and in the case of the first tenor, Maipinepine, especially melodious. The charm lies in the naturalness. The "Wind Song," given as an encore, as well as their music throughout, is strongly tinged with the gentle pathos and rhythm of the negro melodies.[7]

While the Volcano Singers were an artistic success, the panorama lost money, which Thurston blamed on the Panic of 1893.[8] The biggest musical hit of the fair was "After the Ball," Charles K. Harris' "unavoidable, omnipresent accompaniment of the World's Fair summer" that became a staple of the Sousa Band's repertoire.[9]

Despite the historic significance of the Volcano Singers' appearances, it was on the West Coast that the ʻukulele and the new Hawaiian music developed their first real following on the mainland. Because of its proximity to the Islands and because

Music performed by the Volcano Singers was central to the ballyhoo at Lorrin Thurston's Kilauea panorama on the Midway Plaisance at the 1893 Chicago World's Fair. Courtesy of Jeff Carr.

of San Francisco's historic role as the chief port of the Pacific seaboard, California had long been Hawaii's principal point of contact with the mainland. It was the residents of "Kaleponi" who provided the first enthusiastic audiences for the 'ukulele and its music. California, after all, was the scene of the first documented hula performance on the mainland (in Monterey in 1792) and of the first mainland appearance of a professional hula troupe (in San Francisco, Sacramento, and the gold rush country in 1862).[10]

Although a novelty in Chicago, the Volcano Singers were only one of a number of such groups in the Islands, where the singing and playing of string orchestras was regularly featured at social events and at Honolulu hotels. "Scores of 'glee clubs'—quartets, quintets, and sextets—are to be heard almost any evening, in almost any place, filling the air with the sweetest and most soul haunting vocal melody, to stringed instrument accompaniment," one newspaper correspondent wrote.[11] Although renowned for its instrumental prowess under the baton of Bandmaster Henry Berger, one of the best-known singing groups was the Royal Hawaiian Band. The band regularly set aside its instruments and sang Native Hawaiian songs in four-part harmony.[12] At the band's weekly concerts in Honolulu—held at the Hawaiian Hotel, Thomas Square, and Emma Square—the program "generally consists of ten numbers, with intervals between, during which native airs are sung and the men in the audience join in the chorus," an American visitor noted in 1880. "Some of the songs are 'Aloha Oe' (Greeting or Love to You), 'Leilehua' (Garland of Flowers), 'Aina Hau' (Land of the Snow), and 'Ahi Wela' (Burning Love). These natives have very good voices and never force them or strain at the notes. Every concert winds up with the national anthem 'Hawaii Ponoi.'"[13]

More often, tourists heard the same native airs sung by smaller groups—at a hotel reception or dance, a luau, a Waikiki swimming party, or floating through the windows on the night air. "Returning to the hotel we are impressed by the gay and lovely picture of life it represents," Charles Taylor wrote of an 1896 stay at the Hawaiian Hotel. "Parlor, reception and ballroom are beautiful and fragrant with flowers, and dozens of happy young people are gliding gracefully through the modern waltz, to the music of four Kanaka men, who sing and play at the same time. The instruments are a violin, a banjo, and two guitars."[14] Because of tourists' lack of familiarity with the 'ukulele and taro patch, they often were described as guitars, mandolins, or even banjos. When Solomon Hiram's quintet entertained a visiting group of mainland Shriners at the Damon estate in Moanalua in 1901, it was described as playing a violin, two guitars, two banjos, and a flute; a photo of the group shows clearly that one of the instruments is a 'ukulele.[15] In the summer of 1898, less than a year before her untimely death, Princess Kaiulani employed a native quartet to entertain Charles Philips Trevelyan, eldest son of the distinguished English historian, during an outing spent near Koko Head. "There we spent the day talking, eating, bathing, and listening to a choir of four natives who sang to us most beautifully native songs, with very fine voices," Trevelyan wrote in a letter. "We enjoyed ourselves greatly and then rode home, a funny cavalcade, first the princess driving with her pretty niece and a handsome young American, then the four musicians singing and twanging hard."[16]

In turn-of-the-century Hawaii, missionary complaints about the appalling lack of musical talent among the natives were long forgotten; now all Hawaiians were described as having an inborn taste and talent for music.[17] Everyone, it was said, could play or sing. "They are natural musicians and their plaintive, semi-barbaric music once heard will never be forgotten," one visitor wrote in 1899. "There are few natives who cannot play upon the taro patch or ukelele, a sort of guitar."[18] Visitors routinely reported hearing snatches of music through an open window or out in the street, as Charles Warren Stoddard described it in 1883, from "a troop of troubadours strumming a staccato measure that dies away in the distance like a shower of sparks." [19] Serenading parties were often encountered in the Islands, as they were in the streets of Funchal.[20] Nor was this strictly a Honolulu phenomenon. In 1882, a Hilo newspaper correspondent reported that its Fourth of July celebration had included "a party of natives [that] serenaded the various houses at an early hour in the morning."[21] The first time songwriter and musician Sam Kia Kalainaina heard a violin—the instrument that instantly captured his imagination—was around 1889 when a traveling group of musicians playing guitar, 'ukulele, and violin visited his home in the remote Waipio Valley on the Big Island's northern shore.[22] In May 1896, as famed mainland journalist Kate Field lay dying in the stateroom of an interisland steamer off the coast of the Big Island, "some native Hawaiians began singing on deck outside her window, accompanying themselves on the guitar and the native *ukuleli.*"[23] One travel writer remarked how at twilight "the natives gather in groups to talk and sing. There is a plaintive melody about their singing that is very pleasant . . . and the native songs sound very well in the open air and upon the water."[24]

Just as they often had difficulty describing a 'ukulele, visitors struggled to describe the music it made. Michael Shoemaker, who heard some songs sung in Hilo by Hawaiian women, wrote afterward that the music sounded like "a strange mingling of the quaint sounds of Norway with the plaintive murmurs of our own South, through which clashes now and then a strain of barbaric music from the Orient."[25] American artist John La Farge was more prosaic, calling the music he heard on the Big Island in 1890 "melancholy chants adapted to European airs"— except one song, which reminded him of "a sad romantic sort of cakewalk."[26] "Soft," "sweet," and "plaintive" were the adjectives most often used to describe both the singing and the playing of Hawaiian musicians. The Hawaiian language itself— once regarded by missionaries as a source of moral contamination so foul that their children were not allowed to speak it—was now regarded as an essential part of the charm of the new music.[27] Actress Nance O'Neil, a tourist of 1899, described the singing of Hawaiian songs "as only natives can sing them. They have such a wail of plaintive sadness running through them that it almost breaks the heart of those

who listen."[28] In a musical era when a sharp line was drawn between instrumental-
ists and vocalists, observers routinely commented on the novel ability of Hawaiian
musicians to sing to their own accompaniment. "Now, this ability to play and sing
is very unusual," Robert J. Burdette noted in discussing the Royal Hawaiian Band.
"[Sousa's band members] can whistle most excellently, but indeed they cannot sing
acceptably before even a mildly critical audience. But the Hawaiian band or orchestra sings as well as it plays."[29]

Early recordings give some idea of what tourists heard, although the technical limitations of the acoustic recording technology of the time left much to be
desired. "We have heard the cruel travesties of Hawaiian music that some phonographs give, and wondered why an instrument that can reproduce Caruso should so
insult the Hawaiian voice and the Hawaiian strings," Katherine Fullerton Gerould
complained in 1916.[30] The problem was that acoustic recording could successfully
reproduce only a narrow band of sound, with the result that stringed instruments
like the 'ukulele were difficult to record. Most early cylinders and discs are dominated by the sounds of military bands, leather-lunged tenors, and the metallic, pen-
etrating sound of banjos and xylophones.[31] On early recordings of Hawaiian music,
the 'ukulele is almost always used in a strictly rhythmic role, with the melody being
played by steel guitar, violin, or flute.

It is the earliest 'ukulele methods that give the clearest idea of what contemporary playing techniques were like. Although Edward Holstein's chord book
appeared in 1894, Ernest Kaai was the first to offer a complete method in *The Ukulele: A Hawaiian Guitar, and How to Play It,* published in Honolulu by Wall, Nichols
Co. in 1906.

The son of Simon Kaai—member of the House of Nobles, former minister of
the interior and finance for Kalakaua and a staunch royalist—Ernest was a pivotal
figure in the development of the 'ukulele.[32] A self-taught musical virtuoso, teacher
of 'ukulele, guitar, and mandolin, impresario, music publisher, and entrepreneur, by
1906 Kaai was competing successfully with singer and musician John Ellis (1877–
1914) as one of the chief packagers and bookers of Hawaiian music in Honolulu.[33]
That year, for example, he organized a tour of Kauai that included Nani Alapai, the
Royal Hawaiian Band's singer, and fourteen-year-old Johnny Noble, the famous
composer and bandleader who at the time was known as an artistic whistler.[34] By
the following year, Kaai had opened up an office in the Alexander Young Hotel and
was advertising himself as a teacher of guitar, mandolin, banjo, zither, 'ukulele, and
taro patch, as well as conductor of "the best Glee-Club in the Islands, Authority on
Hawaiian Music, and Concert Soloist."[35]

Kaai's method, which uses C tuning, largely ignores standard musical notation
in favor of a system of tablature to lead pupils through such Hawaiian standards as
"Aloha Oe," "Sweet Lei Lehua," "Hawaii Ponoi," and "Tomi Tomi," hapa haole hits
such as "Honolulu Tomboy" and "Waikiki Mermaid," and a few mainland tunes
that included "The Swanee River" ("Old Folks at Home") in a range of keys and

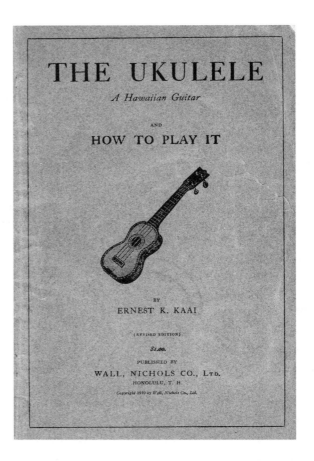

Ernest Kaai's *The Ukulele*, published in Honolulu in 1906, was the first true 'ukulele method. Subsequent method writers borrowed liberally from Kaai.

As early as 1907, Ernest Kaai billed himself as an authority on Hawaiian music.

using a variety of strokes. "Some would call the Ukulele an insignificant instrument, and yet we have all there is necessary to make and cover an accompaniment for the most difficult opera written," he insisted.[36]

Driving the new music was a generation of younger musicians—a remarkable mix of reform school boys and aristocrats, many of whom grew up with the 'ukulele and treated it not as a foreign import but as an integral part of Hawaiian musical culture. Mekia Kealakai (1867–1944) of Honolulu, trombone player, guitarist, and flautist, composer, bandleader, and teacher, and David Nape (1870–1913) of Hilo, gifted musician, singer, and composer, were both alumni of the Reformatory School in Honolulu and of the Royal Hawaiian Band.[37] Like Kaai, 'ukulele virtuoso George Kia Nahaolelua (1877–1929) came from a royalist background: The grandson of Paul Nahaolelua, former governor of Maui, he was the son of Elizabeth, a lady-in-waiting to Liliuokalani.[38] William (b. 1874) and John Ellis, both of whom performed with the Royal Hawaiian Band and with Kaai, were the sons of High Chiefess Nancy Wahinekapu Sumner.[39] Pianist, composer, and arranger Albert "Sonny" Cunha (1879–1933), although part-Hawaiian on his mother's side, was neither aristocratic nor delinquent. A football and baseball star while at Yale Law School, Cunha was the son of an Azorean sailor who married the boss' daughter, took over the family business—Honolulu's Union Saloon—and invested wisely in real estate.[40] There also were other lesser-known artists, such as Antonio Abreu Santos, better known as "Batata" (Potato), who wowed a crowd at a 1910 concert at the Honolulu YMCA with his solo renditions of John Philip Sousa's "Stars and Stripes Forever" and "Under the Double Eagle" on the 'ukulele.[41]

The rise of these young, innovative musicians and the growing popularity of the 'ukuleles that were an integral part of the music they made coincided with the overthrow of the monarchy and annexation to the United States—all of which fostered a new interest in the Islands on the mainland and intensified efforts in Hawaii to promote tourism. Coverage of Hawaii dramatically increased after 1893, not only in newspapers and weighty journals such as the *Nation* and *North American Review,* but in popular magazines such as *Cosmopolitan, Scribner's,* and *Lippincott's.*[42] New books poured off the presses; in the summer of 1898, the *New York Times Book Review* listed three dozen recent books and forty magazine articles about Hawaii, including Liliuokalani's own *Hawaii's Story by Hawaii's Queen.*[43] "We are pitching scores of manuscripts on Hawaii and the Philippines out of our office every day," a well-known publisher was quoted as saying a week later. "Other houses are deluged in the same way, they tell me."[44] The 'ukulele made its mainland literary debut in Richard Hamilton Pott's 1893 short story, "Kulamea," in which the heroine of that name fascinated young Francis Balfour by singing "her pretty native songs to the accompaniment of her ukelele, bringing out all the sad, weird charm of which they were capable."[45] Edison and other film companies featured footage of Honolulu scenes and "Hula Hula dancers as they go through the dance characteristic of the nation."[46] Public curiosity about Hawaii was great, given how little was known about the Islands. As a freshman at Yale in 1898, missionary grandson Henry Judd was astonished by the ignorance of Yale debaters as they prepared to take on Harvard on the question of whether Hawaii should be annexed. "Some of the statements were ludicrous and some absolutely false, such as . . . 'There is only one island,' 'The islands are too hot for Germanic or Anglo-Saxon people to live in.'"[47] Many had no idea how to pronounce "Hawaii." A *New York Times* reporter recorded a dozen different versions during a debate on the floor of the U.S. Senate two years after annexation, including "Hah-way-eye," "Ha-wi," and "Ha-wi-ah."[48]

By the turn of the century, Honolulu had regular, twice-monthly steamship service to and from San Francisco, half-a-dozen guidebooks in print, its own promotional magazine—*Paradise of the Pacific*—and was welcoming a small but steady stream of tourists, including tours from the leading Boston excursion agency of Raymond & Whitcomb.[49] In 1903, with financial support from the territorial government, the Honolulu Chamber of Commerce and Merchants Association created the Hawaii Promotion Committee to sell the Islands as a tourist attraction and investment opportunity, opening offices in Los Angeles and San Francisco.[50] By then, three major hotels had opened to complement the thirty-year-old Hawaiian Hotel: the Moana at Waikiki, the Alexander Young in downtown Honolulu, and the Haleiwa in Waialua at the northern terminus of the Oahu Railway & Land Co.'s line.[51]

As natives of an Atlantic island that had catered to tourists for generations, Santo, Nunes, and Dias needed no convincing about the value of appealing to the tourist trade. By 1898, the three pioneering luthiers—all listed as guitar manufacturers in the city directory—were wholesaling "native Hawaiian" instruments to retail outlets outside Chinatown.[52] Wall, Nichols Co. called itself "Headquarters for Hawaiian Ukuleles and Taro-patch Guitars," while the Hawaiian News Co. advertised that its music department—headed by Edward Holstein—"is complete with all kinds of musical instruments, including Native Ukuleles and Taro-Patch Guitars," and Bergstrom Music Co. boasted that it had "all the latest Hawaiian Songs and Music, Hawaiian Taro Patch and Ukulele Guitars."[53]

Less than two decades after its introduction to the Islands, the 'ukulele had become a staple tourist souvenir, "which in many places in the States is synonymous with Hawaii."[54] The instruments "peculiar to the islands are the ukulele or taropatch," explained the *Hawaiian Almanac and Annual* in 1899. "They are small guitar shaped instruments, made of native woods, hundreds of which are sold to visiting tourists, and are now scattered all over the world."[55] Among the first to take a 'ukulele home was Mabel Andrews of Brooklyn, a cousin of Lorrin Thurston. Andrews accompanied Thurston and the other provisional government commissioners on their 1893 trip to Washington, D.C., to press for immediate annexation after the overthrow of the monarchy, and she was spotted during a stop in Chicago caressing "a miniature guitar, which in the native language is known as the 'ukulele.'" She was quoted as saying, "One thing that struck me particularly was the fact

DO YOU WANT

Hawaiian Songs, Set to Music,
Books on Hawaii,
Photographs of Hawaiian Scenery,
Ukuleles, or Taro Patch Guitars,
The Tourists' Guide,
In fact, anything as a

Hawaiian Souvenir

If so, Call on, or Write to

The HAWAIIAN NEWS COMPANY,
(LIMITED)

Merchant Street, Honolulu, H. I.

- - Publishers, Booksellers and Music Dealers. - -

`Ukuleles quickly became a standard Hawaiian souvenir, as this 1894 guidebook advertisement shows.

that all natives seem to be natural musicians," unaware that much of what she heard voiced protests against the overthrow of the monarchy. "They get exquisite music from the ukuleles."[56] Fifteen years later, the *Pacific Commercial Advertiser* pointed out that the ubiquity of the 'ukulele "is proven by the display in every music store and curio shop in the country."[57]

Not surprisingly, many of the tourists picking through the stock at the Hawaiian News Co. were from California. While spending the winter of 1889–1890 in California, Helen Mather was repeatedly asked "if I should not visit 'the islands' before going away. . . . From the familiar way people spoke of 'running down' to them [I thought it was] perhaps the kind of excursion one takes when going from New York to Coney Island."[58] Thousands of Masons from across the country got their first taste of modern Hawaiian music during the Royal Hawaiian Band's first-ever mainland appearance at the Twenty-Second Triennial Conclave of the Knights Templar in San Francisco in August 1883. Although public interest was initially stimulated by false rumors that some of its thirty members were infected with leprosy, the band's musicianship is what left the most lasting impression.[59] Playing at a series of conclave events, as well as at gigs at the Palace Hotel (official headquarters of the conclave) and city theaters, the band and its mix of Hawaiian, American, and European instrumental and vocal music was a hit, "acknowledged by the Press and the Public to be the best Band that has ever visited San Francisco," crowed

Woodward's Garden, a popular pleasure resort that featured the band in concert.[60] In the conclave's Grand Parade and review, the Royal Hawaiian Band was selected from among the more than twenty bands present to march as special escort to the Grand Master and the Grand Encampment of the United States. "The dusky sons of the distant islands bid fair to outdo their competitors on this coast in regard to skill and merit as musicians," the *San Francisco Chronicle* commented.[61]

When the Chicago World's Fair ended in October 1893, Thurston's cyclorama was shipped west to be exhibited at the San Francisco Midwinter Fair, where what was now called the Pele Quartet was a featured part of the program. Fairgoer Phil Weaver Jr. described how he paid his 50 cents, went in, and "listened to the lecture and the sweetest Hawaiian quartet singing in the moonlight among the volcanic rocks of the great Kilauea to the accompaniment of the 'taro-patch fiddle.'"[62] In a performance at the fair's recreation grounds in front of a crowd estimated at ten thousand, the quartet, "nattily attired and carrying guitars . . . rendered one of those strangely beautiful native songs which have delighted thousands who have visited the Hawaiian concession. Storms of applause greeted the rendition, indicating that the vast throng appreciated something good in the musical line when it heard it." For an encore, the quartet sang, in English, the comic song, "The Midway Plaisance."[63] *Paradise of the Pacific* proudly reported on the success of the "sweet strains from the 'taro patch fiddle,' banjo and guitar skillfully played" by the quartet. "No small number of fair pupils from San Francisco's 'swell set' have been for weeks industriously practicing the 'taro patch fiddle' under the tuition of the dusky player at the Hawaiian Village."[64] The cyclorama and the quartet appeared in Boston in April 1895 in the Tremont Street building that once housed Paul Philippoteaux's famous cyclorama of the battle of Gettysburg. "These natives are fine-looking fellows, dressed in neat white flannel suits," the *Boston Daily Globe* reported. "They are dark-skinned, with intelligent faces, flashing eyes and rows of exquisite teeth. Their voices are exceedingly mellow and sweet and their singing is most delightful."[65] Appropriately, Liliuokalani herself was featured in an early East Coast performance, albeit an amateur one: a private concert at her Washington, D.C., hotel for a few select guests in February 1897. The queen accompanied herself on the autoharp; it was left to Grace Hilborn, daughter of the anti-annexationist Republican congressman from California, to sing Hawaiian songs while playing "the ukulele, a native instrument that looks and sounds like a diminutive guitar, and upon which she plays with great skill."[66]

At the same time the Volcano Singers were appearing in Boston, the former members of the Royal Hawaiian Band—now calling themselves Ka Bana Lahui, or the Hawaiian National Band—launched a tour of the mainland with the financial backing of sugar magnate John D. Spreckels.[67] Having refused offers from Thurston to appear in Chicago in 1893 and San Francisco in 1894, the band was on a mission—"to let the people of this country judge whether the natives of the islands are a barbarous, ignorant, uncivilized tribe, with cannibalistic tendencies, or an enlightened and educated race of people who have been deprived of their property, their liberty and their country by an intriguing lot of foreigners masquerading before the world in the virtuous garb of the missionaries."[68] When the band arrived in San Francisco on May 15, 1895, nationalist feeling was still running high in the wake of January's failed armed uprising against the newly declared Republic of Hawaii and the subsequent arrest, imprisonment, and forced abdication of Liliuokalani.[69]

Starting with a series of concerts in San Francisco and San Jose followed by several days in Los Angeles, the forty-piece band under the direction of bandmaster and saxophone soloist Jose S. Libornio dazzled California audiences. "They were good musicians—entirely different from any other band I've seen," said their manager (and future Honolulu mayor) Johnny Wilson, son of former Hawaiian marshal and royalist Charles Wilson. "They'd open a regular concert using their band instruments. Then during intermission they would entertain by singing—they were outstanding singers. In the next half of the program, they would be a symphony of strings. Everyone in the band played two or more instruments."[70]

Wilson's enthusiasm was matched by the crowds that turned out to hear the Hawaiians play, dressed in their uniform of white pants and blue coats. The band drew "an immense crowd" to the Sutro Baths in San Francisco, where "all the space within hearing distance of the band was packed with people who enjoyed the sweet sounds produced by the musicians from the islands," the *Call* reported.[71] An estimated five thousand people took the train to Redondo Beach for the band's final southern California appearance. "In the afternoon the Hawaiians assembled in the bandstand, with their guitars and violins, and gave many songs to the delighted throng of listeners," the *Los Angeles Times* reported. "Some of the men have magnificent voices, and the Hawaiian music is quaint and bewitching enough to stir the most sluggish pulse to quicker movement."[72]

Over the following eighteen months, the band traveled thousands of miles to play hundreds of dates in the Midwest and South, introducing new audiences to Hawaiian music and earning excellent reviews for its singing as well as its playing.[73] In Chicago, the band played with "great spirit, qualified by sympathy and marked by finish. . . . They also sang their quaint, melodious songs in an agreeable and delightful fashion."[74] Dallas praised the band's music as being "of the highest order. . . . As vocalists they are very fine. Their rendition of several numbers is fully in keeping with their instrumental efforts."[75] In Denver, the band played to a City Park audience estimated at twenty thousand. "Of course, some of the instruments were new to many present, as for instance the 'taro patch' fiddle, from which come the most beautiful strains imaginable when in the hands of the artist," enthused the *Rocky Mountain News*.[76] Each appearance was an opportunity to tell the story of the band's refusal to sign the Provisional Government's oath of allegiance and to emphasize the Native Hawaiians' continued opposition to annexation. "Do you think we want to be regarded as a sort of Indian agency, and that we want to be

TATTERSALL'S—*Sixteenth and State-sts.*

Today at 2:15, Tonight at 8:15, and Every Afternoon and Night Until May 2d.
DOORS OPEN ONE HOUR BEFORE EACH PERFORMANCE.

RINGLING BROS.'
WORLD'S GREATEST SHOWS.

Tremendous Success! Unexampled Amusement Triumph! More thousands
of patrons than ever before attended a Circus in one week. Greater applause
and more new features than ever before seen under roof or canvas.

HAVE YOU SEEN——
THE LOCKHART ELEPHANTS?
ELLA ZUILA AND LU LU?
THE FLYING DACOMAS?
THE 6 FAMOUS JORDANS?
SPEEDY'S GREAT DIVE?
MLLE. IRWIN, THE HUMAN TOP?

And the scores of
Other Exclusive
features of the

Greatest Circus, Menagerie, and Hippodrome Ever Seen on Earth?

See What the Chicago Dailies Say of the Show.

There was more in the show than ever before offered.—Daily News.
The most redoubtable competitors in the whole tent world.—Dispatch.
The show was far ahead of anything in the circus line that has been here for years.—Journal.
It is the fault of the Ringlings that they provide too much.—Times-Herald.
If there is an exclusive circus feature in existance which the "World's Greatest Shows" have not captured it is because no inducement could bring it to this country.—Record.
A Score of Great Riders. Real Roman Hippodrome. Finest Zoological Collection on Earth. Gorgeous Introductory Tournament. One Hour of Concert Music before each Performance by the

Far more in the way of the unique, intrepid, and interesting than any one person could comprehend.—Tribune.
Really merits the title, "The World's Greatest Shows."—Post.
Ringling Bros.' show is larger and better than ever. It would take a gallon of ink and a ream of manuscript to describe the show.—The Inter-Ocean.
The best circus performance money and experience could produce. Not a man or woman was disappointed.—Chronicle.

ROYAL HAWAIIAN BAND.

Reserved Seats, 50c, 75c, and $1.00. Box Seats, $1.50. On sale at Lyon & Healy's and at Tattersall's.
Gallery, 25c. Children, half price, at matinées only. Telephone, 1163 South.

> During its 1895–1896 mainland tour, the Hawaiian National Band played a three-week engagement with the Ringling Brothers' Circus in Chicago.

referred to as wards of your nation, to be fought over by the Bryans and the McKinleys?" cornetist Samuel K. Kamakaia asked in an 1896 newspaper interview. "Never, so long as there is Hawaiian blood in our veins."[77]

By the turn of the century, Hawaiian music and musicians were not the only exports from the Islands. Annexation had spurred new efforts to seek mainland markets for Hawaiian goods. Taroena, "the great Hawaiian health food," appeared on Los Angeles grocery shelves even before annexation, followed by Hawaiian coffee—"the finest product of Uncle Sam's Pacific garden"—stylish women's hats for summer wear, and papayas, coconuts, and other tropical fruits, as well as jams, jellies, pickles, and chutneys.[78] Slowly things Hawaiian began to acquire a certain social cachet. In Los Angeles, for example, Hawaiian luncheons, afternoon receptions, and evenings began to appear in the newspaper society columns—entertainments and benefits built around Hawaiian flags and leis, potted ferns and bamboo, curios, and "Hawaiian" zither solos and orchestras of mandolin, banjo, and guitar.[79] Among the curios on display might be found "an odd little ukalili, or Hawaiian guitar . . . about eighteen inches in length and said by connoisseurs to possess a remarkably sweet tone."[80]

While most of the professional Hawaiian musicians were men, those on the mainland most likely to have "an odd little ukalili" at home tended to be well-to-do women. In the fall of 1896, Mrs. C. R. Templeton—who three years earlier had visited Hawaii—entertained the Portland, Oregon, Women's Club by singing "Aloha Oe," to which she played "an accompaniment on the ukulele—a native musical instrument—which looks like a small violin."[81] Two years later, a sextet of young society ladies in San Francisco offered "three Hawaiian songs, sung to the accompaniment of two taropatches and four ukuleles" at the California Club's elaborate Hawaiian Day.[82] The following summer, during a moonlight cruise off the southern California summer resort of Catalina Island, Miss Daisy Cartwright of Oakland "contributed greatly to the pleasure of the evening by playing several numbers on the ukulele, a Hawaiian instrument similar to the guitar, and by singing Hawaiian songs. She was assisted in singing by Miss Harriet E. Howe of Los Angeles."[83] The 'ukulele began to make appearances up and down the West Coast in the hands of young ladies: at a 1902 meeting of the San Jose Women's Club; in the hands of Mrs. Lucie May Hayes of East Oakland in 1903; at a 1905 meeting of the Women's Missionary Society of the First Presbyterian Church in Bellingham, Washington; in Portland, where Miss Helen Brigham "charmingly accompanie[d] herself on the terrapatch and the eucalali"; at a charity musical in Juneau, Alaska, that same year; and at a church benefit in Boise, Idaho, in 1907.[84]

Like the guitar, the 'ukulele was regarded as an appropriate instrument for women: It was soft in volume, pitched to correspond to a soprano voice, and small in size, allowing for a graceful, ladylike posture while playing and requiring a minimum of exertion.[85] Women were the chief market for sheet music and other forms of popular musical culture; one contemporary study found that women made the final decision in the purchase of phonographs more than three-quarters of the time.[86] In the 1912 catalog of the San Francisco music firm of Sherman, Clay & Co., women are the only customers shown in a photo of the firm's Victrola demonstration room.[87] Retailers generally—and the new department stores particularly—marketed themselves to women, who made up as much as 80 to 90 percent of their customers. Edward A. Filene of Boston was only half joking when he called his store "an Adamless Eden."[88] Marketer James H. Collins took a similar view: "The advertiser talks vaguely of a creature which he calls, variously, 'he,' 'it,' 'clientele,' and 'the public'; yet that creature is woman, pure and simple."[89]

In particular, young women of high school and college age found the new instrument attractive. Long before the Roaring Twenties, the period inescapably associated with the 'ukulele, young people in California had adopted the "eucalili." At a reception for Stanford University faculty and trustees at Jane Stanford's San Francisco home in January 1900, the entertainment was provided by "the Honolulu band," dressed in native costume and accompanying themselves on native instruments. "Mrs. Stanford is very fond of Hawaiian music, and the guests by their applause echoed her sentiments," one account of the reception said.[90] Hawaiian music was often heard at college events in the Bay Area that year—at a Stanford student reception in Palo Alto and at Phoebe Hearst's annual garden party for graduating seniors at the University of California.[91] At Mills College, the Bay Area women's college founded by a former Oahu College president and his wife, music by Hawaiian students was featured at a 1900 fundraising fair, and four years later the Kapiolani Club offered an evening entertainment that featured a Hawaiian quintet to help raise money for a scholarship for Hawaiian students.[92]

On its 1911 tour of Europe, one of the first by a glee club from an American college, the University of California Glee Club featured Hawaiian songs in its repertoire—a prominent part of the program "reminiscent of home" that at least one listener greeted as a relief from the crash and blare of German military bands.[93] The 'ukulele was equally popular in Los Angeles—whether at an Alpha Chi Omega sorority rush, a vaudeville benefit staged by local debutantes, or a garden party benefit at which a couple of Occidental College girls "thrum[med] the ukuleles, drawing sweet strains of Hawaiian melodies from these plaintive-toned instruments."[94] As part of the Hawaiian program at the January 1913 meeting of the Hollywood Woman's Club, a quartet of local high school girls "lightly fingered the ukeles [*sic*], the favorite Hawaiian musical instrument, which resembles a baby banjo. To this accompaniment, a charming young girl, Miss Esther Olsen, sang the Hawaiian national song, 'Aloha [Oe]'—and she sang it with just the right cadence, throwing into it the soft, lilting, plaintive tones which characterize the native Hawaiian melodies."[95]

The popularity of the 'ukulele and Hawaiian music among young Californian women also is reflected in Jack London's 1913 novel *The Valley of the Moon*—the first novel in which the 'ukulele makes an appearance on the mainland.[96] Saxon Brown, a twenty-four-year-old Oakland laundry worker who marries teamster Billy Roberts, learned "the loose-wristed facility of playing accompaniments on the ukulele" from Mercedes, a neighbor. When Saxon and Billy left Oakland on a search for a new life in the country, they eventually wound up on the beach in Carmel with a group of young bohemians. "The girls lighted on Saxon's ukulele and nothing would do but she must play and sing. Several of them had been to Honolulu, and knew the instrument. . . . Also, they knew Hawaiian songs she had learned from Mercedes and soon, to her accompaniment, all were singing 'Aloha Oe,' 'Honolulu Tomboy' and 'Sweet Lei Lehua.'"[97]

Although Saxon is a fictional example, the 'ukulele was well adapted to California's outdoor lifestyle, where families spent weeks at a time camped out on the beach or up in the mountains during the summer.[98] London—who was first introduced to the 'ukulele during his 1906 trip across the Pacific aboard the *Snark*—drew on real life for his fiction. For example, in August 1911 more than three dozen young people held a cookout on a Catalina Island beach. "The steaks were fried over driftwood fires, and were declared to surpass anything ever served on the island," it was reported. "After the 'eats' a dozen or so mandolins, guitars and ukuleles were produced and 'harmony' indulged in."[99] Four years earlier, George Freeth had arrived from Honolulu and begun to put on well-publicized surfing exhibitions at Venice and Redondo Beach—the first in southern California.[100] From the start, whether fashions in ladies' hats, water sports, or musical trends, Hawaiian products and Hawaiian culture were associated with the beach and the outdoors.

Californians drew their musical inspiration not only from trips to Hawaii but from visiting Hawaiian musicians, who steadily developed a West Coast audience during the first decade of the new century.[101] One of the first groups to perform in California—made up of William Ellis, July Paka [Parker], William Kai, Thomas Hennessey, and Thomas Kiliwa—became a fixture in San Francisco in 1899–1902, making it the first mainland city to enjoy the services of a Hawaiian orchestra on a regular basis.[102] The Hawaiian Quintet, as it was known, performed in local theaters and played at dances, private dinners, gatherings of fraternal organizations, charity galas, insurance company banquets, and serenaded Liliuokalani when she passed through San Francisco in May 1900.[103] As the only California city with direct steamer service to Honolulu, San Francisco quickly became a center of Hawaiian music.

In 1905, the city hosted both Mekia Kealakai's Kawaihau Orchestra and Glee Club—"the 10 finest musicians, both vocal and instrumental, in the Islands"—and John Ellis' Hawaiian Orchestra, which played at Techau's Tavern, while a sextette headed by Sonny Cunha played in the beach resort of Santa Cruz to the south for the entire summer season.[104] Across the bay in Oakland, the Royal Hawaiian quartette featured "the sweet melodies of the far off Paradise of the Pacific" at the Bell Theater.[105]

After the devastating April 1906 earthquake and fire that leveled much of San Francisco, the scene shifted south to Los Angeles. In 1907 a series of anonymous Hawaiian groups—billed only as the Hawaiian Band, the Hawaiian Orchestra, the Hawaiian Sextette, and so on—appeared in Los Angeles at the Orpheum Theater, the Venice Auditorium, the Chutes (a local amusement park), the opening of new real estate subdivisions, as part of a Hawaiian promotion at a downtown grocery store, and at society birthday parties.[106] When visiting club women stepped off the streetcars during a July 1907 outing to the beachside resort of Venice, "Hawaiian

A 1907 portrait of Mekia Kealakai (with flute) and his Kawaihau Club Orchestra at the Oregon Grill in Portland, Oregon. Courtesy of Rosa Portell.

music saluted their ears, and immediately the Venice Hawaiian Quartette was surrounded by a group of interested listeners. The music was played on guitars, and the Hawaiian instrument, the ukulele, the musicians wearing the leis of royal orange around their necks."[107] Just one week earlier, George J. Birkel Co. ran a newspaper advertisement that asked readers, "Have You Seen the Bouncing Flea?" announcing the imminent arrival of a shipment of 'ukuleles, "the most charming of all the Hawaiian instruments," at its South Spring Street music store.

"Shaped like a guitar, but much smaller, it is played by strumming and skipping the fingers from one side of the instrument to the other, hence the name Ukulele—meaning a bouncing flea," explained the ad—the earliest known example of retail sales on the mainland. "The instrument is easily mastered—the learner gets more pleasure out of it in a month than he could with a guitar or other string instrument in a year."[108] By May 1909, Hawaiian music was fashionable enough that Estelle Doheny, wife of the millionaire oilman Edward Doheny, employed several Hawaiians to sing "the pretty native airs" at a garden party at her Chester Place mansion.[109]

Hawaiian musicians covered the entire West Coast during the first decade of the new century. The Royal Hawaiian Band sailed to the mainland to play the Lewis

Have You Seen the Bouncing Flea?

Prof. Kia, a native Hawaiian musician, has introduced to the Pacific Coast the most charming of all the Hawaiian musical instruments. It is the Ukulele, shaped like a guitar, but much smaller. It is played by strumming and skipping the fingers from one side of the instrument to the other, hence the name Ukulele—meaning a bouncing flea.

The instrument is easily mastered—the learner gets more pleasure out of it in a month than he could with a guitar or other string instrument in a year.

A shipment of these popular instruments is now on the way to our store. They will be on sale next Wednesday. See them in our window.

GEO. J. BIRKEL COMPANY
STEINWAY, CECILIAN AND VICTOR DEALERS.
345-347 SOUTH SPRING STREET

George J. Birkel of Los Angeles was the first mainland retailer to advertise 'ukuleles in 1907.

and Clark Centennial and American Pacific Exposition and Oriental Fair in Portland, Oregon, in 1905. The band performed in front of large crowds throughout its four-week engagement that summer, drawing enthusiastic reviews. "People can hear a brass band any day—but they cannot hear music like this more than once in a lifetime," cheered the *Oregon Journal*.[110] "Berger has built up a band that is an orchestra, a mandolin club, a glee club, a minstrel show, a brass band and several other things in one," raved another listener.[111] Critics in San Francisco, where the band played several dates while traveling to and from the fair, were equally positive. "Several attractive numbers were also given by the Hawaiian Glee Club, who accompanied themselves on guitars, violins and native instruments," one account read. "One homesick Hawaiian yelled, 'Makai' (good) from the gallery at the favorite 'Tomi Tomi,' and the club waved back to him."[112] Kealakai's Kawaihau Orchestra and Glee Club played at Ye Oregon Grille in Portland's Hotel Oregon in 1907. A studio portrait of the group—formally dressed in black tie—shows the instrumental lineup as two guitars, banjo, bass, violin, flute, and taro patch.[113] They were the first in a series of Hawaiian groups that would play at the Grille for the next several years.[114] In February 1908, an unnamed Hawaiian group appearing at Portland's Grand Theater drew strong reviews, even though "Hawaiian singers are no longer a novelty here."[115] That same year, a Hawaiian sextette appeared in Reno, Nevada, and Salt Lake City had its own resident band, the Hawaiian Troubadours, that played local dances.[116] Hawaiian music also was featured in the Hawaii Building at the 1909 Alaska-Yukon-Pacific Exposition in Seattle, this time an eight-member orchestra under the direction of Ernest Kaai. "They sang almost constantly, and soon became one of the most popular attractions on the grounds," one account said. "Visitors never seemed to tire of their music, and one song especially, 'Aloha Oe,' the Hawaiian dirge, was demanded over and over every day. The amiability of the singers in courteously acceding to such frequent requests was a source of gratification to those in charge of the building."[117] Kaai's musicians performed throughout the three-hundred-acre fairgrounds on "Hawaii Day," for Washington governor M. E. Hay at a special luncheon, and at a gala dance given by the Hawaiian commissioners.[118] The following year, the Royal Hawaiian Orchestra—Kealakai's latest aggregation—became the resident band at the Owyhee Hotel in Boise, Idaho, after a six-month engagement at the Savoy Hotel in Denver. "Evidently there were a number of globe-trotters in the audience who were familiar with the significance of the tunes, as they cried 'Villa-ka-hau' [sic], an Hawaiian expression of applause which literally means 'hot iron,'" one member of the opening night audience wrote.[119]

After annexation, with all hopes of restoring the monarchy extinguished, Hawaiian music no longer represented a political threat. Instead, as Lorrin Thurston recognized as early as 1893, it represented a powerful form of marketing for the Islands. One of the first proposals from the Hawaii Promotion Committee after its formation in 1903 was for a quintette club to accompany the Hawaiian polo team on a trip to California "to advertise the Islands . . . with delightful native music."[120] At the Alaska-Yukon-Pacific Exposition, Kaai and his orchestra quickly proved to be "a great attraction, and [to] very noticeably stimulate the pineapple business," Will J. Cooper reported to the Promotion Committee. "They occupy a stand elevated above the corner where the pineapple is served, and when they play the only difficulty is to keep the tables cleared for all who want [some]."[121] As Adria Imada has shown, Hawaiian dancers and musicians eagerly sought opportunities to perform on the mainland, work that gave them a measure of autonomy and a promise of "fame, glamour and middle-class status difficult for them to achieve in the plantation and service industries" at home.[122] Few managed to make a full-time living from music, however. For example, John "Jack" Ailau, leader and manager of the Hawaiian Quintet Club—one of Honolulu's top ensembles in the early 1890s—was a printer by trade who also sold curios in space he leased in W. F. Reynolds' Golden Rule Bazaar.[123] By 1909, the *Hawaiian Gazette* reported that many of the singers and musicians in Honolulu "are young men who have not had the opportunity to receive the best education, and their occupations often do not command big wages. The opportunity to play and sing in quintet clubs opens the way to earn all the way from $1.50 to $3 a night, affording a fund with which they can almost support a family."[124]

Despite the growing popularity of Hawaiian music on the West Coast, the first years of the new century appear to have been lean ones for 'ukulele makers in Hawaii—the source of all 'ukuleles played or purchased on the mainland. From 1901 to 1905, Santo, although working from his home, was the only original maker consistently listed as a guitar maker in Honolulu directories. He died prematurely of blood poisoning in June 1905.[125] Nunes was listed as a cabinetmaker in 1902 and as working out of his home as a guitar maker in 1904 before opening a shop on Beretania in 1905. Dias, who lost his shop in the devastating Chinatown fire of 1900, worked at the Porter Furniture Co. from 1901 to 1903, returning to instrument making at his home the following year. Two new competitors, Jose Vierra and Manuel Fernandez, surfaced briefly during this period, but each was listed in the city directory for just a single year.[126]

As the decade drew to a close, conditions appear to have improved and competition increased. Dias opened a shop on Union Street in 1907; by 1909, Kaai was advertising himself as "maker of the finest ukuleles in the world."[127] That same year, Nunes announced the opening of M. Nunes & Sons in the Kapiolani Building on Alakea Street with sons Julius and Leonardo.[128] In 1911, although Dias had retired as a result of the tuberculosis that would eventually kill him four years later, three new makers opened up shop in Honolulu: James N. Anahu, Ishiga Sakai, and Jonah Kumalae.[129] Kumalae—politician and former schoolteacher, farmer, and clerk— reportedly began making 'ukuleles as early as 1895 and eventually became one of the most prolific of the early manufacturers.[130]

The first major boost for 'ukulele sales outside the West Coast did not come from Hawaii but from a tourist from California—a stage-struck Berkeley graduate and former theater usher who captured the public's imagination with a play about the ill-fated love between a Hawaiian princess and a Yankee adventurer. Richard Walton Tully's play, *The Bird of Paradise,* boasted elaborate stage effects, an erupting volcano, and a quintet of Hawaiian musicians—including at least one veteran of the Chicago Exposition—that put Hawaiian music before its first real national audience. "How many incantatory ukuleles it set to strumming in the national moonlight will never, of course, be known, but for better or worse their source is definite," the *New York Times* observed some years later.[131]

CHAPTER 5

A Landscape Set to Music

The wonderfully sweet voices and weird melodies of these ukalele players strike a plaintive heart-note never to be forgotten once heard.

—*Hartford Courant,* February 4, 1913

Theatrical impresario Oliver Morosco was hunting deer in the Tehachapi Mountains north of Los Angeles when word reached him that his latest production, *The Bird of Paradise,* had flopped on opening night. Morosco raced back to town to discover that playwright Richard Walton Tully had not made any of the many cuts he had ordered during rehearsals. The result was a play that dragged on for more than four hours. Furious, Morosco took matters into his own hands. Working from his own version of the script, he personally rehearsed the cast the following afternoon in preparation for that evening's performance. "The patient rallied finely from the blue-penciled anaesthetic," Julian Johnson, the *Los Angeles Times* drama critic, reported approvingly on September 13, 1911. "The novelty and beauty of the story; the newness of its locale, and the really fine touches of 'atmosphere' both human and material were much more apparent last evening."[1]

After a successful four-week run in Los Angeles and a stop in Rochester, New York, the *Bird* opened on Broadway four months later to tepid reviews. The first night's box office barely topped $300. Convinced of the play's merit—he called it "one of the most exquisite plays ever written"—Morosco papered the house to give it a boost. Despite his efforts, the play's New York run was fairly short, but real success for the Hawaiian-themed play with authentic Island music and dancing was to come on the road. By 1924, when efforts to produce the first movie version were underway, profits from the *Bird* were estimated to be more than $1 million, "as the play was one of the most successful in recent years and has been produced in nearly every city of the United States," the *New York Times* reported. "Almost every season three or four companies have had it on the road. It also met with great success in a London production and has been produced in Austr[ali]a and in India."[2] A perennial favorite in Los Angeles, the *Bird* returned at least six times between 1913 and 1921.[3] "Plays may come and plays may go, but 'The Bird of Paradise' . . . seems destined to go on forever," one Washington, D.C., critic wrote.[4]

Although Morosco was proudest of the erupting volcano effect at the play's climax, the *Bird*'s Hawaiian quintet was the "touch of atmosphere" that was to have the longest and most lasting impact on its audiences. "Throughout the play Mr. Tully . . . has interwoven with great delicacy and appropriateness the weird and fascinating melodies of the Hawaiians," wrote one early reviewer. "These songs, to the accompaniment of strangely floating airs from stringed instruments (already familiar to vaudeville lovers, but new to patrons of legitimate drama), were more effective in the establishment of the langorous, alluring, hypnotic atmosphere which the author describes, than all the costumes, native faces, odd properties, and elaborate scenery combined."[5]

Although Hawaiian acts had become increasingly common in vaudeville, for many on the mainland Tully's play was their first exposure to modern Hawaiian music and the first time they had seen or heard the 'ukulele. "This is the play that made the ukulele famous," a Morosco press agent boasted in 1918, two years after

Hawaiian music and dancing was always featured prominently in the advertising for *The Bird of Paradise*, beginning with the original Los Angeles production in 1911.

the Honolulu Chamber of Commerce presented Tully with a letter of thanks and a "specially made and decorated" 'ukulele.[6] Among those the *Bird* introduced to Hawaiian music were two figures who would later play a major role in defining Hawaii to American audiences: Nebraska-born songwriter and bandleader Harry Owens, who saw *Bird of Paradise* at the Missoula, Montana, Opera House in 1913, and writer-poet Don Blanding of Oklahoma, the "Father of Lei Day," who was inspired to travel to Honolulu after seeing the play in Kansas City in 1916.[7] The music that the original quintet—B. Waiwaiole, S. M. Kaiawe, A. Kiwala, William B. Aeko (who played with the Volcano Singers in Chicago in 1893), and Walter Kolomoku—played on 'ukulele, guitar, steel guitar, and *ipu* quickly became a major selling point of the production. "Hear the Hawaiian Singers," urged the newspaper ads Morosco ran in the *Los Angeles Times* after the play's debut: "A Quintet of vocalists who render the songs of this beautiful island paradise of the Pacific in such a manner as to call forth round after round of applause."[8] Sheet music from the production, including such songs as "Aloha Oe," "Mai Poina Oe," and "Ahi Wela" (with English lyrics) reportedly sold more than two million copies, and Victor Records released twelve sides of the play's music—"sure to charm every listener, as the accompaniments are given by the Hawaiian instruments."[9] While tourists had been visiting Hawaii for years and returning with 'ukuleles tucked under their arms, the *Edison Phonograph Monthly* observed that "it was not until Tully's opera 'The Bird of Paradise' was produced that musicians gave any serious attention to the instrument and its music."[10]

Bird of Paradise's success was due not only to its novelty and musical effects but to the engines of a true mass American culture that had emerged by the turn of the century: a national railroad network that made it possible for *Bird* troupes to crisscross the country; national theater chains where they performed; recorded music; movies; and the rise of department stores, amusement parks, and other new forms of mass merchandising and amusement. In 1893, when modern Hawaiian music made its debut in Chicago, the first vaudeville theater opened in New York, offering continuous and respectable entertainment for middle-class audiences; Tin Pan Alley was born when M. Witmark & Sons moved its offices to Manhattan's West 28th Street; and Emil Berliner successfully produced a flat disc for recorded music—the first phonograph record.[11] Popular entertainment was becoming a standardized product marketed to a growing national middle-class audience by a group of culture industries headquartered in New York.[12] All this made it possible for the 'ukulele and Hawaiian music—an otherwise obscure form of tropical exotica heard by a few thousand adventuresome tourists each year—to become familiar to mainland audiences, whose image of Hawaii became inexplicably entwined with the music and musicians they heard.[13] "The power of the Hawaiian imagery above all has to do with the fact that this was the first really mass-mediated paradise," observes Orvar Lofgren, "a landscape not only to experience through colored postcards and illustrated magazine features but also a landscape set to music."[14] Or as one observer put it more bluntly, "Hawaiian music from Hawaiian musicians is the keystone of the Island tourist ballyhoo, the universally recognized signature of the whole grass-skirt-bottom-wriggling-beach-at-Waikiki complex."[15]

Adding to the *Bird*'s impact was its use of Hawaiian settings in a melodrama, rather than as objects of comic condescension. The play and its *Madame Butterfly*–influenced plot, set on the island of Hawaii in the early 1890s, tells the story of Luana, a Hawaiian princess, who falls in love with newly arrived American physician Paul Wilson. Luana refuses to travel to Honolulu and assume the throne, preferring to stay with Paul, a well-bred but careless young haole. When Paul finally shakes off his tropical lethargy and travels to Honolulu, Luana accompanies him. Unable to cope with modern civilization and believing she stands in the way of her lover's opportunities, she returns to the Big Island and commits suicide by throwing herself into Kilauea Volcano.[16] While Tully said his play was a dramatization "of the well-known fact that though we dress, educate, and polish the members of a lower race to the superficial religious and social equality with the Caucasians, at heart he is still the fetish-worshipping savage who will become atavistic in every moment of stress," it stood in dramatic contrast with the comic opera image of Hawaiians that had dominated the American stage for the previous twenty years.[17] Tully's innovation marked the end of an era: Los Angeles car dealer Earle Anthony's comic musical *The Pearl Maiden*, which opened in New York two weeks after *The Bird of Paradise*, closed after just twenty-four performances.[18]

The first theatrical portrayal of Hawaii on the New York stage had been staged more than a century before: *The Death of Captain Cook*, a "Grand Serious Pantomime" based on the French original that opened in May 1793 and was presented in various forms for almost twenty years.[19] It was the arrival of Gilbert and Sullivan's hit operetta *HMS Pinafore* in 1878 and the subsequent success of *The Mikado*, however, that sparked an American rage for comic opera.[20] The result was a string of homegrown productions set in a bewildering array of foreign locales—Cuba, Egypt, China, the Philippines, Japan, Iraq, Algeria, Peru (the setting for John Phillip Sousa's *El Capitan*)—and Hawaii.[21] *King Kaliko*, a three-act operetta set in Honolulu, opened in June 1892 but closed after only twelve performances.[22] In response to the political turmoil surrounding the overthrow of the Hawaiian monarchy, Liliuokalani was mocked in newspaper parodies such as "Lilli Walkee Lanny, or, Saving the Ham Sandwich Queen," on the stage by Lottie Gilson, "The Little Magnet," who sang "Queen Lily Ouki-Ouk-Alani," and in an 1895 musical comedy, "Queen Lil."[23] An 1894 collaboration between Sousa and Chicago newspaper columnist and poet Eugene Field on a comic opera entitled *Honolulu* fizzled, but an 1897 production by two Californian unknowns, *Captain Cook*, scored a coup when Liliuokalani, then on a tour of the East Coast, sat patiently through the premiere at Madison Square Garden and was quoted as politely saying she enjoyed it very much.[24] *Captain Cook* proved as ill-fated as *King Kaliko*: It closed after fourteen performances, leaving behind a trail of unpaid bills.[25] At the turn of the century, a trio of young ladies known as "The Hawaiian Queens" presented "a pocket edition operetta" titled *King Moo's Wedding Day,* in which they played what passed for Hawaiian maidens with "characteristic songs and dances."[26] As late as 1911, Portland, Oregon, audiences could see "the latest cyclone of merriment" from the Lyric Musical Comedy Co., *Dillon and King in Honolulu.*[27]

As Amy Kaplan has pointed out, turn-of-the-century Americans had a habit of viewing foreigners through the lenses of racial categories at home, which meant that Hawaiians were depicted with the same ugly, big-lipped, kinky-haired caricatures as American blacks.[28] Such attitudes were not new: As a young man traveling in Washington, D.C., the future Kamehameha IV had been insulted by a train conductor who thought he was black. Back in Honolulu, some Americans in the 1850s repeatedly referred to Hawaiians and the royal family as "niggers."[29] "The negro and the Polynesian have many striking similarities," Samuel Chapman Armstrong, the son of missionaries and founder of the Hampton Institute, wrote in 1884. "Of both it is true that not mere ignorance, but deficiency of character is the chief difficulty."[30] Later, as part of the annexationist campaign to undermine the monarchy, both Kalakaua and Liliuokalani were rumored to be the illegitimate children of an emigrant African-American shoemaker named Blossom.[31] In 1896—the same year that the U.S. Supreme Court ruled racial segregation was legal—Chicago's Strauss Music Co. published "Ma Honolulu Queen," one of the first in a series of "coon songs," cakewalks, and ragtime instrumentals that treated Hawaiians and African-Americans interchangeably.[32] Bert Williams, the pioneering singer-songwriter, actor, and comedian who became the first African-American Broadway star, took this confusion a step further when in one of the first jobs of his career he posed as a Hawaiian musician at San Francisco's 1894 Midwinter Fair.[33] Five years later, in his musical farce *The Policy Players,* two young African-American dancers in his troupe performed as Kioka and Kama, the "Honolulu Belles."[34]

Still, Hawaiians posed less of a threat to mainland audiences than blacks. As Jane C. Desmond has written, Hawaiians "were outside time, memory, and important mainland events, such as slavery and its aftermath. They escaped the legacies of fear and potentially violent hatred which lay submerged in the black-white mainland interactions."[35] Despite almost a century of "Christian civilization," many Americans shared Tully's belief that Hawaiians were still primitive savages destined for extinction. As Karen Linn has shown, this kind of antimodern aesthetic was popular in the rapidly changing, increasingly industrialized and urbanizing United States.[36] The adoption of the guitar and the 'ukulele by Hawaiian musicians neatly tied together late Victorian stereotypes of the guitar as an expressive, sensual, and even dangerous instrument and Americans' view of Hawaiians as sensuous savages.[37] Vaudeville—created by people from immigrant and working-class backgrounds to provide something for everyone—was an ideal vehicle for helping to bring the 'ukulele and the new Hawaiian music to a national middle-class audience.[38] A business built on novelty, vaudeville was constantly in search of new acts, acts encouraged by the fact that it took very little capital to get one's foot in the door of the entry-level, five-shows-a-day circuits. The creation of the Association of Vaudeville Managers and of the United Booking Office at the turn of the century made New York the industry's national headquarters and the chief arbiter of what audiences would see.[39]

Toots Paka's Hawaiians was probably vaudeville's best-known Hawaiian act, thanks to their success in becoming a regular "name" artist on the Orpheum and Keith-Albee circuits, which dominated the big time.[40] Toots (Hannah Jones, 1877?–1942), a Michigan-born dancer who had never been to Hawaii, married Iolai "July" Paka (1874–1943), a talented young Hawaiian musician who played with William Ellis in San Francisco in 1900 and had been a member of Mekia Kealakai's orchestra at the Pan-American Exposition in Buffalo in 1901. Together they put together a new act.[41] The earliest documented appearance of the Pakas was in December 1906 at the Grand Theater in Bellingham, Washington, where they were billed as "July & Paka—Hawaiian Duo, Singers & Dancers."[42] Toots and July were eventually joined by steel guitarist Joseph Kekuku, widely regarded as the originator of steel guitar technique, and they played dates up and down the East Coast and as far south as Kentucky, performed at private parties in Manhattan, and recorded a series of cylinders for Edison, the company's first Hawaiian recordings.[43] By 1910, the troupe's standing was such that it made appearances as a specialty act in two Broadway shows, *The Young Turk* and *The Echo,* the latter a Charles Dillingham production that toured the Midwest and eastern cities that summer.[44]

Although the size of Paka's troupe varied, as did the instrumentation, a review of a 1912 show as headliners at the Los Angeles Orpheum gives some idea of how Hawaiian music was first presented to mainland vaudeville audiences:

> The curtain arises upon a tropical scene. There is an expanse of baby-blue water, a riotous sunset and some palm trees. On a bench are seated three native musicians with guitars and mandolins. Against the sunset reclines Toots Paka in an uncomfortable hammock. She wears a costume resembling a robe de nuit. There is some music built on thirds and continually recurring to C major. It is not thrilling. Then a nervous young man sings a sentimental song, and he is followed by a young man who plays the guitar in a unique manner. He is joined by another guitar player, and ragtime—good ragtime—holds forth for a spell. The feature of the act, however, is the Hawaiian dance performed by Toots Paka herself. It is a primitive affair with little or no artistic significance in its present form, but from certain suggestions it would seem that it has been expurgated for Los Angeles consumption, and so, perhaps, should not be judged as an expression of the folk tradition of the Hawaiians. As it is now being given, it is scarcely more than an elaborate wiggle—Salome with delirium tremens. The act is fulfilling, nonetheless, and receives long and enthusiastic applause.[45]

Toots Paka's Hawaiians was only one of a growing number of 'ukulele-playing Hawaiian string bands that performed in front of appreciative mainland audiences. Few are identifiable today, having been billed generically as "The Hawaiian Quintette" or "The Hawaiian Orchestra," as if each were the only one of its kind. As early as 1899, a group of seven Hawaiian *paniolo*—cowboys—appeared with Buffalo Bill's Wild West Show, singing as well as demonstrating their riding skills. Yale sophomore and Honolulu native Henry R. Judd caught the show with his sister Agnes in New York and was not impressed. "They entered the arena mounted on horses, singing 'Ahi Wela' with harsh voices and thereby creating a poor impression of what Hawaiians were," Judd wrote afterward. "They did not add any glory for Hawaii."[46]

Paving the way for Toots Paka's troupe in mainland vaudeville was Kealakai's orchestra. Assembled to perform at the 1901 Buffalo Exposition, various members of the group continued to make appearances on both sides of the country long after the exposition closed in November.[47] One contingent led by Johnny Wilson that included Kealakai, Paka, and David Nape played the Orpheum circuit, performing in cities such as Kansas City and Omaha before touring the West Coast—the earliest Hawaiian orchestra known to have toured in vaudeville. "The Hawaiian Glee Club, now performing in this country, is a surprise," said the *Kansas City Journal*. "Its music is a delight . . . unlike any heard here in many a day, if at all." The *Los Angeles Times* was equally enthusiastic: "The Hawaiians have made one of the most pronounced hits ever scored at the Orpheum."[48] Meanwhile, a second group led by Joe Puni that included George Kia and Jack Heleluhe took a disastrous trip through the South, banking on a booking at the South Carolina Inter-State and West Indian Exposition in Charleston that never materialized. After months of struggling to find work in South Carolina, Florida, and Georgia, they made their way to Washington, D.C., where they finally found appreciative audiences. "Thousands in the Capitol during the last six months have been charmed by the melody of a group of dark-hued visitors, the melody of far-off Hawaii," the *Washington Post* reported. "One uses a flute, two employ guitars, and three play upon the peculiar little string instrument called 'ukelele,' which in native Hawaiian means 'the flea.'"[49]

Members of these groups likely made up "the Famous Hawaiian Sextette from the Pan-American Exposition" that appeared in Los Angeles at The Chutes in June 1902; the Honolulu Sextette that played in Philadelphia's Woodside Park that July; and the Royal Native Hawaiian Glee Club that performed in A.M. Rothschild & Co.'s department store in Chicago in November.[50] Hawaiian string bands subsequently performed in Manhattan in April and October 1903, at New York's Glen Island resort, and at Philadelphia's Ninth and Arch Street Museum the following year; headlined at Huber's Museum in Manhattan in 1905, at Kansas City's Forest Park and Chicago's Café Savoy in 1907, and at a Duluth, Minnesota, restaurant, theaters in Omaha, Nebraska, and Syracuse, New York, and Coney Island by 1908; and in segregated theaters in Atlanta, the resorts of Atlantic City, and on the boardwalk

MR. SOUSA STOPPING TO CHAT WITH THE HAWAIIAN BAND.

Famed composer John Phillip Sousa poses with the Hawaiian Orchestra at the 1901 Buffalo Pan-American Exposition. Courtesy of SUNY Buffalo Library.

at Asbury Park in New Jersey in 1910–1911.[51] As early as 1906, Hawaiian orchestras had become such a familiar urban presence that a Hawaiian singer was featured as the protagonist of a short story published in the *Boston Globe*.[52] Two years later, it was estimated that almost two hundred Hawaiian musicians were performing on the mainland "from Atlantic City to the pleasure resorts of the Pacific Coast."[53] President William Taft, who as secretary of war had been entertained by Hawaiian musicians during a stop in Honolulu on his 1905 goodwill tour of the Far East, invited Frank J. Vierra's Hawaiian quintet to perform a series of "melodious and mysterious songs and renditions on stringed instruments" at a White House reception for Prince Tsai Tao of China in April 1910.[54]

1906 was the year the Royal Hawaiian Band (together with what was billed as the Royal Hawaiian Glee Club, directed by Sonny Cunha) toured much of the West and Canada.[55] "It is not only a brass band but also an orchestra and a glee club, the second part of the programme consisting of Hawaiian songs accompanied by their characteristic stringed instruments," the band's promotional materials reminded audiences.[56] According to one account, instrumentation for glee club performances included ten violins, three cellos, two bass viols, fifteen guitars, and fifteen 'ukuleles.

"Nobody ever saw so many ukuleles being played at one time before, and it was a surprising novelty, even in Hawaii."[57] 1906 also was the year that the Honolulu Students, a sextette of singer/musicians led by Lu Thompson Keouli, performed in New York, Philadelphia, and Boston, which led to their being booked on eastern and midwestern Lyceum circuits in 1907–1908 and 1908–1909.[58]

The Honolulu Students, who sang to the accompaniment of guitar, violin, flute, "and the native instruments, 'ukulele' and 'Taropatch,'" introduced small-town audiences in such places as Baldwinsville, New York, Bristol, Vermont, Logansport, Indiana, and Emporia, Kansas, to Hawaiian music. The educational quotient of the show was boosted by a series of stereopticon slides of the Islands. "Their entertainment is first-class in every particular," one audience member wrote. "The native music is fascinating in its plaintive sweetness and in the liquid quality of the language. The faculty with which the Students play and sing at the same time without any aid of printed music is charming."[59]

The charm of the Students' performances was captured on what were among the first recordings of Hawaiian music—a series of songs recorded in New York in 1905 or 1906 for the American Record Co. Although the first recording of Hawaiian

The Honolulu Students, shown here in a ca. 1909 promotional brochure, were among the first Hawaiian groups to step into the recording studio. Courtesy of Redpath Chatauqua Collection, University of Iowa Libraries, Iowa City, Iowa.

music appears to have been made in Honolulu by the Royal Hawaiian Band on March 14, 1891—a performance of Berger's "Liliuokalani March" and "Hawaii Ponoi" during a phonograph demonstration at the Opera House—the more than two dozen songs recorded by the Students under the name Royal Hawaiian Troubadours were among the first to be made available to mainland audiences (and subsequently in England).[60] In 1906, the Victor Talking Machine Co.'s catalogue featured more than four dozen Hawaiian selections recorded in Honolulu the previous year by such artists as Nani Alapai of the Royal Hawaiian Band, William and John Ellis, the Ellis Brothers Quartette and Glee Club, and a cappella performances by a "Quartette of Hawaiian Girls" from Kawaiahao Seminary. Like Paka's subsequent 1909 recordings for Edison and a 1912 series from Columbia, Victor's novel Hawaiian sides were released as part of a special "foreign" series, marketed under the slogan "The Language You Know Best."[61]

Sophisticated or merely curious New Yorkers who bought the new recordings were doomed to disappointment if they went to a Manhattan music store to find sheet music of any of the songs they heard. With the exception of Liliuokalani's "Aloha Oe," the only "Hawaiian" music available were the Broadway or Tin Pan Alley versions—songs such as "My Honolulu Queen," sung by stage star Anna Held in *Papa's Wife,* an 1899 farce set in Paris; "My Hula Lula Girl," a 1903 number in which an exotic tropical dancer turns out to be an Irish shopgirl; "My Hula Hula Girl" from the 1907 musical comedy *The Grand Mogul,* which related the comic adventures of George Washington Barker, a circus fakir stranded in Honolulu with a tent show; or "Honolulu Rag," performed in the 1910 Broadway production of *Girlies,* a comedy set at Hightonia Coed College.[62] *The Grand Mogul* was billed as "the first stage production of any character, musical or dramatic, in which any attempt has been made to accurately represent the Hawaiian people."[63] The genuine article was available only in Honolulu and to a lesser extent on the West Coast.

The first piece of sheet music published in Hawaii was Liliuokalani's "He Mele Lahui Hawaii" ("Hawaiian National Anthem"), which appeared in 1867; her "Nani Na Pua" ("Beautiful Are the Flowers") was the first Hawaiian song published on the mainland, by Oliver Ditson of Boston in 1869.[64] The first folio collection of Hawaiian songs, Henry Berger's 1884–1891 *Mele Hawaii,* "marks an era in the musical world of this city [Honolulu]," the *Hawaiian Gazette* noted at the time. "In times past there have been a few Hawaiian compositions published, but they never have been put in distinctive form."[65] Berger's pioneering work was followed by Charles A. K. Hopkins' *Aloha Collection of Hawaiian Songs* (Oliver Ditson, 1899) and Sonny Cunha's *Songs of Hawaii* (Bergstrom Music, 1902), the latter of which featured a winsome art nouveau Hawaiian maiden playing a ʻukulele on the cover.

"The instruments of the Old Hawaiians have succumbed to the onward march of civilization," the preface to Cunha's collection said. "The guitar, the banjo, the mandolin, the ukulele (modification of a Portuguese fiddle), and the flute have taken their place and have come to stay."[66] It was after *Songs of Hawaii* appeared

Sonny Cunha's 1902 song compilation, *Songs of Hawaii*, featured a ʻukulele-playing Hawaiian maiden on its art noveau-style cover.

that Bergstrom Music Co.—where Cunha worked from 1908 to 1914—published several of his hapa haole songs that appear among the earliest of Hawaiian recordings.[67] Songs such as "Honolulu Tom Boy," "My Waikiki Mermaid," and "My Hawaiian Maid" were the first to popularize a combination of English and Hawaiian lyrics set to a ragtime beat that Cunha soaked up as a teenager.[68]

However, all this music was arranged for piano, which dominated the home music market as a symbol of middle-class respectability until the end of World War I. By 1910, when more efficient assembly line methods had reduced their price and player pianos made lessons superfluous, one of every 252 Americans owned a piano.[69] As historian James Parakilas has pointed out, turn-of-the-century Americans lived in a society when pianos were found not only in front parlors but everywhere people gathered—in schools, churches, saloons, hospitals, department stores, and steamship lounges.[70] But for those who had heard "Ahi Wela" or another *hula kui* song performed by Hawaiian musicians on ʻukulele and guitar, the effect when played on a piano just wasn't the same. In August 1905, when the Taft party was touring a sugar plantation outside Honolulu, it was serenaded by a group that "stirred every man having warm blood in his veins with the native airs and native dances," one reporter wrote. "Several members of [the] party hastened to a music store as soon as they got back to Honolulu and were successful in buying sheet music representing these native tunes. But when reproduced on the piano on shipboard, they were far from the real thing. The stringed instruments are lacking, and the voices of the natives which are always introduced cannot be reproduced by Americans."[71]

The first mainland manufacturer to experiment with building ʻukuleles was the venerable C.F. Martin & Co., which in December 1907 sold six "Hawaiian Ukeleles made to sample as a trial lot to calculate price" to Bergstrom Music Co. of Honolulu for $6.50 each—the same year George G. Birkel Co. of Los Angeles became the first mainland retailer to offer ʻukuleles.[72] But there is no evidence that Martin pursued the new product any farther at that early date. In New York, the engine of American popular culture, Charles H. Ditson & Co. advertised "Hawaiian Ukuleles" as a novelty in 1910, part of a collection of odd musical instruments that included Arabian war drums, Turkish cymbals, and Scottish bagpipes.[73] The previous year, the Boston music house of Oliver Ditson issued *Method for the Ukulele (Hawaiian Guitar)*—the first ʻukulele method to be published outside of Hawaii.

Thomas Rollinson's *Method for the Ukulele*, published in Boston in 1909, was the first ʻukulele method produced on the mainland.

Its editor, Thomas Rollinson (1844–1928), was a cornet player, band leader, arranger, and composer who headed Ditson's band and orchestra and banjo, mandolin, and guitar departments. He offered a brief introduction to the strange new instrument ("The Ukulele is principally used for accompanying songs") and tried to ground its instructions in the familiar—telling students it should be held like a mandolin, that a "sweeping chord stroke" is more effective than a picked chord stroke, and a mandolin pick can be used, although "it is doubtful if the mandolin tremolo would be effective."[74] In addition to some scales for practice, Rollinson offers a decidedly old-fashioned set of songs without a single Hawaiian tune, all in standard musical notation: "Old Folks at Home," "America," "Blue Bells of Scotland," a polka, two waltzes, and a schottisch.[75] The 1910 promotion was a short-lived one: Neither Ditson firm advertised 'ukuleles again until 1912, the year of *The Bird of Paradise*.[76] A few other adventurous retailers decided to give the Hawaiian novelty a try in 1911: E.P. Droop & Sons, the oldest music retailer in Washington, D.C., and Sampson Music Co. in Boise, Idaho.[77] However, it was on the West Coast where the Hawaiian music fad first developed, where the first major retailing efforts took place, and where the first identifiable mainland manufacturer began production.

In the fall of 1911, Birkel began to advertise "genuine Hawaiian ukuleles" on a regular basis. Just before Christmas, the downtown Los Angeles retailer offered five 'ukulele models made of "Coa wood" ranging from $8 to $25, prominently displayed by the front entrance in its small goods department.[78] The following summer, Birkel was aggressively pushing 'ukuleles ("a favorite with everybody"), advertising a "vacation music ukulele special"—a genuine Hawaiian 'ukulele, a case, and an instruction book for just $10.[79] That same year, Sherman, Clay & Co., the San Francisco wholesaler and retailer with branches in Washington, Oregon, and throughout California, offered three models of Hawaiian 'ukuleles, "The Hawaiian Guitar," for $15, $20, and $22.50. "The following Ukuleles are manufactured especially for us by the most expert makers in the islands, from koa which has been seasoning for more than half a century. . . . The frequent coast tours of native Hawaiian organizations in recent years [have] created an enormous demand for the Ukulele, and it has come to be recognized that as an accompaniment to the voice the quaint little instrument, with its tropical coloring and altogether delightful individuality of sound, has no superior." Sherman, Clay also offered cases and a choice of either Kaai's or Rollinson's 'ukulele method.[80]

For the most part, we can only guess as to who made the earliest 'ukuleles sold on the mainland. In 1912, according to the city directory, there were five 'ukulele makers active in Honolulu—Nunes, James Anahu, Joseph Kumalae, Kaai, and Ichiga Sakai—but music store newspaper ads and catalogues rarely identified the maker.[81] Birkel ads from that year are the lone exception—they made it clear the pioneering music house was selling Nunes instruments, although it couldn't always spell the name correctly.[82]

The first identifiable mainland maker was Leonardo Nunes (1874–1944) of Los Angeles, son of 'ukulele pioneer Manuel Nunes. Born in Madeira, Leonardo grew up in Honolulu and worked in the family business with his father and brother Julius until around 1912; the following year, Birkel began advertising "the famous L. Nunes Native Hawaiian instruments, made expressly for the Birkel Company."[83] Why he left Honolulu to strike out on his own and why he chose to open up shop in Los Angeles rather than San Francisco is not clear. The move and his willingness to trade on the family name put his "Ukulele O Hawaii" in direct competition with his father, whose instruments were being sold one block down the street at Southern California Music Co. "We have just received a large consignment of the genuine Hawaiian Ukuleles from the M. Nunes & Sons Co. of Honolulu," one Southern California Music advertisement advised in July 1914. "These are the genuine Hawaiian instrument invented and manufactured first by M. Nunes. Insist on getting the genuine—they cost no more and are unquestionably better."[84] Leonardo's modest output from his San Pedro Street factory meant that like his father and the other Honolulu manufacturers, he was never in a position to challenge the market dominance of the big mainland firms.[85]

The year after Leonardo Nunes made his debut in Los Angeles, three 'ukulele method books were published in California to meet the rising demand for the instrument anyone could learn to play without a teacher: Kealakai's *Self Instructor for the Ukulele and Taro-Patch Fiddle,* published by the Southern California Music Co.; George Kia's *Self Instructor for the Ukulele and Taro-Patch Fiddle,* published in Los Angeles by R. W. Heffelfinger, a former Birkel department manager turned publisher; and N. B. Bailey's *A Practical Method for Self Instruction on the Ukulele,* published in San Francisco by Sherman, Clay & Co. The 'ukulele "has invaded the Pacific Coast states to such an extent that one is sure to hear its soft tones wherever young people congregate. In one university alone, there are over one thousand of these charming little instruments," Bailey's introduction said.[86]

By 1913, demand had grown to the point that Leonardo Nunes was joined by other mainland-based manufacturers. "Remember, there is a great difference between the Hawaiian Ukulele of genuine Koa wood and the American factory-made instrument—a difference as radical as the chasm between daylight and darkness," Birkel warned its customers in October 1913.[87] By the end of the following year, a visitor noted that "the Hawaiian instrument, the Ukulele, is cutting a very wide swath in the west—one Los Angeles firm sold 26 of these instruments over the counter in one day, at prices ranging from $10 to $15 each. Some business!"[88] 'Ukuleles became available to more than four million rural customers nationwide via mail order in 1914 when mail-order giant Sears Roebuck listed two mahogany models, complete with instruction book, for $3.75 and $4.45 in its fall catalog. "The Ukulele is creating a sensation in this country, especially on the Pacific Coast, where it is exceedingly popular," the copy ran. "It is a sweet toned instrument that anyone can learn to play without the aid of a teacher and is especially suitable for vocal accompaniments. Also used to good advantage in mandolin clubs. With a little study and practice one can produce beautiful harplike effects on it."[89] According to one estimate, from twenty to twenty-five thousand 'ukuleles were sold on the mainland in 1914, 90 percent on the Pacific Coast, "where they are becoming quite commonly used."[90]

As the market heated up, so did the competition between Birkel and Southern California Music. Birkel, which in September 1913 proclaimed in no uncertain terms that "this Store is headquarters for Ukuleles," took an early lead.[91]

Los Angeles' George J. Birkel Company proclaimed itself "ukulele headquarters" as early as 1913.

That summer, as part of "an unusual opportunity never offered by a Music House in Los Angeles," it offered 'ukulele purchasers free lessons from Professor George Kia, "the Hawaiian virtuoso whose talent is so widely known."[92] The following year, Southern California Music offered not only free 'ukulele lessons from Ernest Kaai, "Internationally Known as the Greatest Authority on Hawaiian Music," but free steel guitar lessons from Joseph Kekuku, "Originator of the Hawaiian System of Steel Guitar Playing."[93]

Not to be outdone, Birkel sponsored a free concert by Kia and his pupils in Westlake Park that September that attracted a huge crowd. "Several thousand persons, taking advantage of the warm evening, congregated around the lake illuminated by Japanese lanterns to listen to the tinkle of the ukulele and the haunting notes of a Hawaiian love song," the *Los Angeles Times* reported. "Seventh Street, from Alvarado west to the limits of the park, was lined with machines [automobiles], in some portions two deep."[94] While the concert was sponsored by Birkel, Kia clearly had more in mind than selling 'ukuleles. At a concert at the Gamut Club three months earlier that also featured the Los Angeles High School Glee Club,

Ernest Kaai offered 'ukulele lessons at Southern California Music Co. in Los Angeles in 1914.

Kia "attempted, not unsuccessfully, a solo interpretation of 'Il Trovatore,' showing how far a ukulele expert can go in the use of his favorite instrument."[95] In San Francisco, Sherman, Clay modestly advertised "the largest stock of ukuleles in the world" as music stores in Portland, Oregon; Tucson, Arizona; Racine, Wisconsin; Des Moines, Iowa; and Cleveland, Ohio were suggesting 'ukuleles, "the greatest little melody instrument ever invented," as Christmas gifts.[96]

Such was the popularity of Hawaiian music that some mainstream music teachers decided to add the 'ukulele and steel guitar to their repertoire. One of the first in Los Angeles was Charles De Lano, who as a newly minted graduate of the University of Wisconsin had arrived in 1886 and offered his services as a teacher of guitar.[97] He founded the Ideal Guitar, Banjo and Mandolin Club in 1890, a society-page staple that offered as many as ten concerts each season, served on the music faculties of USC and the Throop Institute (today's Caltech), and was elected president of the newly formed Los Angeles Music Teacher Association in 1907.[98] By his own account, De Lano began studying the 'ukulele and steel guitar around 1909–1910, taking advantage of the large numbers of Hawaiian musicians playing and teaching in Los Angeles.[99] He first advertised 'ukulele lessons in the 1912 city directory, the same year Mae Muntz, a prominent San Jose music teacher, publicly added the 'ukulele to her repertoire.[100] By 1913 he had formed his own 'ukulele club and during the following year was performing on the 'ukulele and steel guitar in duets and larger ensembles in a variety of venues.[101] Convinced Hawaiian music was not a fad, De Lano advertised correspondence courses in both the 'ukulele and steel guitar for $12 each and even offered to help select "a choice genuine Hawaiian made ukulele" for his colleagues. "Do you know by teaching the Ukulele and Hawaiian Steel Guitar you can increase your income $100 per month as I have done?" he asked readers of *Cadenza,* the Boston-based music magazine aimed at professionals. "Don't let the other fellow get ahead of you. Be the first teacher in your city."[102] By the end of 1915, at least four other music teachers were advertising 'ukulele and steel guitar methods to national audiences; growing competition had driven the price down to as low as 50 cents.[103] "As both a solo and accompanying instrument, the possibilities of the ukulele are almost unlimited," Los Angeles music publisher Frank Littig insisted.[104]

At that point, the youthful trend had spread to the East Coast as well. In the fall of 1912, Charles Ditson of New York reported the sale of "a great many Ukuleles the past few months. Many of these instruments go to the leading young ladies' schools in this country."[105] That same year, a program by the Dartmouth Musical Clubs in Hartford, Connecticut, featured "vocal duets by Messrs Geller and Ickes, who will accompany themselves on the Ukalalies, the Hawaiian musical instruments noted for their tone qualities."[106] At an Oriental bazaar organized by Barnard coeds in 1914, Edna Henry and a band of singers "sang haunting Hawaiian melodies and some merry ones as well. . . . Miss Henry and Ray Levi played a Hawaiian instrument, Katherine McGiffert a mandolin, and Edith Roland and Eleanor von Elts the guitar."[107] Later that year, an MIT Glee Club concert in Boston featured a Hawaiian quartet "playing on their strange ukuleles and tonoharps. As the music from their instruments is weird and the words of their songs rather odd, the effect produced is unique."[108] A few months later, a performance by the Princeton Glee, Banjo, and Mandolin Clubs included an appearance by a Hawaiian sextette "with its unusual effects and the use of the much-talked of 'ukulele.'"[109] Californians helped carry the banner here, too: at a March 1914 meeting of the National California Club at the Waldorf Astoria Hotel in Manhattan, the program featured Hawaiian music, the same time that Charles H. Ditson & Co. of New York was reporting "a really surprising demand for ukuleles."[110]

But it was at a world's fair in San Francisco, the city where Henry Berger and the Royal Hawaiian Band first introduced modern Hawaiian music to the mainland in 1883, that the diminutive instrument became a national phenomenon. As early as 1904, a proposal was floated to the San Francisco Merchants Association to put on "the greatest World's Exposition ever attempted" in 1915 to celebrate the anticipated completion of the Panama Canal.[111] In the aftermath of the disastrous 1906 earthquake and fire, the exposition idea was embraced as a means of advertising the city's remarkable recovery, which as one modest booster put it, "swept away the vestiges of a calamity greater than befell Rome under Nero, or London under Charles."[112] San Franciscans persevered despite financial depressions, a toe-to-toe political battle with New Orleans' competing exposition bid, and even the outbreak of World War I to open the Panama Pacific International Exposition on schedule on February 20, 1915. Music was to be central to the fair experience—the board of directors, which included Philip T. Clay of Sherman, Clay & Co., built four outdoor bandstands and budgeted almost $700,000 for musical talent so fairgoers could enjoy "music that would appeal to all classes—not trash for that purpose, but good, popular compositions, and especially things that were new."[113] The runaway hit of the fair, however, came not from Sousa's or Creatore's bands in the Festival Hall or the Court of the Universe, but from a lei-bedecked quintet playing on a small platform in the fair's Hawaiian Pavilion.

CHAPTER 6

A Craze of the Frisco Exposition

The country has all of a sudden gone mad over Hawaiian music.
—SAN FRANCISCO CHRONICLE, AUGUST 27, 1916

Among the thousands of exhibits at London's Crystal Palace Exhibition of 1851 was a koa table inlaid with the Hawaiian coat of arms, a gift to Queen Victoria from Kamehameha III. At the queen's direction, it was placed on display "so as to shew to the vast assemblage of foreigners now in London the Beauty of the Woods grown in the Hawaiian Dominions."[1] The Great Exhibition of the Works of Industry of All Nations launched the world's fair movement, and Hawaii quickly realized the value of such exhibitions as a vehicle to sell itself and its products to international markets. "In our estimation, their usefulness and importance cannot be overvalued," one Honolulu newspaper editorialized in 1876.[2] Although the kingdom's plans did not always come to fruition, Hawaii had some kind of presence in at least ten international expositions in Europe, the United States, and Australia by the time the World's Columbian Exposition opened in Chicago in 1893.[3] Up to that point, the Hawaiian presence at fairs had always been static—displays of sugar, coffee, and other agricultural products, collections of ferns, shells, and lava, native manufactures including tapa, *kahili*, capes, and calabashes lent by the Hale Naua Society, photos of island scenery, and in Paris in 1889, a surfboard.[4] When music first appeared in the Hawaiian exhibit at New Orleans in 1884, it was in the form of sheet music and a showpiece guitar made of eight kinds of native woods, "which is not only beautiful to look at, but pronounced, by those who know, to be of very fine tone."[5]

Although the overthrow of the monarchy dashed Hawaii's elaborate plans for the Chicago fair, Lorrin Thurston's privately funded concession marked a major departure—the first time Hawaii had been represented by live music.[6] Rather than a sedate display under glass in an exhibition hall, the Volcano Singers appeared on the

Midway—the mile-long amusement zone that included villages of Africans, Native Americans, Japanese, Turks, Egyptians, "South Sea Islanders," and other peoples, ostensibly operated under the formal auspices of the fair's Ethnology Department.[7] "What an opportunity is here afforded to the scientific mind to descend the spiral of evolution, tracing humanity in its highest phases down almost to its animalistic origins," the *Chicago Tribune* wrote.[8] However much the Midway served to reinforce white Americans' feelings of racial superiority, it also signaled a major shift in the official attitude toward popular culture. As Robert Rydell has shown, officials at the Philadelphia fair in 1876 had barred such entertainment from the fairgrounds and actively fought to eliminate it outside the Centennial Exhibition's gates.[9]

Despite the Volcano Singers' positive reviews, it was the hula that initially made the biggest impression on mainland audiences. In Chicago, Kini Kapahu (Jennie Wilson) remembered standing on the Midway, playing the 'ukulele, wiggling seductively, and singing,

On the Midway, the Midway, the Midway Plaisance
Where the naughty girls from Honolulu do the naughty hula dance.[10]

She and her troupe also performed at the Madison Street Opera House as part of Sam T. Jack's Creole Co., performing with "queer native instruments" as well as "mandolins and guitars of native make, but well-tuned and finely finished."[11] Wilson and some of her fellow dancers went from Chicago to New York, where they performed at Doris's Museum on Eighth Avenue with acts that included a legless gymnast and a two-headed cow, before traveling to Boston and eventually to Europe for a prolonged tour.[12] Hula dancers became a regular feature of Hawaiian villages at other American fairs, to the extent that one turn-of-the-century newspaper commentator writing in anticipation of the latest fair remarked that "the hula-hula dance . . . by many, has been thought to be about the only fruit that grew in that portion of our national domain. But the Midway without the h-h won't seem like the same old smile."[13]

The 'ukulele-playing musicians that accompanied the dancers drew mixed reactions. In Omaha, at the Greater America Exposition of 1899, Johnny Wilson brought a "crack native quintet club"—Jim Shaw, John Edwards, W. B. Jones, Thomas Hennessey, and Mekia Kealakai—that played in the theater of the Hawaiian Village (a replica of Iolani Palace) on the Midway.[14] "This is beyond comparison with any other music at the exposition," the *Omaha World-Herald* reported. "Ever since the evening the Hawaiian musicians were heard on the lagoon, they have been the talk of the town and hundreds visit the Hawaiian Village every evening for no other reason than to hear the beautiful instrumental and vocal selections of this company."[15] In Buffalo, an anonymous correspondent of the *New York Times* was underwhelmed with what he heard and saw at the Hawaiian Village—despite the fact that the band managed by Johnny Wilson at the fair boasted such outstanding musicians as Mekia Kealakai and David Nape. "On a stage at the far end of this hall some native Hawaiians dance what is called the houla-houla, which appears to be a mild sort of danse de ventre, and there is some plaintive singing to mandolins," he wrote. "The curtain falls after about ten minutes of this performance, and the audience, finding nothing more to see, retires the same way it entered."[16] Two years later, when Wilson tried to line up a band for a Hawaiian Village at the 1904 Louisiana Purchase Exposition in St. Louis, he came up empty. Because of their success in vaudeville following the Buffalo exposition, "the boys held me up and wanted too much," said the chagrined Wilson.[17] When a political dispute in the Territorial Legislature tied up the appropriation for the Hawaiian Pavilion, Hawaii's elaborate plans for St. Louis amounted to nothing more than a single showcase shared with Puerto Rico in the U.S. Government Building.[18]

Although Hawaii had a substantial presence at the Portland fair of 1905 and Seattle's Alaska-Yukon-Pacific Exposition in 1909, both were largely regional affairs that attracted just a fraction of the crowds that flocked to Chicago—1.5 million in Portland and 3.7 million in Seattle.[19] When the Territorial Legislature allocated $100,000 in 1913 for a Hawaiian Building at San Francisco's 1915 fair, the Panama-Pacific International Exposition, it signaled the Islands' intent to move beyond the Midway, as it had done for the first time in Seattle, with an ambitious program that rivaled those mounted by some mainland states.[20] The exhibit planned by the Territorial Exposition Committee "promises to exceed in beauty, interest and educational value anything hitherto attempted by Hawaii," the Honolulu Chamber of Commerce enthused in 1911.[21] Hawaii-born architect C. W. Dickey designed a French Renaissance–style building for a prime location—opposite the Fine Arts Palace and the California Building and just down the street from the fair's Baker Street entrance.[22] The search for a musical organization to perform at the fair led to a fierce competition between the glee clubs of Jonah Kumalae and Ernest Kaai, one that after many miscues resulted in Kumalae's group—Henry Kailimai (whose "On the Beach at Waikiki" was to be one of the hits of the fair), William Lincoln, Robert Waialeale, Frank Kema, and Gordon Hiianaia—being chosen to "discourse Hawaiian music in the Hawaiian building."[23]

Fish, not music, were the chief attraction that initially lured crowds to the Hawaiian Building. Large tanks lining three walls of the main hall were filled with "the most beautiful fish ever seen . . . [and] some of the most fascinatingly hideous eels and devilish-looking devil fish nature ever invented," the exposition's official history recorded. "People could not help talking about it and telling their friends they must see it, and crowds of them flocked to the Hawaiian Building and had to be admitted in lines and kept moving by guards. . . . The building was not large, yet it is said to have been visited by as many as 34,000 people in a single day."[24] Once in the building, however, visitors were serenaded by Kailimai and his group, playing on a small bandstand in the center of the entrance hall, surrounded by tree ferns, queen palms, and other tropical flora.[25]

A Hawaiian quintet featuring Henry Kailimai (center) was fea-
tured in the Hawaiian Building at San Francisco's Panama-
Pacific International Exposition in 1915. Courtesy of Hawaii
State Archives.

Hawaiian music was not limited to the confines of the Hawaiian Building.
Some three dozen musicians participated in the building's dedication ceremonies,
which included a parade through the exposition grounds. On Hawaii Day, June
11, 1915, musicians on barges towed by outriggers on the Fine Arts Lagoon played
"the languorous, throbbing harmonies of that strange and gentle people."[26] Large
crowds also were entertained by musicians in the Hawaiian Gardens in the Horticultural Building, where free samples of pineapple and other Hawaiian products

were served. Author Laura Ingalls Wilder was among the fairgoers who dropped by, and she described the

> large pavilion where Hawaiian coffee and pineapple juice and salad and other combinations of pineapple are served at little tables. There is a fountain in the center and water vines and shrubs and flowers around the fountain's rim. The fountain and a little space are enclosed with golden ropes and there are marble pedestals inside with canaries in cages on them. At one side is a balcony where a Hawaiian band plays and sings their native songs, which are lovely. The canaries have heard the music so long that at certain places they take up the tune and sing an accompaniment. It is beautiful. The waiters are Hawaiian men and girls and it's a delightful place to sit and rest, listen to the music and sip either coffee or delicious pineapple juice.[27]

Because of the 'ukulele's widespread popularity on the West Coast, the Hawaiian presence at the Panama-Pacific International Exposition already was a familiar one to many of the locals. For a special train excursion from Los Angeles to San Francisco during the early days of the exposition, the Los Angeles Chamber of Commerce hired a group of Hawaiian singers to provide entertainment. During Southern California Day in July, a Hawaiian orchestra serenaded visitors to the Southern California portion of the California Building.[28] But Hawaiian music had a profound impact on many other of the fair's more than 18 million visitors, one of whom fondly recalled, years later, listening to the Hawaiian orchestra in the Horticultural Building. "Remember, there was no radio, no TV in those days, no music at all that was really live, unless you went to a concert. . . . Kids like us didn't have the money to go to concerts. The first live music I remember enjoying so much was this daily concert they had. Oh, that Hawaiian girl, can you imagine, a beautiful young girl doing the hula and singing. What it meant for a hick from the country, drinking pineapple juice to the tune of Hawaiian music!"[29]

Another visitor captivated by the Hawaiians' music was Henry Ford, whose Ford Motor Company had one of the most popular exhibits at the fair: a replica assembly line in the Palace of Transportation that turned out twenty cars a day.[30] At Ford's request, Kailimai and a group of fellow musicians moved to Detroit after the fair ended to perform for company promotions and social events throughout the Midwest.[31] Renamed the Ford Hawaiians, Kailimai and his group went on to record for Edison and perform on Ford's Dearborn radio station, WWI.[32]

Although Kumalae apparently did a good business selling 'ukuleles, taro patches, calabashes, and other curios at the fair, winning a gold medal featured prominently in subsequent advertising, 'ukuleles had been available in San Francisco music stores for quite some time.[33] In the fall of 1914, just before the fair opened its doors, both Sherman, Clay and Byron Mauzy, "Everything in Music," stocked 'ukuleles.[34] "We carry the largest stock of Ukuleles in the world," Sherman, Clay proclaimed, advertising instruments priced from $5 to $20.

The San Francisco music house of Sherman, Clay enthusiastically plugged 'ukuleles after the Panama-Pacific International Exposition opened in 1915.

Business boomed during the course of the fair: So great was the popularity of Kailimai, Awai, and the other Hawaiian musicians that "dealers in San Francisco are already increasing their orders in the Hawaiian Islands for these little instruments," one observer wrote in August 1915. "One of the largest San Francisco firms placed an order a while back for 200 instruments; he has now increased this order to 500."[35] Sherman, Clay was quick to realize the potential of the new fad, advertising the 'ukulele nationally that summer with a promise that they "can be sold at a very low price and [you] can still make big profit."[36]

The 'ukulele had become "the most popular instrument of the day. . . . Society fad of the hour," as one national music house put it in November 1915, shortly before the fair's nine-month run came to a successful close.[37] By the end of the year, 'ukuleles—"the new musical instrument, a craze of the Frisco Exposition"—and 'ukulele lessons were being advertised in Kansas City, Detroit, Fort Worth, New

Orleans, Duluth, Minnesota, Anaconda, Montana, and Columbus, Georgia.[38] The ʻukulele and Hawaiian music offered a welcome diversion from the grim war news from Europe, where German and Allied armies had reached a bloody and increasingly frustrating stalemate. "In these days of strain and stress, the music of Hawaii comes with peculiar pleasure," Columbia Records soothed in advertising its latest releases.[39] The sickening realities of modern warfare, together with the rapid and often bewildering pace of urbanization and industrialization of the United States, made preindustrial music like that of Hawaii a welcome form of escapist exoticism—particularly when it was seized upon in New York, the country's official arbiter of popular culture.[40] "Nothing new in the way of social diversion ever comes from London or Paris these war-stricken days, consequently society has to look to other climes for novel suggestions," a New York society writer wrote while noting the popularity of "Hawaiian entertainments."[41]

Tin Pan Alley, vaudeville, and the burgeoning recording industry adopted the ʻukulele and Hawaiian music, elevating what had been a regional fad into a trend that swept across the United States and into Canada.[42] In December 1915, just three weeks after the fair ended, "On the Beach at Waikiki"—Kailimai's hapa haole song about stealing a kiss from a "sweet brown maiden"—was being featured in two Broadway productions simultaneously: Irving Berlin's *Stop! Look! Listen!* and *Very Good Eddie* (a young Jerome Kern wrote a new verse for the hit Hawaiian tune).[43] Six months later, when Florenz Ziegfield unveiled the 1916 edition of his *Follies*, the revue included what one critic called an "inevitable" Hawaiian number in which two cast members imitated "that insinuating musical instrument which the wags never seem to tire of calling the eucalyptus."[44] The rest of the country was quick to see the results of the new trend. "We've had these lei-bedecked Hawaiians and their ukuleles working for their board around at the pork-and-bean hunger cures, and thought nothing of their artistic writhings and plaintive wailings at all, until lo, New York took up the fad, and now the simplest little 'sidewalk' act in vaudeville has to have its Honolulu number," critic Grace Kingsley noted in the *Los Angeles Times* in 1916. "There are only two acts on the Orpheum bill this week which haven't a Hawaiian number."[45] Entire shows were inspired by the craze, with such titles as *Hello Honolulu, The Garden of Aloha, My Honolulu Girl,* and *The Ukulele Girl.*[46] By the end of the year, one writer reported with a touch of hyperbole that the fad had stripped Honolulu of musicians and dancers. During the height of the cabaret season, "Honolulu is deserted, save for the tourists and motion-picture actors. The sight of a native walking along the streets set the city agog with wonder and amazement."[47]

The number of songs with Hawaiian themes grew exponentially in the wake of the San Francisco fair—from about a dozen published in 1915, most from local firms in Honolulu, San Francisco, and Chicago, to almost four times that number in 1916, penned by such names as Berlin, Al Dubin, Harry Von Tilzer, and Bert Kalmar—men who had never been to Hawaii and never picked up a ʻukulele.[48]

"Oh Honolulu, America loves you/O Honolulu, we're thanking you too, we do!" proclaimed one verse of "Honolulu, America Loves You," a 1916 offering. "You've made our poorest of families/Dance to your beautiful melodies/Our millionaires are playing Ukaleles too." W. D. Adams, president of Honolulu's Bergstrom Music Co., reported after a 1916 trip to the mainland that he was able to sell four hundred thousand copies of two unnamed Hawaiian songs, and that one New York publisher reported that he had sold half a million copies of the sheet music for "Aloha Oe" each year since 1909. "Everywhere I visited—music halls, vaudeville shows, hotels, cafes and cabarets—Hawaiian songs are sung," Adams said.[49] In February 1917, three-quarters of the dance orchestra playlists published in a popular New York music journal included one or more Tin Pan Alley Hawaiian numbers.[50]

The market also was flooded with Hawaiian recordings, featuring what Columbia Records called "the Haunting Charm of Hawaiian Music." In an August 1916 newspaper advertisement, readers were urged to "listen to the strange, throbbing plaintiveness of voices, the all-but-human notes of the Hawaiian guitar and the throbbing of the *ukalele* in these Columbia Records, and you will feel the weird enchantment of night in the South Sea Islands."[51] Victor, which dominated the record market, asked Adams to address a national convention of Victor wholesalers during his 1916 trip. In response to his queries, "every jobber was unanimous in stating that the Hawaiian records placed on the market the last year had reached larger sales with them than any other popular records," he reported.[52] C. Bruno & Son of New York, one of the country's largest musical wholesalers, noted that "The 'craze' for Ukuleles, Hawaiian Guitars, and Saxophones has largely been created by the publicity given these instruments by the Talking Machine."[53] While the artists Columbia and Victor were promoting included David Kaili, Pale K. Lua, and Robert Kaawa, most of the "Hawaiian" music coming out of New York was standard Tin Pan Alley fare that had no relationship to real Hawaiian music—just as the *stilo alla turco* music popular throughout Europe in the eighteenth century bore little resemblance to that actually played by Turkish military bands that inspired it.[54] "Songwriters are a meretricious race," music publisher Edward Marks once observed. "They write according to the market."[55] Customers walking into music stores could buy recordings of "The Honolulu Hicki Boola Boo" by the American Quartet, "I Can Hear the Ukuleles Calling Me" by the Victor Military Band, and "Aloha Oe" by opera star Alma Gluck.[56]

One of the biggest successes of the genre was "Yaaka Hula Hickey Dula (Hawaiian Love Song)," introduced by Al Jolson in *Robinson Crusoe Jr.* in February 1916, a song recorded for Columbia and introduced to a countrywide audience during that year's national tour of the popular Broadway production.[57] Such ersatz fare—"Oh, I don't care if you've loved the ladies far and near/You'd forget about them all if you could hear/Yaaka hula hickey dula,/Yaaka hula hickey dula"—helped confuse the public about what constituted real Hawaiian music, as Charles M. Bregg of Pittsburgh learned when he visited Hawaii in 1917. "A lot of so-called Hawaiian music

Columbia Records featured Toots Paka, Helen and Frank Ferera, and other Hawaiian artists during the summer of 1916.

The Haunting Charm of Hawaiian Music

HAWAIIAN music has a fascination that *grows*. Listen to the strange, sobbing plaintiveness of voices, the all-but-human notes of the Hawaiian guitar and the rhythmic throbbing of the *ukalele* in these Columbia Records, and you will feel the weird enchantment of night in the South Sea Islands:

A1616 | ALOHA OE. Toots Paka Hawaiian Company.
10-inch | HAWAIIAN MEDLEY.
75c. | Toots Paka Hawaiian Company.

A1967 | MAUNAKEA. Henry N. Clark. Tenor and Octette.
10-inch | KAALA. Robert Kaawa, Baritone, and
75c. | Octette.

A1935 | ON THE BEACH AT WAIKIKE. Helen Louise and Frank Ferera. Ukalele Duet.
10-inch | HAPA HAOLE HULA GIRL. Helen Louise
75c. | and Frank Ferara. Ukalele Duet.

Columbia Grafonola
Price $150

The perfect reproduction of Hawaiian music, with all its strange fascination, is proof of the power and *truth* of Columbia recordings.

Test this in *any* form of music—Columbia Records will *prove* it. There is a Columbia dealer near you—let him produce the proof *tomorrow*.

*New Columbia Records on sale the 20th of every month.
Columbia Records in all Foreign Languages.
This advertisement was dictated to the Dictaphone.*

COLUMBIA
GRAFONOLAS and DOUBLE-DISC
RECORDS
Columbia Graphophone Co.
174 TREMONT ST., BOSTON TELEPHONE OXFORD 1893

COMPLETE STOCK OF COLUMBIA GRAFONOLAS AND RECORDS FOR SALE BY is made in New York, as I found out when I asked the native leader of a Hawaiian band playing in the Casino at Waikiki Beach what 'Yuka [*sic*] Hula Hickey Dula' meant. He looked puzzled. I repeated the phrase, thinking I would get the translation of the title of this popular Hawaiian song from him. He smiled and replied in perfect English, 'I'm very sorry, sir. You see, I'm not very well educated. I don't know any foreign languages.'"[58] Public confusion extended to such matters as spelling (ukalele, eukalele, ukalali, akalele), pronunciation (the sheet music for Irving Berlin's 1915 composition "My Bird of Paradise" provided a helpful guide, "Pronounced 'You-ka-la-ly,' Definition—Hawaiian Guitar"), the difference between a 'ukulele and steel guitar (confusion between the two was "a rather common error among laymen," *Cadenza* magazine noted condescendingly in 1917), and life in Hawaii generally. "It is apparent that a misleading conception of Hawaii has been drawn by many from popular songs and light literature," one mainland newspaper reported without a trace of irony.[59]

Confused or not, New York high society embraced the new fad. Hawaiian orchestras entertained at dinners at the Ritz Carlton and were featured at musical recitals at the Waldorf-Astoria, debutante affairs at Sherry's, a dance at Mrs. Cornelius Vanderbilt's Fifth Avenue mansion, and at dinner-dances for the elite at Newport, Rhode Island.[60] Late-night lobster palaces in Manhattan featured Hawaiian music; in March 1917 the bill at Reisenweber's near Columbus Circle included both the South Sea Troubadours and the Original Dixieland Jazz Band, the group credited with launching the new craze for jazz.[61] In November 1916, the *New York Tribune* devoted an entire page of its Sunday edition to cartoonist L. M. Glacken's depiction of "Ukulele Square, the Hawaiian Quarter of New York," with its statue of a 'ukulele-playing Queen Liliuokalani, a 'ukulele-strumming snow removal squad, a junk man specializing in 'ukuleles, and a smart society wedding party stepping down the aisle in grass skirts to a 'ukulele accompaniment.[62] The following spring, Canadian humorist Stephen Leacock's imagined encounter with Father Knickerbocker in Manhattan took place in a fashionable restaurant where they heard "a burst of wild music, pounded and thrummed out on ukuleles by a group of yellow men in Hawaiian costumes."[63] The fad spread to high society's servants as well: So popular was the 'ukulele among maids of families vacationing in Atlantic City that hotel proprietors felt compelled to post signs banning them on the premises.[64]

In the South, the 'ukulele phenomenon took a little longer to catch on. In the spring of 1915, the *Washington Post* felt obliged to inform its readers that the instrument resembling a small guitar used to produce the "weird and alluring" music featured in *The Bird of Paradise* was known as the 'ukulele.[65] Several months later, the *Atlanta Constitution* could still adopt the role of an onlooker as it described "the ukalali Hawaiian love songs and dances which are now the rage in the north and west."[66] But it was only a matter of time. "There are a lot of fellows I know who would be sniffing it and shooting it up the arm if Hawaiian music was dispensed in packages instead of ukeleles," one young writer enthused in the *Constitution* in

1916. When the Brazilian ambassador hosted a birthday party for Vice President Thomas Riley Marshall in Washington, D.C., in March 1916, a Hawaiian orchestra provided the music.[67] By that summer, ʻukuleles could be purchased at Stieffer's Music House in Charlotte, North Carolina, the E. C. Christian Music Co. in Lexington, Kentucky, and at S. Ernest Philpitt in Miami.[68] The 1916–1917 edition of Al G. Fields' Minstrels featured the young Bobbie Henshaw as the "Human Ukulele."[69] The following year, Western Automatic Music Co. of Dallas, Texas, was proudly advertising itself as "Ukulele Headquarters of the South."[70]

High school and college students all over the country embraced the ubiquitous ʻukulele, which began to appear everywhere: at a birthday party of a young socialite in Atlanta; at high school graduations in Washington, D.C., and Dallas; at a Sunday evening musical service in a Boston church; and in Bemidji, Minnesota, where it was reported that "nearly all the high school girls can strum jazzy numbers on the ukulele."[71] ʻUkulele orchestras "have sprung up here, there and everywhere," the *Memphis Commercial Appeal* lamented in 1917. "The Ukulele infects this otherwise pleasant republic like a plague of grasshoppers."[72] Hawaiian trios and quartets became a featured turn in college glee clubs, from the University of Nevada and the University of Texas to Mount Holyoke and Cornell.[73] "The old time mandolin club has been renovated and fitted with modern improvements until in its present form as 'Ukelele Club' it would scarcely recognize its old self," one Pennsylvania reviewer wrote of a 1916 performance by the Lafayette College Glee Club.[74] "What has become of the old-fashioned boy—beg pardon, we mean college man—who used to play the banjo?" editorialized the *Kansas City Star*. "Its honest plunkings reflect young America better than the lascivious slurrings of the South Seas."[75]

Guitarist William Miles, a Toronto native, is believed to have been the first to introduce Hawaiian music to Canada around 1903, after having heard it in Honolulu as a traveling circus musician.[76] The first Hawaiian troupes did not arrive until a decade later, including Clark's Royal Hawaiians, who arrived in Toronto in 1915; Ben Hokea decided to stay and became a major force in Hawaiian music in Canada as a teacher, performer, and recording artist.[77] However, the full force of the ʻukulele craze does not appear to have hit until 1916–1917. In Winnipeg, for example, the Strand Theatre presented Pauline Thurston, together with Leo Hemming and the Royal Hawaiians, in June 1917 because "for the past few months [management has] received requests from patrons to incorporate an Hawaiian act in one of the vaudeville bills shown at this house."[78] ʻUkuleles could be had at Whaley, Royce & Co., "Canada's Greatest Music House," which asked patrons, "Do You Ukulele?" or at Mclean & Co., Ltd., which boasted "Everything in Music."[79] Owners of newly purchased ʻukuleles could take lessons from Miles at Whaley, Royce or from Miss Mabel Downing, who offered "rapid, up-to-date tuition."[80]

Despite considerable skepticism as to how long the fad would last—as late as 1920, one executive referred to the ʻukulele as a "freak instrument"—mainland manufacturers kicked production into high gear to meet the new demand, part of a broader interest in making music that saw production of all instruments (other than pianos and organs) rise dramatically between 1914 and 1919.[81] Which firm was supplying Sears with its mail-order 'ukuleles in 1914 isn't clear, but Chicago-based Lyon & Healy and Harmony both appear to have been in the business of 'ukulele manufacture by 1915.

Chicago, which by 1910 had replaced New York as the country's largest manufacturer of musical instruments, quickly became the center of mainland 'ukulele production.[82] Major New York wholesalers, including Bruno and Buegeleisen &

The Ukulele

GENUINE HAWAIIAN

Made of Native Koa

LEANDRO NUNES

M. NUNES & SONS MAKERS

Unsurpassed in tone and durability. The Ukulele is the most popular Instrument of the day. The favorite of College men and women everywhere. Society fad of the hour. Ideal voice accompaniment. Easy to learn. We furnish Instruction Book.

PRICES :
$8.00, $10.00, $12.00, $15.00, $20.00 post-paid. Chicago made Ukuleles, $5.00 and up.

LYON & HEALY
CHICAGO

Chicago music wholesaler Lyon & Healy advertised "Genuine Hawaiian" 'ukuleles made by "Leandro" Nunes of Los Angeles in 1915.

Jacobson, quickly followed suit.[83] Gut strings manufactured specifically for 'ukuleles appeared as early as 1917.[84] Big-city department stores began to stock 'ukuleles—"America's most popular musical instrument"—including the Fair in Chicago, the Broadway in Los Angeles, and Lit Brothers and Wanamakers in Philadelphia.[85] 'Ukuleles were even sold in sporting goods, furniture, and jewelry stores.[86] Seeing money to be made, local firms jumped into the market as well. In Los Angeles, for example, the American-made 'ukuleles touted by Southern California Music Co. as "positively the greatest values ever offered for the money" could have come from the Hawaiian Ukulele and Violin Manufacturing Co., the Non-Slip Key Socket and Ukulele Manufacturing Co., or Wood Manufacturing Co., which made phonograph cabinets as well as ukuleles.[87] Overseas manufacturers saw a lucrative opportunity as well; as early as 1918, Japanese firms reportedly were making 'ukuleles.[88]

What would become the mainland's best-known 'ukulele manufacturer didn't enter the market until October 1915, when it sold its first two 'ukuleles to George Stannard of Trenton, New Jersey.[89] Although its instruments retailed for three times or more the price of the product of its chief competitors—its three styles of all-mahogany instruments retailed for $10, $15, and $25 in 1917, when its first 'ukulele catalog was published—the C. F. Martin & Co.'s 'ukuleles were an immediate success, quickly surpassing the company's output of guitars. As a result, the firm's rural Pennsylvania factory had to be expanded the following year.[90] "The additional men required by the demand for this new instrument were at first accommodated in the old buildings by means of the strictest economies of space, but as the Hawaiian music grew in popularity, it became necessary to provide additional floor space," *Cadenza* reported in April 1917.[91] Martin's high-end strategy stood in dramatic contrast to the rest of the mainland market, where the 'ukulele's astonishing popularity and what some critics attacked as wartime profiteers willing to produce and sell instruments "false in tone, flimsy in construction, and made in a cheap, shoddy way" sent prices for instruments steadily downward: from $6 in 1914 to $3.50 in 1915 to a sales price of $1.95 in 1917.[92] Quality suffered in the drive for bargains, professionals complained. "Only about one out of five of the ukuleles made have a musical tone—due mostly to the quality of the wood," Charles De Lano observed in 1917. "Even the koa-wood instruments made by the best manufacturers are of varied quality."[93] To their credit, some retailers sounded a note of caution about the cheapest mainland models. Philadelphia distributor Fred C. Meyers & Co. pointed out that their least expensive American-made instrument "looks like an ukulele, that's all we'd care to say about it," but that "those ranging from $7.50 upwards are genuine Hawaiian, made by Hawaiians in the Hawaiian Islands. Hawaiians make them by hand, they use only native Koa wood. They 'know how.' You'll never regret buying a genuine."[94]

Production in Hawaii expanded dramatically in an attempt to meet the demand for the genuine—from an estimated five to six hundred 'ukuleles per month in August 1915 to sixteen hundred per month just one year later.[95] In 1916–1917, the

New York wholesaler Buegeleisen & Jacobson offered eighteen different 'ukulele models in May 1917, including taro patches and harp models.

six major firms in Honolulu—James N. Anahu, the Hawaiian Ukulele Co., Kinney & Mossman, Jonah Kumalae, M. Nunes & Sons, and Singers Ukulele Manufacturing Co.—together employed more than a hundred workers.[96] It was during this boom that Samuel K. Kamaka Sr. launched the family firm that is today Hawaii's oldest 'ukulele company.[97] But the small scale of Hawaiian production and mainland retailers' practice of selling cheaper mainland-made instruments side by side with the pricier Hawaiian models made it difficult for the islanders to compete effectively, even though there is evidence they quickly moved through West Coast wholesalers to gain access to national distribution networks.[98] For example, having signed with H. C. Churchill of San Francisco as exclusive agent for the United States and Canada, by 1920 Jonah Kumalae's 'ukuleles were distributed by Sherman, Clay of San Francisco, Lyon & Healy in Chicago, Oliver Ditson in Boston, and C. Bruno & Son of New York.[99] Predictably, the Hawaiians emphasized the higher quality of "genuine" 'ukuleles and complained about the tactics of quick-buck artists on the mainland. "Unfortunately, the demand for this little instrument has been so great throughout the States that the concerns in the Islands have been unable to supply the market fast enough," Thrum's *Hawaiian Almanac* said in a 1917 overview of Hawaiian music. "This condition has given unscrupulous manufacturers everywhere the opportunity to put on the market an imitation of the ukulele, being machine made, of cheap American woods, the result of course being a poorly made and poorly toned instrument. . . . There will always be a class of people in the States who will demand a genuine Hawaiian article, and this is the trade we should endeavor to supply."[100] Bergstrom's, the Honolulu music store, took out ads on the mainland urging customers to "Buy Your Ukuleles Direct from the Country Where They Are Made."[101]

Not only were mainland companies manufacturing a cheap imitation, some were passing them off as Hawaiian-made, much to the consternation of the islanders.[102] In 1916, Tom May, acting secretary of a booster group known as the Honolulu Advertising Club, filed an application to trademark a "Made in Hawaii" tabu mark, featuring crossed *puloulou* or *kapu* sticks, surmounted by a *hoaka,* or crescent, a symbol intimately associated with *alii,* and the royal Hawaiian crown.[103] Southern California Music Co., "sole U.S. selling agents for the Genuine M. Nunes & Sons' Ukuleles," prominently featured the new tabu mark in a November 1916 newspaper ad, telling customers, "For Your Protection When Purchasing Your Ukulele Look for this Trade-Mark. It signifies that the instrument is a genuine Hawaiian-handmade Ukulele. Refuse all substitutes."[104] In addition to M. Nunes, makers who subsequently used the mark were Aloha Ukulele Manufacturing Co., James Anahu, Manuel Nunes, Paradise Ukulele and Guitar Works, and, curiously, Los Angeles-based Leonardo Nunes.[105]

Hawaiian manufacturers also were hampered by America's entry into World War I in April 1917; the Pacific was quickly stripped of every ship that could be put to use in the Atlantic, making it more difficult and expensive to ship ukuleles to

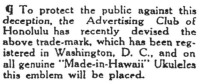

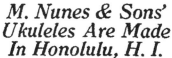

Southern California Music Co. featured the Honolulu Ad Club's Tabu mark as the sign of the genuine Hawaiian-made article in November 1916.

the mainland until some semblance of normalcy was restored in 1920.[106] The war destroyed Hawaiian dreams of a new tourist boom, as envisioned by the *Star-Bulletin* in August 1914: "Hawaii now faces a golden, a stirring, an unprecedented and never-to-be-repeated opportunity to go after and get a large share of the world's tourist traffic."[107] The war also cut off almost all European musical imports, which meant that "for all practical purposes, . . . American manufacturers virtually have the entire small instrument trade in this country at their disposal," one trade publication observed.[108] America's declaration of war on Germany also had a completely unanticipated effect: It introduced the 'ukulele to Europe.

Only a small number of Hawaiians actually served overseas during the war, including fifty naval militiamen who served aboard the USS *St. Louis* in the Atlantic. A group photo taken at the Boston Navy Yard makes clear they took their music with them: It includes a display of four guitars, two 'ukuleles, and a violin.[109] Larger numbers of the more than twelve thousand men in regular army units stationed in Hawaii were shipped back to the mainland during the war, bedecked with leis and carrying 'ukuleles.[110] When John Dos Passos shipped out from New York in June 1917 to serve as an ambulance driver in France, a Hawaiian band played on the wharf—a scene he later incorporated in the opening pages of his first novel, *One Man's Initiation: 1917*.[111] But the 'ukulele did not arrive in Europe directly from Hawaii; rather, it was through the entertainment-starved doughboys from the mainland and the good offices of the Young Men's Christian Association and other service groups. 'Ukuleles were often found in army training camps, both in the hands of the recruits themselves and those entertaining them.[112] "There is nothing like the ukulele to drive the 'blues' away when a boy begins to think of home and sweethearts," said Isabelle Works of Los Angeles, who in 1918 mounted a drive to put a 'ukulele into every army tent in southern California.[113]

Army regulations forbade soldiers from bringing instruments with them, and instruments were scarce and expensive overseas. Convinced that "entertainment is not a luxury to the modern man . . . it is a necessity as vital to him as sugar in his food," the YMCA organized its entertainment bureau in New York in September 1917 to recruit entertainers for overseas service and collect musical instruments and sheet music. When bureau chief Thomas McLane issued "a call for everybody to take down 'that old ukulele' from the top shelf and send it to the boys 'over there,' the public threatened to bury him under mounds of instruments."[114] McLane's plea was echoed by President Woodrow Wilson, who said in a statement that "the man who disparages music as a luxury and non-essential is doing the nation an injury. . . . Music now more than ever before is a national need."[115]

Music retailers happily joined in the spirit of things, urging customers to "Send One to Your Soldier Boy" (Barlow's Music of Trenton, New Jersey) and telling them "Our Boys 'Over There' Would Appreciate a Ukulele" (S. Ernest Philpitt in Miami) or "Send Him a Ukulele or Taropatch Fiddle for Christmas!" (Southern California Music Co.).[116]

Many Officers and Men

In our camps are enjoying their little "UKULELES" which they thoughtfully included in their equipment.

Now Is the Time to Prepare

For the convenience of the boys at the front and those that will shortly join them we offer the largest and best selected stock in the city.

UKULELES, American Made, Price, $6.50 and up

The Genuine Original Nunes Ukuleles, Price $15 and Up. Carrying Cases, Books of Instruction and Ukulele Music Collections.

THE HAWAIIAN or Singing Guitars, $10.75 and up

Band, Fife and Drum Corps Supplies

Popular Sheet Music, 10c Per Copy

Collections of Patriotic Songs of All Nations

E. F. Droop & Sons Co., 1300 G St.

After the United States entered World War I in 1917, music retailers sensed a new sales opportunity for the Hawaiian music fad.

During the war and its aftermath, the YMCA shipped more than 18,000 musical instruments and 450,000 pieces of sheet music to the troops as part of what was modestly billed as "the greatest entertainment enterprise in the world's history."[117] Prisoners of war were not forgotten: Between March 1915 and June 1917, the American YMCA spent 20,000 German marks on musical instruments for Allied POWs.[118] Among the entertainers recruited by the Y were the Liberty Belles, three "charmingly talented young ladies" who featured the 'ukulele as part of an act "pulsating with Patriotism," and Irene Wright, who, when a piano or organ was not to be had, "proved her versatility by making use of her ukulele, upon which she played accompaniments for arias from the great operas, duets and for popular songs dear to the hearts of the 'doughboys.'"[119]

When the Americans arrived, they discovered the 'ukulele was largely unknown in Europe, despite the fact that William Kanui, Joe Puni, and other Hawaiian musicians had played in Paris in late 1913 and early 1914, and Kanui and Puni had been touring English music halls since 1914.[120] The Paris edition of *Stars and Stripes* reported in February 1918 under the pointed headline "Ignorance Is Bliss": "The average American high school girl, who must have her ukulele, would not feel at home in France, for the ukulele is unknown here. A ukulele hunt through the

All three of the multitalented Liberty Belles—Vera Krake, Elsie Bemont, and Kathleen Le Baron—played the "uke-lele." Courtesy of Redpath Chatauqua Collection, University of Iowa Libraries, Iowa City, Iowa.

biggest stores of Paris failed to bring to light one of these instruments, even with the use of English, bad French, eloquent arms, a dictionary, and an illustrated catalogue from a music dealer."[121] Yet the 'ukulele managed to penetrate even further on the continent after the war when American troops stationed in Germany as part of the Army of Occupation were followed by the faithful YMCA, which distributed more than four thousand musical instruments there.[122] "Guitars, mandolins, uke-leles, and even our own southern banjoes have sprung up from nowhere at all and each one of them has found a manipulator," reported an AEF member on occupation duty.[123] At least one vaudeville duo got its start with a 'ukulele donated to the troops: Harry Jans and Harold Whalen, who went on to become a popular team working in musical comedies and reviews, met in post-armistice France when Jans was entertaining his outfit by strumming a 'ukulele and making up nonsense lyrics to fit the tunes, and Whalen literally jumped in and began to dance.[124]

In the summer of 1918, a Philadelphia officer assigned to a French antiaircraft school near Verdun reported that the French "were enthusiastic over my ukulele which, although derided in the States as a woman's musical instrument, is never-theless very popular among the boys."[125] Back home, women—particularly young women—had been the first to embrace the little Hawaiian import, whether Mabel Andrews of Brooklyn in 1893, Mrs. C. R. Templeton in Portland, Oregon, in 1896, Grace Hilborn in Washington, D.C., in 1897, Daisy Cartwright of Oakland in 1899, or the scores of women's club members up and down the West Coast after the turn of the century. In 1916, one San Francisco reporter described how "the newfangled girl" had embraced the 'ukulele to the extent that dozens gathered in Golden Gate Park each day at noon "to while away their lunch hour charming birds and buf-faloes and the young men who happen by" with their 'ukulele strumming.[126] Mid-western girls caught the bug, too. "Hundreds of her have the craze," reported the *Kansas City Star*.[127] But the war to end all wars unwittingly played a pivotal role in transforming the 'ukulele from a largely feminine fad to an instrument men wanted to play. With few other musical alternatives available overseas, tens of thousands of servicemen were introduced to the little "eucalyptus" and found they liked it. "It seems the Germans won't believe our boys are in the trenches because they haven't heard the ukuleles," one newspaper joked six months after America's entry into the war.[128] It was a transformation that set the stage for the Roaring Twenties, when the popular stereotype placed a 'ukulele in the hands of every college man.[129]

At the end of the war, London and New York also found their traditional roles reversed: It was to New York that London looked for new diversions. "The jazz band, which arrived in London with the American troops, is now being followed by Hawaiian ukulele players; the advent of the hula dancer is predicted," the *New York Times* reported in the summer of 1919. "'London is war-weary,' the dispatch comments, 'and having more money than ever before is looking for amusement.'"[130] Among the first postwar Hawaiian musicians in London were Joseph Kekuku and Mekia Kealakai, who both left New York in June 1919 aboard the SS *Baltic* with contracts to play at the swank Savoy Hotel.[131] "The orchestra gave a refined and charming entertainment, accompanying their songs with the ukuleles, an instru-ment specially adapted for harmonizing with the human voice," reported the *London Times*.[132] A long-delayed production of *The Bird of Paradise* was mounted in London that September, a play "that seemed to give the audience . . . immense gratification."[133] The enthusiasm for things Hawaiian quickly became a cliché: In the fall of 1921, under the headline "New and Original Features for the Season's Reviews," *Punch* wearily noted that audiences could expect to see "A Scene in Honolulu."[134]

What the British came to identify as the 'ukulele, however, was known in the States as the "banjo ukulele," an instrument of murky origins that first emerged in 1916 and was popularized in England by the peripatetic Keech brothers, Alvin (b. 1890) and Kelvin (1895–1977).[135] The earliest known appearance of 'ukulele banjos was in an October 1916 advertisement for Chicago distributor Frank Pallma and Son, which it billed as "the successor to the Hawaiian Ukulele."[136]

The banjo-ukulele, also known as the banjuke and the banjulele, was the next big thing—or was being marketed as such—
in 1917.

An accompanying article identified the ukulele banjo as the invention of
"Joseph" Bolander. Although John Bolander of Berkeley filed a U.S. trademark
application for the term "Banjo Uke" in January 1917, saying he had been using the
term for eighteen months, it is unclear what his relationship was to the "Ukulele-
Banjos" first advertised by Kohler & Chase in San Francisco and Southern California Music Co. in June 1917 ("isn't it the classiest little instrument you ever saw?"),
the "Banjuke," manufactured by Edward and F. A. Norton of Berkeley and advertised by Sherman, Clay that same month ("has all the 'jazz' and 'pep' of a banjo . . .
[with] the appealing sweetness of the ukulele"), or the Keech "Ukulele Banjo"
advertised by Birkel Music of Los Angeles in February 1918.[137]

Born in Hawaii, where Kelvin was a star pupil in the Ernest Kaai Music School in Honolulu, the Keeches moved to San Francisco sometime prior to the opening of the Pan-Pacific International Exhibition, where they opened the Keech Studios on Powell Street and sold the "Keech Art Ukulele" and Hawaiian music, offered lessons, and supplied Hawaiian musicians for parties, concerts, and other occasions.[138] They are listed in Los Angeles city directories in 1916; early the following year, Alvin appeared there with the De Lano Steel Guitar and Ukulele Sextette and "introduced" the ukulele banjo playing "My Flower of Hawaii."[139] Kelvin joined the army after the United States entered the war, was shipped to France in September 1918, and stayed after his discharge in April 1919, playing in a jazz band called the White Lyres.[140] Alvin remained in Los Angeles making, selling, and demonstrating his banjo ukulele until 1920, when meeting with unspecified business reverses, he left town and shipped to Antwerp as a common seaman to join his brother in Europe.[141] By the spring of 1921, the two were in London, where Keech Brothers once again began manufacturing banjo ukuleles—what they now called banjuleles—with considerable success.[142] Other British firms also manufactured 'ukuleles and banjo ukuleles, including Aladar de Vekey of Bournemouth, who for more than two decades had been the sole English dealer for Gibson mandolins.[143]

When America entered the war in 1917, many had predicted that "the days of the dreamy, snaky Hawaiian airs are gone forever," to be replaced by patriotic war songs. "Now these ukuleles are being laid away on the shelf with the Teddy bears and all the rest of the obsolete fads of yesterday," wrote one observer with apparent relief.[144] But at the end of the war, it became clear that the 'ukulele was no longer an exotic novelty but had become part of mainstream American culture. For example, it was used to sell Victrolas: "It will transport you . . . to the beach at Hawaii, where lithe girls dance to plaintive ukuleles"; player pianos: "The Euphona contains the miniature keyboard, transposing device, ukulele attachment and other exclusive features"; and social acceptance: "With the aid of the Ukulele you can play yourself right into popularity."[145] Its ubiquity was such that it began to appear in the latest novels—Sinclair Lewis' *Babbitt* used a music school pitch for 'ukulele lessons as an example of American anti-intellectualism—in pawn shops, and even in the presidential sickroom: After Woodrow Wilson was prostrated by a stroke, a phonograph played "a number of Hawaiian melodies, the weird strain of the ukulele sounding through the White House."[146] In 1922, when Manuel Nunes, the last of the original makers, died in Honolulu, it marked the end of one era—and the beginning of another. That same year, a young New York divorcée named May Singhi Breen was given a 'ukulele for Christmas, was unable to exchange it, and decided to take lessons instead.[147] On a navy warship in the Mediterranean, a young sailor named Arthur Godfrey was practicing on a 'ukulele that a Hawaiian colleague had shown him how to play back at the radio school at the Great Lakes Naval Training Station in Illinois.[148] And all across the country, a new phenomenon called radio was quickly building an audience of millions—and providing a powerful new platform for the 'ukulele.

CHAPTER 7

The Height of Its Popularity

The whole face of the earth has bloomed with ukuleles this summer.

—*Music Trade Review,* September 21, 1921

O riginally a hobby pursued by a small group of enthusiasts, radio's explosive growth after World War I left contemporary observers struggling for adjectives. The *Review of Reviews* said it "has possibly not been equaled in all the centuries of human progress." *Radio Broadcast* called it "almost incomprehensible." Herbert Hoover, then secretary of commerce, found it "astounding."[1] KDKA of Pittsburgh, the country's first commercial station, went on the air in November 1920; by the fall of 1922, there were almost five hundred stations nationwide.[2] That year, $60 million in radio sets and parts were sold; just two years later, total sales had increased almost sixfold, to $358 million.[3]

From the beginning, Hawaiian music and the 'ukulele were a staple of what one radio historian has called the "somewhat chaotic jumble of different types of music" offered in the early make-it-up-as-you-go days of broadcasting.[4] In 1922, the Schenectady Hawaiian Trio broadcast on WGXP in Schenectady; Frank W. May offered Hawaiian guitar selections in Springfield, Massachusetts; in Chicago, KYW listeners heard Janey Hickey and the Mele Hawaiian Quartet; Los Angeles listeners heard steel guitarist Wiki Bird and Anita Ransom on 'ukulele performing a medley of popular tunes; Messrs. Schrader and Lensner, Hawaiian guitarists, presented vocal and instrumental selections in Pittsburgh; and in New York, Virginia Burt, soprano and Hawaiian guitar imitator, offered her own compositions and Hawaiian novelties.[5] "The radio listener is certain to tune in on some ukulele playing somewhere or other before any evening is over," one music industry analyst observed.[6]

The intimate nature of a radio broadcast that gave rise to a natural, casual style of singing labeled as "crooning"—a style the young Bing Crosby rode to success—also favored the 'ukulele. The new technology made it possible for the small instrument to be heard effortlessly in a way that was impossible on stage or in early recordings. "Stringed music has become highly popular with listeners-in," the *Los Angeles Times* noted in June 1923 in reporting an on-air performance of Kenelle's Iolani Hawaiian Orchestra. "It broadcasts perfectly, sounding perhaps better by radio than at close range."[7] Cultural critic Charles Merz reached a similar conclusion: "It is the brass bands, the harmony boys and the ukuleles that have made the radio famous. And it is to the brass bands, the popular airs, the harmony boys and the ukuleles that the radio gives most of its treasured time."[8] 'Ukulele makers were quick to pick up on the trend, advertising their instruments' "broadcasting qualities" and the endorsements of the radio performers who used them.[9]

The 'ukulele's radio resurgence came at a time when, weary of the fad that burst onto the scene in 1915–1916, some welcomed the idea that 'ukulele's time had come and gone. "Ukulele No Longer Favored by the Public," the *Hartford Courant* proclaimed with obvious relief in the summer of 1921, after a reporter visited a local music store "and saw hanging upon the walls almost a score of ukulele, all of them covered with the dust of time." But the obituary proved premature: Ten days later, the *Courant* quoted a local music dealer as saying the 'ukulele "is still one of the most popular instruments today and we are selling as many of them as we were at the time the Hawaiian song was the height of its popularity."[10] Some predicted that with the rise of radio, interest in playing the 'ukulele and other musical instruments would decline; but music dealers reported that the effect was quite the opposite. "Whenever one of the popular 'mike' artists thumps a new song hit on his guitar or ukulele, the dealers said there were many who resolved to master the magic of the melodic strings," a survey of Chicago music retailers found.[11]

The speed with which the 'ukulele became a staple of radio entertainment helped complete its transformation from an exotic novelty to a staple of popular culture. No longer was it regarded chiefly as a Hawaiian instrument played by Hawaiian musicians performing Hawaiian music. Now it was an American phenomenon—a perception popular not only at home but abroad. Americans "all are accomplished jazz singers; they sing the newest Broadway song hits all the day, accompanying themselves on the ukulele," German cartoonist Hans Michaelis wrote in a comic 1929 account of European stereotypes of America.[12] When composer Aaron Copland was in Paris in 1926, contemplating the idea of incorporating jazz into his work with the intent of creating new music "that would be recognizably American within a serious musical idiom," he wrote "Two Pieces for Violin and Piano," the second of which, "Ukelele Serenade," included "arpeggiated chords in the right hand of the piano part [to] simulate a ukelele sound."[13] Copland, composer George Gershwin (who cowrote "Ukulele Lorelei"), and their contemporaries were part of a new generation of singers, songwriters, and producers who grew up with the 'ukulele and helped push it into the mainstream. Prolific songwriter ("Sonny Boy," "California, Here I Come") and longtime Broadway and film producer

Buddy De Sylva (1896–1950) launched his career as a ʻukulele-playing "Hawaiian" at the Vernon Country Club—a popular nightspot just outside Los Angeles—where he was discovered by a touring Al Jolson. De Sylva's first published song was "The Honolulu Pa-ki-ka," a ragtime number he wrote in 1916 while a student at the University of Southern California.[14]

The ʻukulele's popularity on radio was paralleled by its status as a fixture in Hollywood, one of the other new incubators of popular culture. Beginning in 1914, studios produced dozens of "South Seas" films, including such productions as *Sirens of the Seas,* a 1917 drama that featured the beautiful Sybil and her female companions "all donned in seaweed in lieu of bathing suits, playing ukuleles and dancing about on the beach."[15] More than seventy-five South Seas films were produced between 1917 and 1930. As a result, "to most of us, the South Seas mean simply cannibals and naked girls," one writer neatly summarized in 1921.[16] ʻUkuleles were not limited to the South Seas, however: One of its earliest appearances on screen came in Essanay's 1916 comedy, *The Beach Combers,* in which traveling salesman Andy Laffin's ʻukulele skills make him a favorite with girls on the beach.[17] Fatty Arbuckle pulled a ʻukulele out of his capacious pants and serenaded a young ingenue in his 1919 comedy two-reeler, *Backstage.*[18] Paramount produced a newsreel short that showed ʻukuleles being made in Honolulu, as did the Ford Motor Co.[19] Hawaiian orchestras were a regular feature at fashionable Hollywood parties; directors such as D. W. Griffith often favored Hawaiian music to set the mood while filming; and it was a Hawaiian trio that played at producer/director Thomas Ince's 1924 funeral at Hollywood Cemetery.[20] Bessie Love, who played one of her own ʻukuleles in the 1929 Academy Award–winning musical, *A Broadway Melody,* had a large collection at home.[21] Mabel Normand, Buster Keaton, and Lupe Velez played the ʻukulele, and Gary Cooper and cowboy star Hoot Gibson performed with their own Hawaiian bands.[22] When heartthrob Ramon Novarro made his sound debut in *The Pagan* in 1929, faulty synchronization led audiences to wonder whether it was really his voice as he strummed a ʻukulele and sang "The Pagan Love Song." It turned out that Novarro actually was singing—it was the ʻukulele playing that was somebody else's.[23] For attractive young ingenues like Gloria Swanson—who serenaded Teddy the dog with her ʻukulele in the 1917 Keystone comedy *Teddy at the Throttle*—Clara Bow, and even Greta Garbo, posing with a ʻukulele became a standard publicity shot.[24] Joan Crawford was a judge at a 1927 ʻukulele contest at a Los Angeles movie theater, and Clara Bow presented an autographed ʻukulele to the winner of a San Jose, California, contest that same year, two of dozens of such contests held at theaters across the country.[25]

But of all the mainland images associated with the ʻukulele, none has been more indelible or lasting than that of the callow college student of the twenties strumming away—an image captured by artist Elbert Jackson in a *Saturday Evening Post* cover showing a nattily dressed young man and an elegantly gowned young woman seated on a paper moon—he fingering a ʻukulele and singing, she listening with her eyes closed.[26] In the popular imagination, collegiate quickly came to mean "wide trousers, coonskin coats and hip flasks, ukuleles and high-powered cars, pep meets and cheerleaders"—to the extent that some college students complained. "Lord knows we are funny enough," wrote one Wisconsin undergraduate. "But we do not wear battered old hats turned up in front, thank you, nor do we run up and down stairs tooting saxophones, nor do we play ukuleles any more generally than any other section of the public, including journalists."[27] Such protests proved futile—the 'ukulele-carrying undergraduate had become a staple of fiction in novels by P. G. Wodehouse and Sinclair Lewis, short stories by F. Scott Fitzgerald and Booth Tarkington, and in movies such as Harold Lloyd's 1925 comedy *The Freshman,* in which Lloyd, having seen his favorite college movie six times, steps off the train for his first year at Tate University fully prepared with golf clubs, a tennis racket, and a 'ukulele.[28] The artist who epitomized the youthful 'ukulele player was English novelist and poet Malcolm Lowry (1909–1957). After picking up his first 'ukulele at age sixteen, it was his constant companion as he serenaded his first love, drove roommates and landlords mad with his incessant strumming, performed in Cambridge pubs, and took a star turn in the university's 1932 *Footlights Review.* In 1940, from Canada, he sent mentor Conrad Aiken his "Epitaph":

Malcolm Lowry
Late of the Bowery
His prose was flowery
And often glowery
He lived, nightly, and drank, daily
And died playing the ukulele.[29]

Just as historian Lyn Dumenil has shown that many of the sweeping changes so evident during the 1920s actually predate World War I, so too does the identification of teenagers and the 'ukulele.[30] The stereotypes of the twenties reflected the convergence of a variety of factors, chief among them the arrival of postwar prosperity and acceptance of the relatively new concept of adolescence as a distinct developmental stage (the term itself wasn't coined until 1898). The end of government-enforced wartime frugality and the rapid expansion of the American economy created a sense of optimism—one that American business worked hard to encourage. "Buy What You Need Now!" urged the National Prosperity Bureau in 1919. A higher standard of living made it possible for more students to attend college—the number more than quadrupled between 1890 and 1924—at a time when, as Jon Savage put it, "America's young were granted a new status as the vanguard of the consumer revolution," one dedicated to leisure and self-expression.[31] It was during the twenties, Mark Sullivan observed, that "an emphasis was placed on the young, simply because they were young, that has probably never been equaled in the history of the world."[32]

The 'ukulele—marketed as easy to play and effortlessly portable in an era of easy prosperity and automotive mobility—was an ideal tool of adolescent self-expression. The piano was inseparable from the parental parlors in which it sat, and the mandolin, despite the never-say-die marketing of the Gibson Company, was too closely associated with the old-fashioned swains parodied by George Ade in his prewar *Modern Fables.*[33] The fact that many adults regarded the 'ukulele as a twanging, whanging nuisance associated with the moral and social threat of jazz music merely made it more attractive—an attitude embedded in the opening lines of Viña Delmar's 1928 novel, *Bad Girl:* "Someone had brought a ukulele. Someone who hit the strings with a gay discordancy, a gleeful insistence that seemed to say, 'Sure, it's out of tune. Who cares?'"[34] Music dealers recognized the importance of the 'ukulele as a means to reach the youth market. "The importance of catering to the youthful trade cannot be overestimated," counseled the *Music Trade Review.* "Many dealers feature ukuleles for no other reason than they bring into their business place a desirable element, which is the trade of the younger people of the community."[35]

Adolescent self-expression aside, the 'ukulele's ubiquity during the twenties was inescapable. Not only did it appear regularly in theater, movies, and on radio, but 'ukulele arrangements became a standard feature of sheet music, thanks in large part to the efforts of prolific performer, composer, and arranger May Singhi Breen (1891–1970), radio's "Ukulele Lady."[36] Dozens of 'ukulele methods and songbooks flooded the market—some edited or arranged by such national figures such as Breen or bearing the name of well-known entertainers such as Ukulele Ike (Cliff Edwards)—but many by relative unknowns or anonymous musicians and published in places as diverse as Milwaukee, Denver, and Altoona, Pennsylvania.[37] These methods, ranging from the *EZ,* the *Practical,* the *Guaranteed,* and the *Simplified* to the *Conservatory* and the *Symphonic*—were rolled out regularly to meet a strong demand that also was responsible for a myriad of songbooks: popular songs, comic songs, camp songs, college songs, and ballads.[38] In 1925, New York music publisher Robbins-Engel announced the formation of a new 'ukulele department. "The lowly and unpretentious ukulele, in my opinion, looms as a saviour to the music industry," said company head Jack Robbins.[39] Even guitar virtuoso Vahda Olcott-Bickford, who viewed the 'ukulele as beneath "the really artistic fretted instruments," published her own 'ukulele method in 1920.[40] Only a handful of songbooks and methods were authored by Hawaiian players or published in Hawaii, and few included Hawaiian songs, apart from "Aloha Oe."

'Ukuleles could be found everywhere, from campgrounds to Folsom Prison—convicted murderer Chick Galloway was labeled the "Ukulele Slayer" for killing a friend in a drunken brawl and stealing his ukulele—and even aboard the battleship *Arizona.*[41] In professional baseball, where players such as pitcher Jack Bentley of the New York Giants and Charlie Grimm, first baseman for the Chicago Cubs, acquired a reputation for their 'ukulele playing as well as their play on the field, the term "ukulele umpire" came to be applied to the third-base umpire in major series, "because he doesn't have much to do and ought to have a ukulele out there to while the time away."[42] By 1925, the 'ukulele was reported to be the country's top-selling instrument, surpassing the banjo and the saxophone.[43] When *Don Juan,* the first talking motion picture, premiered with much fanfare in 1926, it was accompanied by a series of Vitaphone shorts—including *His Pastimes,* featuring multi-instrumentalist Roy Smeck playing guitar, steel guitar, banjo, and his Martin 'ukulele. Two years later, the first public demonstration of television broadcasting in Schenectady featured radio announcer Louis Dean strumming a 'ukulele and singing "Ain't She Sweet?"[44]

Smeck (1901–1994), of Binghampton, New York, vaudevillian, radio performer, and recording artist known as "The Wizard of the Strings," was part of a new generation of pop artists who relied on the 'ukulele in their work. Many entertainers often began their careers with a 'ukulele—Freeman Gosden, for example, was part of a 'ukulele-piano duo with his partner Charles Correll before they enjoyed their phenomenal radio success as *Amos 'n' Andy.*[45] Smeck's command of the instruments he played, as well as his showmanship—he twirled and tapped his 'ukulele as he played, blowing across the soundhole between a variety of showy strokes—made him arguably the greatest string virtuoso of his time.[46] However, other 'ukulele artists achieved greater fame, including Wendell Hall (1896–1969) of Chicago, "The Red-Headed Music Maker," a guitar- and 'ukulele-playing vaudevillian and songwriter who broke into radio in Davenport, Iowa, before becoming a national figure in 1923 with his immensely popular Victor release, "It Ain't Gonna Rain No Mo," a 'ukulele-backed number he plugged on a national tour of radio stations.[47] Almost half a century before Tiny Tim drew one of the largest late-night television audiences ever for his marriage on the *Tonight Show,* Hall's 1924 marriage to Marion Martin was broadcast live on the radio.[48]

Johnny Marvin (1897–1944) of Oklahoma, "The Ukulele Ace," donned blackface and joined a Hawaiian troupe as a teenager to play 'ukulele, guitar, and musical saw.[49] Marvin went on to become one of the best-selling recording artists of the late twenties, recording for a wide range of labels under his own name and a variety of aliases, including "Honey Duke and his Uke."[50]

After a successful stint on Broadway in *Honeymoon Lane,* Marvin traveled to England in 1928 where he played several months of club dates, bringing with him a specially made presentation tenor 'ukulele for the Prince of Wales as a publicity stunt.[51] Frank Crumit (1889–1943), an Ohio native and graduate of Ohio State, also donned blackface early in his vaudeville career, although in his case it was to accompany his banjo playing, "amusing negro dialect stories and his plantation melodies."[52] Crumit began to use a 'ukulele in his act by 1916 and was one of the earliest mainland performers to play the 'ukulele on Broadway—in the 1919 production of *Betty Be Good.*[53] His performance led to a recording contract, the start of a career that lasted throughout the decade as he continued to appear on Broadway in musicals such as *Tangerine, No, No Nanette,* and *Oh Kay.* Paired with his wife,

Recording star Johnny Marvin was one of several artists who
lent their names to mainland-made 'ukulele models in the
1920s.

Broadway actress Julia Sanderson, Crumit went into radio in 1928, where he spent the rest of his career.[54]

Not all popular 'ukulele artists were men. Jennie Durkee (1877–1941), daughter of George B. Durkee, the superintendent of Lyon & Healy's Chicago factory, was a performer and teacher of national reputation who adapted mandolin technique to the 'ukulele, presented in her self-published 1917 method, *The American Way of Playing Ukulele Solos*—using a felt pick.[55] After numerous appearances at Lyon & Healy, Durkee moved to Los Angeles in 1923, where she continued teaching and became a fixture on local radio for the next eight years, favoring a classical repertoire that included pieces by Puccini, Grainger, and Rubinstein to demonstrate the 'ukulele's range.[56] May Singhi Breen, daughter of a New York builder and a pianist, studied the piano originally before being given a 'ukulele that she tried to exchange before deciding to learn how to play it.[57] Breen made her radio debut in 1923 playing the banjo, an instrument she often used in early appearances, but she quickly became a leading 'ukulele evangelist on and off the air. She and her regular partner (and in 1929 her husband), pianist Peter DeRose, rose to national fame as the "Sweethearts of the Air" with their musical duets. Both also were accomplished composers.[58] After Jerome Harris of C. Bruno & Co. (himself a 'ukulele player) successfully lobbied music publishers to include 'ukulele arrangements beginning in 1922, Breen's chord tabs and 'ukulele arrangements appeared on literally hundreds of pieces of sheet music, in addition to the methods and songbooks she published.[59] As a teacher, she offered private lessons and group instruction, reaching even more students with her recording of "The Ukulele Lesson" for Victor.[60] In 1926, Breen—described as a "Radio Star, Victor Record Artist, World's Ukulele Authority"—advertised her International Ukulele Club as a means to become a "master of the Ukulele, not just an ordinary strummer."[61] Breen aggressively fought for the 'ukulele to be taken seriously, generating national headlines. In 1931, when she applied for membership in the Manhattan local of the American Federation of Musicians as a 'ukulele artist, she was refused on the grounds that the 'ukulele was not a musical instrument—a finding that prompted much bemused media coverage. Unwilling to take no for an answer, Breen appealed to the federation's national board.[62] The following year, she was the featured soloist in her husband's symphonic poem, "Inspiration," in which her 'ukulele was backed by Paul Whiteman and his orchestra. The piece was written by Rose and Charles Harold "to demonstrate the instrumental potentialities of the ukulele."[63]

The most famous 'ukulele artist of the twenties, however, was Cliff Edwards (1895–1971), better known as "Ukulele Ike." Star of vaudeville, Broadway, radio, and motion pictures and a prolific recording artist, Edwards counted among his fans a young Bing Crosby, served as a model for such artists as Johnny Marvin, and inspired a host of imitators—including "Ukulele Myke," Nee Wong, "the Chinese Ukulele Ike," and James Manning, "billed as Hartford's Ukulele Ike."[64] Born in Hannibal, Missouri, Edwards dropped out of school before the age of fifteen and

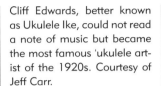

Cliff Edwards, better known as Ukulele Ike, could not read a note of music but became the most famous 'ukulele artist of the 1920s. Courtesy of Jeff Carr.

got his first show business job at the People's Palace in St. Louis, where he sang and drummed twelve hours a day for $4 a week.[65] During his teens, he traveled widely as a carnival entertainer and struggled to get by, driving a milk truck, painting freight cars, selling newspapers and magazine subscriptions, and working as a counterman in a Manhattan diner.[66] By 1917 he was working in Chicago at Mike Fritzel's Arsonia Café; it was there he acquired his nickname when a waiter who couldn't remember his name called out, "Hey, Ukulele Ike!" But it wasn't until 1918 that he was first identified as "Cliff Edwards, the Boy with the Ukulele" during a vaudeville appearance in Miami.[67]

After a brief appearance with comedian and dancer Joe Frisco in New York, Edwards paired with dancer Pierce Keegan to present an act called *Jazz Az Iz,* which caught the eye of longtime Ziegfeld producer Gene Buck and resulted in their appearance in *Ziegfeld's Midnight Frolic* in the fall of 1919.[68] The following year, Edwards joined a new partner, Lou Clayton (later a partner of Jimmy Durante's) in a blackface act that toured vaudeville for more than three years, appearing briefly with Mae West in the Broadway revue, *The Mimic World of 1921.*[69] Edwards' first success as a recording artist came with Pathe in 1923, but it wasn't until he starred with Fred and Adele Astaire in George Gershwin's first smash-hit Broadway musical, *Lady Be Good,* in 1924 that his career really took off. "Ukulele Ike was doing his stuff with the 'Lamb Chop' as he called it. . . . [He] stopped the show with his speciality," a second act solo turn in which he sang one of three or four songs, Astaire remembered.[70]

Edwards' role in *Lady Be Good*—he sang "Fascinating Rhythm" with the Astaires and soloed on two other numbers written for him by Gershwin, "Little Jazz Bird" and "Singing Pete"—was a remarkable achievement for the self-taught musician who couldn't read a note of music. "Every time I get a new piece of music, I have to go over it with a piano player and memorize it," he admitted in a 1946 interview. Certainly there were other 'ukulele players who had greater technical skills; Edwards was primarily a strummer. But as jazz historian Will Friedwald has pointed out, Edwards "was the first pop star to display genuine jazz rhythmic virtuosity." Edwards is also widely credited with being among the first jazz artists, if not the first, to use scatting—wordless vocal improvisation—and make it a cornerstone of his style.[71]

He recorded more than 150 sides during the 1920s, including such hits as "It Had to Be You" and "Fascinating Rhythm" (1924), "Paddlin' Madelin' Home" (1925), and "Singing in the Rain" (1929), as he continued his stage and radio career, including appearances in Oscar Hammerstein and Jerome Kern's hit 1925 musical *Sunny* and the *Ziegfeld Follies of 1927*.[72] After making two movie shorts for MGM in 1928, Edwards moved to Los Angeles and began a film career that spanned two decades and led to his best-known performance as the voice of Jiminy Cricket in Walt Disney's 1940 classic, *Pinocchio*.[73]

So pervasive was the influence of Edwards and other popular artists that the 'ukulele was no stranger to musicians in the emerging category of "hillbilly music"—what was eventually to become known as country music. As music historians Bill C. Malone and Elijah Wald have shown, musical boundaries in the 1920s were far more fluid than they are today.[74] What may have been the first radio barn dance was broadcast on WBAP of Fort Worth, Texas, in January 1923 featuring square dance music played by a string band that ordinarily played Hawaiian music: Fred Wagner's Hilo Five Hawaiian Orchestra. The 'ukulele was part of the instrumental mix for Fiddlin' Powers and Family on their early 1924 Victor sessions, for the pioneering band the Hill Billies, for Crockett's Kentucky Mountaineers, and Ernest Thompson, the blind multi-instrumentalist who recorded for Columbia.[75] The great Jimmie Rodgers (1897–1933) toured the Midwest in 1925 with his own Hawaiian band, posed for a 1927 studio portrait in Asheville, North Carolina, with a 'ukulele, played 'ukulele on a recording session the following year, recorded with Hawaiian musicians, and toured the South in 1930 with an opening act known as the Waikiki Hawaiians.[76] In the Piedmont region of North Carolina, the influence of touring Hawaiian bands, records, and sheet music meant "Tar Heel Hawaiians sprang up everywhere," Bob Carlin has pointed out.[77] The 'ukulele even occasionally made an appearance with white gospel groups, most notably the Speer Family of Lawrenceburg, Tennessee.[78]

Although he was already in his thirties when his recording career took off, Ukulele Ike was successfully marketed as a teen sensation.

The 'ukulele also made inroads into the African-American community after World War I, although available evidence suggests it was not to the extent that it did among white mainlanders. When the all-black Field Remount Squadron of the 331st Service Battalion returned from its service in France during World War I, it boasted what it called "the jazziest jazz band in the A.E.F.," with "ukuleles and banjos predominating" in its instrumentation—a configuration likely due to the unavailability of other instruments in wartime Europe.[79] In the twenties, black music teachers offered 'ukulele lessons in Baltimore and Philadelphia, community centers formed 'ukulele clubs and offered lessons in Baltimore, Cleveland, Norfolk, Virginia, and McKeesport, Pennsylvania, and enterprising teachers at Baltimore's School 107 taught their children how to build 'ukuleles from cigar boxes as part of a unit on construction and musical appreciation in 1924.[80] A reader of the *Chicago Defender* wrote in to complain about a group of high school students on Chicago's Indiana Avenue, "all members of our group . . . causing a great disturbance by playing ukuleles, singing and dancing out there in the open."[81] Retailers occasionally advertised 'ukuleles and Hawaiian guitars in African-American newspapers, most notably George and Cornelius Dorsey, who while students at the University of Pittsburgh opened the Dorsey Music Shoppe in 1923 and offered a complete range of 'ukuleles, including Martins.[82] Although closely identified with jazz in the popular imagination, the 'ukulele only occasionally appeared with black ensembles or vaudeville acts. Denny (or Danny) Small and Harry Mays, "The Ukulele Boys," appeared on both coasts in 1926–1927; "Ukulele Bob" Williams recorded for Paramount and appeared in vaudeville; Sterling Grant of the Silvertone Quartet recorded a version of "It Ain't Gonna Rain No Mo," strumming "a hot ukulele" for Emerson in 1924; pianist Clarence Williams cut two sides with a 'ukulele accompaniment for OKeh the following year; and some regional performers also featured the 'ukulele, including Billie Brown in Los Angeles and Lewis "Rabbit" Muse in Virginia, but such examples are not easy to find.[83] Perhaps the best-known African-American performer to adopt the 'ukulele is Ella Jenkins of Chicago, the "first lady of children's music" and recipient of the Recording Academy's 2004 Lifetime Achievement Award.[84]

Having been transformed into an American instrument, the mainland became the center of 'ukulele production. Mass production techniques, aided by electrification of production, ensured that 'ukuleles became part of the flood of consumer products that were widely available in the 1920s. "Modern methods of production incorporating standardization and elimination of waste have enabled the company to turn out stringed instruments like automobiles," said a 1927 account of Lyon & Healy's new Chicago stringed instrument factory, said to be capable of producing several hundred 'ukuleles a day.[85] Martin dominated the upper end of the market with its Style 1, 2, and 3 mahogany 'ukuleles retailing for $10, $15, and $25 respectively; a large order from Southern California Music Co. led it to introduce koa models in 1919. The firm subsequently expanded its product line at both the

Blues artist and musical entrepreneur Clarence Williams jumped on the 'ukulele bandwagon in 1925.

The one and only Clarence Williams doing something different!

CLARENCE WILLIAMS, who taught the piano to talk, is doing new musical tricks. His latest is a duet with Clarence Dodd and a ukulele. Listen to those two Clarences as they wail "Just a Cotton Picker's Blues." Then turn the record over and let the Williams boy keep you happy with "Temptation Blues."

It's the biggest crowd of high, wide and handsome blues you ever heard. Scamper north or south, or east or west, but be sure you get OKeh Record No. 8204.

GENERAL PHONOGRAPH CORPORATION
25 West 45th Street, New York City

OKeh Race Records

upper and lower ends, introducing the now-legendary 5-K model, "a select article . . . with a finish like satin" and a steep $50 price tag, in late 1921 and the plain all-mahogany Style 0 in January 1922. A larger concert 'ukulele was introduced in 1925 and an even larger tenor 'ukulele in 1928, the culmination of years of development aimed at increasing the 'ukulele's volume and tone, driven by the demands of growing numbers of stage and radio performers.[86] Lyon & Healy appears to have introduced the tenor 'ukulele in 1923, advertising it as having "double the volume of the ordinary ukulele."[87] Schulz & Moenning, also of Chicago, also debuted what it called a concert-size 'ukulele in the fall of 1925, "of unusually big tone and carrying power."[88] The following year, the Standardization Committee of the National Association of Musical Instrument and Accessories Manufacturers drafted a series of specifications for 'ukulele, including string lengths—13 to 13.75 inches for standard (soprano), 13.75 to 15.5 inches for concert, and 14.5 to 15.75 inches for tenor. Instruments that measured up would carry the association's seal of approval. "A good talking point is afforded the dealer handling the standard approved ukulele because he can truthfully assure the consumer that it has been examined and tested by a committee fitted by knowledge and experience to judge fretted instrument quality."[89]

While Martin clearly succeeded in terms of popularity and quality, it was impossible for the firm to meet more than a small percentage of the demand that by the fall of 1924 totaled four million instruments, according to E. C. Mills, head of the Music Publishers Protective Association and ASCAP chairman.[90] By 1925, a year in which the firm sold almost eleven thousand 'ukuleles, many new customers had to be turned away "in justice to our old customers whose orders we are not now able to supply with reasonable promptness," Martin wrote to one disappointed vendor.[91] Far more instruments were being manufactured by Lyon & Healy (after 1928, J. R. Stewart Co.), Harmony, Slingerland, Regal, Gretsch, and other large firms.[92] Unwilling to give up on the mandolin, Gibson was a latecomer to the field, not producing its first 'ukulele—a $30 ukulele banjo—until 1924.[93] 'Ukuleles were as popular with retailers as with their customers. "This little, unobtrusive instrument is a mighty good friend of music merchants," one trade publication observed in 1923. "They are so easy to sell and there are so many people to sell them to! Little technical knowledge is needed and a small investment. And they sell for cash at a good margin of profit."[94]

In 1926, Los Angeles residents could pick from a dazzling selection of 'ukuleles ranging in price from $1.39 to $75.

As the competition increased, so did the number of styles: Just before Christmas 1926, Southern California Music Co. advertised a stock of one thousand 'ukuleles of fifty different varieties, including "Ukaholas" with round bodies in three fancy colors (Chinese red, jade green, and lavender) for $1.39, Wendell Hall's Red Head 'ukulele at $3.95, an octagonal banjo-ukulele for $3.99, and an array of eight-string taropatches priced at $11.95, $15, and $20.[95] Down the street at Birkel Music Co., a customer could buy two new Washburn models—the Venetian 'ukulele, "small enough to carry in one's pocket and a novelty that is most desirable," for $4.95, or at the other end of the spectrum, the Artist's Model 'ukulele, priced at $40 to $75.[96] The files of the U.S. Patent Office are full of examples of ideas for new 'ukulele designs, including heart-shaped, Chinese-style, peanut-shaped, and teardrop-shaped instruments.[97] One unusual design actually built and marketed by the Stromberg-Voisinet Co. of Chicago in 1930 was the Aero Uke, "which as closely as possible resembles an aeroplane."[98] Competition also continued to drive down the price of low-end ukuleles: At Birkel's annual clearance sale in fall 1928, 'ukuleles could be had for as little at 50 cents each.[99]

Overwhelmed by mainland production, Hawaiian makers simply couldn't keep up with demand. As early as 1916, Ernest Kaai acknowledged that "it is true Hawaii cannot supply the demand for ukuleles. . . . There are more ukuleles being made on the mainland than in Hawaii at present."[100] Four years later, after the end of World War I had freed up Pacific shipping once more, former musical impresario and newly elected Honolulu mayor Johnny Wilson optimistically reported that "the Hawaiian ukulele crop is the greatest in history. . . . Hawaii is enjoying its greatest tourist season, and the ukulele factories are working night and day."[101] But customs figures show that exports to the mainland declined by more than half the following year, while imports of musical instruments to Hawaii almost doubled.[102] Tragedy struck Jonah Kumalae in October 1922 when a fire of unknown origin destroyed his Honolulu factory, causing an estimated $10,000 in damage and the loss of four thousand instruments.[103] In an effort to compete, Hawaiian makers diversified their product lines. In 1925, the Niu Kani 'ukulele, made in part of coconut shell, made its debut; the following year, Kumalae developed his own banjo-ukulele model; Samuel Kamaka Sr. trademarked his famous (and patented) pineapple-shaped 'ukulele in 1927; and the same year George Mossman introduced his Concert Belltone 'ukulele, which the maker claimed could be heard for up to half a mile away.[104] To help publicize the new model, after a 1927 Honolulu recital Mossman presented Ignace Jan Paderewski with what the famed pianist and former Polish prime minister described as a "super-ukulele."[105]

In April 1927, five of the major Hawaiian manufacturers—Kumalae, Mossman, Kamaka, the Aloha Manufacturing Co., and the Hawaiian Mahogany Co.—formed the Ukulele Manufacturing Association of Hawaii, with the intent to "study production methods and go after mass volume of business," it was reported. "The members are aiming ultimately at an export business of $500,000 instead of the

The Hawaiian Mahogany Co. sold $3 'ukuleles to compete with cheaply made, mass-produced models built in Chicago and other mainland cities. Courtesy of Jeff Carr.

present $50,000."[106] These efforts seem to have come to naught, however, as little was heard of the association after the original announcement.

Ironically, even as Hawaiian makers were competing for a bigger piece of the estimated $12 million annual market for 'ukuleles, what had come to be regarded as traditional Hawaiian music—the kind played by string orchestras that helped launch the 'ukulele craze—was slipping away in the Islands, increasingly overshadowed by jazz played with saxophones.[107] In 1920, when Johnny Noble (1892–1944) took over Dan Pokipala's orchestra at the Moana Hotel in Waikiki, "immediately he began rehearsing the men, quickening the tempo of their playing, re-arranging some of their best numbers to a jazz tempo, putting in 'blue notes,' and giving their music a new lilting, syncopated swing."[108] The collaboration between Noble and Sonny Cunha that yielded the hit "Hula Blues" was a sign of things to come. "Since Waikiki Beach has been rhapsodized by Tin Pan Alley, jazz has made a hit with Honoluluans," the *New York Times* reported in 1922. "The Hawaiians appreciate the music written about themselves, and to repay the compliment are now busy fox-trotting along their famous moonlit shores."[109] A 1925 guidebook cautioned that "there are numerous [musical] organizations calling themselves Hawaiian, and not a few—Hawaiians and make-believe Hawaiians—that 'jazz' Hawaiian music out of all resemblance to the real."[110] Composer Charles King, who in 1926 brought his production, *The Prince of Hawaii,* a light opera entirely in Hawaiian with "a haunting native orchestra," to the mainland, hated the new trend. "The tendency now, simply because people do not discourage it, is to play noise," he complained. "The dance orchestras today, using largely the saxophone, do not produce melody. . . . [It's] all noise and no music."[111]

Although King's *Prince of Hawaii* did nothing to halt the saxophone's advance, a different prince played a major role in popularizing the ʻukulele in England. As in the United States, many Britons were introduced to the ʻukulele and Hawaiian music by touring productions of *The Bird of Paradise,* followed by various Hawaiian acts. "In their search for the new and startling, certain theatrical people are going to give London an orgy of ukulele music and Hawaiian dancing," the *Manchester Guardian* reported early in 1921.[112] But it was the ʻukulele's adoption by Edward Windsor, Prince of Wales, that truly made it fashionable. Kelvin Keech claimed to have taught the prince how to play; it may be Keech who is referred to in a December 1924 news report that "the Prince of Wales is learning to play the banjolele. . . . The Prince, who is somewhat of a jazz dilettante, recently took a few tips on thumping the banjo from an American master of the instrument who happened to be performing in a London cabaret."[113] The prince took his banjo ukulele with him on his widely reported 1925 South African tour and reportedly asked singer Sophie Tucker to teach him how to play "Ukulele Lady" that summer.[114] "Certainly the thing has gone beyond reasonable limits," complained "Feste," a columnist for the *Musical Times.* "The banjulele and ukulele have become fashionable, and their tonal spewings are induced even by the hands of Royal Highnesses."[115] Reported to be among those taking ʻukulele lessons were actresses Beatrice Lillie and Gertrude Lawrence and novelist Michael Arlen.[116] As in America, the ʻukulele became a radio staple during the late twenties, featured in on-air performances by such artists as Keech, Earl Collins, Gilbert Highet, Sydney Nesbitt, and American expatriate Art Fowler.[117] By the mid-twenties, the ʻukulele had reached as far east as Berlin. "The ukulele craze has hit Berlin with a bang," said a July 1924 news report. "Music dealers appear determined to put a little ukulele in every home."[118] Franz and Josef Kollitz of Rothau, Sudetenland, added ʻukuleles and banjos to their production of violins in the thirties, a family-owned firm that today is Brüko, Germany's oldest ʻukulele manufacturer.[119]

The ʻukulele also traveled far to the west in the twenties, thanks in large part to the pioneering efforts of Ernest Kaai. Kaai led what is believed to be the first troupe of Hawaiian musicians to tour Australia and New Zealand in the spring and summer of 1911.[120] "They have such a wealth of musical accomplishment to draw upon, and they do so with such modesty, that seekers of new musical expression will find them a most refreshing change from the stereotyped concert programme," the *Sydney Morning Herald's* anonymous critic wrote. The ʻukulele, the *Herald* explained, "is shaped like a very small guitar. It is light in tone, and has no bass to it, but lends itself agreeable to accompaniments."[121]

MUTT AND JEFF—Mutt's Ukulele Must Have a Swiss Movement. . . . By BUD FISHER.

Bud Fisher, originally of San Francisco, was one of the first newspaper cartoonists to grasp the comic potential of the 'ukulele.

Henry A. Peelua Bishaw of Honolulu (1889–1972?), who was a member of Kaai's 1911 Royal Hawaiian Troupe and had been a partner in the firm created in 1917 to take over Kaai's musical manufacturing business, managed the musicians who toured Australia and New Zealand in 1917–1919 as part of *The Bird of Paradise* and afterward stayed on in Australia.[122] Living in Sydney, he became "the only genuine Hawaiian teacher in Australia" of 'ukulele and steel guitar at the Albert College of Music, arranging music and assembling a 'ukulele method published by J. Albert & Son.[123] In 1919, Kaai took a group of musicians for a pioneering three-year tour through Java, China, India, and the Philippines, publishing a portfolio titled *Hawaiian Songs* in Java in 1921.[124] He returned to the Far East in 1923 for another two years, spending much of his time performing in Australia and New Zealand. He returned yet again in 1926 for almost a decade, traveling to Australia, Singapore, Ceylon (now Sri Lanka), Japan, and China before retiring to Ceylon in the 1930s, finally returning to Hawaii in 1937.[125]

During the twenties, the 'ukulele reached the apex of international popularity. Yet at the same time, it was the target of a steady stream of invective—like most fads, the victim of its own overwhelming success. Even before the Panama-Pacific Exposition, the 'ukulele had become a favorite target of comics. Joe Cook (1890–1959), one of the most acclaimed comedians of his era, poked fun at the "Hawaiian eucalyptus, cheapest instrument of its kind in the world" in his *One Man Vaudeville Show* sketch in New York in October 1914.[126] Cook was best known for his routine, "Why I Will Not Imitate Four Hawaiians," his meandering explanation of why he can but won't imitate four 'ukulele players that later became a book of the same name.[127] In 1916, when music stores were still touting the 'ukulele as a "sweet-toned little melody instrument . . . more popular today than ever before," the *New York Times* made reference to "the whining ukelali music to which the New York stage is heir just now" and followed with a poem entitled "Hawaii," which included these immortal lines:

Oh, my Hawaiian fay,
I'll serenade you daily,
Having learned to play
Upon the ukulele;
It certainly is more than queer
That I should journey over here
To advertise my passion,
And be irrevocably bent
On twanging this freak instrument
But, maiden, it's the fashion![128]

This was tame stuff compared to the scathing denunciation delivered by symphony orchestra advocate Waldemar Lind before the state convention of the Oregon Federation of Women's Clubs that fall: "As long as music has been uplifted by the pioneer representatives of the art, let us now not retrograde by giving aid to the low and vulgar instruments, such as the ukulele and the banjo and the stuff mis-called music, which cannot but poison the body and soul of our younger generation and will have its marked effect with regard to higher medical development on the future men and women of America."[129]

'Ukulele putdowns quickly became a staple of editorial writers and city editors after the war. "A cruel Congress has voted absolute prohibition in Hawaii, and what the people will do now to deaden themselves to the tortures of the ukulele, the good Lord only knows," the *Ft. Wayne News and Sentinel* said in a representative 1918 jab.[130]

Comic-strip artists quickly joined in the fray: Among the earliest was Bud Fisher, whose popular *Mutt and Jeff* strip—the first regular daily newspaper comic—was spoofing the 'ukulele as early as 1917.[131] Newspapers happily reported 'ukulele bans: In Chicago's Lincoln Park in 1921, where its influence was judged "disturbing and vicious"; at the University of Moscow in 1923: "It would seem here is a higher civilization than our own"; and in Saudi Arabia in 1928 (saxophones and banjos also were targeted).[132] Court reporters contributed accounts of late-night strumming sessions that resulted in charges of disturbing the peace or even assault. One such case led to a 1927 ruling by the Nebraska Supreme Court that upheld an Omaha city ordinance barring a fraternity from maintaining a chapter house in an exclusive residential neighborhood. "[Neighbors] said they did not wish their slumbers disturbed by the nocturnal revels appertaining to fraternity house life, the long lines of motor cars that appeared only after nightfall, the tinkle of the ukulele and the moan of the saxophone," it was reported.[133]

Faced with a suspect charged with stealing five 'ukuleles from a freight car in 1923, a New York City judge quipped that he didn't know whether to regard the man "as a malefactor or benefactor. . . . I am tempted to give you my address instead of sending you to prison. In the house next to mine there is a young man who plays

Henry Bishaw's 1919 'ukulele method was Australia's first.
Courtesy of the National Library of Australia.

one of these instruments."[134] *Los Angeles Times* columnist John Steven McGroarty proposed the ultimate penalty in 1927: "They say that for many years no one knew who invented the ukulele. It remained a dark mystery. . . . At last the offender, conscience stricken, surrendered himself to the authorities and was duly hanged."[135] And woe betide any music professional who proposed taking the 'ukulele seriously. Robert E. Sault, supervisor of music in the public schools of Lawrence, Massachusetts, made that mistake when he reported on the results of a statewide survey of school music at a 1923 music educators conference in Boston. When he told of two teachers "holding classes on instruction in the ukulele, the educators laughed," the *New York Times* reported. "They fairly roared when Mr. Sault added that one of the teachers found her instruction so popular that she had to hold five classes in ukulele playing." Ultimately, reason was restored: "It was agreed that music should be taken more seriously in school curricula, but that instruction should be in more old fashioned form."[136]

On screen, despite its initial popularity in Hollywood, the ʻukulele received the same treatment and often ended up the worse for wear. In his 1928 silent comedy, *Steamboat Bill Jr.,* Buster Keaton plays the son of a rough-edged steamboat captain. A Harvard graduate of diminutive stature who sports a thin mustache, a beret, and a ʻukulele on his return home from college, Keaton quickly becomes ashamed to be seen with this embarrassing symbol of collegiate frippery and stomps on his ʻukulele in disgust.[137] The ʻukulele meets a similar fate in Laurel and Hardy's *Sons of the Desert* (1933), in which the instrument is part of an elaborate scheme to convince the boys' wives that they took a trip to Hawaii rather than to the Sons of the Desert convention. In this case, however, Ollie trips over Stan's luggage and falls on top of his ʻukulele with predictable results.[138]

The same lack of respect also could be found in popular literature. The plot of P. G. Wodehouse's 1934 comic novel, *Thank You, Jeeves,* turns on Bertie Wooster's enthusiastic embrace of the banjolele and the complications that ensue when his faithful butler, Jeeves, gives notice rather than listen to him play such tunes as "Singin' in the Rain" and "I Want an Automobile With a Horn That Goes Toot-Toot." Jeeves' announcement follows on the heels of a visit by an irate Sir Roderick Glossop, who blasts Bertie as "a public menace. For weeks, it appears, you have been making life a hell for all your neighbours with some hideous musical instrument. I see you have it with you now. How dare you play that thing in a respectable block of flats? Infernal din!"[139]

The ʻukulele simultaneously suffered from an authenticity crisis. Sold to the mainland public as a Native Hawaiian instrument, it was regularly dogged by would-be exposés of the open secret that it wasn't.[140] One of the first was a March 1917 magazine article that revealed that the ʻukulele was "a diminutive Spanish guitar which some roving Portuguese seems to have introduced about 40 years ago."[141] It was quickly followed by newspaper stories with headlines such as "Not to Blame for the Ukulele."[142] A 1922 account alleged that all the grass skirts in Honolulu were manufactured in Connecticut and the ʻukuleles in Chicago and New Jersey, while a 1927 story claimed that the paper leis worn by musicians were manufactured in San Francisco.[143] Distorted accounts began to circulate that the ʻukulele was introduced to Hawaii by a German (an apparent reference to Henry Berger, leader of the Royal Hawaiian Band), by a Yale undergraduate—likely a garbled reference to Sonny Cunha, the pioneering hapa haole composer and Yale Law School alumnus—or by Portuguese sailors shipwrecked in Hawaii in the seventeenth century.[144]

Regardless of its purported origins, the ʻukulele's popularity persisted, providing a measure of vindication for poor Robert Sault. During the twenties, ʻukulele bands became a fixture on public playgrounds across the country as a recreational program that helped teach children the rudiments of music and music appreciation. Los Angeles, for example, boasted of fourteen playground ʻukulele clubs less than a year after the city's Playground and Recreation Department launched its Division of Musical Activities in February 1927. "The work of the numerous ukulele clubs has been recognized as a means toward bringing out latent musical talent and as furnishing a starting point for more serious endeavor," the division reported. By the following year, 'ukulele clubs could be found on playgrounds across the country, including Lincoln, Nebraska; Fall River, Massachusetts; Wilmington, Delaware; Birmingham, Alabama; Houston, and even Winnipeg.[145] The music industry, always alert to new opportunities, created a *Simplified Course in Ukulele Playing* for use by the National Playground and Recreation Association, YMCAs, and other youth organizations.[146] Despite its popularity, the National Recreation Association insisted in 1932 that the 'ukulele was a "low grade" or "inferior" instrument "that many musicians and other music lovers scorn." Its chief virtue was as a path to better things for "many a person—especially among adolescent boys—who cannot carry a tune or who can carry it accurately but not satisfyingly, and who never has had enough interest to learn to sing well or to play one of the standard instruments, may, through a simple instrument, be led happily into admirable kinds of music to which he had always been indifferent."[147]

However, by 1932, in the depths of the Depression, few people were buying 'ukuleles. The stock market crash three years before had dealt a hammer blow to the music industry in general. In 1921, Americans bought 110 million records; in 1933, sales had plummeted to just 10 million.[148] Chart-topping Johnny Marvin and his 'ukulele were reduced to working on a session-by-session basis, paid a flat fee for each recording, rather than receiving any royalties.[149] On Broadway, *Luana*, the latest musical adaptation of *The Bird of Paradise*, closed in September 1930 after just twenty-one performances.[150] One month later, Ukulele Ike was quoted as saying that he wanted to get rid of his 'ukulele and be taken seriously as an actor "and not merely as a song and dance man."[151] When Wendell Hall resurfaced on the radio in 1935 after an absence of several years, his famous 'ukulele was seldom in evidence. "Where is the instrument today?" asked one entertainment columnist at the time. "One scarcely hears it, even on Major Bowe's or Fred Allen's amateur hours. The trend today seems to run toward guitars, violins, clarinets, saxes, trumpets and accordions. . . . The 'uke' apparently is going rapidly into the limbo of the mandolin."[152]

CHAPTER 8

Made of a New Gleaming Plastic Material

> We used to think a Hawaiian originally invented the ukulele. Now we're convinced it's Arthur Godfrey.
>
> —The *Vidette-Messenger*, Valparaiso, Indiana, March 18, 1953

In November 1948, as postwar consumer demand fueled an unprecedented economic expansion, the *Honolulu Advertiser* reluctantly printed an obituary for the 'ukulele. Quoting Emerson Strong, vice president of the Brooklyn-based Gretsch Manufacturing Co., the *Advertiser* reported that "the ukulele, outside of Hawaii, today is 'deader than a doornail.'" Although he didn't say so, Emerson likely based his dour opinion on the disappointing sales of Gretsch's own frankly unappealing postwar model with a "warp-proof, crack-proof body of laminated hardwood in an attractive two-tone shaded lacquer finish," instruction book, and carrying case that it had begun marketing two years earlier for the relatively high price of $9.[1] "Its popularity today is practically nil," Emerson said. "I can honestly say it is deader than a doornail. Which is surprising, considering that it is the least expensive of all stringed instruments and easiest played."[2] Yet one week later, the *Long Beach Press Telegram* reported a remarkable increase in 'ukulele sales. "Guess what is coming back in popularity as a musical instrument that was in its heyday when mother was a girl?" the newspaper asked its southern California readers. "Long Beach merchants report remarkable sales in ukuleles, of all things. In a large range of prices, but still within the reach of a modest pocketbook, the instruments are reported to be selling well in the $6 model."[3]

What Emerson and Gretsch had not foreseen was how the convergence of two new technologies—television and modern plastics—would combine to kick off a new 'ukulele revival, one that would sell millions of instruments over the next decade. Arthur Godfrey, the era's red-headed king of all media, played a critical role in driving the revival with his ubiquitous presence on both radio and television, unique flair as a pitchman, and lifelong fondness for the 'ukulele. Godfrey's rise coincided with an era of innovation in the chemical industry, which had been subsidized by the federal government during World War II to develop new synthetic polymers in support of the war effort. An endless procession of new plastic products emerged from wartime research, including 'ukuleles and other musical instruments. But unlike in the jazz era, when the 'ukulele was an adolescent fad, the chief market for the instrument in the 1950s was children, who accounted for up to 90 percent of sales, according to one contemporary estimate. Plastic 'ukuleles, which made up the vast majority of instruments made during this decade, helped define the instrument for baby boomers as a toy—a reputation it still struggles to overcome today.

At the time, however, the boom was a welcome alternative to the grim years of the 1930s, when the entire music industry struggled to survive the Great Depression. One of the speakers at a Chicago music convention in April 1930 tallied the losses: "four out of five professional musicians out of work; many studios half filled; concert bureaus, lyceums, and chatauquas diminishing; legitimate theaters and vaudeville houses closing everywhere . . . the sale of pianos and of musical instruments declining precipitously; decline of congregational singing and home made music."[4] In an era of big band music dominated by horns and reeds, sales of stringed instruments plummeted. Chicago-based J. R. Stewart, maker of Le Domino 'ukuleles and (since 1928) Washburn stringed instruments, was forced into receivership in the spring of 1930, the same year Lyon & Healy reported an operating loss of more than $350,000.[5] In Kalamazoo, Michigan, Gibson shifted most of its factory production to making toys for more than two years.[6] Martin and other manufacturers actually saw an increase in 'ukulele sales at the beginning of the Depression, but the Pennsylvania-based firm cut its prices in 1930 in response to the rapidly shifting market. By 1933, annual production had dropped more than 80 percent to fewer than 750 instruments, which contributed to the grim necessity of laying off all but thirty workers.[7] The evaporation of mainland markets on higher-priced Hawaiian exports was catastrophic: In 1931, instruments worth just $2,119 were shipped to the mainland—a drop of almost 95 percent from five years earlier.[8] By the latter part of the decade, 'ukuleles—"the collegiate lyre of the Scott Fitzgerald days"—were said to be making a comeback based on eye appeal.[9] The Metropolitan Music Co. wholesale catalog of the period offered low-priced birch 'ukuleles in a variety of colors and finishes, including the "Art Moderne" model, "a modernistic ukulele finished in blue, red and yellow colors" that sold for $2 wholesale. But in 1938 it was reported that demand for 'ukuleles and other stringed instruments had dropped off significantly, even as sales of pianos, reed instruments, and drums grew.[10]

Record sales, which peaked in 1921, also shrank as radio's popularity grew: By 1933, jukeboxes, not individual consumers, had become the single largest market.[11] Movies became the chief medium for selling music, symbolized by Warner

Brothers' purchase of M. Witmark & Sons, the archetypical Tin Pan Alley firm, and ten other music publishing houses.[12] In 1935, seven of the top ten songs heard most frequently on the radio were from such movies as *Top Hat* and *Gold Diggers of 1935*.[13] That same year, Warner Brothers, MGM, and Twentieth Century Fox controlled more than half of the music ASCAP licensed.[14] When Bing Crosby, the country's top recording artist, appeared in *Waikiki Wedding* in the spring of 1937, it was not only one of the year's top-grossing films but spawned a hit single, Harry Owens' "Sweet Leilani," that dominated the charts for six months, selling millions of copies of sheet music and earning Crosby his first gold record and Owens a best song Oscar. As Crosby biographer Gary Giddins pointed out, "As the best-selling American disc in eight years, it was acclaimed as a turning point for the recording industry and a good sign for the national economy."[15] Seizing what seemed like a golden opportunity, that summer the first week of August was designated "National Ukulele Week" in an effort to boost sales.[16] But it was a last gasp: Two years later, the president of the National Association of Musical Merchandise Wholesalers referred to "the limbo of the forgotten product, like the banjo, ukulele and other instruments which once enjoyed great popularity."[17]

"Sweet Leilani" also triggered a new wave of popularity for Hawaiian music in the United States, defining it for an entire generation just as Al Jolson's "Yaaka Hula Hickey Dula" had done two decades earlier. In 1959, when New York humorist H. Allen Smith announced he was planning a trip to Hawaii, a friend told him he'd love it, that it was "a Bing Crosby sort of place." Smith "knew immediately what she meant—Hawaii was actually a mythical land, a place invented and devised and dressed up for Crosby to sing about."[18] Once again, California helped set the stage for the national trend. By the time of *Waikiki Wedding*'s release, Ernest Beaumont-Gantt had created the first tiki bar, Don the Beachcomber in Los Angeles, a city that boasted Polynesian-themed restaurants (King's Tropical Inn, opened in 1930 with a performance by Sol Hoopii's Hawaiian Orchestra), a cafeteria (Clifton's Pacific Seas, opened in 1931 with music by Bob Canfield's Hawaiian Beach Boys), and a nightclub that served as one of the mainland's most important venues for Hawaiian music (the Seven Seas, opposite Grauman's Chinese Theatre on Hollywood Boulevard.)[19] Three months after the movie's release, the Hawaiian Room opened in the basement of Manhattan's Lexington Hotel, a supper club with a floor show featuring some of the Islands' best dancers and a talented band led by Ray Kinney. The timing was ideal, and other Hawaiian clubs and lounges followed across the country as Hollywood released a host of *Waikiki Wedding*–inspired films, including *Hawaiian Buckaroo* and *Hawaii Calls* (1938), *Honolulu* and *Hawaiian Nights* (1939), and *Moonlight in Hawaii* (1941).[20]

Back in Honolulu, Hawaiian music was seen as playing an essential role in attempts to revive the tourist business, which like the sugar and pineapple industries had been hit hard by the Depression. "Every year, some 20,000 trippers spend $11 million to loll on the beach at Waikiki when, from Los Angeles, they could streetcar to Venice at 35 cents a head. It's glamour that makes the difference, and glamour, in 'Paradise,' comes wrapped in Hawaiian music," the *Los Angeles Times* reported in 1937. "Island music, as much as any other factor, is responsible for skyrocketing the territorial tourist crop."[21] *Hawaii Calls,* the weekly international shortwave radio broadcast that the *Honolulu Advertiser* once called "the greatest public relations program ever seen," was launched on July 3, 1935, with a subsidy from the Hawaii Tourist Bureau, funding that was later replaced with an annual appropriation from the Territorial Legislature.[22] Created by Webley E. Edwards (1902–1977), the show—which would be on the air for the next forty years—featured live performances by some of the Islands' best musicians, even though Edwards once acknowledged that "the songs are not important. It's the atmosphere we're striving for."[23]

More traditional Hawaiian music could be heard at Lalani Hawaiian Village in Waikiki. Created by hapa haole 'ukulele maker George Paele Mossman in 1932, Lalani offered tourists a recreated Hawaiian village of thatched huts where they could enjoy a luau and see traditional hula performed—all of which served to finance his efforts to preserve traditional Hawaiian culture.[24] But even at Lalani, visitor Sigmund Spaeth was struck by "the entertainers' catholicity of taste. When the Hawaiian musicians are putting on a show they make no distinctions as to periods or materials. At one moment you may be watching an ancient ritual dance . . . the next number may be a modern song of the Tin Pan Alley type, by Harry Owens or Johnny Noble or Alex Anderson, the ruling triumvirate of Hawaii's popular song-writers."[25] With the rise of such musical leaders as Owens (a native of Nebraska) and Edwards of *Hawaii Calls* (born and raised in Oregon), it was increasingly evident that "the new Hawaiian music which appeared was no longer the music of Hawaiians," Noble's biographer wrote. "As the haoles had eventually come to dominate other aspects of island life and culture, they also controlled its musical output and performance."[26]

As a new generation of mainland writers and musicians reshaped audiences' perception of Hawaiian music, Lancashire comic-turned-singer George Formby (1904–1961) shaped a generation's view of the 'ukulele in England.

Born William Booth, son of a successful music hall comic who went by the name of George Formby, the younger Formby followed his father into the family business, incorporating a banjo-ukulele into his act in 1923.[27] It wasn't until 1932 that he hit the big time with his second Decca release, "I Told My Baby with a Ukulele," and made his first movie, *Boots! Boots!* two years later.[28] The homely Formby was an unlikely star—like Cliff Edwards, he was unable to read music or even tune his own instruments—but his air of artless enthusiasm made him hugely popular in England. By 1942, he had topped the *Motion Picture Herald*'s popularity poll for five consecutive years.[29] "There can hardly have been a single moment of any day from 1935 until the end of the war when the voice of George Formby was not to be heard somewhere in England," Formby biographer John Fisher wrote.[30]

George Formby, Britain's most popular movie star of the late 1930s, shaped the popular perception of the 'ukulele in Britain. Courtesy of Jeff Carr.

His stardom puzzled contemporary Americans—in a review of his 1940 feature "Let George Do It," the *Los Angeles Times* called Formby "a peculiar personality, not at all good-looking or even particularly magnetic"—but his high-speed strumming, on display in eighteen films and on more than two hundred recordings, defined the 'ukulele in England.[31] "It's impossible for an entertainer to walk on stage with a ukulele under his arm [in England] without the audience, young, middle-aged or elderly, expecting him to play Formby songs," one Formby biographer wrote in 1974.[32]

While Formby was entertaining British troops with his 'ukulele during World War II, the war brought new challenges for 'ukulele makers who managed to survive the Depression. Unable to obtain wood and other essential supplies, Sam Kamaka Sr., who had started growing flowers in Kaneohe in the 1930s to supplement his slender 'ukulele sales, rented out his South King Street shop, worked part-time at Pearl Harbor, and began growing mangoes on a farm in Waianae.[33] But in the long run, the war was to have the same unintended effect on the 'ukulele as the First World War had, despite wartime restrictions that limited the manufacture of new instruments. Early on, the U.S. War Department organized a music section in its Special Services Division whose efforts to bring entertainment to the troops included distributing songbooks arranged for piano, guitar, and 'ukulele, ten-minute instructors for 'ukulele, harmonica, and ocarina, and the instruments themselves.[34] At one point, the U.S. Navy found itself in the peculiar position of shipping 'ukuleles to Honolulu for morale purposes.[35] As they had done a generation before, retailers advertised 'ukuleles as the perfect gift for the troops: "Boys in the service have a grand time with them," May Co. department stores assured Los Angeles customers in advertising a victory model in red, white, and blue for $1.95.[36] However, with domestic musical instrument production down an estimated

75 percent—Gibson spent the war making such items as radar assemblies and precision rods for submachine guns—multiple organizations began soliciting donations of 'ukuleles and other small instruments for the troops.[37] Red Cross Camp and Hospital Services, the Musical Instruments Committee of the War Prisoners Aid of the YMCA, the Chaplains Service Corps, the National Federation of Music Clubs, and the Metropolitan Opera Guild of New York all collected 'ukuleles.[38] "All kinds of instruments can be used, but small ones such as ukuleles [and] mandolins, easily played by convalescents, are in greatest demand," read one appeal for instruments for hospitals and hospital ships.[39] Servicemen spread the 'ukulele far and wide, including Papua New Guinea, where it and the guitar became the basis of a postwar form of popular music known as "stringband."[40]

As production shortages continued after the war's end—Lyon & Healy was reduced to offering Christmas shoppers gift certificates for such items as pianos, organs, and band instruments redeemable at an unspecified future date—'ukuleles were among the items still in stock for Christmas presents.[41] Just before Thanksgiving 1945, Chicago's Wurlitzer Music advertised 'ukuleles of unknown provenance made of "plastic bonded to prevent warping in a damp climate. A fine instrument, complete with waterproof cover, felt pick, extra strings and instruction book," all for $7.75—the earliest known offering of a plastic 'ukulele.[42] Less than six months later, a clear plastic 'ukulele and other instruments were on display at the Society of Plastic Industries Show in Los Angeles, where more than two hundred companies demonstrated how they were "turning strange resinous compounds, certain special fabrics, and modern techniques into such widely different items as trout-fishing boats and artificial limbs."[43]

During the war, the U.S. government had encouraged the chemical industry to invest in plastics research to provide urgently needed substitutes for scarce natural materials and to perform critical functions in new technologies. The first American polystyrene, a thermoplastic polymer that could be ground into a molding powder with the ability to reproduce detailed molds with great accuracy, was introduced in 1933. But it was the federally subsidized production of such items as aircraft cockpit covers, helmet liners, and mortar fuses that left the industry poised for a tremendous postwar surge as it moved to convert to civilian production.[44] Because polymers are infinitely variable, minor and inexpensive modifications can alter their properties significantly, making it possible for companies to offer manufacturers a product that was specifically tailored to a customer's needs—including toy and instrument makers.

Another key factor in turning the 'ukulele into a national phenomenon was Arthur Godfrey (1903–1983), the radio and television personality whose folksy and unpredictable style dominated the postwar airwaves. Godfrey made his radio debut on Baltimore's WFBR in 1928 as Red Godfrey, the Warbling Banjoist, but the New Jersey native from modest circumstances had been a 'ukulele player since a fellow sailor from Maui showed him how at the Naval Radio School at Great Lakes,

Illinois. "He had a steel guitar . . . and I was fascinated with the thing, and I wanted to learn," Godfrey remembered. "'No, no,' he said. 'You learn to play the ukulele and you can accompany me. We'll make a little Hawaiian music.' So he somehow procured a small ukulele . . . and taught me the chords on it. And I began to play with him, pretty nice Hawaiian songs."[45]

The 'ukulele became an integral part of Godfrey's style, in which he shared his enthusiasms and candid opinions with listeners. His spontaneous, unscripted approach made commercial sponsors squirm but sold millions of dollars of product. As a late-night announcer in Baltimore, Godfrey would occasionally offer fifteen minutes of 'ukulele solos instead of playing records.[46] When he hit the big time on April 30, 1945, with the debut of *Arthur Godfrey Time* on CBS radio, he naturally brought his 'ukulele with him. "That summer is here also would seem borne out by one aspect of Arthur Godfrey's new divertissement at 9:15 a.m. weekdays on CBS. On a coast-to-coast network in 1945 he has been heard playing the ukulele," the *New York Times* reported, with a hint of disdain.[47]

Over the next five years, Godfrey steadily increased his audience share, launching *Arthur Godfrey's Talent Scouts* on CBS radio in the summer of 1946; a variety show, *Arthur Godfrey Time,* in 1948; television simulcasts of both a few months later; and finally a television musical variety show, *Arthur Godfrey and His Friends,* in January 1949, on which he continued to feature the 'ukulele.[48]

Godfrey was one of the first major radio stars to move to the new medium of television; almost everyone else followed over the next three years as Americans embraced TV. By 1952, 15.3 million American households had televisions, up from only 350,000 in 1948. As Gary Edgerton has noted, television was adapted more quickly than any previous new communications technology had been.[49] In his heyday, in addition to the six Top 20 hits he recorded for Decca Records, Godfrey was on air ninety minutes each weekday on CBS radio and another hour on CBS television, accounting for an estimated 12 percent of the network's total annual revenues.[50] As one of the most popular personalities on television, Godfrey's 'ukulele evangelism had an enormous impact. His greatest contribution to the postwar 'ukulele revival is often said to be the lessons he offered on his fifteen-minute television program, *Arthur Godfrey and His Ukulele,* which ran for three months in the spring of 1950.[51] But his influence on shaping public demand had been made clear years before.

In 1946, Elliot and Ruth Handler were just getting started in the toy business in Los Angeles when Elliot took note of the "stir of interest" Godfrey was creating in the 'ukulele. The result: the first plastic 'ukulele to be distributed and sold nationwide. Mattel's Uke-A-Doodle, which was fourteen inches long, "blue and coral-colored, made music (sort of) and came complete with floral decals and a classy and colorful 'set up' box," was introduced in January 1947.[52] More than a decade before Mattel introduced its blockbuster Barbie doll, the Uke-A-Doodle quickly became Mattel's first big seller—so big that it launched what Ruth Handler

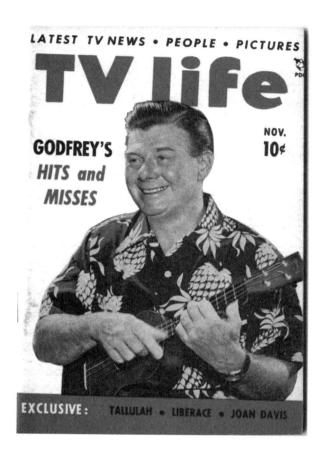

Arthur Godfrey, America's king of all media in the late 1940s and early 1950s, inspired a new wave of 'ukulele popularity. Courtesy of Lex Passaris.

would later call "the 1947 Ukulele War."[53] In March, Elliot Handler traveled to New York for the annual toy fair, only to find that "a large firm, Knickerbocker Plastics, had buffed off the Mattel name and was using the Uke-A-Doodle as a sample to pre-sell their own ukulele, which would be an exact replica of ours," Ruth Handler remembered with ire years later. "And Knickerbocker was offering theirs at a suggested retail price that was 30 cents less!"[54] (Knickerbocker was not the only competition: American Plastic Products of Los Angeles introduced its own Uke-a-Tune in April 1947.)[55] Originally priced by Mattel at $1.49, Knickerbocker's knock-off triggered a price war. By Christmas, plastic 'ukuleles were being sold across the country at Montgomery Ward, hardware, auto parts, and variety stores for as little as 59 cents.[56] "Imagine the fun youngsters will have with a toy ukulele that can be played like a real instrument," Murphy's, "the Store Packed with Holiday Values," told its customers in Indiana, Pennsylvania. "It has strong wire strings and is made of plastic. Instructions on the box. . . . Easy as can be to play."[57] Ultimately, Mattel was able to make a small profit on the toy that year and later claimed sales of 11 million Uke-A-Doodles and its descendants over the following decade.[58]

For millions of baby boomers, this was their introduction to the 'ukulele: an inexpensive plastic toy sold at the local drugstore or an item demonstrated by a cowboy in the toy department of Gimbel's Department Store.[59] As a result, for years afterward 'ukulele makers and retailers often felt compelled to emphasize that what they were offering were real musical instruments. "Full Size Ukulele—Not a miniature! Not a toy! Actually a Full Size Genuine Musical Instrument Made of a New Gleaming Plastic Material That Has a Wonderful Tone," one retailer advertised in 1951.[60] The fact was, however, that children made up the vast majority of the postwar 'ukulele market, accounting for 80 to 90 percent of sales, according to the *Wall Street Journal*.[61] By December 1948, when syndicated columnist Robert Ruark was mourning his lost youth, the 'ukulele revival had not yet extended beyond the children's market. Ruark sent a spy to the music stores on Manhattan's West 48th Street to see if she could find a 'ukulele, "which used to be as vital to the way of a man with a maid as springtime. . . . Most everybody she talked to about ukuleles thought she was nuts. 'Only the older people ask for them anymore,' [one dealer] said."[62] Ruark would have written a different column if he had sent his spy to Newberry's or a National Dollar Store.[63]

The following year, reports differed as to the cause of it all. Some attributed the 'ukulele's resurrection to Godfrey, others to the popularity of the Rodgers and Hammerstein musical *South Pacific,* which opened in April 1949 to rave reviews and ran for six years—but all agreed that sales were rising.[64] "The ukulele and banjo are making a strong comeback, the American Music Conference reports, and adds that interest in the two strummed instruments is greater now than at any time since the Twenties," the *New York Times* reported that summer. At the annual convention of the National Association of Musical Merchandise Manufacturers, president Jay Kraus told of "an amazing revival in the last few months" and predicted that 'ukulele sales would rise to three hundred thousand by the end of the year, six times the average sales during the war years.[65] Arthur Cremin, director of a chain of music schools in the New York area, shook his head as he described the 'ukulele's new popularity: "Four months ago, it was nothing. Today we've got 300 people—all learning to play the ukulele!"[66] That fall, the Music Publishers Protective Association urged its members to revive the practice of including 'ukulele and guitar chords on sheet music in light of booming instrument sales.[67] Not everyone welcomed the new trend. "But the uke? Spare us the uke," editorialized the *Claremont* [New Hampshire] *Eagle.* "We had thought this so-called musical instrument was an unlamented relic of the past."[68]

A chance meeting with Godfrey by the swimming pool of the swank Kenilworth Hotel in Miami that year would lead to the creation of the era's best-known 'ukulele, the perfect fusion of postwar plastics and the power of Godfrey's celebrity: Mario Maccaferri's Islander. Maccaferri (1900–1993)—a master luthier trained as a youth in his native Italy, a classical guitarist, Columbia recording artist, entrepreneur and inventor, friend and colleague of Andres Segovia, Benny Goodman, and Les Paul—was struggling financially when he met Godfrey.[69]

When Arthur Godfrey plugged his plastic 'ukuleles on the air, Mario Maccaferri couldn't keep up with the orders that poured in. Photo by Ed Wergeles.

In France before the war, Maccaferri had partnered with Henri Selmer to create the Maccaferri-Selmer guitar, the first mass-produced cutaway guitar that became a favorite of famed jazz guitarist Django Reinhardt. After a dispute with Selmer, the protean Maccaferri went into the reed manufacturing business, based on his newly patented method of cutting reeds with a diamond-cutting machine. Fleeing Europe just before the German invasion of Poland in September 1939, Maccaferri set up the French American Reed Manufacturing Co. in the Bronx, secured the endorsement of Goodman and other major musicians for his product, and success-fully switched to plastic when supplies of natural reed disappeared during the war.[70]

Maccaferri's contract to provide reeds for military bands and his contacts with Dow and Monsanto gave him early access to plastic manufacturing, which he turned to great advantage when he created a popular plastic clothespin to address a shortage of the wooden article. However, the founding of Mastro Plastic Corp. in 1945 and the expansion of his manufacturing plant came just as postwar competi-tion cut deeply into his markets, leaving him deep in debt and facing bankruptcy.[71] Maccaferri was still paying off that debt, having expanded into plastic wall and ceil-ing tiles, clothes hangers, and toilet seats, when he met Godfrey:

During our conversation, I mentioned that I play guitar, and we soon wound up in his room playing music. The guitar and a few drinks made us quite talkative. He said that he liked the uke very much and would like to encourage young people to play it. He felt that if only someone could produce a uke that fingered well, had a passable tone, and could retail for under $10, he could sell a million of them. I did not tell him at that time of my background in musical instrument making. . . . Back in New York, I called Charlie Sonfield of the Bruno Company. I asked him how many ukes were sold last year, in 1948. He said, "About 26,000." I told him I was thinking about a plastic ukulele, that the necessary tooling would cost about $25,000 and when completed, I would be able to produce about 26,000 per week.[72]

Maccaferri was not the only manufacturer seeking to develop a plastic ʻukulele that was more than a toy. George Finder of San Diego had his patented two-piece Diamond Head Fin-Der ʻukulele on the market by the spring of 1950, "beautifully finished in two-tone ebony and cream plastic" and featuring nylon strings of four different colors.[73] Later that year, Chris-Kraft Instrument Co. of Union, New Jersey, introduced its Flamingo model, BW Photo Utilities of Pasadena, California, its Mauna Loa, and Lapin Products Inc. of Newark, New Jersey, its Happy Tunes ʻukulele.[74]

But Maccaferri's Islander was truly the Stradivarius of plastic ʻukuleles. Said to be modeled on Martin's Style 0, the Islander had eight-part construction, a carefully designed fingerboard with overmolded frets, and a conically shaped soundhole to create "a desired volume and fidelity of tone to compare favorably with the best of the wood instruments."[75]

Islander sales exploded when Godfrey gave Maccaferri an on-air plug, which the company quickly included in its advertising; by March 1950, Mastro was producing 2,500 ʻukuleles a day and had a backlog of 100,000 orders for the $5.95 uke.[76] By the end of the year, Mastro had shipped 350,000 ʻukuleles, including the Sparkle Plenty Ukette, a smaller children's instrument named after a character in the popular Dick Tracy comic strip and accompanied by a thirty-six-page comic book-style method by May Singhi Breen that together sold for $2.98.[77] "Local musical instrument dealers have been unable to satisfy the demand here, especially since a New York man tossed his plastic uke on the market to supplement the wooden variety, admirably timed to the TV pulse of Mrs. Godfrey's big fat boy, Arthur," one Massachusetts newspaper reported. "When the shiny ukes hit the market, about three weeks ago, Lowell dealers had to scribble out waiting lists and shake up the jobbers to get out and deliver the goods."[78] Music dealers across the country reported the same phenomenon. "Don't know exactly how to account for it, but we can't hardly keep them in stock any more," a dealer in Harlingen, Texas, said. "Guess it's because of this new plastic ukulele which recently hit the market."[79]

While Maccaferri was the immediate beneficiary of Godfrey's endorsement, his was an enthusiasm that lifted all boats. The 1950 National Association of Musical

Lapin Products assembled an impressive list of celebrity endorsements for its plastic Happy Tune 'ukulele.

Merchandise Manufacturers (NAMMM) convention was buzzing with news of increased sales. Association president C. Frederick Martin III was quoted as saying that Godfrey "is the greatest thing that ever happened to the ukulele."[80] Gretsch, which eighteen months before had claimed the 'ukulele was deader than a doornail, reported producing one thousand a week, with a good-sized list of back orders.[81] By August, total 'ukulele sales for the year were reported to have reached 1.7 million, including the new oversize baritone 'ukulele created by Eddie Connors at the behest of Godfrey. (Connors played the new baritone to convince New York's Local 802 of the American Federation of Musicians that 'ukulele players belonged in the union. He succeeded.)[82] Hailed as a hero on a July 1950 trip to the Islands, Godfrey and his enthusiasm for the 'ukulele had a major impact on Hawaiian makers as well. Longtime woodworker John S. Perry, whose Honolulu plant was described as Hawaii's largest, also had a backlog of orders and at one point even turned down a mainland order for ten thousand 'ukuleles.[83] It was chiefly the plastic variety, however, that Howard K. Morris apparently used to give 'ukulele lessons aboard the Matson Lines' SS *Lurline* on trips between the West Coast and Honolulu after he was hired as entertainment director in 1952.[84]

The national fad also revived the careers of many 'ukulele artists of the 1920s, whose methods were reissued and whose names began to reappear on new 'ukuleles.[85] "Since Arthur Godfrey brought the ukulele back to life, Cliff Edwards has a whole new career," Hedda Hopper wrote in the fall of 1950. "Everybody wants him." Edwards and Wendell Hall both landed "sing and chat" television shows— Edwards a fifteen-minute, three-nights-a-week spot on CBS in May 1949 and Hall a five-days-a-week show on Chicago's WBKB the following year. Wielding a baritone 'ukulele, former silent movie actress Carmel Myers had a similar show in New York in 1951.[86] Bobby Henshaw landed TV guest spots and a theater tour in Texas in 1950 and presided over a weeklong 'ukulele talent search in Amarillo; Art Fowler, who had been making a living as an actor in low-budget Westerns, made appearances with Arthur Godfrey and at Manhattan's fashionable Stork Club; and Roy Smeck picked up new dates, including an appearance at Macy's flagship store as part of the chain's hundredth anniversary celebration.[87] The 'ukulele outbreak gave new artists a chance as well: A performer by the name of Jackie appeared on Ed Sullivan's *Toast of the Town* in March 1952 standing on his head and playing the 'ukulele and harmonica simultaneously. "It makes Godfrey pale by comparison," a newspaper critic wrote.[88]

The 'ukulele revival and the resurrection of such twenties artists as Ukulele Ike and Wendell Hall came when Eastern Europe and China had fallen under communist domination, the American monopoly on nuclear weapons had ended, and communist aggression in Korea bred fears of World War III. Faced with the possibility of nuclear annihilation and communist subversion at home, such comforting nostalgia was a widespread response to what historian David Halberstam has called "a mean time."[89] As Louis Armstrong biographer Terry Teachout pointed out, Cold War America longed for musical comfort food.[90] Dixieland jazz made a comeback in the early 1950s, as did the Charleston, flapper parties, and twenties fashion, including bobbed hairstyles and cloche-style hats.[91] Vaudeville, in the form of Milton Berle and the top-rated *Texaco Star Theater,* dominated prime-time television. It seems likely, however, that the refugees housed at Fort Kilmer outside New Brunswick, New Jersey, after the abortive 1956 Hungarian revolution were puzzled to find two hundred banjos and 'ukuleles among the supplies waiting for them. "No one here could explain why these instruments were donated for Hungarians," the *New York Times* reported.[92]

The revival also prompted a new interest in the 'ukulele in the classroom, although it did little to improve its second-class status. As early as 1949, T. P. Giddings bravely advocated the 'ukulele as the best means of teaching both vocal and instrumental music. "It took me fifty-two years of school music teaching to discover that the most useful instrument of the whole list is—don't faint—*the ukulele!*" he told readers of the *Music Educators Journal.* "It plays rhythm, melody and harmony—all three of the elements of music. One can sing as he plays. Now where is there another instrument with all of these qualifications?"[93] In Alliance, Ohio, schoolteacher William Milhalyi used the 'ukulele as a stepping-stone to interest his fourth graders in moving up to "more advanced instruments."[94] A teacher in Paris, Texas, organized a one-hundred-piece 'ukulele orchestra at her elementary school that performed for students at the high school.[95] The Music Department of the Southwestern Louisiana Institute in Lafayette used the 'ukulele to give its elementary music majors "practical musical knowledge that can be acquired and applied in a short time without previous knowledge of music."[96] Because of its ubiquitous presence, the 'ukulele was the first instrument for dozens of baby boomer musicians who helped shape popular music in the 1960s and 1970s, including Jimi Hendrix, Johnny Winter, George Benson, and Bob Seger in the United States and Led Zeppelin's John Paul Jones, Jethro Tull's Ian Anderson, and Peter Frampton in England.[97] In Toronto in 1958, a teenaged Neil Young would close the door to his room at the top of the stairs with his 'ukulele "and we would hear *plunk,* pause while he moved his fingers to the next chord, *plunk,* pause while he moved again, *plunk.*"[98] As a fourteen year old in the southern California citrus town of Redlands, Joan Baez's first public performance was at a high school talent show, playing the 'ukulele and singing "Earth Angel."[99] In Queens, New York, future Greenwich Village folkie Dave Van Ronk picked up a 'ukulele and learned the chords for "Cool Water." "I must have played that thing a hundred times a day just for the pleasure of hearing it come out right. (I suspect the pleasure was all mine)," he remembered. "Still, by assiduous application I managed to acquire a reputation as the second-hottest twelve-year-old ukulele player in Richmond Hill."[100]

The 1950s also gave rise to a sophisticated new style of 'ukulele playing, exemplified by Lyle Ritz and Eddie Kamae. Both were talented musicians who pushed the 'ukulele past its Hawaiian and pop roots and into explorations of jazz and Latin idioms. Ritz was a music student and tuba player at the University of Southern California when he took a part-time job at Southern California Music Co. in downtown Los Angeles.

Working at the small goods counter on the first floor at the height of the Godfrey-fueled 'ukulele boom, Ritz picked up the instrument and began to work out tunes, eventually buying a Gibson tenor for himself.[101] Drafted during the Korean War, he spent two years playing in an army band at Fort Ord, California, where he learned to play the acoustic bass under the tutelage of Lenny Niehaus, a fellow draftee who had been the lead alto saxophone player for Stan Kenton.[102] After his discharge, Ritz returned to Los Angeles to study auto design at the Art Center College of Design, but his love of music finally won out, and he began to work professionally as a bass player in local clubs and piano bars. His first solo recording, however, was the album *How About Uke?* for Verve in 1957, which was the result of guitarist Barney Kessel, the label's West Coast A&R representative, having heard Ritz play the 'ukulele at Southern California Music.[103] Recorded at Capitol Records in three three-hour sessions, the album featured a mix of jazz standards such as "Don't Get Around Much Anymore," "Lulu's Back in Town," and a few Ritz originals. "The music chosen for the album is not of traditional uke repertoire, but includes some of jazz's most interesting and difficult tunes," the liner notes explain. "No quarter is asked; Lyle meets jazz on its own ground."[104] The album was a revelation to serious 'ukulele players in Hawaii. "All of a sudden, here comes Lyle with all these fantastic chord harmonies that just took music to a whole new level on the ukulele," said Roy Sakuma.[105]

Bass player Lyle Ritz of Los Angeles pioneered a sophisticated jazz style of 'ukulele playing in the 1950s. Courtesy of Elizabeth Maihock Beloff.

In Hawaii, simultaneously but independently, Eddie Kamae was exploring the same musical territory. Born in the Kauluwela neighborhood of Honolulu, near the harbor, Kamae was a fifteen-year-old student at Farrington High School when his oldest brother, a driver for Honolulu Rapid Transit, gave him a 'ukulele that had been left on his bus.[106] Like Ritz, Kamae was drafted into the army and served two years, practicing constantly and working out instrumental versions of favorite songs such as "Stardust" and "Tico Tico." Although his father Sam, who loved Hawaiian music, encouraged his son's music making, "I thought I was smarter than him," Kamae said. "I liked jazz and swing and the Latin numbers. For a long time that's all I played."[107] One of his major influences was Jesse Kalima (1920–1980), a fellow Farrington alumnus who was fascinated by the 'ukulele as a child and followed in the footsteps of Ernest Kaai and George Kia to became an evangelist for the 'ukulele as a solo instrument. Kalima's arrangement of Sousa's "The Stars and Stripes Forever" won the 1935 Territorial Amateur Contest at Honolulu's Princess Theater, which earned him his first job as a professional at the theater's *Potluck Show.* Kalima, credited with being the first to amplify a 'ukulele on stage, had a successful career working clubs in Honolulu and on the mainland, featuring his solo work on the 'ukulele with such distinctly non-Hawaiian recordings as "Jalousie," "Dark Eyes," and "Under the Double Eagle."[108]

While making his first public appearances at weekend music sessions at Charlie's Cab Stand on South King Street, Kamae met Shoi Ikemi, whose similar views on the 'ukulele's possibilities led them to form the Ukulele Rascals. The instrumental-only duo quickly picked up work around Honolulu, while the ambitious Kamae took private lessons in music theory at the University of Hawaii, eventually adding excerpts from Ravel and Rachmaninoff to his repertoire.[109] The Rascals broke up after a mainland tour with Ray Kinney in 1949, and Kamae, discouraged by the rigors of touring, wound up serving three years in prison for conspiracy to defraud after getting caught up in a fake medicine scheme. Once again he turned to his music, and on his release he landed a solo spot at the Biltmore Hotel. Throughout the 1950s, Kamae continued to perform and offer lessons, and in 1959 he recorded *Heart of the Ukulele,* which showcased his favorite pop and Latin tunes and the "chord soloing" technique he and Kalima developed: By plucking all four strings at the same time, one can simultaneously hear the chords and melody.[110]

Regardless of the artistry of musicians like Ritz and Kamae, a decade of marketing the 'ukulele in drug and auto parts stores as children's toys made it difficult for the public to take it seriously. Most 'ukuleles manufactured in the late 1940s and throughout the 1950s were made of plastic, and plastic in postwar America increasingly was associated with cheapness, low quality, and artificiality.[111] By 1956, plastic 'ukuleles literally were cheap: Dart Drug in Washington, D.C., was offering three "TV ukuleles" for 99 cents.[112] Maccaferri's claim that his Islanders could be played underwater was not just a public relations stunt—it was a response to the fact that thermoplastics were sensitive in varying

The baby boomers' perception of the 'ukulele as a toy was shaped by manufacturers' decision to market almost exclusively to children. Courtesy of Cyril LeFebvre.

degrees to heat, chemicals, water, and sunlight, factors that had become a serious marketing problem.[113] Plastic 'ukuleles seemed even more childlike when compared to the guitars played by Elvis Presley and other rock 'n' roll stars. "If a kid has a uke in his hand, he's not going to get in much trouble," Arthur Godfrey proclaimed in a 1950 interview. For teenaged baby boomers listening to Elvis, Bill Haley, and Chuck Berry, nothing could be less appealing.[114] As early as 1951, NAMMM reported that a rise in guitar sales could be attributed to "the desire of persons who learned to play the ukulele in its recent popularity upswing to master the more advanced instrument."[115]

No more powerful symbol of the 'ukulele's irrelevance could be found than on the *Ed Sullivan Show* of Sunday, February 9, 1964. The popular variety show featured a typical lineup: a magician, an impressionist, a selection from the latest Broadway musical, and Tessie O'Shea, the veteran English music hall artist clad in lamé singing and playing her Gibson banjo-ukulele.[116] O'Shea seemed hopelessly old-fashioned, bracketed by the Beatles playing "She Loves You" and "I Saw Her Standing There" in their live American debut.[117] For the show's estimated 74 million viewers—the largest television audience in American history, with almost 60 percent of households with televisions tuned in—it was guitars that mattered now.[118] Canny businessman that he was, Mario Maccaferri recognized the seismic shift that had just occurred: By April, he had acquired the licensing rights and issued a whole catalog of Beatles instruments, including 'ukuleles marketed as guitars with the Beatles faces molded on their soundboards.[119] Rock 'n' roll guitars were sweeping all before them.

CHAPTER 9

The Growing Underground Movement

The expectations are so deliciously low for all of us that it's only up from here.
—JIM BELOFF, 1998

Tiny Tim's prime-time television debut—a medley of "A Tisket, A Tasket" and "The Good Ship Lollipop" while strumming a 'ukulele fished out of a shopping bag—left *Laugh-In* cohost Dick Martin openmouthed in mock disbelief. "A little surprise for you there," said his partner Dan Rowan after the long-haired performer had exited, blowing kisses to the studio audience. "You searched high and low for that one, didn't you?" Martin said with a grin. "It kept him out of the service," Rowan replied—a reference to the Vietnam-era military draft that drew a big laugh.[1]

The next morning, the *Los Angeles Times'* television critic reported that Tiny Tim "has to be seen to be believed," referring to what he thought was intended as a spoof of rock 'n' roll singers.[2] But within six months of his startling appearance on the January 22, 1968, premiere of the irreverent comedy-variety show, Tiny Tim (1934–1996) had become a full-fledged pop culture sensation, with six network television appearances, a best-selling LP (*God Bless Tiny Tim*), a book (*Beautiful Thoughts*), a movie (*You Are What You Eat*), and bookings at venues ranging from San Francisco's Fillmore to the Royal Albert Hall in London.[3] From the beginning, Tiny Tim inspired hyperbole, both from his critics and his admirers. To Albert Goldman of the *New York Times,* Tiny Tim offered "the most perfect impersonations of old singers ever heard." *Life* called his LP "one of the most dazzling albums of programmed entertainment to come along since . . . Sergeant Pepper," while *Time* called him "the most bizarre entertainer this side of Barnum & Bailey's sideshow" and a *Chicago Tribune* reviewer wrote that "his efforts at entertaining are so fraudulent that an audience is embarrassed before it turns resentful."[4]

While Tiny Tim's instrumental technique was rudimentary and he occasionally had trouble keeping time, contemporary reviewers rarely mentioned his 'ukulele playing, focusing instead on his shoulder-length hair, extraordinary looks, fluttering hands, falsetto voice, and encyclopedic knowledge of vintage Tin Pan Alley tunes. Even so, Tiny Tim—who credited Arthur Godfrey for spurring him to pick up the 'ukulele—defined the instrument for modern audiences.[5] It's almost impossible for American journalists to write about the 'ukulele today, more than forty years later, without mentioning Tiny Tim.[6] As with his inspiration Godfrey, television played a critical role in his career: Building on his previous appearances, his wedding to Miss Vicki, broadcast live on the *Tonight Show* on December 17, 1969, attracted one of the largest late-night audiences ever.[7] Despite his inescapable association with the instrument, however, Tiny Tim has been largely irrelevant to the international 'ukulele revival that began to pick up momentum in the 1980s. Some critics would argue that the new interest in the 'ukulele took place despite his role in shaping the public's perceptions.

Tiny Tim was not the first performer to swim against the popular music tide of the sixties with a 'ukulele. English native Ian Whitcomb (b. 1941) launched his career with a piano-driven falsetto novelty, "You Turn Me On," which was a top-ten hit on the American charts in the summer of 1965. The following year, he scored a regional hit in southern California with his remake of Al Jolson's 1916 recording of "Where Does Robinson Crusoe Go with Friday on

Ian Whitcomb defied popular music trends in the 1960s by performing with his pawnshop 'ukulele—years before Tiny Tim. Courtesy of Ian Whitcomb.

Saturday Night," accompanying himself on the Martin 'ukulele he had picked up in a Los Angeles pawnshop three years earlier.[8] That September, at a well-reviewed show at the Troubadour in Los Angeles, Whitcomb showcased a series of English music hall and ragtime songs—"A Lemon in the Garden of Love," "She Was Poor but She Was Honest," "I'm Shy, Mary Ellen"—accompanying himself on the 'ukulele and piano.[9] "I was reviving the ukulele in the era of rock 'n' roll, but doing it in a straight and unfreaky way," said Whitcomb, who appeared playing the 'ukulele and singing the Beatles' "You Won't See Me" on Dick Clark's *Where the Action Is* in 1966—probably the first rock musician to feature the 'ukulele on U.S. network television.[10]

Whitcomb was among the best-known artists in the small and loosely defined "new vaudeville" movement that briefly flourished in 1965–1966: the Nitty Gritty Dirt Band (their 1965 debut album featured such songs as "I Wish I Could Shimmy Like My Sister Kate" and "Crazy Words, Crazy Tune"); Jim Kweskin & the Jug Band (their second album, also released in 1965, included "Ukulele Lady"); San Francisco-based Sopwith Camel (Tiny Tim covered their first single, "Hello Hello"); the Bonzo Dog Band (on "The Intro and the Outro," Vivian Stanshall pretends to introduce "Eric Clapton on ukulele" as a member of the band); and the New Vaudeville Band ("Winchester Cathedral" went to the top of the U.S. charts in December 1966).[11] But new vaudeville disappeared almost as quickly as it arrived. Indeed, one could argue that Tiny Tim's complete identification with the 'ukulele in the popular mind was possible because he had so little competition in a decade dominated by rock 'n' roll. In 1968, when Tiny Tim made his prime-time debut, total annual 'ukulele production at Martin was just seventy-five instruments, the lowest level since the firm first began to make 'ukuleles in 1916.[12] At that point, to hear the 'ukulele one's best bet would have been to attend one of Mel Torme's New York club dates.[13]

In Hawaii, it was the same story: Rock dominated, and few musicians were interested in playing Hawaiian music.[14] "It wasn't cool to be playing Hawaiian music," remembered Roland Cazimero, who with his brother Robert played in a rock band in the late 1960s after graduating from Kamehameha School. "If you were playing that, you were dead."[15] In the big hotels in Waikiki, "hapa-haole music did fine, everyone knew the 'Wedding Song,' but . . . singing something really Hawaiian, something you really enjoyed, just wouldn't sell," said Kahauanu Lake, who beginning in 1955 spent more than twenty years entertaining tourists in Waikiki hotels with his baritone 'ukulele.[16] By 1969, the mainland's interest in traditional Hawaiian music had waned to the extent that Capitol and Decca dropped the Hawaiian category completely. In the Islands themselves, as late as 1975 the total industry output was a meager five albums for the entire year.[17] One of the few exceptions was 'ukulele virtuoso Herb Ohta, a former student of Eddie Kamae who scored a major hit on the charts in 1964 with the instrumental "Sushi" and signed a five-year contract with Decca.[18] The 'ukulele has unusual qualities that have not been properly exploited, Ohta told the *New York Times* in 1966. "It has the range of a flute, but it also can be chorded. And you can't strum a guitar the way you can a ukulele."[19] But two years earlier, Ohta's anticipated mainland tour in support of "Sushi" was suddenly canceled because "the Beatles were coming," Ohta said. "I didn't understand what he was saying. I thought he was talking about an insect invasion."[20]

By 1971, historian and Hawaiian cultural advocate George Kanahele lamented in the *Honolulu Advertiser* that "popular Hawaiian music is in its death throes. . . . The signs of the end are as clear as they are frightening. Hawaiian musicians are rapidly disappearing. . . . There are fewer and fewer Hawaiian bands and shows. Only one major hotel in Honolulu comes close to featuring a simon-pure Hawaiian show. Few people, after all, care to listen to Hawaiian music today; it is now passé. . . . Ask any kid in Hawaii and he will say Hawaiian music is a drag—it's out, it's dead."[21]

But just as Kanahele was sounding the alarm for Hawaiian music, a new political and cultural consciousness was developing among Native Hawaiians. The influence of the civil rights movement on the mainland, protests against the war in Vietnam, the decolonization of former European possessions in the Pacific—all helped set the stage for the "Hawaiian Renaissance," a term coined by Kanahele and described by Amy Kuuleialoha Stillman as "the vigorous assertion of native Hawaiian ethnic identity."[22] On the political level, the movement is generally regarded to have begun with a 1970 protest over the eviction of Native Hawaiian farmers from Oahu's Kalama Valley by the Bishop Estate to make way for expensive new housing, a protest that evolved into a broader effort to assert the rights of Native Hawaiians.[23] Music was not far behind. As was the case during the last days of the monarchy, Hawaiian politics and musical culture were closely entwined. "The new interest in the music is tied to the diminishing factor of the Hawaiian lifestyle," singer/songwriter Jerry Santos of Olomana said. "With the buildings and the condominiums and the thousands of people, a lot of the older things are vanishing quickly. There is more of an urgency to remember the old values correctly."[24] Kanahele, the moving force behind the creation of the Hawaiian Music Foundation in 1971 "to perpetuate, develop and promote Hawaiian music," agreed: "Viewed in the broadest perspective, while the foundation's focus is Hawaiian music, it can be no less concerned with the development and preservation of the whole culture from which Hawaiian music receives its essential meaning."[25]

Pioneering the revival of traditional Hawaiian music was Eddie Kamae, whose jamming with slack key guitarist Gabby Pahinui in 1959 convinced him to abandon his jazz and Latin repertoire and organize the Sons of Hawaii with bassist Joe Marshall, steel guitarist David "Feet" Rogers, and Pahinui. By 1971, the Sons had released four critically acclaimed albums of Hawaiian music in Hawaiian, using traditional arrangements and instrumentation. Kamae, known earlier for his picking skills, used his 'ukulele primarily as a rhythm instrument.[26] Building on the foundation laid by the Sons, what really kicked off the musical renaissance was the release of Sunday Manoa's 1971 album, *Guava Jam,* with Peter Moon and the brothers Cazimero, Robert and Roland, playing traditional Hawaiian music with a contemporary edge.[27] "Everybody knows, Sunday Manoa revolutionized Hawaiian music," said chanter and musician Kelii Taua.[28] "It was like, 'OK, I am Hawaiian, I am different. I've been raised differently and there's no reason I shouldn't say what I want to say,'" said Santos.[29] Among the attractions of Sunday Manoa was the 'ukulele playing of Moon, who has cited Kamae, Ohta, and Lyle Ritz as his major influences.[30] "The 'ukulele solo in 'Pualilia' should be in the Hall of Fame of 'ukulele solos," 'ukulele virtuoso Jake Shimabukuro said.[31]

As a result of all these factors, what was now regarded as traditional Hawaiian music exploded in the late 1970s: From a mere five albums in 1975, some fifty-three were released in 1977.[32] Roy Sakuma, a groundskeeper with the Honolulu Parks and Recreation Department and a student of Ohta's, launched an annual 'ukulele festival in 1971 (now in its forty-first year); the centennial of the arrival of the 'ukulele in the Islands was celebrated with a formal ceremony at the state capitol, concerts, and an exhibition at the Bishop Museum that featured instruments from the important collection of Leslie Nunes, great-grandson of 'ukulele pioneer Manuel Nunes.[33] But it wasn't until the early 1990s that the stylings of Kelly Boy Delima of Kapena, Troy Fernandez of the Kaau Crater Boys, and Israel Kamakawiwoole of the Makaha Sons of Niihau inspired a new generation of players in Hawaii.

Up to that point, pupils at the 'ukulele studios Sakuma first opened in 1974 were interested primarily in learning how to play pop tunes. Then "Iz, Kapena, [and] Ka'au Crater Boys changed all that," Sakuma said. "Troy came out playing the 'ukulele like no one had ever heard before. Suddenly all these kids were coming in to learn what Troy was doing on the 'ukulele."[34] Although he lacked the instrumental

Israel Kamakawiwoole's music helped redefine the 'ukulele as "cool" in Hawaii. Courtesy of Mountain Apple Co. Hawaii/Big Boy Records.

pyrotechnics of Delima and Fernandez, Kamakawiwoole became an enormously influential solo artist, whose songs such as "Hawaii '78" and "E Ala E" ("Wake Up") spoke eloquently to the cultural trauma experienced by Native Hawaiians.[35] His 'ukulele-backed "Over the Rainbow/What a Wonderful World" medley became the "Sweet Leilani" of his generation, featured on mainland television shows (most notably on the 2002 episode of *ER* in which Dr. Mark Green dies), soundtracks, and advertisements, exposure that made his *Facing Future* album Hawaii's first platinum musical release.[36] When the thirty-eight-year-old musician died in 1997, the state government took the unusual step of flying state flags at half-staff and allowing his body to lie in state in the courtyard of the capitol, where tens of thousands came to pay their respects.[37] "You'd be hard-pressed to find a local kid who doesn't think playing the 'ukulele is cool," one local writer noted four years later.[38]

At the same time Delima, Fernandez, and Kamakawiwoole were reenergizing the 'ukulele in Hawaii, a widely scattered group of enthusiasts on the mainland and in Canada, England, and Japan also were embracing the 'ukulele. Jim Beloff was a lifelong guitarist who, impressed with his father-in-law's chops on a family 'ukulele, bought a Martin tenor at the Rose Bowl Flea Market for $250 in 1992. The associate publisher of *Billboard* magazine, he was quickly captivated by his new purchase, but he had a hard time finding sheet music or songbooks. Coming from a family of entrepreneurs—his family operated a Meriden, Connecticut, department store for years—Beloff and his wife Liz decided to do something about it and utilized his music industry contacts to publish a collection of his own, *Jumpin' Jim's Ukulele Favorites* in 1993. Other songbooks, the first book on the history of the 'ukulele, and a compilation of sixty years of 'ukulele music for Rhino Records followed, and by early 1998 the Beloffs had quit their jobs to launch Flea Market Music and make the 'ukulele their full-time job.

The following year, working with brother-in-law Dale Webb, a talented engineer, they introduced a new low-cost, high-quality plastic 'ukulele they called the Fluke.[39] Debuted at the 1999 National Association of Music Merchants (NAMM) show in Los Angeles, the Fluke was a big hit, thanks in large part to the 'ukulele's renewed popularity in Japan.[40] Hawaiian music and the 'ukulele had been introduced to Japan in the 1920s and developed by such pioneers as Ernest Kaai and Yukihiko and Katsuhiko Haida, both natives of Hawaii, who formed the Moana Glee Club in 1929.[41] Public interest peaked after World War II, spurred by a series of annual summer tours during the sixties by Hawaiian musicians that included 'ukulele virtuosos Herb Ohta and Eddie Bush, but it declined by the mid-seventies, a victim of the popularity of rock music.[42] Thus it was with a sense of skepticism that the Ukulele Orchestra of Great Britain traveled to Japan in 1994 after being signed by Sony Music Japan. "I was rather dubious about whether we'd actually get to Japan, and the next thing I know we're being waved at by girls in the street," said bassist Jonathan Bankes. "Whole groups kept stopping us to sign their CDs, t-shirts and

Jim Beloff's purchase of a Martin tenor at a flea market in 1992 marked a turning point for the modern 'ukulele revival.

ukuleles."[43] By 1999, a 'ukulele boom was underway in Japan, with young women making up a large part of the market that was moving an average of three hundred 'ukuleles a month at the Tokyo store Akio Gakki.[44]

Founded in 1985, the seven- (now eight-) member Ukulele Orchestra of Great Britain (UOGB) became one of the most visible manifestations of a similar boom in England, although the early going wasn't easy. Early on, UOGB members complained that they were ostracized because of their staunch refusal to perform Formby tunes (the group plays conventional 'ukuleles rather than banjo ukuleles).[45] The self-proclaimed "anarcho-syndicalists of the ukulele world" instead played an eclectic repertoire that runs from the Sex Pistols and Nirvana to Wagner and Beethoven. "We were tired of the technological bias of the rock gig, and later of those performers who stared at a laptop," said cofounder George Hinchliffe. "We yearned for a gig in which people simply play the music. . . . Today's explosion in uke playing is reminiscent of back-to-basics movements such as skiffle, or punk even, and like those, it's open to all. The audience goes home and thinks, 'I could do that.'"[46] From playing in London pubs, the UOGB has moved to Royal Albert Hall, where it performed to a sold-out crowd at the BBC Proms music festival in August 2009. "Their witty, deadpan style and well-honed flippancy conceal a consummate skill, and the sophisticated sound they produce—both percussive and melodic—is at once hilarious and heartfelt," the *Financial Times* enthused.[47]

The modern Canadian 'ukulele movement, older than that in the United States or England, was driven not by irony but pedagogy. In 1962, during his second year as a music teacher in the public schools of Halifax, Nova Scotia, J. Chalmers Doane organized his first 'ukulele ensemble, convinced it was an ideal method of bringing musical literacy to young students. As music supervisor for Halifax schools from 1967 to 1985, Doane became a 'ukulele evangelist, traveling across Canada, demonstrating his courses, training teachers, designing a distinctive triangular teaching 'ukulele, publishing a method and even a magazine—*Ukulele Yes!*—that led to thousands of students in all ten provinces receiving their first musical training on the 'ukulele. "I rather enjoyed the skeptics. Most of the time," he said. "I was getting people started in music who would never have had a door open to music. Now, if they decided because of what they had on the ukulele that they [wanted to pursue music further], the world was open to them."[48] The movement began to fade in the late eighties and early nineties because of cutbacks in school funding, but it continues to thrive in Nova Scotia, its original home, and in British Columbia, home to the Langley Ukulele Ensemble, which has produced such noted 'ukulele artists as James Hill, winner of the Canadian Folk Music Awards' 2009 Traditional Album of the Year.[49]

Beginning in the mid-nineties, these and other widely scattered players, teachers, and entrepreneurs began to find each other online. Web sites like the Beloffs' fleamarketmusic.com, launched in 1997, made it possible for individual enthusiasts to not only buy and sell instruments, strings, songbooks, instructional videos, and CDs but to ask questions, share information, and participate in the give-and-take of an increasingly far-flung virtual community.[50] The Web has played a key role in fostering what has become known as the "third wave" of 'ukulele popularity. Just as radio and the recording industry sustained the first wave in the teens and twenties, and television helped create the second wave in the fifties, technology—in this case, the Internet—played an important role in the 'ukulele's latest resurrection. The 'ukulele community quickly picked up on the launch of YouTube in 2005, posting thousands of videos of individual performances and sharing vintage clips of such artists as Roy Smeck and Johnny Marvin as well as from current movies and television.[51] As Gary Peare has pointed out, the 'ukulele's small size makes it an ideal instrument for self-made, point-and-shoot videos. Today there are tens of thousands of 'ukulele videos on YouTube and hundreds of 'ukulele Web sites, blogs, and bulletin boards that originate in the United States, Canada, England, France, Germany, the Netherlands, Finland, Brazil, Japan, Australia, and New Zealand.[52] In Thailand, the 'ukulele was virtually unknown until Pasapum Naonan launched UkuleleThai.com in 2009; by the following year, he had more than 2,500 members.[53]

Over the past decade, although the 'ukulele has not achieved the ubiquity of the Roaring Twenties or the Godfrey era, its popularity has continued to grow. In the absence of a major pop culture figure like Godfrey or Ukulele Ike, the modern revival has been a more viral, grassroots affair. Consistent with its historic role,

California has led the way. The mainland's first annual 'ukulele festival, founded in 1994 in Hayward, was followed by more than two dozen others in the United States, Europe, Australia, and New Zealand.[54] "We think it's time to have one here," organizer Lee Ann Harper told a reporter on the eve of the first-ever Midwest UkeFest in 2003. Like many other festivals, the Indianapolis event grew out of what Harper called "the growing underground movement, especially among the young, in playing ukuleles."[55] More than 150 'ukulele clubs have sprung up across the country, in part aided by the ease with which individual players can find each other online. "I'm pretty much a loner," said Ron Chamberlin, explaining how he ended up at the 2004 Inland Empire Ukulele Festival in Loma Linda, California. "I developed my own style and then I found this group on the Internet. It's fun to play with a group."[56] One of the standard festival attractions is performances and classes by such talented performers as Lyle Ritz, James Hill, Bryan Tolentino, and Kimo Hussey, as well as the opportunity to jam with other players. The mainstream press has taken notice: Over the past decade, major accounts of the 'ukulele revival have appeared in the *New York Times, Los Angeles Times, USA Today,* on National Public Radio and CBS's *Sunday Morning,* and overseas in the *Ottawa Citizen, Financial Times, Der Spiegel,* and the *Age* in Melbourne, Australia, among other outlets.[57]

The renewed interest in the 'ukulele has led to a revival of interest in its value in the classroom as an effective and inexpensive way to promote musical literacy. The most impressive example of this approach is found in Langley, British Columbia, where for more than thirty years students have been trained as musicians and developed impressive playing skills as members of the Langley Ukulele Ensemble.[58]

The talented James Hill is a leading advocate of using the 'ukulele as a way to teach music.

Langley alumnus James Hill has picked up where Doane left off, reviving his *Ukulele Yes!* magazine online and urging schools to incorporate the 'ukulele into the music curriculum. "What I'm hoping to cultivate is an array of musically literate people," he says. "I don't really care what they end up playing."[59] More modest efforts have been reported elsewhere, as well: in elementary and intermediate schools in Lakeland, Florida, Morton, Illinois, Seattle, Washington, Ottawa, Canada, and Mt. Roskill, New Zealand.[60] In England, the growing movement to replace recorders—long a staple of primary music instruction—with 'ukuleles has attracted a flurry of attention in the national press. "I offered the lessons as an experiment, but found the children were so enthusiastic that, within a few months, I had enough players for an entire ukulele orchestra," Tim Lewis, a teacher at Holway Park Primary School in Taunton, Somerset, told the *Guardian.* "It was amazing: there was so much interest [from other schools], not just from across Somerset, but from as far afield as Newcastle and Suffolk."[61]

The third wave also has given rise to a new generation of 'ukulele virtuosos, of whom the best known is Jake Shimabukuro. Like Kaai, Kia, Kalima, and other noted performers who preceded him, Shimabukuro has sought to demonstrate the full range of his instrument and in so doing "is challenging every last preconception about the ukulele," one profiler wrote.[62] "I love to play things that people don't expect and totally blow them away," Shimabukuro says.[63] Born in Honolulu in 1976, Shimabukuro first picked up the 'ukulele at the age of four, encouraged by his mother. Seven years of lessons under the tutelage of Tami Akiyami at Roy Sakuma Studios followed. Insight gained from playing drums in the Kaimuki High School marching band ("When I played the drums, I was only twisting my wrist. So I transferred that to the 'ukulele and strummed by twisting at the wrist like I'm drumming") and working at a local music store, which allowed him to experiment endlessly with pedals and processors, helped shape his high-speed, unconventional approach.[64] "Basically, I wanted to be like Edward Van Halen," he says.[65]

His professional career began with Pure Heart, the trio that won four Na Hoku awards with its eponymously titled 1998 debut album. Shortly after he launched his solo career in 2001, he was signed by Epic, reportedly the first Hawaiian artist to join the major label owned by Sony Music.[66] Although many of his tour dates are at relatively small venues, he has toured with Jimmy Buffett, appeared on *Late Night with Conan O'Brien* and the *Tonight Show,* and a video of his version of George Harrison's "While My Guitar Gently Weeps" posted online in 2005 has been viewed more than 8.7 million times.[67] His latest high-profile gigs were a performance at the Royal Variety Performance in London before Queen Elizabeth II, accompanying Hawaiian-born singer Bette Midler, and an appearance at the 2010 Playboy Jazz Festival in Los Angeles.[68]

The 'ukulele has begun to make inroads into the world of mainstream rock and country music as well—and this time not as a nostalgic novelty. Paul McCartney, Bruce Springsteen, Elvis Costello, Roger Daltrey, Todd Rundgren, Aimee Mann,

Jake Shimabukuro has become the modern era's best-known 'ukulele virtuoso. Courtesy of Hisashi Uchida.

and Taylor Swift have all used the 'ukulele while on tour—McCartney during his 2002 tour as a tribute to his old Beatles bandmate George Harrison, a serious 'ukulele player and George Formby fan. (Harrison's posthumous 2002 album, *Brainwashed,* has 'ukulele in the mix on every track.)[69] Eddie Vedder of Pearl Jam bought a Kamaka on a whim during a 1988 trip to Hawaii and fell in love with its musical possibilities. "Music just started coming out of this thing," he said in an interview. "Somehow, melodies happen on the uke that I just wasn't pulling out of the guitar." After dabbling with the 'ukulele in the studio and on stage ("Soon Forget" is a 'ukulele-only track on Pearl Jam's 2000 album, *Binaural,* and Vedder once played a 'ukulele version of Black Sabbath's "Iron Man" in concert), he released *Ukulele Songs* in June 2011, a solo album featuring Vedder and his 'ukulele.[70] The 'ukulele-driven track "Hey, Soul Sister" by Train reached No. 3 on *Billboard's* Hot 100 list in the spring of 2010, boosted by its use in a Super Bowl commercial.[71] The modern pop artists most closely associated with the 'ukulele, however, are Stephin Merritt of the Magnetic Fields, Steven Swartz and Alan Drogin of Songs from a Random House, and Zach Condon of Beirut. Merritt, whom some critics have called "the Cole Porter of indie rock," featured the 'ukulele prominently in his critically acclaimed 1999 three-disc song cycle, *69 Love Songs* and in subsequent live performances.[72] Swartz and Drogin, who play baritone and soprano 'ukulele, respectively, also made it a mainstay of their music. "When you get up on stage and you have a guitar, people are going to make judgments about what they're going to hear just based on what kind of guitar it is," Swartz said. "But with the ukulele the field's open, and it's a much more musically versatile instrument than people are aware of."[73]

'Ukulele players seeking validation have been quick to point to a new generation of Hollywood celebrities who have picked up the instrument—Daniel Craig, William H. Macy, Zooey Deschanel, Emily Blunt, Cybill Shepherd, and Pierce Brosnan among them—as well as politicians (English prime minister Tony Blair made headlines in England when he played a 'ukulele on a 2005 vacation) and business executives, including master investor Warren Buffett, who first picked up a 'ukulele in Omaha, Nebraska, in 1949 to compete with the 'ukulele-playing boyfriend of a girl he was pursuing. Today Buffett is famous (or infamous) for playing at the annual meeting of Berkshire Hathaway, his investment firm.[74] The 'ukulele also has made a number of unusual stage appearances of late: in the Rockettes' annual Christmas show at Radio City Music Hall; in New York's Classic Stage Company's 2004 adaptation of Sophocles' *Antigone;* in Chen Shi-Zeng's staging of the seventeenth-century Chinese opera *Peach Blossom Fan;* and in the Flying Karamozov Brothers' juggling act.[75]

As a result of this new visibility, 'ukulele production boomed in the 1990s as established manufacturers ramped up production and dozens of new boutique makers in Hawaii and on the mainland entered the business. "We're selling twice as many as 10 years ago, easily," Stan Werbin, owner of Elderly Instruments, a leading dealer based in Lansing, Michigan, said in a 1998 interview. "Twenty years ago, you couldn't give them away. Now, some are going for up to $11,000."[76] 'Ukulele sales have continued to grow. "It's exploded," Sammy Ash of Sam Ash Music Stores said in fall 2010. "Five years ago we stocked two no-name [brands], but now we stock over 30 models."[77] Sutherland Trading, one of the largest distributors in the UK, imports three thousand 'ukuleles each month.[78] Founded in 2001, the Honolulu-based 'Ukulele Guild of Hawaii now boasts an international membership of more than 350.[79] As arguably the world's oldest 'ukulele company, family-owned and -run Kamaka Hawaii remains the industry leader, with a sizeable waiting list despite its annual production of 4,200 instruments in the cinder block shop on Honolulu's South Street it has occupied for the past fifty years.[80] Martin, which once set the standard for mainland production, dropped most of its 'ukulele models by 1965 and went out of the business altogether in the 1970s, only to resume production in Navojoa, Mexico, in 2003 when the market demand for its vintage instruments grew too great to ignore.[81] Six years later, Fender—southern California–based maker of the iconic electric guitar—went into the 'ukulele business for the first time, marketing three moderately priced models with a Telecaster headstock.[82] Other major manufacturers that have entered the field include Hohner, the German harmonica maker who produces the Lanikai line of 'ukuleles; Illinois-based U.S. Music Corp, which now makes Oscar Schmidt 'ukuleles; and the Japanese guitar maker Takamine, which introduced its new Shimabukuro-designed MIGM 'ukulele at the 2010 NAMM Show in Los Angeles.[83] Even Candelas Guitars of East Los Angeles, for seventy years a respected maker of classical, flamenco, and mariachi guitars, now makes 'ukuleles.[84] Because of the cost of traditionally made instruments, which generally range from $500 to $2,000, production has begun to move overseas to factories in Indonesia, Portugal, and China in an attempt to provide more affordable models.[85] However, most 'ukulele makers continue to handcraft their own instruments, whether long-established luthiers such as Sonny Dahlins and David Gomes in Hawaii or newer firms such as Palm Tree Ukuleles in Colorado Springs (established in 2005) and Kepasa Ukuleles of Middlesex, Vermont (launched in 2004).[86]

The market for vintage 'ukuleles also has grown enormously. "Especially over the last 10 years, interest in collecting vintage musical instruments has exploded," Jim Beloff noted in his pioneering 1997 'ukulele history, fueled by what collectors half-jokingly refer to as "UAS"—'ukulele acquisition syndrome—and eBay.[87] Once a routine part of the stock of pawnshops and flea markets, 'ukuleles have become collector's items. The rarest examples of early Hawaiian 'ukuleles and the much-sought-after Martin 5K model now command four- and five-figure prices when they come on the market.[88] At least two vintage 'ukuleles have appeared on the popular PBS series, *Antiques Roadshow,* including an early Dias soprano appraised at up to $15,000.[89] "Today, I couldn't afford to buy the 10 best ukes I once had in my collection," said Melbourne, Australia–based Chuck Fayne, an online ukulele expert and collector for fifty years who once amassed eight hundred instruments.[90] Low-end mainland-manufactured 'ukuleles of the twenties through the early sixties also are eagerly sought after, in many cases for their period graphics or unusual design rather than their playability.[91] The work of modern luthiers has mirrored this interest in vintage instruments, including new 'ukulele lines modeled on historic examples (Kenny Hill's Ukebrand instruments are based on Jonah Kumalae's) and building replicas of early Hawaiian instruments (Dave Means of Annapolis and Michael Da Silva of Berkeley are among the leaders in this area).[92] Collectors' enthusiastic interest in vintage instruments also has made possible a series of museum exhibits over the past decade.[93] Both the Ukulele Hall of Fame Museum Foundation and the 'Ukulele Guild of Hawaii are pursuing plans to create museums devoted exclusively to the 'ukulele.

Despite a higher profile, the growth in sales, the museum exhibits, and ventures into high culture—at least two recent works for 'ukulele and symphony orchestra have been composed and performed, and choreographer Doug Varone premiered his "Beyond the Break (7 Dances for Ukulele)" at Wolf Trap in 2007 to Shimabukuro's music—the 'ukulele is still perceived as a comical novelty or children's toy.[94] Reviews of Shimabukuro's mainland tours, while positive, give a clear idea of how the 'ukulele is perceived: "a Hawaiian souvenir more suited for collecting dust than creating cutting-edge sounds," "the small, four-stringed instrument more often associated with plinking out children's songs," "an instrument most people regard as a novelty better suited for Tiny Tim impersonators or as a prop at a luau party."[95] Even in the face of impressive artistry, preconceptions have proved hard to overcome. "Despite their effectiveness, it's hard to ignore the constant mechanical manipulation required to extract rich harmonies from a relatively limited instrument," the *Los Angeles Times* wrote of the 2001 jazz collaboration of Lyle Ritz and Herb Ohta, *A Night of Ukulele Jazz Live at McCabe's.* "The amazement, as someone once said, is not how it's done, but that it's done at all."[96]

Mainland audiences continue to get plenty of reinforcement for their idea of the 'ukulele as a toy or a musical joke. It is the favored instrument of SpongeBob Squarepants, one of American television's most popular cartoon characters: One verse of SpongeBob's "F.U.N. Song" declares that "U is for ukulele." It continues to be featured as a comic prop on Broadway: Tom Selleck played one in the 2001 revival of the musical comedy *A Thousand Clowns;* on television: Victoria Jackson took her 'ukulele to her *Saturday Night Live* audition and played a nutty 'ukulele-playing character on Nickelodeon's *Romeo;* and in the movies: in Christopher Guest's *A Mighty Wind,* one character describes how she learned to play the 'ukulele when making "a short film of a mature nature," titled *Not So Tiny Tim.*[97] Tellingly, in two recent best-selling novels for young adults, Jerry Spinelli's *Stargirl* (2000) and Mark Peter Hughes' *Lemonade Mouth* (2007), unconventional heroines play the 'ukulele; Stella Penn, one of Hughes' protagonists, describes herself as an "embattled ukulele-toting maverick."[98] "Well, let's face it," wrote newspaper columnist Lex Van Den Berghe. "When you think of the ukulele, 'cool' is not the first word that springs to mind."[99]

The past ninety years have not been kind to the 'ukulele in the sense that what was regarded as an instrument of exotic enchantment in 1916 is now seen on the mainland as a children's toy and a party prop. But just as it did in the 1890s, the 'ukulele operates on several different levels simultaneously. It remains central to the marketing of the Hawaiian fantasy to tourists, found in tour package brochures, hotel and cruise line advertisements, on museum brochures, and in free literature distributed to visitors.[100] "The sweet sounds of Hawaii's music seem to rise from the heart of the Islands, keeping time with the swaying palms and the rhythm of waves, casting a romantic spell that immediately brings to mind pictures of paradise," one recent tourist publication purred beneath a photo of a ukulele.[101] Yet even as artists like Shimabukuro—who in 2004 was hired by Hawaii Tourism Japan to be the spokesperson for a reinvented marketing program—help sell the tourism industry, others, as did Israel Kamakawiwoole, use the 'ukulele to protest the second-class status of Native Hawaiians, many of whom regard tourism as one of Hawaii's biggest problems.[102] An instantly recognizable symbol of Hawaii, a promise of an island paradise, a tourist souvenir, an instrument central to a rich and celebrated musical culture, a tool of political protest, a highly sought-after collectible, a remarkable synthesis of Western and Pacific cultures, the butt of jokes—the 'ukulele is all these things. "I don't think it's a gimmicky novelty, I think it's a whole culture," singer/songwriter Stephin Merritt says. "And it doesn't seem particularly funny to me."[103]

APPENDIX A

Chronological List of Early Hawaiian Luthiers

Augusto Dias (1842–1915), flourished (fl.) 1884–1910

Dias is the first ʻukulele maker for whom there is any documentation: He appears in the 1884–1885 *Honolulu City Directory* as a guitar and furniture maker at 11 King St. Burned out in the 1886 Chinatown fire, he and Jose do Espirito Santo were working as partners in 1887 on Nuuanu Street. He is listed at various addresses on Nuuanu and King through 1900, when he lost everything for the second time in the Chinatown fire of that year. After three years as an employee of the Porter Furniture Co., he was once again listed as a guitar maker in the 1904–1905 city directory, opening his own shop on Union Street in 1907. He retired from active business ca. 1911, dying four years later of tuberculosis. His instruments are the rarest of the early makers: To date, only twelve have been identified.

Manuel Nunes (1843–1922), fl. 1885–1917

Listed as a cabinet maker with C. E. Williams in the 1884–1885 *Honolulu City Directory*, Nunes advertised his "cabinetmaking shop of string instruments, guitars and machetes" in Honolulu's new Portuguese-language newspaper in August 1885. His directory listings at various addresses alternate between guitar maker and cabinet maker through 1903, after which he is always listed as a guitar maker. His claim to be the inventor of the ʻukulele first surfaced in 1909, around the time the firm of M. Nunes & Sons was formed, and it was featured in all subsequent advertising. Nunes ʻukuleles were among the first Hawaiian-made instruments to be distributed and sold on the mainland. Southern California Music Co. of Los Angeles first advertised M. Nunes ʻukuleles in July 1914 and became Nunes' national distributor. Nunes appears to have gone out of business in 1917, after which all directory listings cease; Southern California Music announced it was no longer Nunes' U.S. representative in November 1917.

Jose do Espirito Santo (1850–1905), fl. 1885–1905

Santo does not appear in the *Honolulu City Directory* until the 1888–1889 edition, but he first advertised his services as a cabinet and guitar maker in 1885. He is the only one of the three original makers who is consistently identified in the city directory as a guitar maker throughout his career. A partner with Dias in 1887 and again in 1896, he otherwise worked alone. He continued to produce instruments until his sudden death in 1905. Santo was the most aggressive marketer of the original makers, advertising in Portuguese and English in Honolulu newspapers and in the city directory.

Naapohou, fl. 1898–1899

Nothing is known about the first Native Hawaiian 'ukulele maker, apart from his brief listing in the 1898–1899 *Honolulu City Directory*: "Naapohou, guitar maker, resides Queen north of Richard."

Jose Vierra, fl. 1900–1901

Vierra makes only a single appearance as a guitar maker: "Jose Vierra, guitar maker, resides west side of Pauoa Valley Road north of Punchbowl" (1900–1901 *Honolulu City Directory*).

Manuel Fernandez, fl. 1903

Like Vierra, Fernandez makes only a single appearance as a guitar maker: "Manuel Fernandez, guitar maker, resides 1417 Canavarro Lane" (*Honolulu City Directory*, 1903–1904).

Leonardo (Leandro) Nunes (1874–1944), fl. 1912–1930

The second son of 'ukulele pioneer Manuel Nunes, Leonardo is listed as working in his father's Honolulu firm from 1908 to 1912, when he moved to Los Angeles and began building his own instruments—the first known mainland 'ukulele maker. George J. Birkel Co. of Los Angeles sold L. Nunes 'ukuleles in 1913 (and possibly earlier); by 1915, his instruments were being distributed nationally in direct competition with his father's instruments (Lyon & Healy carried his 'ukuleles that year). He introduced his Uka Pila and Ki Pila (eight- and ten-string, respectively) models in 1923 and his Radio Tenor model ca. 1925. Leonardo is listed as a 'ukulele or instrument maker in the *Los Angeles City Directory* through 1929. He appears to have been out of the business by 1930.

Nunes Ukulele Company, fl. 1915

In 1915, Julius Nunes, son of Manuel Nunes, is listed as manager of what appears to be a rival 'ukulele company: "Nunes Ukulele Co., Jules Nunes Manager. Manufacturers of Hawaiian String Instruments, 1124 South Beretania, Telephone 4026"

(*Honolulu City Directory,* 1915). The listing disappeared the following year; nothing more is known about this firm.

James N. Anahu, fl. 1910–1922

James Anahu first appeared in the city directory as a cabinetmaker in 1909 and as a guitar maker the following year. In 1912 he was associated with Ernest Kaai in the formation of the Kaai Ukulele Manufacturing Co. The association appears to have been a short one, as Anahu was again listed individually as a maker of stringed instruments from 1913 to 1917. In October 1917, Anahu formed the Anahu Ukulele Co. in partnership with John F. Soper. The company was listed in the city directory from 1918 to 1920 and was formally dissolved in 1926.

Ichiga Sakai, fl. 1911–1912

The 1911 *Honolulu City Directory* lists him as follows: "Ichiga Sakai, guitar maker, 1287 River, resides same."

Jonah Kumalae (1874–1940), fl. 1911–1940

Politician (Democratic member of the Territorial House of Representatives and the Honolulu Board of Supervisors) and poi maker, Kumalae reportedly began to make ʻukuleles as early as 1895 but isn't listed in the city directory as a ʻukulele maker until 1911. He is best known for having won a gold medal for his ʻukuleles at the 1915 Panama-Pacific International Exposition in San Francisco. Kumalae signed with piano salesman H. C. Churchill of San Francisco as his exclusive agent for the United States and Canada; by 1920, his ʻukuleles were distributed by Sherman, Clay of San Francisco, Lyon & Healy in Chicago, Oliver Ditson in Boston, and C. Bruno & Son of New York. Kumalae's Liliha Street factory was destroyed by fire in 1922; despite this setback, he was one of the few early makers who continued production through the Depression. The company shut down on his death in 1940.

Ernest K. Kaai (1881–1962), fl. 1912–1920

Although an advertisement in the 1909 city directory identified Kaai as "Maker of the Best Ukuleles in the World," it wasn't until 1912 when the Kaai Ukulele Manufacturing Company, a partnership between Kaai and James Anahu, was listed. Kaai sold his manufacturing business to the Paradise Ukulele and Guitar Works in 1917 and became a shareholder in the newly formed Aloha Ukulele Manufacturing Co. The Kaai company continued to be listed in the directory until 1920, so it's not clear who the actual maker of Kaai ʻukuleles was after 1917.

João M. Soares, fl. 1913–1923

João Maria Soares, an immigrant from Ponta Delgada, São Miguel, Azores, who arrived in Hawaii in 1895, is the earliest-known ʻukulele maker on the Big Island. Listed as a carpenter in the 1910 federal census, he first appears as a ʻukulele maker in the 1913 city directory. Located in Honokaa, on the coast northwest of Hilo, Soares had a small shop that made ʻukuleles, five-string *rajãoes,* six-string guitars, and "violas pelo systema Michaelense"—Azorean-style guitars, according to a 1917 article in *O Luso.*

Kinney & Mossman, fl. 1914–1918

George Paele Mossman, a former house carpenter, and Clarence W. Kinney, a former mail carrier, first appear as Kinney & Mossman, ukulele makers in the 1914 directory. In the 1917–1918 directory, they are listed as "Expert Makers and Instructors of Ukuleles, Repairing of Guitars, Mandolins and Violins a Specialty, Also Makers of Leis, Calabashes, Canes and Hawaiian Curios." A careful analysis of the listings in the 1917–1918 directory by John King reveals that twenty-four men and women are listed as employees of Kinney & Mossman, as compared to twenty-three at Kumalae, twelve at M. Nunes & Son, and eleven at James Anahu, making Kinney & Mossman one of the largest ʻukulele manufacturers in the Islands. The partnership dissolved ca. 1918.

Jonah P. Davis, fl. 1915

The 1915 *Honolulu City Directory* lists him as follows: "Jonah P. Davis, Cabinet-maker, High-Grade Koa Furniture and Ukuleles Made to Order, Also Calabash Repairing, mauka 809 Richards, resides same."

Ernesto Machado, fl. 1915–1917

"Ernesto Machado, Ukuleles," is listed in the 1915 and 1916–1917 city directories at 680 South Beretania.

Hawaiian Ukulele Company, fl. 1916–1917

This company is listed in the *Honolulu City Directory* in 1916 and 1917: "Hawaiian Ukulele Co., Makers of 'Royal' Ukuleles, Fort at the corner of Kukui, Telephone 3028."

Ukulele Company, Ltd., fl. 1916–1918

This company was incorporated in 1916 by L. M. Fishel, E. J. Botts, John S. Grace, Harry E. Hoffman, and C. H. Hou to make and sell ʻukuleles and other musical instruments and Hawaiian curios and souvenirs. The owners filed for dissolution of the company in 1918. It is not listed in the city directory.

Pahu Ukulele Manufacturing Co., Ltd., fl. 1916

The November 25, 1916, issue of the *Music Trade Review* reported the formation of the Pahu Co. by D. S. K. Pahu, Ernest Kaai, F. L. Hadley, and Allan McGowan with a capitalization of $20,000 to build from five hundred to a thousand ʻukuleles per month. Nothing more is known about this enterprise.

Ross & Kapio, fl. 1917

The 1917 *Honolulu City Directory* has the following listing: "Ross & Kapio (Benjamin Ross, Lot K. Kapio), Makers of Koa Ukuleles, 1282 Nuuanu."

Singers Ukulele Manufacturing Company, fl. 1917

The 1917 *Honolulu City Directory* has the following listing: "Singers Ukulele Manufacturing Co., D. Y. Lee Manager, Manufacturers of Ukuleles, Calabashes, and Walking Canes, 267 North Vineyard, Telephone 4058, P. O. Box 1035."

Lot K. Pelio, fl. 1918

The 1918 *Honolulu City Directory* has the following listing: "Lot K. Pelio, Maker and Repairer of String Instruments, Leis, Canes, Calabashes, and Ukuleles a Specialty, 1282 Nuuanu, resides same."

Samuel [Kamuela] K. Kamaka, fl. 1916–1953

According to his son Samuel Jr., the elder Kamaka began making 'ukuleles ca. 1914 in his basement but didn't launch his business until 1916. The Kamaka Ukulele & Guitar Works doesn't appear in the city directory until 1920, but Kamaka 'ukuleles began to appear in mainland stores as early as 1919. Kamaka managed to stay in production during the Depression but suspended operations during World War II when labor and materials became unavailable. Today, Kamaka is the oldest Hawaiian 'ukulele manufacturer; it and C. F. Martin & Co. are the world's oldest 'ukulele makers.

Paradise Ukulele and Guitar Works, Ltd., fl. 1917–1926

Paradise was incorporated in 1917 with the stated purpose of taking over Ernest Kaai's musical instrument manufacturing business by A. W. Mather, H. A. Bishaw, and A. A. Feiereisel. It was listed in the city directory only in 1917 and dissolved in 1926.

Aloha Ukulele Manufacturing Company, fl. 1917–1935

Aloha was incorporated on October 30, 1917, by Chu Gem, Wong Chow, Wong Chee, Goo Kim Fook, and Lung Mon-Chow with the objective of manufacturing 'ukuleles and other stringed instruments. Ernest Kaai owned 5 percent of the company. It's possible Aloha manufactured 'ukuleles marketed under the Kaai label from 1918 to 1920. Tai Chong Goo, who used the pseudonym Akai, worked for Aloha. After the company was dissolved in 1935, Tai continued to make 'ukuleles under the name of Akai Ukulele and Curio Co.

David W. Kaiwa, fl. 1919–1920

The 1919 *Honolulu City Directory* has the following listing: "D. W. Kaiwa, Ukuleles, 560 South."

P. F. Ungson, fl. 1919–1920

The 1919 *Honolulu City Directory* has the following listing: "P. F. Ungson, Ukuleles, 1345 Liliha."

Clarence W. Kinney, fl. 1919–1922

After dissolving his partnership with George Mossman, Clarence Kinney contin-ued to be listed as a 'ukulele maker in the city directory through 1922.

George P. Mossman, fl. 1919–1930

The bulk of Mossman's production appears to have been sold to Honolulu hotels and music stores. He manufactured the Belltone 'ukulele, a name he copyrighted on January 3, 1928, claiming first use for the name on February 1, 1927. To promote his 'ukuleles, Mossman presented a Belltone to pianist Ignace Jan Paderewski after a 1927 recital in Honolulu. However, it was the puff piece on his new concert Bell-tone ukulele and its purported ability to be heard half a mile away published in the *Advertiser* in January 1928 that got him the most publicity: It was picked up by wire services and resulted in a brief notice in *Time* magazine. After the opening of Lalani Village in Waikiki in 1932, Mossman appears to have devoted most of his time to running his new family-owned and -operated tourist attraction.

Chang Lau Cheong, fl. 1920–1925

The 1922 *Honolulu City Directory* has the following listing: "Chang Lau Cheong, ukulele manufacturer, 2481 Sakura Ave, resides 2466 Maui."

Author's note: Three other early 'ukulele makers not listed in the directory have been identified through their labels:

Heilborn Manufacturing Co.

"Kaai/Ukulele/Heilborn Manufacturing Co./Honolulu, T.H."—'ukulele label.

Enos Kealoha

"Genuine Hawaiian Ukulele / Made By / Enos Kealoha / 552 Hotel St. / Honolulu, Hawaii"—'ukulele label.

Nuuanu Ukulele Company

"Guaranteed / Genuine Koa / Made In / Hawaii / by the / Nuuanu / Ukulele Co. Honolulu"—'ukulele label.

APPENDIX B

Annotated Checklist of Selected 'Ukulele Methods and Songbooks, 1894–1920

When mainland retailers began selling 'ukuleles, it quickly became the custom to offer a self-instructor with each instrument sold (in addition to those stores that provided in-house lessons). As early as July 1912, the Los Angeles music house of George J. Birkel Co. was advertising a "ukulele outfit"—a genuine Hawaiian ukulele, case, instructor, and extra set of strings—for $10. However, which tuning one learned depended on the method or instructor one happened to have. "I have been studying the method of Mr. [Charles] Delano in which the strings are tuned to A, D, F sharp and B," a perplexed Cora L. Butler of Port Richmond, New York, wrote *Cadenza* in October 1916. "A few days ago I bought a method at Carl Fischer's published by Sherman, Clay & Co. of San Francisco . . . and the strings are to be tuned G, C , E, A. A method by William J. Smith sold by John Wanamaker is for the first tuning mentioned. Now, unless something is done at once we are going to have two sets of players unable to play from the same score and no end of trouble." C tuning—the familiar "my dog has fleas"—eventually won out.

1. E. C. Holstein, *Chords of the Taro-Patch Guitar* (Honolulu: Hawaiian News Company, 1894), 16 pp. Chord diagrams only; C tuning. The only known copy is in the Hawaii State Archives.
2. Ernest K. Kaai, *The Ukulele: A Hawaiian Guitar and How to Play It* (Honolulu: Wall, Nichols Company, 1906), 40 pp. Chord diagrams and rudimentary tablature; C tuning. The first real 'ukulele method. Copy in the Hawaiian Mission Children's Society Library, Honolulu.
3. *Ukulele Method* (Honolulu, T.H.: Bergstrom Music Co., n.d. [ca. 1907]), 8 pp. Chord diagrams only; C tuning. Copy in the Paul Weber collection. Although undated, the sheet music listed for sale on the inside back cover (including J. K. Aea's "Honolulu Hula Hula Heigh," 1906) suggest a ca. 1907 publication date for this anonymous pamphlet.

4. T. H. Rollinson, ed., *Method for the Ukulele (Hawaiian Guitar)* (Boston: Oliver Ditson Co., 1909), 16 pp. Standard notation; C tuning. The first method published on the mainland. Rollinson (1844–1928) was a cornet player and prolific composer and arranger for Oliver Ditson Co. of Boston.

5. Mekia Kealakai, *Chords of the Ukulele* (no publisher, place, or date of publication is listed; the copy in the Library of Congress was received July 23, 1909), 13 pp. Calling itself "the only Book of its kind ever been Published," it advocates D tuning and provides chords for eleven major keys and their relative minor keys.

6. Ernest K. Kaai, *The Ukulele: A Hawaiian Guitar and How to Play It,* rev. ed. (Honolulu: Wall, Nichols Company, 1910), 44 pp. Reengraved edition based on the 1906 method.

7. Major [Mekia] Kealakai, *Self Instructor for the Ukulele and Taro-Patch Fiddle* (Los Angeles: Southern California Music Company, 1912–1914), 45 pp. Chord diagrams and standard notation; D tuning for 'ukulele (what became known as "mainland tuning"), C tuning for taro-patch. Kealakai was living in San Francisco in 1913, advertising his ability to furnish Hawaiian music for all occasions, as well as 'ukulele, taro-patch, and guitar lessons. (*San Francisco Chronicle,* March 23, 1913). A subsequent revised edition (ca. 1917) is titled *The Ukulele (Ukulele Banjo) and How to Play Them.*

8. Jos. V. Christy, *Self Instruction Book for the Ukulele or the Banjo-Uke* (San Jose, CA: Ferguson Music House, 1912), 8 pp. C tuning. With banjo-uke in the title, this edition was published ca. 1917 or later, but the copyright date suggests the original title was *Self Instruction Book for the Ukulele.*

9. C. S. Delano, *Instructions for Playing the Ukulele* (Los Angeles, ca. 1913), 2 pp. D tuning, how to read standard notation, pick the strings, stroke technique, triple fingering. In the January 1914 issue of *Cadenza,* Delano advertised his courses for 'ukulele and steel guitar, "every detail explained in full," for the premium price of $12. "I have the only solos for either instrument by note." In a January 1917 *Cadenza* profile of Delano, it was reported that twenty thousand copies of his solos and methods had been sold during the previous year; Delano offered a new, enlarged edition in an advertisement in the same issue.

10. N. B. Bailey, *A Practical Method for Self Instruction on the Ukulele* (San Francisco: Sherman, Clay & Company, 1914), 38 pp. Chord diagrams; C tuning. According to the May 13, 1916, issue of *Music Trade Review,* "A circumstance which aids materially in selling these books is the association of the name Bailey, with 'Old Bill Bailey,' who played the ukulele in the recent popular song. It's not the same man." According to Sherman, Clay advertisements, almost two hundred thousand copies of the Bailey method had been sold by the summer of 1917; by June 1925, sales reportedly topped 2 million. Editions published ca. 1917 and later were titled *A Practical Method for Self*

Instruction on the Ukulele and Banjo Ukulele. Bailey, who is listed in San Francisco city directories as a Sherman, Clay employee from 1913 to 1919, also authored steel guitar and saxophone methods for the firm.

11. Kelvin K. Keech, *A Standard Method and Self-Instructor on the Ukulele* (San Francisco: Keech Studios, 1914), 23 pp. Keech, a pupil of Kaai, advocates D tuning, which he calls the "new way" to tune the 'ukulele. He and his brother Alvin also published a method in England: *The Keech Banjolele . . . and Ukulele Tutor* (London: Keith, Prowse & Co., 1922).

12. George Kia, *Self Instructor for the Ukulele and Taro-Patch Fiddle* (Los Angeles: R. W. Heffelfinger, 1914), 48 pp. Chord diagrams and standard notation; D tuning. Kia notates the fourth string an octave below pitch. The October 9, 1915, issue of the *Music Trade Review* reported that "since the date of its first publication, April 1914, [the Kia method] has sold 4,300 copies." Los Angeles city directories show Kia was living in Los Angeles from 1914 to 1916, his occupation listed as "musician" or "music teacher."

13. George Kia, *Ukulele Solos and Hawaiian Songs with Ukulele Accompaniment* (Los Angeles: R. W. Heffelfinger, n.d. [ca. 1915]), 36 pp. Chord diagrams and standard notation; D tuning. Kia notates the fourth string an octave below pitch. Advertised in the December 1916 *Cadenza.*

14. Frank Littig, *Correspondence Course for the Ukulele.* (Los Angeles, 1915); not seen. Advertised in the April 1915 issue of *Cadenza* as "a correct and comprehensive system . . . fully explaining all styles of solo, ensemble, and accompaniment playing." In the June 1915 issue of *Cadenza,* Littig offered a "complete outfit"—'ukulele, canvas case, and correspondence course—for $5.

15. Frank Littig, *Ukulele Method* (Los Angeles, 1915); not seen. Advertised in the July 1915 issue of *Cadenza;* his June 1916 *Cadenza* advertisement contained an endorsement from Zarh Myron Bickford. Littig's publications were acquired by W. A. Quincke & Co. of Los Angeles in 1918.

16. Will D. Moyer, *National Self Teacher for Hawaiian Ukulele* (Chicago: Chart Music Co., 1915), 16 pp. D tuning. Advertised in the January 1916 issue of *Cadenza.* In the February 1917 issue of *Cadenza,* advertised as "a simple, comprehensive instructor, with well-arranged exercises and melodies."

17. M. Muntz, *Universal Ukulele Instructor* (San Jose, CA: Muntz-Elmer Music Company, 1915), 28 pp. Standard notation; C tuning. Muntz notates the fourth string an octave below pitch. Muntz was secretary of San Jose Chapter No. 1 of the American Guild of Banjoists, Mandolinists, and Guitarists.

18. A. A. Santos and Angeline F. Nunes, *Original Method and Self-Instructor on the Ukulele* (Honolulu: Santos-Nunes Studios, 1915), 23 pp. Standard notation and chord diagrams. The only known 'ukulele method to adopt the original Madeiran machete tuning, D-G-B-D.

19. N. B. Bailey and Keoki Awai, *The Ukulele as a Solo Instrument: A Collection of Ukulele Solos with Full Instructions for Playing* (San Francisco: Sherman,

Clay & Co., 1916), 71 pp. Standard notation, chord diagrams, and Italian-style tablature; C tuning. Also published for 'ukulele in D tuning. The February 12, 1916, issue of the *Music Trade Review* reported that Sherman, Clay's book of ukulele solos "will be along in about a week." George "Keoki" Awai (1891–1981) was one of the Hawaiian musicians who performed at the 1915 Panama-Pacific International Exposition.

20. N. B. Bailey, arr., *Songs from Aloha Land* (San Francisco: Sherman, Clay & Company, 1916), 94 pp. Standard notation and Italian-style tablature; C tuning.

21. Ernest K. Kaai, *The Ukulele and How It's Played* (Honolulu: Hawaiian News Company, 1916), 58 pp. Standard notation and Italian-style tablature; C tuning.

22. Dave Langlands, *Famous Ukulele Solos* (Los Angeles: Southern California Music Company, 1916), no page numbers. Chord diagrams; D tuning. Contains twenty-two solos based on Hawaiian songs using chord diagrams and an inadequately explained, proprietary rhythm notation. Langlands was an employee of the Southern California Music Co.

23. D. Mansfield, *The Bridal School for the Hawaiian Ukulele* (New York: D. Mansfield, 1916); not seen. Mansfield, of 244 West 114th St., New York, advertised four 'ukulele books and six Hawaiian guitar books (no titles are listed) in the September 1916 issue of *Cadenza*.

24. James F. Roach, comp., *Ukulele Instructor* (Cincinnati, OH: Roach-Frankland Music, 1916), 21 pp. Not seen. Advertised in the November 1916 *Cadenza* as featuring selections from *Bird of Paradise*. Roach served as a director of the American Guild of Banjoists, Mandolinists, and Guitarists.

25. William J. Smith, *The New Kamiki Ukulele Method* (New York: William J. Smith & Company, 1916), 63 pp. Standard notation and chord diagrams; D tuning. Smith notates the fourth string an octave below pitch. Smith, formerly with C. H. Ditson, opened his first retail outlet at 56 E. 34th St., New York, in late 1915, specializing in stringed instruments (*Music Trade Review,* December 4, 1915). By the summer of 1919, Smith claimed sales of more than 200,000 (*Music Trade Review,* July 26, 1919).

26. E. N. Guckert, *The Original Guckert's Chords for the Ukulele at Sight Without Notes or Teacher* (Chicago: Lyon & Healy, Inc., 1917), 20 pp. Chord diagrams; C tuning. Guckert was a Toledo, Ohio–based banjoist and former music store owner who at one point worked for the National Music Publishing Co. of Chicago. He published a series of methods, including guitar, banjo, mandolin, and steel guitar.

27. Ernest K. Kaai, *Simplified Chords of All the Major and Minor Keys for the Ukulele, Guitar, Steel Guitar* (Honolulu: Ernest K. Kaai, 1917), 2 pp. C tuning. Includes tonic, subdominant, and dominant chords in all twenty-four major and minor keys; diminished chords.

28. Leon Coleman, *The Ukulele and How To Play It Including Instructions for the Taro Patch Fiddle* (New York: Carl Fischer, 1917); not seen. In the April 1917 issue of *Cadenza,* Coleman was identified as a "prominent teacher and solo-ist of the Pacific Coast, has practically all of his life associated with native Hawaiian soloists." Fischer advertised the Coleman method in the May 1917 issue of *Cadenza*; it was featured in the fall 1917 Sears, Roebuck catalog, and in all subsequent editions through the 1920s.

29. Jennie M. Durkee, *The American Way of Playing Ukulele Solos* (Chicago: Jennie M. Durkee, 1917), 56 pp. Standard notation and Italian-style tabla-ture; D tuning. "The American way of playing . . . consists of using a *thick felt plectrum* in the same manner in which a mandolin plectrum is used." A later edition was published by Lyon & Healy.

30. William J. Smith, ed., *Songs for the Ukulele* (New York: William J. Smith & Co., 1917), 71 pp. Standard notation and chord diagrams for "38 of the best songs ever written"; D tuning. Smith notates the fourth string an octave below pitch.

31. Myrtle Stumpf, *Stumpf's Ukulele-Method and Solo Book* (Los Angeles: Southern California Music Co., 1917), 66 pp. Standard notation; D tuning. Stumpf notates the fourth string an octave below pitch. A Los Angeles music teacher, Stumpf (ca. 1880–1919) was a pupil of Joseph Kekuku and com-piled what may be the first published steel guitar method, *Original Hawaiian Method for the Steel Guitar* (Southern California Music Co., 1915).

32. *Self Instructive Course of Twenty-Five Lessons for the Ukulele and Taro-Patch Fiddle*. Not seen. Described in the fall 1917 Sears, Roebuck catalog thus: "Combines the notation and diagram system, so simply arranged that the student can learn to play accompaniments in two or three lessons. Contains many beautiful selections, including many Hawaiian airs and several splen-did solos."

33. Henry A. Peelua Bishaw, *The Albert Ukulele Hawaiian Guitar Complete Instructions* (Sydney: J. Albert & Son, 1919), 50 pp. Chord diagrams, stan-dard notation, and some Italian-style tablature; C tuning. Believed to be the first Australian 'ukulele method. Bishaw was a member of the first troupe of Hawaiian musicians to tour Australia and New Zealand in 1911, under the leadership of Ernest Kaai.

34. William C. Hodges, ed., *California-Hawaiian Souvenir Collection of Songs and Views* (Los Angeles: William C. Hodges, 1919), 56 pp. Includes eight Ernest Kaai arrangements. Standard notation, with two-page "Kaai's Simpli-fied Chords" tablature for ukulele, guitar, and steel guitar. An abbreviated 32-page edition was published for S. H. Kress & Co.

35. H. Kahanamo, *Modern Method for the Ukulele* (St. Paul, MN: W. J. Dyer & Bro., 1919), 43 pp. Standard notation; D tuning. Kahanamo notates the fourth string an octave below pitch.

36. Will D. Moyer, *Moyer's Up-to-Date Collection of Solos for the Ukulele* (Chicago: Chart Music Publishing House, 1919), 34 pp. Standard notation; D tuning. Moyer notates the fourth string an octave below pitch. Moyer "is well qualified to edit a book of solos for this popular instrument, having been a teacher of stringed instruments for 25 years and an expert performer on all of them. . . . Two forms of playing are treated in this book—the finger or guitar and banjo style, and the plectrum or mandolin style" (advertisement, *Cadenza,* March 1919).

37. Vadah Olcott Bickford and Zarh Myron Bickford, *Bickford Method for the Ukulele* (Boston: Oliver Ditson Co., 1920), 74 pp. Standard notation; D tuning. The Bickfords notate the fourth string an octave below pitch. Olcott Bickford was a preeminent American guitarist of the early twentieth century.

NOTES

Chapter 1: These Little Instruments, of Which They Are So Fond

1. Helen H. Roberts, *Ancient Hawaiian Music,* Bulletin No. 29 (Honolulu: Bernice P. Bishop Museum, 1926); George H. Kanahele, ed., *Hawaiian Music and Musicians: An Illustrated History* (Honolulu: University Press of Hawaii, 1979) 334–335; Charlotte J. Frisbie, "Helen Heffron Roberts (1888–1985): A Tribute," *Ethnomusicology* 33 (winter 1989), 99–100; Lorin Tarr Gill, "Portuguese Were First to Introduce Ukulele in Hawaii Says Miss Roberts," *Honolulu Advertiser Magazine,* August 10, 1924, 3. Roberts, a classically trained pianist, thought modern Hawaiian music "banal." Accounts of the ʻukuleleʼs Portuguese origin appeared sporadically, beginning as early as the 1880s. See Augustus Marques, "Music in Hawaii Nei," *Hawaiian Almanac and Annual* (Honolulu: Thos. G. Thrum, 1886) 58; *Paradise of the Pacific,* February 1906, 11; *Pacific Commercial Advertiser,* December 29, 1909, 11; Nathaniel Emerson, *Unwritten Literature of Hawaii: The Sacred Songs of the Hula* (Washington, D.C.: Government Printing Office, 1909), 251; "How the Ukulele Came to Hawaii," *Paradise of the Pacific,* January 1922, 8–10.

2. "Luck Eludes Song Writer," *New York Times,* September 7, 1924, 20:2. In 1923, ʻukuleles could be had for as little as $1.54 at Macy's in New York and for $1.90 at Platt Music Co. in Los Angeles (see *New York Times,* June 8, 1923, 17; *Los Angeles Times,* October 11, 1923, 15.)

3. "Say It with a Ukulele" was released by Columbia in February 1924 per advertisement, *Los Angeles Times,* January 27, 1924, G4. Marvin had his first solo recording session, accompanying himself on the ʻukulele, in June 1924. Michael Pitts and Frank Hoffman, *The Rise of the Crooners* (Lanham, MD: Scarecrow Press, 2002), 161.

4. "Adele Astaire Fascinates," *New York Times,* December 2, 1924, 23; Fred Astaire, *Steps in Time* (New York: Harper and Brothers, 1959), 126–128.

5. Arnold Shaw, *The Jazz Age: Popular Music in the 1920s* (New York: Oxford University Press, 1987), 136; "Ukelele Craze Breaks Out Anew in Waterbury Due to New Germ," *Bridgeport* (CT) *Telegram,* September 20, 1924. Chicago's Regal Musical Instrument Co. showed its Red-Head Ukulele at the October 1924 Illinois Product Exposition. "Seven Manufacturers to Exhibit at Exposition," *Music Trade Review* (September 27, 1924): 49. Hall's song was even the choice of a brave young woman who played her ʻukulele and sang to keep up the spirits of passengers on an ocean liner that caught fire in a fierce storm off the coast of Delaware in 1925. "Liner, Afire in Gale at Sea, Races to Shore Saving 200 Passengers," *Hartford Courant,* January 3, 1925, 1.

6. John Hutchens, "'The Bird of Paradise' on an Eighteen Year Front," *New York Times,* April 6, 1930, 120. The American Film Institute's Catalog of Motion Pictures lists forty-one films with South

Seas settings produced between 1914 (*McVeagh of the South Seas*) and 1924 (*Venus of the South Seas*). Pickford appeared in *Hearts Adrift* (1914); Power in *Lorelei of the Sea* (1917); and Karloff in *The Infidel* (1922).

7. "Prince of Wales a Good Drummer," *New York Times,* August 16, 1924, 11.

8. Manuel Morais, "Os instrumentos populares de corda dedilhada Madeira," in Morais, ed., *A Madeira e a Música: Estudos c. 1508-1974* (Funchal: Empresa Municipal "Funchal 500 Anos," 2008), 62.

9. William Shaw, *Golden Dreams and Waking Realities: Being the Adventures of a Gold-Seeker in California and the Pacific Islands* (London: Smith, Elder and Co., 1851), 249.

10. Francisco Alcafarado, *An Historical Relation of the First Discovery of the Isle of Madera* (London: William Cademan, 1675), 21.

11. Fernando Augusto da Silva and Carlos Acevedo de Menezes, *Elucidario Madeirense* (Funchal: Tipografia "Esperança," 1921) 1:432, 436.

12. T. Bentley Duncan, *Atlantic Islands: Madeira, the Azores and the Cape Verdes in Seventeenth-Century Commerce and Navigation* (Chicago: University of Chicago Press, 1972), 9–11; Alberto Vieira, "Sugar Islands: The Sugar Economy of Madeira and the Canaries, 1450-1650," in Stuart B. Schwartz, ed., *Tropical Babylons: Sugar and the Making of the Atlantic World, 1450-1680* (Chapel Hill, NC: University of North Carolina Press, 2004), 64–67. By 1681, Funchal was Portugal's third busiest port, after Lisbon and Oporto.

13. Hugh Thomas, *The Slave Trade: Story of the Atlantic Slave Trade 1440-1870* (New York: Simon and Schuster, 1997), 70–71; Robin Blackburn, *The Making of New World Slavery: From the Baroque to the Modern, 1492-1800* (London: Verso, 1997), 108–112. As David Hancock's research has shown, slaves continued to be bought and sold in Funchal throughout the eighteenth century, until slavery was abolished in Portugal in 1773. David Hancock, *Oceans of Wine: Madeira and the Emergence of American Trade and Taste* (New Haven: Yale University Press, 2009), 11–12.

14. *Elucidario Madeirense,* 2:552–553; Duncan, *Atlantic Islands,* 31–37; Hancock, *Oceans of Wine,* 19–20.

15. "The Madeira Wine has in it this peculiar excellence, of being meliorated by the heat of the Sun," seventeenth-century visitor John Ovington observed. *A Voyage to Surat in the Year 1689,* ed. H. G. Rawlinson (London: Oxford University Press, 1929), 12. See also John Barrow, *A Voyage to Cochinchina in the Years 1792 and 1793* (London: T. Caddell and W. Davies, 1806), 7; Duncan, *Atlantic Islands,* 38; and Hancock, *Oceans of Wine,* 89–92.

16. *The Writings of George Washington,* ed. John C. Fitzpatrick (Washington, D.C.: U.S. Government Printing Office, 1931), 2:481; *The Papers of Thomas Jefferson,* ed. Julian P. Boyd (Princeton: Princeton University Press, 1954), 9:274; *The Papers of Alexander Hamilton,* ed. Harold C. Syrett (New York: Columbia University Press, 1963), 7:444; *The Works of John Adams,* ed. Charles Francis Adams (Boston: Little, Brown and Co., 1853) 8:127.

17. Desmond Gregory, *The Beneficient Usurpers: A History of the British in Madeira* (Rutherford, NJ: Farleigh Dickinson University Press, 1988), 18, 26; Alan K. Manchester, *British Preeminence in Brazil, Its Rise and Decline: A Study in European Expansion* (Chapel Hill, NC: University of North Carolina Press, 1933), 1–39.

18. Manchester, *British Preeminence,* 39.

19. Robert White, *Madeira, Its Climate and Scenery* (London: Cradock & Co., 1851), 106–107, 185; Isabella de França, *Journal of a Visit to Madeira and Portugal (1853-1854)* (Funchal: Junta Geral do Distrito Autónomo do Funchal, 1969), 543; Duncan, *Atlantic Islands,* 265–266; Hancock, *Oceans of Wine,* 16–19.

20. William H. Koebel, quoted in Gregory, *Beneficient Usurpers,* 15.

21. Henry Nelson Coleridge, *Six Months in the West Indies in 1825* (London: John Murray, 1825), 14–16.

22. In addition to White's handbook, on the market at various times were Cooper's *The Invalid's Guide to Madeira* (London: Smith, Elder & Co., 1840); Vernon's *A Sketch of Madeira, Containing Information for the Traveller, or Invalid Visitor* (London: John Murray, 1851); and *Colloquial Portuguese*

. . . *for the Use of English Visitors in Madeira* (Funchal: Typographia da Ordem, 1854). The earliest guidebook, *A Guide to Madeira . . . with Instructions to Such as Repair to That Island for Health,* was published in London in 1801 by T.N. Longman and O. Rees.

23. de França, *Journal,* 46–47.

24. Rev. John Overton Choules, *The Cruise of the Steam Yacht North Star* (Boston: Gould and Lincoln, 1854), 330.

25. S. G. W. Benjamin, *The Atlantic Islands as Resorts of Health and Pleasure* (New York: Harper and Brothers, 1878), 101–102.

26. As historian Castelo Branco Chaves has noted, visiting foreigners came with preconceived ideas: "They built up a picture of the two nations [Spain and Portugal] that they were superstitious, fanatical, backward, barbarous, and ridiculously ignorant." Chaves, *Os livros de viagem em Portugal no Século XVIII e sua projecção europeia* (Lisbon: Instituto de Cultura e Lingua Portuguesa/Ministério da Educação, 1987), Biblioteca Breve 15 (2nd ed.), 11–12, cited in Manuel Morais, ed., *Collecção de Peças para Machete por Cândido Drumond de Vasconcelos* (Casal de Cambra: Caleidoscópio, 2003), 72.

27. *The Resolution Journal of Johann Reinhold Forster 1772–1775,* ed. Michael E. Hoare (London: The Hakluyt Society, 1982), 144–145. Forster was the son of George Forster, Cook's naturalist.

28. Fanney Anne Burney, *A Great-Niece's Journals,* ed. Margaret S. Rolt (Boston: Houghton Mifflin, 1926), 282–283. In 1768, Joseph Banks, a naturalist on Cook's first voyage, repeated a story reportedly told by the late governor of Madeira: "It was very fortunate, said he, that this island was not Eden, in which Adam and Eve dwelt before the Fall, for had it been so the inhabitants would have never been induc'd to put on Cloaths; So much are they resolved in every particular to follow the paths of their forefathers." *The Endeavour Journal of Joseph Banks 1768–1771,* ed. J. C. Beaglehole (Sydney: Angus and Robertson, 1962), 2:162.

29. White and Johnson, *Madeira,* 1860, 123; Francis M. Rogers, *Atlantic Islanders of the Azores and Madeira* (North Quincy, MA: Christopher Publishing House, 1979), 345.

30. Ovington, *A Voyage to Surat,* 16. Isabella de França found it difficult to sleep during her first night in the city because a loud chorus of dogs, cats, roosters, frogs, and "occasionally a peasant who had remained late in town could be heard singing, or rather bellowing as he passed on his way home. It is a matter of astonishment to me, how the invalids bear this." *Journals,* 53.

31. Maria R[iddell], *Voyages to the Madeira and Leeward Caribbean Isles* (Salem, MA: N. Coverly, 1802), 10–15. See also N. C. Pitta, M.D., *Account of the Island of Madeira* (London: Printed for Longman, Hurst, Rees, Orme & Brown, and for John Anderson, Edinburgh, 1812), 87–88; William Combe, *A History of Madeira, with a Series of Twenty-Seven Colored Engravings, Illustrative of the Costumes, Manners, and Occupations of the Inhabitants of that Island* (London: Ackermann, 1821), 77; and John Driver, *Letters from Madeira in 1834* (London: Longman & Co., 1838), 9.

32. White, *Madeira: Its Climate and Scenery,* 38. According to White, these were the instruments "in common use." The six-string Spanish guitar first appeared in Europe in the late eighteenth century, and was probably introduced to mainland Portugal by the occupying French during the Peninsular War (1808–1814), hence the name, *viola Francesa* (French guitar). The term viola can be traced to the early Renaissance when certain stringed instruments were known collectively as *vihuelas,* and differentiated according to the manner in which the strings were vibrated: bowed (*de arco*), plucked with a plectrum (*da penhola*) or played with the fingers (*da mano*). The Portuguese viola, or guitar, belongs to the third group of instruments. In 1789, Manoel da Paixao Ribeiro published a method entitled *Nova Arte de Viola* for the five-course, fifteen-string viola. The so-called *guitarra* was not a true guitar, but a cittern: an instrument with a pear-shaped body and six courses of brass and steel strings tuned to an open C chord. The English brought the instrument to Portugal in the eighteenth century, where it became known as the *guitarra Portuguesa.* A good deal of printed music from eighteenth-century England and Portugal exists for the guitarra, including Antonio da Silva Leite's method, *Estudo de Guitarra* (Porto, 1796). In the 1700s the English called the instrument guittar; it's unclear if Forster had seen citterns or violas in Madeira. For a detailed analysis of these issues, see Morais, *Peças para Machete,* 78–84, 93–100.

33. White, *Madeira: Its Climate and Scenery,* 38.

34. João Cabral do Nascimento suggests that the machete was "probably brought to Madeira by Portuguese settlers from Minho" (de França, *Journal,* 77), an opinion with which Ernesto Veiga de Oliveira, author of *Instrumentos Musicais Populares Portugueses* (Lisbon: Fundação Calouste Gulbenkian, 1966) seems sympathetic. See Jose Fernandes' English translation of de Oliveira's chapter on the *cavaquinho* at http://cavaquinho-minhoto.blogspot.com. After his visit to the island in 1843, John Dix stated flatly that the machete was "an invention of the island." John A. Dix, *A Winter in Madeira; and a Summer in Spain and Florence,* 2nd ed. (New York: William Holdredge, 1851), 71. For a modern account of the origins of Madeiran settlers, see David Higgs, "Portuguese Migration Before 1800," in Higgs, ed., *Portuguese Migration in Global Perspective* (Toronto: Multicultural History Society of Ontario, 1990), 9.

35. Raphael Bluteau, *Vocabulario Portuguez e Latino,* Tome 5 (Coimbra: Collegio das Artes da Companhia de Jesus, 1716), 134, cited in Morais, *Peças para Machete,* 18, 80.

36. Alberto Vieira Braga, "Curiosidades de Guimarães," *Revista de Guimarães* 58 (1948), 57–58, cited in Morais, *Peças para machete,* 80.

37. Anthony Baines, *European and American Musical Instruments* (New York: Viking Press, 1966), 49; Anthony Baines, *Victoria and Albert Museum: Catalogue of Musical Instruments* (London: Her Majesty's Stationery Office, 1968) 2:55; and James Tyler, *The Early Guitar* (London: Oxford University Press, 1980), 30. The Renaissance guitar also is the ancient predecessor of the modern six-string guitar. While the *cavaquinho* is often regarded as synonymous with the machete, nineteenth-century sources suggest this was not always so. Isabella de França called the *cavaquinho* she heard in Madeira "a machete with six strings, instead of four, peculiar to Oporto" (de França, *Journal,* 183). An early reference to the *cavaquinho* in Brazil, where it was introduced by Portuguese emigrants, also suggests it had six strings: "Joaquim Manuel, mulâtre de Rio-Janeiro, doué d'un rare talent pour la musique, renommé surtout pour jouer parfaitment d'une petite viole française de son invention, apelée *cavaquinho*" (Joaquim Manuel, a mulatto from Rio de Janeiro, possesses a rare talent for music, and is renowned for his perfect execution upon a little French guitar of his own invention, called the *cavaquinho*). Adrien Balbi, *Essai statistique sur le Royaume de Portugal et d'Algarve* (Paris: Rey & Gravier, 1822), 2:ccxiii. See also de Oliveira, *Instrumentos Populares,* fig. 194.

38. It's impossible to know specifically what kind of instruments are referred to in the earliest references to violas and *guitarras* found in Gaspar Fructoso's *As Saudades Da Terra* (ca. 1584, but not published until 1873) and in the *Relaçam geral das festas qve fez a religiaõ da companhia de Iesus na Provincia de Portugal* (Lisbon, 1623). Morais, "Os Instrumentos," 23–29.

39. Forster, *A Voyage Round the World, in His Britannic Majesty's Sloop Resolution . . .* (London: Printed for B. White, J. Robson, P. Elmsly, and G. Robinson, 1777), 1:19.

40. Burney, *Great-Niece's Journals,* 291.

41. de França, *Journal,* 42; Benjamin, *Atlantic Islands,* 110; Burney, *Great-Niece's Journals,* 291–292.

42. Dix, *A Winter in Madeira,* 71–73.

43. Ute York, ed., *Insight Guides Madeira* (Singapore: APA Publications, 1992), 92.

44. W. R. Wilde, *Narrative of a Voyage to Madeira, Teneriffe, and along the Shores of the Mediterranean* (Dublin: William Curry, Jr. & Co., 1840), 93–95. William Wilde was the father of Oscar Wilde.

45. Lady Emmeline Stuart Wortley, *A Visit to Portugal and Madeira* (London: Chapman and Hall, 1854), 233. Duties on pianos in 1834 ranged from $42 for a square piano to $150 for a grand piano. Driver, *Letters from Madeira,* appendix, ii.

46. de França, *Journal,* 183.

47. Dix, *Winter in Madeira,* 72–73.

48. Ibid., 71–73.

49. *O Defensor,* No. 102, 1841, cited in Carlos M. Santos, *Tocares e cantares da ilha: Estudo do foclore da Madeira* (Funchal: Empreza Madeirense Editora Lda., 1937), 43; Morais, *Colecção de*

peças, 101. Drumond came from a musical family; his brother, Padre Antonio Francisco Drumond de Vasconcelos, wrote several small sacred works. Performances of some of Drumond's works by Manuel Morais' Quinteto Drumond Vasconcellos can be found on YouTube.

50. Sir Richard Francis Burton, *Wanderings in West Africa from Liverpool to Fernando Po* (London: Tinsley Brothers, 1863), 1:54.

51. White and Johnson, *Madeira,* 45. For Manuel Joaquim Monteiro Cabral's *Estudos para machete,* see John King, "Um método desconhecido para o machete Madeirense," in Morais, ed., *A Madeira,* 589–608. It was Cabral who arranged the machete and guitar duets of Candido Drumond de Vasconcelos for the use of his student Joanna Mathilde Beda de Freitas in 1846 (Morais, *Colecção de peças,* 75). Santos also mentions Antonio Jose Barbosa (fl. ca. 1870), a teacher, singer, and composer who also wrote a method, "Principios para machete." Barbosa's manuscript—its current location unknown—contained thirty-three pages of music for popular dances, with Portuguese and English titles and exercises, scales, and a diagram of the machete's fingerboard. Santos' descriptions of Barbosa's exercises, particularly the titles, are not only identical to those found in Cabral's *Estudos* but occur in the same order. See Santos, *Tocares e cantares,* 35–36.

52. Rev. Alexander J. D. D'Orsey, *Colloquial Portuguese; or, the Words and Phrases of Every-Day Life* (London: Trubner & Co., 1860), 93.

53. *Lewis Carroll's Alice: The Photographs, Books, Papers and Personal Effects of Alice Liddell and Her Family* (London: Sotheby's, 2001), Lot 39; Roger Taylor and Edward Wakeling, *Lewis Carroll Photographer: The Princeton University Library Albums* (Princeton: Princeton University Press, 2002), 247.

54. Albert A. Stanley, *Catalogue of the Stearns Collection of Musical Instruments* (Ann Arbor, MI: University of Michigan, 1918), 154, 157, 158, 160, 211.

55. Charles R. Beazley and Edgar Prestage, trans., *The Chronicle of the Discovery and Conquest of Guinea, Written by Gomes Eannes de Azurama* (New York: Burt Franklin, n.d.), 1:9.

56. Combe, *History of Madeira,* 87.

57. Beaglehole, *Endeavour Journal,* 1:160–161.

58. Driver, *Letters from Madeira,* 72.

59. Ellen M. Taylor, *Madeira: Its Scenery, and How to See It* (London: Edward Standford, 1889), 77. See also Burney, *Great-Niece's Journal,* 271, and de França, *Journal,* 64.

60. Charles Thomas-Stanford, *Leaves from a Madeira Garden* (London: John Lane, 1910), 197. In *Madeira & Porto Santo* (London: Cadogan Guides, 1999, 53), Rodney Bolt notes that "the island was once renowned for its furniture makers."

61. For Octaviano and João Nunes, see Carlos M. Santos, *Trovas e bailados da ilha: Estudo do foclore musical da Madeira* (Funchal: Ediçao da Delegação de Turismo da Madeira, 1939), 15–22, and Rene Vannes, *Dictionnaire universal des luthiers* (Brussels: Les Amis de la Musique, 1972), 1:279; for Augusto da Costa and Antonio Quintal, see Vannes, *Dictionnaire universal,* 1:68, 290. See also Morais, "Os instrumentos," 84, 94–95.

62. Forster, *Voyage,* 1:19; Benjamin, *Atlantic Islands,* 110.

63. *History of Madeira* (1821), 46; for the increase in sales prices, see Hancock, *Oceans of Wine,* 70–72.

64. Gregory, *Beneficent Usurpers,* 38; Dix, *Winter in Madeira,* 104.

65. Gregory, *Beneficent Usurpers,* 50, 69–76; Charles E. Nowell, *A History of Portugal* (New York: D. Van Nostrand Co., 1952), 194–200; H. V. Livermore, *A History of Portugal* (Cambridge: Cambridge University Press, 1947), 424.

66. Duncan, *Atlantic Islands,* 25, 61–72; Rui Nepomuceno, *As crises de subsistência na historia da Madeira: Ensaio histórico* (Lisbon: Caminho, 1994), 13–14, 90–92. Wealthy landlords in continental Portugal also favored cash crops. See Carl A. Hanson, *Economy and Society in Baroque Portugal* (Minneapolis, MN: University of Minnesota Press, 1981), 187, 202.

67. J. Willett Spalding, *The Japan Expedition: Japan and Around the World . . .* (New York: Redfield, 1855), 17.

68. de França, *Journal*, 196–197.

69. Mary Noel Menezes, *The Portuguese of Guyana: A Study in Culture and Conflict* (n.p., 1993), 13; Jo-Anne Ferreira, *The Portuguese of Trinidad and Tobago* (St. Augustine: Institute of Social and Economic Research, University of the West Indies, 1994), 10.

70. Quoted in Menezes, *Portuguese of Guyana*, 22.

71. Alberto Vieira, "Emigration from the Portuguese Islands in the Second Half of the Nineteenth Century: The Case of Madeira," in Higgs, ed., *Portuguese Migration*, 53.

72. *Elucidario Madeirense*, 1:412–414; Nepomuceno, *As Crises*, 98–100; Gregory, *Beneficent Usurpers*, 106.

73. *Elucidario Madeirense*, 1:346; Vieira, "Emigration," 51; Jo-Anne Ferreira, "Madeiran Portuguese Migration to Guyana, St. Vincent, Antigua and Trinidad: A Comparative Overview," *Portuguese Studies Review* 14 (2006/7), 66.

74. Gregory, *Beneficent Usurpers*, 96; White and Johnson, *Madeira*, 74, 321. Another estimate placed the number at 35,000: Edward William Harcourt, *A Sketch of Madeira: Containing Information for the Traveller, or Invalid Visitor* (London: John Murray, 1851), 55.

75. Henry Dalton, *The History of British Guiana* (London: Longman, Brown, Green and Longmans, 1855), 1:457.

76. Santos, *Tocares e cantares*, 42; Rudyard Kipling, *Something of Myself for My Friends Known and Unknown* (Garden City, NY: Doubleday, Doran & Co., 1937), 139; Kipling, "Captains Courageous," *McClure's Magazine* 8 (January 1897), 222–225. In Kipling's novella, Manuel, a fisherman who proudly proclaims himself to be "a Madeira man," pulls out "a tiny guitar-like thing with wire strings, which he called a *machette*."

77. Quoted in Gregory, *Beneficent Usurpers*, 106.

78. *Elucidario Madeirense*, 2:108; White and Johnson, *Madeira*, 77; Choules, *North Star*, 342.

79. Gregory, *Beneficent Usurpers*, 41; *Elucidario Madeirense*, 1:254–255; Charles W. March, *Sketches and Adventures in Madeira, Portugal, and the Andalusias of Spain* (New York: Harper and Brothers, 1856), 54.

80. *Elucidario Madeirense*, 1:409–410; Gregory, *Beneficent Usurpers*, 41; Ferreira, *Portuguese of Trinidad*, 18. A Madeiran pipe held 110 gallons. Hancock, *Oceans of Wine*, 20.

81. D. K., "Days Ashore at Madeira," *New York Times*, May 13, 1883, 4.

82. A. Drexel Biddle, *The Land of Wine, Being an Account of the Madeira Islands at the Beginning of the Twentieth Century, and from a New Point of View* (Philadelphia: Drexel Biddle, 1901), 2:108.

83. de França, *Journal*, 190. *Demerarista* remained the term for prosperous returned emigrants for generations afterwards. See Johnson, *Madeira*, 54.

Chapter 2: The Sound of Pa, Ko, Li

1. Frank Vincent Jr., *Through and Through the Tropics: Thirty Thousand Miles of Travel in Oceania, Australasia, and India* (New York: Harper and Brothers, 1876), 53–54. (An houri is a voluptuous, alluring woman; sangaree is a sweet drink of wine and nutmeg.) Forty years earlier, one American visitor marveled, "Could I have forgotten the circumstances of my visit, I should have fancied myself in New England." Samuel Eliot Morison, *The Maritime History of Massachusetts 1783–1860* (Boston: Houghton Mifflin, 1921), 264. A century later, as Charles K. L. Davis, the Julliard-trained opera singer from Hawaii, toured the mainland (1950–1976), he never failed to be astonished at the ignorance of his mainland audiences. "It's crazy.... They think we still live in grass skirts and thatched homes." Burl Burlingame and Robert Kamohalu Kasher, *Da Kine Sound: Conversations with the People Who Create Hawaiian Music*, vol. 1 (Kailua, HI: Press Pacifica, 1978), 89.

2. In his 1860 defense of the missionaries published in the *New York Tribune*, Richard Henry Dana called the Hawaiians "a nation of half naked savages, living in the surf and on the sand, eating raw fish . . . and abandoned to sensuality." Walter F. Frear, *Anti-Missionary Criticism with Reference to Hawaii* (Honolulu: privately printed, 1935), 36.

3. A. Grove Day, ed., *Mark Twain's Letters from Hawaii* (London: Chatto & Windus, 1967), 26.

4. J. C. Levenson, *The Letters of Henry Adams,* vol. 3: *1886–1892* (Cambridge, MA: Belknap Press, 1982), 271–273.

5. Joseph Tracy, *History of American Missions to the Heathen, From Their Commencement to the Present Time* (Worcester, MA: Spooner & Howland, 1840), 79–80, 88–94; Ralph S. Kuykendall, *The Hawaiian Kingdom 1778–1854: Foundation and Transformation* (Honolulu: University of Hawaii Press, 1947), 100–103. The ABCFM was organized in 1810 and did not dispatch its first missionaries (to India) until 1812.

6. Sheldon Dibble, *History and General Views of the Sandwich Islands' Mission* (New York: Taylor & Dodd, 1839), 45. For the image of the South Seas as paradise, see Charles W. J. Withers, "Geography, Enlightenment, and the Paradise Question," in David N. Livingstone and Withers, eds., *Geography and Enlightenment* (Chicago: University of Chicago Press, 1999), 82–84.

7. Karen Ordahl Kupperman, "Fear of Hot Climates in the Anglo-American Colonial Experience," *William and Mary Quarterly* 41 (April 1984), 213–240; Marvin Harris, *The Rise of Anthropological Theory: A History of the Theories of Culture* (New York: Thomas Y. Crowell Co., 1968), 41–42. For the application of this theory in the tropics, see Peter Hulme, "Dominica and Tahiti: Tropical Islands Compared," in Felix Driver and Luciana Martins, eds., *Tropical Visions in an Age of Empire* (Chicago: University of Chicago Press, 2005), 81, 85–86.

8. Hiram Bingham, *A Residence of Twenty-One Years in the Sandwich Islands . . . ,* 3rd ed. (Canandaigua, NY: H.D. Goodwin, 1855), 81.

9. Morison, *Maritime History of Massachusetts,* 264.

10. Kuykendall, *Hawaiian Kingdom,* 1: 84–89.

11. Lance E. Davis, et al., *In Pursuit of Leviathan: Technology, Institutions, Productivity and Profits in American Whaling, 1816–1906* (Chicago: University of Chicago Press, 1997), 19, 39; Kuykendall, *Hawaiian Kingdom,* 1: 93; Charles de Varigny, *Fourteen Years in the Sandwich Islands 1855–1868* (Honolulu: University Press of Hawaii, 1981), 66.

12. Kuykendall, *Hawaiian Kingdom,* 1: 122–123, 161–163; Gavan Daws, *Honolulu: The First Century, The Story of the Town to 1876* (Honolulu: University of Hawaii Press, 2006), 63–66.

13. Charles Roberts Anderson, *Melville in the South Seas* (New York: Columbia University Press, 1939), 121, 130–134.

14. "Kalakaua's Birthday," *New York Times,* December 31, 1874, 5.

15. Dane, *Twain Letters,* 104.

16. Kuykendall, *Hawaiian Kingdom,* 3: 86. One visitor in 1881 found American, English, French, Italian, Russian, Belgian, Mexican, Chilean, and Peruvian coinage in circulation in Honolulu. L. Vernon Briggs, *Experiences of a Medical Student in Honolulu, and on the Island of Oahu 1881* (Boston: David D. Nickerson Co., 1926), 8.

17. Helen Geracimos Chapin, *Shaping History: The Role of Newspapers in Hawaii* (Honolulu: University of Hawaii Press, 1996), 57.

18. Mark Twain, *Roughing It* (Berkeley: University of California Press, 1995), 462, 465. Similarly, Charles Nordhoff called Hawaii a "toy kingdom." Nordhoff, *Northern California, Oregon, and the Sandwich Islands* (New York: Harper & Brothers, 1874), 75. The *New York Tribune* referred to it as "the monkey show of a preposterous monarchy." *New York Tribune,* November 14, 1893, cited in Ellis Paxson Oberholtzer, *A History of the United States Since the Civil War,* vol. 5: *1884–1901* (New York: Macmillan Co., 1937), 337. And John W. Foster called it "the merest mimicry of a monarchy." John W. Foster, *American Diplomacy in the Orient* (Boston: Houghton Mifflin & Co., 1904), 375.

19. Kuykendall, *Hawaiian Kingdom,* 1: 165–166, 206–225.

20. Neither Catholic, Anglican, or Mormon musical practices appear to have been as influential as those of the New England missionaries. Amy K. Stillman, "Beyond Bibliography: Interpreting Hawaiian Language Protestant Hymn Imprints," *Ethnomusicology* 40 (fall 1996): 470.

21. Bingham, *Twenty-One Years,* 124–125. Chester Lyman, himself an ordained minister, found the missionaries' insistence on bonnets ridiculous. "In their native headdresses of full curling hair

bound by a cincture of ribbon or a wreath of flowers they look free & in good taste, but an old fashioned, rumpled, dirty cast-off bonnet . . . on top of the heads transforms them at once into hags." Chester S. Lyman, *Around the Horn to the Sandwich Islands and California 1845–1850* (New Haven, CT: Yale University Press, 1924), 115.

22. Quoted in Kanahele, *Hawaiian Music,* 130. Compare this to the complaint of a New England minister in 1721 about the singing of his congregation: "The tunes are now miserably tortured, and twisted, and quavered . . . into a horrid medly of confused and disorderly noises." Cited in H. Wiley Hitchcock, *Music in the United States: A Historical Introduction,* 2nd ed. (Englewood Cliffs, NJ: Prentice Hall, 1974), 5.

23. Mary Dillingham Freer, *Lowell and Abigail: A Realistic Idyll* (New Haven, CT: privately printed, 1934), 102–103. Not all foreigners found traditional Hawaiian singing awful. Richard Henry Dana described "listening to the musical notes" of a Hawaiian named Mahanna as his crew heaved at a windlass on a merchant ship off San Diego in 1835. "This fellow had a peculiar, wild sort of note, breaking occasionally into falsetto . . . to me it had great charm." Richard Henry Dana, Jr., *Two Years Before the Mast: A Personal Narrative* (Boston: Houghton Mifflin Co., 1912), 152–153. Charles Nordhoff also had a kind word, saying *mele* "have a singular fascination for my ears." Nordhoff, *Northern California,* 87.

24. Bingham, *Twenty-One Years,* 129. To Hawaiians, "the perfection of enjoyment is . . . filthy songs," the Reverend Sheldon Dibble shuddered. Dibble, *History,* 53.

25. Quoted in Elizabeth Buck, *Paradise Remade: The Politics of Culture and History in Hawaii* (Philadelphia: Temple University Press, 1993), 109. As Amy K. Stillman has observed, "The mele is the foundation of all performance." Amy Kuuleialoha Stillman, "Access and Control: A Key to Reclaiming the Right to Construct Hawaiian History," in Andrew N. Weintraub and Bell Yung, eds., *Music and Cultural Rights* (Chicago: University of Illinois Press, 2009), 91.

26. C. S. Stewart relied not only on his own observations but "the communications of others, necessarily to associate [hula] with exhibitions of unrivalled licentiousness, and abominations." C. S. Stewart, *Journal of a Residence in the Sandwich Islands During the Years 1823, 1824, and 1825 . . .* (London: H. Fisher, Son, and P. Jackson, 1830), 120.

27. Bingham, *Twenty-One Years,* 89.

28. Ibid., 97.

29. Edward S. Ninde, *The Story of the American Hymn* (New York: Abingdon Press, 1921), 74.

30. Kanahele, *Hawaiian Music,* 130; Bingham, *Twenty-One Years,* 127.

31. Quoted in Kanahele, *Hawaiian Music,* 131. Ursula Emerson established a singing school in Waialua, Oahu, in 1832, shortly after she and her husband, the Reverend John Emerson, arrived there. Oliver Pomeroy Emerson, *Pioneer Days in Hawaii* (Garden City, NY: Doubleday, Doran & Co., 1928), 60, 66, 90. Missionaries in Hawaii were not alone in their emphasis on music; their colleagues in Bombay were busy translating hymns into Mahratta. Tracy, *American Missions,* 114.

32. Quoted in Stillman, "Beyond Bibliography," 476–477; Freer, *Lowell and Abigail,* 81. A singing school was established at the Oahu Charity School in 1833. Daws, *Honolulu,* 155.

33. Liliuokalani, *Hawaii's Story by Hawaii's Queen* (Rutland, VT: Charles E. Tuttle Co., 1964 [1898]), 30.

34. David W. Forbes, comp., *Hawaiian National Bibliography 1780–1900,* vol. 1: *1780–1830* (Honolulu: University of Hawaii Press/Holdern House, 1999), 396–397.

35. Stewart, *Journal,* 270. Early hymnals went through multiple editions—*Na Himeni Hawaii* (1823) was reprinted four times by 1836; *Na Himeni Hoolea* went through seven printings between 1857 and 1867. Stillman, "Beyond Bibliography," 484, 477.

36. Freer, *Lowell and Abigail,* 125. Smith served as pastor of Kaumakapili Church from 1839 to 1869.

37. Hitchcock, *Music in the United States,* 64; Lloyd Frederick Sunderman, "The Era of Beginnings in American Music Education (1830–1840)," *Journal of Research in Music Education* 4 (spring 1956): 35.

38. Kanahele, *Hawaiian Music,* 130; Freer, *Lowell and Abigail,* 81; Gerrit P. Judd IV, *Dr. Judd, Hawaii's Friend: A Biography of Gerrit Parmale Judd (1803–1873)* (Honolulu: University of Hawaii Press, 1960), 68; Jacob Adler, ed., *The Journal of Prince Alexander Liholiho* (Honolulu: University of Hawaii Press, 1967), 26.

39. Ninde, *American Hymn,* 111–112.

40. Capt. F. W. Beechey, *Narrative of a Voyage to the Pacific and Beering's Strait* . . . (London: Henry Colburn and Richard Bentley, 1831), 1:423–424.

41. Rufus Anderson, *The Hawaiian Islands: Their Progress and Condition Under Missionary Labors,* 2nd ed. (Boston: Gould & Lincoln, 1864), 178. For accounts of music encountered elsewhere on his tour, see 166, 190, 208, 219, as well as the account of his daughter, Mary E. Anderson, *Scenes in the Hawaiian Islands and California* (New York: American Tract Society, 1865), 107, 141, 153, 161, 166.

42. Mary C. Alexander and Charlotte P. Dodge, *Punahou 1841–1941* (Berkeley: University of California Press, 1941), 111–112.

43. One of the first three pianos to arrive in California in 1843 sold for $600. E. D. Holden, "California's First Pianos," *California Historical Society Quarterly* 13 (March 1934): 34–37. The English consul in Honolulu, Richard Charlton, had a piano as early as January 1839. Doyce B. Nunis, ed., *The California Diary of Faxon Dean Atherton* (San Francisco: California Historical Society, 1964), 22.

44. Lyman, *Around the Horn,* 71. Lyman later taught briefly at the Chiefs' School. In 1847, Emma Smith, the young daughter of missionaries, was taking piano lessons. Freer, *Lowell and Abigail,* 200.

45. Barbara E. Dunn, "William Little Lee and Catherine Lee, Letters from Hawaii 1848–1855," *Hawaiian Journal of History* 38 (2004), 74. By 1874, pianos also had made their way to Maui and Kauai. Isabella Bird Bishop, *Six Months Among the Palm Groves, Coral Reefs, and Volcanoes of the Sandwich Islands* (New York: G.P. Putnam's Sons, 1894), 225, 281. "There is probably no other town in the world where, for the proportion of population, so many pianos can be found," Augustus Marques boasted of Honolulu in 1884. "The Future Prospects of the Honolulu Library," *Saturday Press,* June 7, 1884, 1.

46. de Varigny, *Fourteen Years,* 266. Glees are part-songs for three or four unaccompanied voices.

47. Alfons L. Korn, ed., *The Victorian Visitors* (Honolulu: University of Hawaii Press, 1958), 161–162.

48. Stewart, *Journal,* 340. Ships' bands played at the funerals of Liholiho in 1825 and of Princess Harieta Nahienaena in 1837; in the procession that preceded the first officially sanctioned Catholic mass in 1839; at various points during the Paulet affair in 1843; during Fourth of July celebrations in 1845; and for the presentation of a portrait of King Louis Philippe of France in 1848. Mary Ellen Birkett, "The French Perspective on the Laplace Affair," *Hawaiian Journal of History* 32 (1998): 82; Frear, *Lowell and Abigail,* 153; Laura Fish Judd, *Honolulu: Sketches of Life in the Hawaiian Islands from 1828 to 1861* (Chicago: Lakeside Press/R.R. Donnelly & Sons, 1966), 176, 190, 200, 249.

49. Harold Whitman Bradley, *The American Frontier in Hawaii: The Pioneers 1789–1843* (Stanford, CA: Stanford University Press, 1942), 255; Kanahele, *Hawaiian Music,* 335.

50. Lyman, *Hawaiian Yesterdays,* 102–103.

51. John Haskell Kemble, ed., *Journal of a Cruise to California and the Sandwich Islands in the United States Sloop-of-War Cyane* (San Francisco: Book Club of California, 1955), 37.

52. Duncan and Dorothy Gleason, *Beloved Sister: The Letters of James Henry Gleason 1841 to 1859 from Alta California and the Sandwich Islands* (Glendale, CA: Arthur H. Clark Co., 1978), 53–55, 61–64; Pauline King, ed., *The Diaries of David Lawrence Gregg: An American Diplomat in Hawaii 1853–1858* (Honolulu: Hawaiian Historical Society, 1982), 74, 109, 112, 117, 147, 171, 180, 196, 235, 309, 320, 329, 332, 334, 335, 339, 345, 350, 362, 368, 376, 377, 378, 388, 416, 426, 435, 459. See also Daws, *Honolulu,* 234–235.

53. Kuykendall, *Hawaiian Kingdom,* 1:131; George P. Hammond, ed., *The Larkin Papers* (Berkeley, CA: University of California Press, 1951), 1:107–108, 196.

54. Buck, *Paradise Remade*, 105; *Gregg Diaries*, 253–254, 311. The amateur musicians of Honolulu Engine Co. No. 2 put on a minstrel show in 1869. "The Concert of Saturday Night," *Hawaiian Gazette*, March 10, 1869, 3.

55. Forbes, *National Bibliography*, 3:88, 104, 124, 135.

56. Rubellite Kinney Johnson, *Kukini 'Aha'ilono (Carry On the News)* (Honolulu: Topgallant Publishing Co., 1976), 158–159, 292–293.

57. Judd, *Honolulu*, 154. Judd and her family named their Nuuanu Valley home "Sweet Home," after the well-known 1823 song "Home Sweet Home" by John Howard Payne and Sir Henry Rowley Bishop. Ibid., 236.

58. Dane, *Letters*, 51. During an 1867 visit to Hilo, a U.S. naval officer reported a performance by Sunday school children, singing "Marching through Georgia," "Tramp, Tramp," "Rally Round the Flag," and "John Brown's Body" in Hawaiian and English. "The Capitol," *Philadelphia Inquirer*, September 23, 1867, 1.

59. *Foreign Relations of the United States 1894: Affairs in Hawaii*, Appendix 2 (Washington, D.C.: Government Printing Office, 1895), 17.

60. Alfons L. Korn, ed., *News From Molokai: Letters Between Peter Kaeo and Queen Emma, 1873–1876* (Honolulu: University Press of Hawaii, 1976), 80, 183. "What the Wild Waves Are Saying" is an 1850 tune by Joseph Edwards Carpenter and Steven Glover; the Scottish song "Annie Laurie" was first published in 1835. Kaeo also mentions singing "The Dearest Spot on Earth to Me" and "Love Not."

61. For organs and melodeons in churches, see Freer, *Lowell and Abigail*, 220–221, 241; Anderson, *Hawaiian Islands*, 178; and Nordhoff, *Northern California*, 28. For accordions, see Freer, *Lowell and Abigail*, 199; Alexander and Dodge, *Punahou*, 112; Lyman, *Hawaiian Memories*, 36; and Korn, *Victorian Visitors*, 212. In 1846, John Gulick paid $1.50 for a fife from an American sailor; he had hoped for a flute, but at $13 it was too expensive. Alexander and Dodge, *Punahou*, 112. See also Kanahele, *Hawaiian Music*, 274–276.

62. George Leonard Chaney, *"Alóha!" A Hawaiian Salutation* (Boston: Roberts Bros., 1888), 72; Lyman, *Hawaiian Memories*, 36.

63. "Band Music," *Hawaiian Gazette*, November 9, 1870.

64. Kanahele, *Hawaiian Music*, 351–352. For the introduction of the vaqueros, see Kuykendall, *Hawaiian Kingdom*, 1:318, and Billy Bergin, *Loyal to the Land: The Legendary Parker Ranch 750–1950* (Honolulu: University of Hawaii Press, 2004), 31–36.

65. George Vancouver, *A Voyage of Discovery to the North Pacific Ocean and Round the World 1791–1795*, ed. W. Kaye Lamb (London: Hakluyt Society, 1984), 2:733; William Heath Davis, *Seventy-Five Years in California* (San Francisco: John Howell Books, 1967), 45.

66. Dana, *Two Years Before the Mast*, 160. The Reverend Walter Colton mentions the guitar more than a dozen times in his *Three Years in California* (New York, 1850), which covers his experiences in Monterey and the gold country during the years 1846–1849 (see pp. 15, 23, 35, 99, 104, 126, 132, 147, 191, 204, 208, 212, 223). Guitars were offered for sale in Los Angeles in 1858. *Los Angeles Southern Vineyard*, June 19, 1958, cited in Howard Swan, *Music in the Southwest 1825–1950* (San Marino, CA: Huntington Library, 1952), 101.

67. Edward T. Perkins, *Na Motu: Or, Reef-Rovings in the South Seas* (New York: Pudney & Russell, 1854), 134.

68. For Hawaiians as sailors, see Bradley, *American Frontier*, 33, 227. For the extensive trade between Hawaii, California, and such ports as Mazatlán, Guayaquil, Callao, and Valparaiso, see Bradley, *American Frontier*, 75–76; Hammond, *Larkin Papers*, xi, xiii, 4–7; and David Igler, "Diseased Goods: Global Exchanges in the Eastern Pacific Basin, 1770–1850," *American Historical Review* 109 (June 2004): 705–709. As Bradley notes, invoices of cargoes consigned to one American merchant in Honolulu between 1826 and 1830 included cotton goods, fancy goods, stationery, shoes, umbrellas, table covers, towels, cutlery, hatchets, fishhooks, pocket pistols, scissors, files, jackknives, razors, crockery, finger rings, handkerchiefs, twine, champagne, castor oil, soap, blankets, ink, perfume, pantaloons, card tables, pearl buttons, chairs, Dutch pipes, prints, and pictures. Bradley, *American Frontier*, 87.

69. Philip F. Gura, *C. F. Martin and His Guitars 1796–1873* (Chapel Hill, NC: University of North Carolina Press, 2003), 17, 22, 24.

70. Advertisement, *Polynesian,* June 6, 1840, 4. The same ad ran through February 1841. The first reference to steel-stringed guitars—as distinguished from the more common gut strings—dates back to 1865, when Curtis P. Iaukea remembered a group of Portuguese workers from the Azores ("shipwrecked crews of the Whaling fleet which ran afoul of the Confederate Cruiser 'Shenandoah' up north during the Civil War") arriving at the Pioneer Plantation with steel-stringed guitars, "the first we had ever seen." Curtis Piehu Iaukea, "Whaling in the Days of the Kingdom" (*Honolulu Advertiser,* May 7, 1939), editorial page. If Iaukea's memory, more than seventy years after the fact, is correct, these would have been Azorean *viola do dois coraçoes,* twelve-string guitars with two distinctive heart-shaped soundholes that were carried around the world by Azorean whalers.

71. Reverend Walter Colton, *Deck and Port: Or, Incidents of a Cruise in the United States Frigate Congress to California* (New York: A.S. Barnes & Co., 1850), 337.

72. "Musicians Offer Services in Honolulu," *Polynesian,* July 7, 1855, 2. The following year, the *Polynesian* noted that pianofortes, harps, guitars, and accordions could be found in many Honolulu parlors. "Editor Hopkins Describes Evolution of Foreign Community in Honolulu," June 28, 1856, 2.

73. Advertisement, *Hawaiian Gazette,* August 7, 1867, 4. The same ad ran continuously for nearly two years.

74. *Hawaiian Gazette,* June 16, 1869, 2.

75. *Hawaiian Gazette,* September 4, 1878, 2. On November 5, 1881, Wells advertised an inventory in the Hawaiian-language *Ka Nupepa Kuokoa* that included "Gita, Akodiana, Banjo, Ohe, Violina, Pahu Hookani Nunui a Liilii" (guitars, accordions, banjos, flutes, violins, drums large and small).

76. Adolphus, "San Francisco Letter," *Saturday Press Supplement,* November 17, 1883, 1.

77. For guitar advertisements, see C. E. Williams, *Daily Bulletin,* December 8, 1885, 2; Lycan & Co., *Hawaiian Gazette Supplement,* June 11, 1885, 1; Lyons & Levey, *Daily Bulletin,* December 6, 1884, 4; and Dias & Gonsalves, *Daily Bulletin,* September 28, 1883, 4. For the Wood burglary, see "Local & General News," *Daily Bulletin,* November 21, 1884, 3. A year earlier a suspect named Paahana was sentenced to nine months at hard labor for stealing a guitar valued at $10. "Notes of the Week," *Saturday Press,* March 11, 1882, 4. For Babcock, see advertisement, *Daily Bulletin,* June 26, 1885, 3.

78. For Hawaiian Hotel, see "Local & General News," *Daily Bulletin,* November 24, 1883, 3. For housewarming, see "Pleasant Parties," *Daily Bulletin,* December 15, 1884, 3, and "Social Happenings," *Saturday Press,* December 20, 1884, 3. For Kaumakapili, see "Last Night's Concert," *Daily Bulletin,* June 26, 1885, 3. For Kawaiahao, see "Notes of the Week," *Saturday Press,* June 24, 1882, 3. For Waimea, see "Our Princess Regent," *Saturday Press,* August 27, 1881, 2. For Waipio, see Helen E. Lewis, "Waipio and Waimanu," *Saturday Press,* August 15, 1885, 1. For the Maui schooner, see "Island Locals," *Hawaiian Gazette,* June 25, 1884, 12.

79. Agnes M. Burke, "Honolulu," *Daily Bulletin,* January 16, 1886, 4.

80. Roberts, *Ancient Hawaiian Music,* xx.

81. Bingham, *Twenty-One Years,* 619, 580–581. A list of Kalakaua and Liliuokalani's contemporaries at the school can be found in Mary Krout, *The Memoirs of Hon. Bernice Pauahi Bishop* (New York: Knickerbocker Press, 1908), 30–31.

82. Quoted in Kanahele, *Hawaiian Music,* 201. See also Barbara Barnard Smith, ed., *The Queen's Songbook* (Honolulu: Hui Hanai, 1999), 3.

83. Judd, *Honolulu,* 223.

84. Charles Wilkes, *Narrative of the United States Exploring Expedition during the Years 1838, 1839, 1840, 1841, 1842.* (Philadelphia: C. Sherman, 1844), 3:388.

85. Sir George Simpson, *An Overland Journey Round the World, During the Years 1841 and 1842* (Philadelphia: Lea and Blanchard, 1842), Part 2, 42–43. Despite such favorable accounts by visitors, Amos Cooke considered the school a failure. Daws, *Honolulu,* 152–153.

86. Liliuokalani, *Hawaii's Story,* 30–31.

87. Judd, *Honolulu,* 38, 60.

88. Korn, *Victorian Visitors,* 31–32; Adler, *Liholiho,* 30, 38, 59, 66–67, 88, 99.

89. Forbes, *National Bibliography,* 3:297; Bird Bishop, *Six Months,* 187.

90. Day, *Mark Twain,* 124; Korn, *Victorian Visitors,* 31–32. King Lunalilo (William Charles Lunalilo, 1835–1874) was also a composer; he wrote the words to the unnamed closing hymn sung by the Kawaihao Church choir after he took the oath of office in 1873. "The Accession to the Throne," *Pacific Commercial Advertiser,* January 11, 1873, quoted in *Message of the President of the United States with the Accompanying Documents . . .* (Washington, D.C.: Government Publication Office, 1873), 510. Princess Victoria gamely played "God Save the Queen" on her father's piano for Lady Franklin during an 1861 visit. Korn, *Victorian Visitors,* 165.

91. Liliuokalani, *Hawaii's Story,* 6; Korn, *Victorian Visitors,* 31–32; "King Kalakaua," *New York Times,* December 6, 1874, 9.

92. Liliuokalani, *Hawaii's Story,* 52–53.

93. Lorrin A. Thurston, *The Writings of Lorrin A. Thurston,* ed. Andrew Farrell (Honolulu: Advertiser Publishing Co., 1936), 17–19. Thurston reported that after Leleiohoku's death, his Kawaihau Glee Club "went every night for a month to the Royal Mausoleum, where his body was laid, and spent the evening singing songs that they had learned when Leleiohoku was living, as well as others composed in his memory."

94. Edgar Marquess Branch et al., *Mark Twain's Letters,* vol. 1: *1853–1866* (Berkeley, CA: University of California Press, 1988), 334–335. It's also possible Queen Emma supported a choir of her own, as mention is made of an appearance of "Queen Emma's choristers" at a gathering at the royal palace in November 1880. "Miss Sharon's Wedding To-Night," *New York Times,* December 23, 1880, 5.

95. Korn, *Victorian Visitors,* 114. Kalakaua taught the royal bandmaster in Siam "Hawaii Ponoi" by playing it to him on the piano. William N. Armstrong, *Around the World With A King* (Honolulu: Mutual Publishing, [1904] 1995), 131–132. Liliuokalani served as choir director and organist at Kawaiahao Church for several years. Smith, *Queen's Songbook,* 4. 8. See also Kanahele, *Hawaiian Music,* 201, 226, 229.

96. Kalanianaole Collection, Bishop Museum Library MS 8, cited in Kanahele, *Hawaiian Music,* 352.

97. Louise Coffin Jones, "My Journey with a King," *Lippincott's Magazine* 28 (October 1881), 364–365. For Kalakaua on the guitar, see also Isobel Field, *This Life I've Loved* (New York: Longmans, Green and Co., 1937), 175. The Z. K. Meyers family scrapbook contains an undated note from Kalakaua to stationer Thomas Thrum of Honolulu, asking that four harmonicas and a set of guitar strings be sent to him. Bonham's Sale 17520, Fine Books and Manuscripts, October 19, 2009, Session Two, Lot 413. While on a visit to Washington, D.C., in 1897, Liliuokalani was interviewed by a journalist from *American Woman's Home Journal,* who reported that "At her right was a table covered with rare and beautiful flowers, books, papers and periodicals; at her left was a guitar on which she had just been playing." Quoted in "Liliuokalani," the *Independent,* April 1, 1897, 1. For Likelike, see Kanahele, *Hawaiian Music,* 226, 229. The guitar's presence in the royal circle was noted as early as November 1873, when Queen Emma reported that the musical entertainment for King Lunalilo and his guests in Kailua included "singing to Guitar, mouth consatinas [harmonicas] and accordion." Emma to Lucy Peabody, November 22, 1873, quoted in Korn, *News From Molokai,* 163.

98. Alma L. Smith, "Correspondence: Visit of the King's Brother," *The Latter Day Saints' Millenial Star* 38 (January 3, 1876), 58–60. George Chaney wrote of overhearing Leleiohoku and two companions aboard the steamer from Honolulu to the island of Hawaii as "together they solace themselves . . . with songs in their low, sweet, bubbling native tongue. The guitar, touched but never twanged by the skilful sympathetic player, seemed to sing the same sweet liquid words that came from its human companions. I cannot tell what part each took; guitar, prince, friends, all seemed to sing as one voice; and the song they chanted was like the movement of the sea, endlessly repeated in seeming monotony, and yet never twice the same." Chaney, *Alóha,* 56–57.

99. Andrew Farrell, ed., *John Cameron's Odyssey* (New York: Macmillan Co., 1928), 224. William

Armstrong, Kalakaua's attorney general and former schoolmate, agreed: "He was an excellent musician" with a "keen sense of good music." Armstrong, *Around the World,* 10, 217.

100. Liliuokalani, *Hawaii's Story,* 31.

101. Kanahele, *Hawaiian Music,* 100–101, 225. James Fuld notes that the beginning of the chorus is similar to George F. Root's 1847 composition, "There's Music in the Air." James J. Fuld, *The Book of World-Famous Music, Classical, Popular and Folk* (New York: Crown Publishers, 1966), 81. In the 1920s and 1930s, when the popularity of Hawaiian music was at its peak, debunkers often pointed to the similarities between "Aloha Oe" and "The Rock Beside the Sea." See Lee Shippey, "The Lee Side O' L.A.," *Los Angeles Times,* August 17, 1931, A4. During a visit to Honolulu in 1925, the eminent Austrian violinist Fritz Kreisler created "a sensation among Hawaiian enthusiasts when he asserted that 'Aloha Oe' was not a Hawaiian song but really an old Austrian folk song." Louis P. Lochner, *Fritz Kreisler* (New York: Macmillan Co., 1950), 241. Kreisler recorded "Aloha Oe" for Victor that year. T. Malcolm Rockwell, *Hawaiian & Hawaiian Guitar Records 1891–1960* (Kula, HI: Mahina Piha Press, 2007), 665 (CD-ROM).

102. David W. Bandy, "Bandmaster Henry Berger and the Royal Hawaiian Band," *Hawaiian Journal of History* 24 (1990): 74–75. By 1886, there were four bands in Honolulu: Berger's Royal Hawaiian Band; the Reform School band; the St. Louis School band; and the Portuguese band, whose initial practices generated many complaints from neighbors. "The Portuguese Band," *Daily Bulletin,* December 7, 1886, 2.

103. Kanahele, *Hawaiian Music,* 35–36.

104. Kanahele, *Hawaiian Music,* 37. For a description of the relationship between words and music in nineteenth-century Hawaii, see Stillman, "History Reinterpreted," 21–22.

105. Kanahele, *Hawaiian Music,* 35; H. Berger, *Mele Hawaii* (Honolulu: Hawaiian News Co., n.d.). Engraved and printed in San Francisco by the Schmidt Label and Lithograph Co., *Mele Hawaii* features such songs as "Hawaii Ponoi" and "Aloha Oe," arranged for four voices (SATB) with piano accompaniment, as well as Berger's own compositions for solo piano.

106. Kanahele, *Hawaiian Music,* 338; "Kalakaua At Home," *New York Times,* March 31, 1875, 5. The fact that Berger was German likely played a role in shaping the band's reputation; as David Suisman points out, "the German presence [in nineteenth-century] American music was overwhelming." David Suisman, *Selling Sounds: The Commercial Revolution in American Music* (Cambridge: Harvard University Press, 2009), 34.

107. Nordhoff, *Northern California,* 19; Kuykendall, *Hawaiian Kingdom,* 2:173–174 and 3:94, 110–112.

108. Kuykendall, *Hawaiian Kingdom,* 3:29, 40, 47, 83.

109. *Twelfth Census of the United States, Census Reports,* vol. 2: *Population, Part 2* (Washington, D.C.: Government Printing Office, 1902), ccxvi. The size of the Hawaiian nation before the arrival of Captain James Cook in 1778 has been the subject of a vigorous and ongoing debate. See David E. Stannard, *Before the Horror: The Population of Hawaii on the Eve of Western Contact* (Honolulu: University of Hawaii Social Science Research Center, 1989).

110. de Varigny, *Fourteen Years,* 65.

111. Kuykendall, *Hawaiian Kingdom,* 3:117.

112. Kuykendall, *Hawaiian Kingdom,* 3: 117–125.

113. Katharine Coman, "The History of Contract Labor in the Hawaiian Islands," *Publications of the American Economic Association,* Third Series (August 1903), 4:7–8; Kuykendall, *Hawaiian Kingdom,* 1:329.

114. Clarence E. Glick, *Sojourners and Settlers: Chinese Migrants in Hawaii* (Honolulu: Hawaii Chinese History Center and University Press of Hawaii, 1980), 7, 12.

115. Hilary Conroy, *The Japanese Frontier in Hawaii, 1868–1898* (Berkeley: University of California Press, 1953), 21, 67.

116. Ronald Takaki, *Pau Hana: Plantation Life and Labor in Hawaii 1835–1920* (Honolulu: University of Hawaii Press, 1983), 25–28; Kuykendall, *Hawaiian Kingdom,* 3:128–135; "News From

Honolulu," *Los Angeles Times,* May 28, 1899, A13; "Spanish Emigrants Sail for Hawaii," *Washington Post,* April 4, 1907, 4; "Russians for Sugar Fields," *Los Angeles Times,* July 27, 1909, 15; William B. Gatewood Jr., *Black Americans and the White Man's Burden 1898-1903* (Urbana, IL: University of Illinois Press, 1975), 298.

117. Takaki, *Pau Hana,* 23–24; Conroy, *Japanese Frontier,* 49. The Board of Immigration considered the importation of Portuguese laborers as early as 1868—Portuguese, chiefly Azorean sailors from whaling ships, had been present in Hawaii since 1794—but opted instead for less costly Japanese. Conroy, *Japanese Frontier,* 16; John H. Felix and Peter F. Senecal, *The Portuguese in Hawaii* (Honolulu: Privately printed, 1978), 1. Portuguese laborers were needed, the *Planters Monthly* declared in November 1883, "especially as an *offset* to the Chinese; not that the Chinese are undesirable—far from it—but we lay great stress on the necessity of having our labor *mixed.* By employing different nationalities, there is less danger of collusion among laborers, and the employer—on the whole—secures better discipline." Kuykendall, *Hawaiian Kingdom,* 3:147–48.

118. Richard A. Greer, "The Founding of Queen's Hospital," *Hawaiian Journal of History* 3 (1969): 137–141. Perhaps not coincidentally, one of Hillebrand's orderlies at Queen's Hospital in Honolulu was Portuguese.

119. Kuykendall, *Hawaiian Kingdom,* 3:123. Hillebrand's former business partner in Honolulu, J. Mott-Smith, was president of the Board of Immigration at the time. Greer, "Queen's Hospital," 140.

120. *Breve Noticia Àcerca das Ilhas de Sandwich e das vantagens que ellas offerecem á emigração que as procure* (Funchal: Typographia Liberal, 1878), 21–22. This pamphlet apparently was written with Madeirans as its target audience; conditions in Hawaii are repeatedly compared, directly and indirectly, to those in Madeira.

121. Coman, "Contract Labor," 28–29; *Breve Noticia,* 15–16. The monthly wage was paid for twenty-six ten-hour days of work each month.

122. William A. Green, *British Slave Emancipation: The Sugar Colonies and the Great Experiment 1830–1865* (Oxford: Clarendon Press, 1976), 286–287; Caroline Brettell, *Anthropology and Migration: Essays on Transnationalism, Ethnicity and Identity* (Walnut Creek, CA: Altamira Press, 2003), 11–12.

123. Brettell, *Anthropology and Migration,* 10.

124. Felix and Senecal, *Portuguese in Hawaii,* 28–30.

Chapter 3: The National Instrument of Hawaii

1. The original version of this account is an interview with Fernandes that appeared in 1922: "How the Ukulele Came to Hawaii," *Paradise of the Pacific* 35 (January 1922): 8–10. The article was reprinted in *Aloha Land,* a ca. 1924 brochure published by Hawaii Sales Co., Ltd., "Hawaii's Foremost Musical and Novelty Store" (Jack Ford collection). For details on the *Ravenscrag's* voyage, see "Arrival of Immigrants" and "Memoranda," *Hawaiian Gazette,* August 27, 1879. Fernandes' passport application, dated March 17, 1879, lists him as a twenty-four-year-old plumber (*pecheleiro*), married to Carolina Augusta Fernandes, twenty, and living in Funchal's Santa Luzia parish with their month-old daughter Amalia. Passport application, emigration file No. 301, 1879, Arquivo Regional da Madeira (ARM). For da Silva's role, see Bob Krauss, "Hula hoops and ukes," *Honolulu Advertiser,* August 30, 1979, A-3.

2. Portuguese were resident in Honolulu as early as 1811. Gabriel Franchere, *A Voyage to the Northwest Coast of America* (New York: Citadel Press, 1968), 40. Most, if not all, of the early Portuguese were from the Azores and Cape Verde, sailors recruited by American whalers who were abandoned or jumped ship in Hawaii as described by Lorrin Thurston in the early 1870s. Davis et al., *In Pursuit of Leviathan,* 617; Thurston, *Writings,* 38–40. Some accounts claim that Portuguese sailors brought the machete to Hawaii, but the principal folk instrument of the Azores is the viola, or steel-stringed guitar, that J. Ross Browne described aboard the whaler *Bruce* on its 1842–1843 cruise. Browne, *Etchings of a Whaling Cruise . . .* (New York: Harper & Bros., 1846), 43, 46. For an example of the oft-repeated assertion that sailors were the source of the machete, see D. M. Randel, *The Harvard*

Concise Dictionary of Music and Musicians (Cambridge, MA: Belknap Press, 1999), 696. Others have claimed that the machete arrived with the first party of Madeiran contract workers aboard the *Priscilla* in September 1878, but no contemporary evidence has come to light to confirm this (see "Jose Rodrigues Recalls Ukulele's Arrival in 1878," *Honolulu Star-Bulletin,* September 29, 1936, 8).

3. Mr. James Hackett to Gov. Light, July 5, 1841, in *Papers Relative to the West Indies and British Guiana 1841–42,* cited in Menezes, *Portuguese of Guyana,* 23.

4. "Portuguese Musicians," *Hawaiian Gazette,* September 3, 1879, 3.

5. *Livro de Matricula de Cidadanos Portuguezes, Consulado Geral de Portugal em Hawaii,* entries 185, 170, and 193, August 22, 1879; "List of Passengers per 'Ravenscrag,'" entries 300, 358, 383, Series 519, Box 1, Folder 1, Hawaii State Archives.

6. While no contracts have been found for the three men, the names of Santo, Nunes, and Dias all appear on a "List of debts to be paid monthly at Honolulu, HI" dated June 12, 1879: Santo owed 18,000 reis and Nunes and Dias 24,000 reis, apparently for advances on wages. Series 519, Box 5, Folder 4, HAS. Nunes' name also appears on a separate list of passengers from whom promissory notes had been taken. Nunes owed "116.00," presumably dollars, for ship fares and other expenses. Series 519, Box 1, Folder 1, Hawaii State Archives.

7. Of the 124 heads of family and single men aboard the *Ravenscrag* reported in the *Livro de Matricula,* a total of 68, or 55 percent, were from the Funchal parishes of São Roque, São Pedro, São Antonio, Sé, Santa Luzia, Santa Maria Maior, Monte, São Martinho, or São Gonçalo. All but five of the men are listed as *trabalhadores.* In an interview years later, *Ravenscrag* passenger Joaquim Augusto Gonsalves (1855–1931) admitted he had no intention of working on a plantation, "and I've never been sorry, you bet." *Pacific Commercial Advertiser,* May 23, 1912, 16, cited in Lynn Davis, *Na Pa'i Ki'i: Photographers in the Hawaiian Islands 1845–1910* (Honolulu: Bishop Museum Press, 1980), 47.

8. *Breve Noticia,* 11. Compare with average daily wages of 70 to 100 reis for skilled workers just prior to World War I. *Elucidario Madeirense,* 2:409–410.

9. "More Portuguese," *Pacific Commercial Advertiser,* September 27, 1879, 3. "The first Madeira Portuguese . . . were about as peculiar a lot of agricultural emigrants as ever left home and country," said the *Saturday Press* in 1883. "The immediate result was that the Madeira men made, very generally, unprofitable servants in any capacity, and the further result was to give Madeira so bad a name, that planters frequently objected to employ a Portuguese who happened to come from that lovely island, under any circumstances." "Portuguese Immigration," *Saturday Press,* July 14, 1883, 3.

10. According to grandson John Nunes of Wailuku, Maui, Nunes worked on the Big Island. Larry Ikeda, "Ukulele from the Portuguese," *Maui Today* (February 1977): 7. The 1909 marriage certificate for Santo's twenty-six-year-old daughter Emily lists her birthplace as Maui, which places her family there ca. 1883. The 1900 census lists Emily's birthdate as November 1882: Marriage certificate 174, dated August 23, 1909, First Circuit Court, HSA: 183 Emma St., Family 207, page 109, Sheet 20, ED 12, Honolulu, Oahu, Hawaii, 1900 census, Microcopy T623, Roll 1836. Dias' daughter Caroline testified that her father worked on Hawaii and Kauai: Testimony of Caroline Tranquada, Petition for the Registration of the Hawaiian Birth of Charles Francis Gilliland (November 26, 1947), Application 27587, Office of the Secretary of Hawaii. "Augusto Diaz" is listed on tax assessment records as an employee of Lidgate's Plantation in Laupahoehoe on the island of Hawaii in 1880: Tax Assessment and Collection Ledgers (224–2–1880), Vol. 2, District of Hilo: 91.

11. Irving Jenkins, *Hawaiian Furniture and Hawaii's Cabinetmakers 1820–1940* (Honolulu: Daughters of Hawaii, 1983), 93, 138; Frederick Bagot, ed., *McKenney's Hawaiian Directory Including a City Directory of Honolulu, and Hand Book of the Kingdom of Hawaii* (San Francisco: L. M. McKenney, 1884), iv, 83, 102, 107, 110, 132, 134, 181, 205, 214, 222, 246.

12. Jenkins, *Hawaiian Furniture,* 146–147, 150–151. "Emanuel Nunis" is listed as a cabinetmaker with C. E. Williams in the 1884 directory. Bagot, *McKenney's Hawaiian Directory,* 188. Santo does not appear in Honolulu directories until 1888.

13. Dias, Nunes, and Santo were not the first instrument makers in Hawaii. In 1882, J. K. Kaulia, a worker at the Lewers & Cooke lumberyard in Honolulu, was identified as having made guitars.

"Manufactures Creditable Guitars," *Pacific Commercial Advertiser,* December 2, 1882, 5. A generation earlier, a Mr. Lemane, a former employee at the Chickering piano factory in Boston, served as "an excellent repairer and maker of musical instruments" in Honolulu before his death in 1852. *Polynesian,* March 6, 1852, 3.

14. Bagot, ed., *McKenney's Hawaiian Directory,* 113; James C. Mohr, *Plague and Fire: Battling Black Death and the 1900 Burning of Honolulu's Chinatown* (Oxford: Oxford University Press, 2005), 59.

15. Bagot, ed., *McKenney's Hawaiian Directory,* 82, 84, 88–90, 211, 213, 214, 216, 224, 227; Richard A. Greer, *Downtown Profile: Honolulu a Century Ago* (Honolulu: Kamehameha Schools Press, 1966), 5, 37.

16. Both Nunes and Dias ("Manufacturer of guitars and machetes, and all string instruments") advertised in the August 15, 1885, edition of *O Luso Hawaiiano,* Honolulu's newly established Portuguese-language newspaper. For a detailed analysis of Nunes' claim to have invented the 'ukulele, see John King and Jim Tranquada, "The Singular Case of Manuel Nunes and the Invention of the Bouncing Flea," *Galpin Society Journal* 60 (April 2007): 85–95. For Santo's ad, see *Hawaiian Gazette,* September 23, 1885, 3. The ad ran repeatedly through December of that year.

17. Roberts, *Ancient Hawaiian Music,* 9–10. Roberts reported that Gonsalves' account was corroborated by George Nunes, Hawaiian-born son of Manuel. Baptismal records in Funchal show that all three men were born in the parish of Santa Maria Maior and were living there in the early 1870s; by 1879, according to their emigration files, Dias was living in Santa Maria Maior, Nunes in São Pedro, and Santo in Sé.

18. The two men were not brothers—Manuel was the son of Ricardo Antonio Nunes and Maria Augusta of Funchal, while Octaviano's parents were João Antonio Nunes and Ana Maria de Incarnação—but more research is necessary to determine if the two men were cousins. Baptism Book 283, p. 49, ARM; Morais, *A Madeira,* 84.

19. Manuel Nunes, passport application, emigration file No. 316 (1879), ARM; Jose do Espirito Santo, passport application, emigration file No. 302 (1879), ARM; Augusto Dias, passport application, emigration file 105 (1879), ARM.

20. The classic American example of cabinetmaker turned instrument maker is Christian Frederick Martin (1796–1873), founder of C.F. Martin & Co. Several early-American banjo makers also began as cabinetmakers. Philip F. Gura and James F. Bollman, *America's Instrument: The Banjo in the Nineteenth Century* (Chapel Hill, NC: University of North Carolina Press, 1999), 42–43.

21. Kuykendall, *Hawaiian Kingdom,* 3:56–57.

22. Richard A. Greer, "'Sweet and Clean'": The Chinatown Fire of 1886," *Hawaiian Journal of History* 10 (1970): 33–41; "A Deluge of Fire," *Daily Bulletin Summary,* April 30, 1886, 3. A Manuel Nunes helped Dr. Nathaniel Emerson recover the body of an unidentified Chinese man from a King Street house during the height of the fire, but it's not clear whether this was the 'ukulele pioneer. "After the Fire," *Daily Bulletin Summary,* April 30, 1886, 3.

23. *O Luso Hawaiiano,* July 15, 1886.

24. "Reformatory School Boys on the Rampage," *Daily Bulletin,* March 9, 1887, 3. Dias and Santo were subsequently sued by an unhappy customer who claimed they had lost the $25 guitar he left with them to have the neck replaced. *John Brown vs. Dias and Dos Santos,* filed April 15, 1887, Law 2497, First Circuit Court Series 006, Judiciary of Hawaii, Hawaii State Archives. (Thanks to the late Lydia Guzman for finding this file.) Because the burglary took place at a time when it was proposed to turn the twenty-two-year-old school into a military and naval academy—two dozen students were recruited to serve on the *Kamiloa,* Kalakaua's ill-fated attempt to establish a Hawaiian naval presence—it was widely remarked upon by a critical press. For the story of the *Kamiloa,* see Kuykendall, *Hawaiian Kingdom,* 3:334–336. For criticism of the *Kamiloa* and the militarization of the Reform School, see "More Folly," *Daily Bulletin,* July 21, 1886, 2; and "Our Navy," *Daily Bulletin,* April 23, 1887, 2: "Their capabilities for the service have been acquired by long and faithful practice at bumming, beer and the taro-patch fiddle." For references to the burglary, see *Hawaiian Gazette,* March 15,

1887, 4; and "The Flaneur," same date and page; "The Prison System," *Daily Herald,* July 19, 1887, 2; and "The Old Gibsonian Days," *Hawaiian Gazette,* April 24, 1894, 6.

25. As an immigrant in New York City in the 1830s, C. F. Martin carried on a similar trade. See Gura, *C. F. Martin,* 46–52. Nunes, for example, continued with woodworking projects, including an inlaid koa photo album displayed at J. J. Williams' Fort Street photo studio. "A Koa Album," *Daily Bulletin,* October 11, 1888, 3; "Local and General News," *Daily Bulletin,* October 12, 1888, 3.

26. "Eight Youthful Burglars Apprehended," *Hawaiian Gazette,* March 22, 1904, 5.

27. None of the three are listed in the 1880 Honolulu directory. In the 1884–1885 directory, Dias is listed as a guitar and furniture maker and Nunes as a cabinetmaker for C. E. Williams. Santo is not listed. In the 1888–1889 edition, Nunes, Santo, and Dias are all listed as guitar makers.

28. Lane, *Hawaiian Directory* (1888), unpaginated advertisements. Manuel Nunes advertised "Guitars and stringed instruments of all kinds made and repaired" intermittently in the Honolulu *Daily Bulletin* between October 1888 and February 1889.

29. Descriptions of the instrumentation of Hawaiian music in the two decades following the introduction of the machete often use the generic term "guitar" to refer to the 'ukulele, taro patch, and guitar. For example, see M. G. Bosseront d'Anglade (Alfons L. Korn, trans.), *A Tree in Bud: The Hawaiian Kingdom 1889–1893* (Honolulu: University of Hawaii Press, 1987), 50, 86, 101, 105, 130, 162, 184.

30. George Kia, *Self Instructor for the Ukulele and Taro-Patch Fiddle* (Los Angeles: R.W. Heffelfinger, 1914), 23; Mekia (Major) Kealakai, *The Ukulele and How to Play It* (Los Angeles: Southern California Music Co., 1914), 3.

31. "Local News," *Honolulu Daily Press,* November 4, 1885, 3.

32. Charles C. Burnett, *The Land of the O-O; Figures, Fables, and Fancies* (Cleveland: Cleveland Printing & Publishing Co., 1892), 96; Albert A. Stanley, *Catalogue of the Stearns Collection of Musical Instruments* (Ann Arbor: University of Michigan Press, 1918), 161.

33. At a concert at the Hawaiian church in Lihue, Kauai, by the combined glee clubs of the area, the men of the Lihue club played "Yankee Doodle" on violin, guitar, banjo, and 'ukulele. "A Rural Fete," *Hawaiian Gazette,* December 11, 1888, 1.

34. Sidney Colvin, ed., *The Letters of Robert Louis Stevenson* (New York: Scribner's, 1915), 3:144. The use of "taro patch" to describe both the 'ukulele and the five-string taro patch helps explain why some accounts claim the 'ukulele was developed from the larger taro patch. For examples of this claim, see "Ukulele Not Hawaiian at All, but Portuguese," *Morning Oregonian,* May 30, 1920, 5; "An Erroneous Ukulele Idea," *Presto,* May 19, 1923, 21; Alan Randall and Ray Seaton, *George Formby: A Biography* (London: W.H. Allen, 1971), 45; Mike Longworth, *Martin Guitars: A History* (Cedar Knolls, NJ: Colonial Press, 1975), 95.

35. "Stories on Kanaka Land," *Tacoma* [Washington] *Daily News,* January 30, 1893, 1. Guitars normally have six strings, not five.

36. Emerson, *Unwritten Literature,* 251; Gill, "Portuguese Were First," 3. See also Isabel Anderson, *The Spell of the Hawaiian Islands and the Philippines* (Boston: Page Co., 1916), 94.

37. This same relative tuning appears as early as 1760 in Andres de Soto's tiple method and also is documented in de Oliveira's 1966 survey of Portuguese instruments. Andres de Soto, *Arte Para Aprender, Con Facilidad, y sin Maestro, a templar a taner rasgado La Guitarra . . . y tambien el Tiple* (Madrid: Lopez y compañia, 1760), 61–63; de Oliveira, *Instrumentos Populares,* 141.

38. Edward Charles Holstein, *Chords of the Taro-Patch Guitar: A New System for learning to play the chords of the taro-patch guitar without a teacher* (Honolulu: Hawaiian News Co., 1894), 3. Holstein, b. 1868 of a Danish father and Hawaiian mother, was the compiler of the Hawaiian News Co.'s *Ka Buke Mele o na Himeni Hawaii* (1897), an early songbook. He was head of the company's Hawaiian music department for more than thirty-five years. 1900 Census, Dwelling 134, Family 140, Vineyard St., Sheet 16, ED 18, Honolulu District, Hawaii, June 8, 1900; Forbes, *National Bibliography,* 4:660; Holstein, *Ka Buke Mele o na Himeni Hawaii* (Honolulu: Bishop Museum Press, 2003), xiii. In 1898, he advertised his availability to give guitar lessons: "Business Locals," *The Independent,* January 6, 1898, 4. The origin of the association of the phrase "my dog has fleas" with GCEA tuning is unknown. One

early reference is a song by George Kroesling and Claude Malani copyrighted in 1939, "Say my dog has fleas, when you tune an ukulele."

39. Wortley, *Portugal and Madeira,* 233; Robert White and James Yate Johnson, *Madeira: Its Climate and Scenery* (Edinburgh: Adam & Charles Black, 1856), 77–78. This same D-G-B-D tuning is found in Veiga de Oliveria: *Instrumentos Populares,* 141; and in Lambertini's Encyclopedia: Michael'angelo Lambertini, "Portugal," in *Encyclopedie de la Musique* (Paris: Librairie Delagrave, 1920), 2466.

40. A. A. Santos and Angeline Nunes, *Original Method and Self-Instructor on the Ukulele* (Honolulu: Santos-Nunes Studios, 1915), 3.

41. Helen Mather, *One Summer in Hawaii* (New York: Cassell, 1891), 159–160.

42. Lorrin Andrews, *A Dictionary of the Hawaiian Language* (Waipahu, HI: Island Heritage Publishing, 2003), 109; Glen E. Haas, P. Quentin Tomich, and Nixon Wilson, "The Flea in Early Hawaii," *Hawaiian Journal of History* 5 (1971), 59–61; Bingham, *Sandwich Islands,* 176.

43. "[The female Hawaiian] can take down her ukililli—'jumping flea'—a machine of the guitar breed, almost eighteen inches long, but like a four-year-old boy, very noisy for its size." Conflagration Jones, "Kanaka Melody," Chicago *Sunday Inter Ocean,* March 6, 1892, 22. The same definition is given in Jean A. Owen, *The Story of Hawaii* (London: Harper & Bros., 1898), 212.

44. Jack London, *The Cruise of the Snark* (New York: MacMillan, 1932), 113.

45. Ernest K. Kaai, *The Ukulele: A Hawaiian Guitar and How to Play It* (Honolulu: Wall Nichols Co., 1906), 4.

46. Nancy Oakley Hedemann, *A Scottish-Hawaiian Story: The Purvis Family in the Sandwich Islands* (Privately printed, 1994), iii, 264.

47. Gill, "Portuguese Were First," 3; Hedemann, *Scottish-Hawaiian Story,* 276. Helen Roberts' account of how the 'ukulele got its name is the original published version of this story and the first to cite Purvis' role. Pukui and Elbert cite this account in their dictionary: Mary Kawena Pukui and Samuel H. Elbert, *Hawaiian Dictionary* (Honolulu: University Press of Hawaii, 1975), 339. Another possibility is that Purvis got his nickname from the instrument rather than the other way around, just as James A. Wilder was nicknamed "ukulele" by his Harvard classmates in 1890–1891 (although a Boston newspaper reporter heard it as "kukai"). "Skirt Dance and High Kicking," *Boston Daily Globe,* April 13, 1891, 3.

48. Gill, "Portuguese Were First," 3; Hedemann, *Scottish-Hawaiian Story,* 276. The machete apparently was brought by newly arrived Portuguese workers delivered to the Purvis plantation on Kauai. Purvis was supposed to have been proficient on the piano, guitar, violin, and mandolin. Hedemann, *Scottish-Hawaiian Story,* 244. He also could sing, having appeared as The Defendant in an 1882 Honolulu performance of Gilbert & Sullivan's *Trial by Jury.* The *Daily Bulletin* singled out his singing and acting as "especially good." "Third Performance of the Amateur Dramatic Club," *Daily Bulletin,* December 14, 1882, 2; "Local Items," *Saturday Press,* December 16, 1882, 3.

49. Kuykendall, *Hawaiian Kingdom,* 3:346; Hedemann, *Scottish-Hawaiian Story,* 319–321; Jacob Adler and Gwynn Barrett, eds., *The Diaries of Walter Murray Gibson* (Honolulu: University Press of Hawaii, 1973), 65. Gibson's entry for August 8, 1886, reads, "At [former attorney general Paul] Neumann's house. He intimated that he could prove the authorship of hostile articles in the Gazette—Purvis. The King at my house—will remove Purvis & Judd too, if he has proof."

50. Forbes, *National Bibliography,* 4:215. Purvis' satire, which may have been inspired in part by an 1882 Honolulu performance of a burlesque of Offenbach's comic opera *The Grand Duchess of Gerolstein,* was not the first such publication; Sanford B. Dole published *Vacuum: A Farce in Three Acts* in 1885. Dale E. Hall, "Opera and Operetta in Nineteenth Century Hawaii," *Hawaiian Journal of History* 31 (1997), 90–91; Kuykendall, *Hawaiian Kingdom,* 3:346.

51. Mather, *One Summer,* 159–160; Hedemann, *Scottish-Hawaiian Story,* 359; "Death of E. W. Purvis," *Daily Bulletin,* August 29, 1888, 2. There are a number of conflicting claims as to the origin of the name "'ukulele." In 1920, E. R. Adams credited Henry M. Whitney for originating the name, based on the resemblance of strumming the instrument to jumping fleas. E. R. Adams, "From the Azores

Came the Ukulele to Hawaii," *Aloha* (San Francisco: Matson Navigation Co., October 1920), 6. Twelve years later, David M. Kupihea gave a newspaper interview in which he credited Gabriel Davion with coming up with the name. "Doc" Adams, "Old Fisherman Tells How Steel Guitar Originated; Also How Ukulele Got Name," *Honolulu Advertiser,* January 24, 1932, 5 (first cited in Kanahele, *Hawaiian Music,* 395).

52. "Old Fisherman Tells," *Honolulu Advertiser,* January 24, 1932, 5.

53. Original in the possession of William Voiers of North Egremont, MA.

54. Advertisement, *Evening Bulletin,* July 18, 1895, 3.

55. Day, *Mark Twain,* 120.

56. "The Legislative Assembly," *Hawaiian Gazette,* August 7, 1888, 3. "We cannot blame the youngsters," the *Independent* editorialized a decade later. "It is a great deal more pleasant to sing Tira Mola with the accompaniment of an Ukulele to standing over the wash tub or broiling a piece of steak." "Over-Education," the *Independent,* June 23, 1899, 2.

57. Examples include the Dias ʻukulele owned by the May family of Honolulu ("'Oldest' Ukulele Turns Up," *Honolulu Advertiser,* May 19, 1956, A8); by Steve Soest of Orange, CA, pictured in Richard R. Smith et al., *Inventing Paradise: Hawaiian Image and Popular Culture* (Fullerton Museum Center, 2001), 21; and the example pictured in Don R. Severson, Michael D. Horikawa, and Jennifer Saville, eds., *Finding Paradise: Island Art in Private Collections* (Honolulu: Hawaiian Academy of Arts/University of Hawaii Press, 2002), 254.

58. Examples of *kapu* stick pegheads include the Soest Dias and the Dias pictured in Severson et al., eds., *Finding Paradise;* banjo-style pegheads can also be seen in *Finding Paradise,* 257, including a Santo taro patch with a tuning peg located halfway down the fingerboard in imitation of a five-string banjo (*Finding Paradise,* 258).

59. Early examples of crown pegheads include a Santo owned by Andy Roth, which based on its label dates to ca. 1897–1898, and a Nunes with a label with an address at 219 ½ King, an address Nunes used in 1898–1899.

60. "Local and General News," *Daily Bulletin,* April 10, 1884, 3. At a YMCA speech the same week, Supreme Court judge A. Francis Judd warned virtuous youth against what he called the dreamy life of the sybarite: "Is the white boy of Honolulu to succumb to the tendency, and prefer the lei and the Portuguese guitar to the school book and the implements of the artisan?" "A Timely Warning," *Saturday Press,* April 19, 1884, 2.

61. "Women's Christian Temperance Union," *Daily Bulletin,* November 27, 1885, 2.

62. Marques, "Music in Hawaii Nei," 58. The following year, a Boston newspaper correspondent reported Hawaiians' fondness for nocturnal serenades, usually accompanied by an instrument "of the Portuguese variety, carrying four strings, and with no great volume of tone, but fitting enough for this simple lay." "In Kalakaua's Kingdom," *Boston Daily Advertiser,* July 12, 1887, 4.

63. "A Weird Scene," *Daily Herald,* October 30, 1886, 3.

64. Lee Meriwether, *The Tramp At Home* (New York: Harper & Brothers, 1889), 264. John Cameron, chief officer of the Inter-Island Steam Navigation Co.'s *James Makee* and *Iwalani* from 1881 to 1886, described a similar scene: "What a run that was! Entertainments by the crew from the hour of sailing, four o'clock in the afternoon, until eight o'clock at night; ukuleles strummed, songs sounded over a moonlit sea; hula dances evoked roars of applause from white and brown alike." Farrell, *Cameron's Odyssey,* 216.

65. Holstein, *Taro-Patch,* 2. The Hawaiian News Co., Publishers, Booksellers, and Music Dealers, advertised "Ukuleles and Taro Patch Guitars" as Hawaiian souvenirs in the 1895 edition of Henry M. Whitney's *Tourist Guide Through the Hawaiian Islands,* 2nd ed. (Honolulu: Hawaiian Gazette, 1895), advertisement opposite p. 65.

66. Liliuokalani, *Hawaii's Story,* 342.

67. BPBM 1967.289.06, cited in Roger G. Rose, *Hawaii: The Royal Isles* (Honolulu: Bernice P. Bishop Museum, 1980), 173.

68. Burnett, *Land of the O-O,* 97. For example, this image appeared in Bertha E. Herrick's article,

"Life in Honolulu," *Californian* (April 1892): 386; *Atlanta Constitution,* May 12, 1895; *Philadelphia Inquirer,* August 1, 1897, 27; and Australia's *North Queensland Register* on December 22, 1897, 50. The three dancers have been tentatively identified as being from Kalakaua's court. Jane C. Desmond, *Staging Tourism: Bodies on Display from Waikiki to Sea World* (Chicago: University of Chicago Press, 1999), 44–45. The photos are an early example of what Aeko Sereno has termed the "hula girl," not a dancer expressing an ancient culture but a fantasy figure signaling "the path to a forbidden paradise . . . a creation of imagination, not reality." Aeko Sereno, *Images of the Hula Dancer and the "Hula Girl": 1778–1960* (University of Hawaii Ph.D. dissertation, 1990), 189, 194. The artificiality of the image is underlined by the presence of the instruments—hula dancers do not play while they dance. For a more recent compilation of hula girl images, many with 'ukulele, see Jim Heiman, ed., *Hula: Vintage Hawaiian Graphics* (Cologne: Taschen, 2003).

69. "Mr. Vos at Work," *Hawaiian Gazette,* April 26, 1898, 3. In a review of a 1979 show of Vos portraits, critic Vivien Raynor dismissed this portrait as "quite terrible." "Period Pieces," *New York Times,* July 1, 1979, CN10.

70. Severson et al., eds., *Finding Paradise,* 230.

71. Frank Ward Hustace, *Victoria Ward and Her Family: Memories of Old Plantation* (Honolulu: Victoria Ward, Ltd., 2000), 52. 'Ukuleles also appear in the hands of young men and women in snapshots of social gatherings at Samuel M. Damon's Moanalua estate and of Dr. John S. McGrew's country home in Aiea taken in the 1880s and 1890s. Edward B. Scott, *Saga of the Sandwich Islands* (Crystal Bay, NV: Sierra-Tahoe Publishing Co., 1968), 821, 841. Clarence Macfarlane named his new twenty-foot boat *Ukulele* in 1896. "A New Yacht," *Hawaiian Gazette,* February 14, 1896, 5.

72. "Listening Ladies," *Boston Daily Globe,* April 29, 1890, 2. Four years later, when the *Hawaiian Gazette* reported Wilder's admission to Harvard Law School, it noted that he "has done credit to his 'Aina Hanou' with his 'ukulele' and Hawaiian songs." "Hawaii at New Haven," *Hawaiian Gazette,* February 2, 1894, 7. During a 1920 visit to the mainland, James Wilder was identified as "the man who introduced Hawaiian music into the United States." "March Brings Increasing Business to New Orleans," *Music Trade Review* (March 20, 1920): 21. He was the youngest son of Samuel G. Wilder, member of the House of Nobles and interior minister under Kalakaua. John William Siddall, ed., *Men of Hawaii,* vol. 1 (Honolulu: Honolulu Star-Bulletin, 1917), 285. James' older brother Gerrit reportedly owned the first 'ukulele made in Hawaii. Clifford Gessler, *Hawaii: Islands of Enchantment* (New York: D. Appleton-Century Co., 1937), 331. Taro patches also were in evidence among the members of Yale's Hawaiian Club in 1893. "The Seventeenth at Yale," *Hawaiian Gazette,* February 9, 1894, 3.

73. "Welcome Home," *Daily Bulletin,* February 17, 1890, 3.

74. The adoption of the 'ukulele by Hawaiians is an example of what the Cuban historian Fernando Ortiz called transculturation—the complex interaction between cultures that produces unique offspring, both like and unlike its parents. Fernando Ortiz, *Cuban Counterpoint: Tobacco and Sugar* (Durham, NC: Duke University Press, 1995), xxvi, 97–103. For a more extended discussion of syncretic musics, see Margaret J. Kartomi, "The Processes and Results of Musical Culture Contact: A Discussion of Terminology and Concepts," *Ethnomusicology* 25 (May 1981): 227–249.

75. *Foreign Relations of the United States 1894,* Appendix 2: *Affairs in Hawaii* (Washington, D.C.: Government Printing Office, 1895), 257; "Statistics About Hawaii," *New York Times,* July 11, 1898, 7; *Twelfth Census of the United States, Census Reports,* vol. 2: *Population* (Washington, D.C.: GPO, 1902), ccxvii. In 1900, some 68.5 percent of the Hawaiian workforce was made up of laborers, servants, and other blue-collar workers.

76. Holstein, *Taro-Patch,* 2. W. F. Reynolds' Golden Rule Bazaar in Honolulu offered American-made guitars priced from $11 to $25 in 1892 (*Hawaiian Gazette,* November 29, 1892, 8); in its 1894 catalog, Sears, Roebuck and Co. offered guitars ranging from $4.50 to $26, plus express charges. *Sears, Roebuck and Co. Consumer's Guide for 1894* (Sears reprint, n.d. [ca. 1976]), 247.

77. "Local News," *Daily Honolulu Press,* October 3, 1885, 3.

78. *Aurora Hawaiiana,* August 3, 1889. Madeiran immigrants continued to bring machetes and *rajãos* to the Islands, as was the case with those aboard the *Thomas Bell* in 1888. See Lucille da

Silva Canario, "Destination, Hawaiian Islands," *Hawaiian Journal of History* 4 (1970): 8, 10, 14, 15, 20, 25.

79. Between 1884 and 1890, the Portuguese population in the Islands *decreased* by more than 1,500, despite the fact more than 3,100 immigrants from Madeira and the Azores arrived during that same period. Lorna H. Jarrett, *Hawaii and Its People* (Honolulu: Honolulu Star-Bulletin, 1933), 40. See also Donald Warrin and Geoffrey L. Gomes, *Land, As Far As the Eye Can See: Portuguese in the Old West* (Spokane, WA: Arthur H. Clark Co., 2001), 314–315; "Lack of Laborers Hampers Hawaii," *New York Times,* September 24, 1912, 10.

80. *Foreign Relations 1894,* 1000.

81. Ibid., 256.

82. Photo 100, "Iolani Days" Photo Album 87B, Wallace R. Farrington Collection, SAH.

83. Field, *This Life I've Loved,* 175.

84. Mary H. Krout, *Hawaii and a Revolution: The Personal Experiences of a Correspondent in the Sandwich Islands during the Crisis of 1893 and Subsequently* (New York: Dodd, Mead & Co., 1898), 260. (Krout's original account, "Hawaiians at Home," appeared in the *Daily Inter Ocean* on March 1, 1893.) Visitors often struggled to describe the 'ukulele; Krout's description of a native instrument "somewhat like a mandolin" might be based on a familiarity with the mandolinetto or guitar mandolin, shaped like a small guitar but strung, tuned, and played like a mandolin, with a metal tailpiece.

85. Field, *This Life I've Loved,* 175. This account first appeared in Field's (née Strong) 1905 novel: Isobel Strong, *The Girl From Home: A Story of Honolulu* (Honolulu: Crossroads Bookshop, 1912), 95–96.

86. "How the Ukulele Came to Hawaii," *Paradise of the Pacific* 35 (January 1922): 9.

87. "Aunt Tina of Kailua Helped Kalakaua Direct Making of Island's First Uke," *Pali Press,* July 31, 1963. In a 1960 interview, Jennie Wilson remembered seeing Dias at Healani, Kalakaua's boathouse. Elma T. Cabral, "The Ukulele's Real Story," *Honolulu Magazine,* November 1978, 165.

88. Julius Palmer, the queen's private secretary during a portion of her 1897 trip to Boston and Washington, D.C., reported from Washington that "Her Majesty is pleasantly entertaining friends with her own beautiful voice and the accompaniments of guitar, ukulele, or autoharp." "Hawaii's Queen," the *Independent,* April 10, 1897, 3.

89. "Reception," *Daily Bulletin,* January 26, 1889, 2; J. Cumming Dewar, *Voyage of the Nyanza R.N.Y.C. . . .* (Edinburgh: William Blackwood and Sons, 1892), 275. Widemann, married to Mary Kaumana, was a former Kauai planter who served as a member of the House of Nobles and an associate Supreme Court justice who served in the cabinets of Kalakaua and Liliuokalani. Kuykendall, *Hawaiian Kingdom,* 3:476; Bob Krauss and William P. Alexander, *Grove Farm Plantation: The Biography of a Hawaiian Sugar Plantation,* 2nd ed. (Palo Alto: Pacific Books, 1984), 104–105, 112–116, 152.

90. Hawaii State Archives.

91. "Oldest Ukulele Turns Up," *Honolulu Advertiser,* May 19, 1956, A8.

92. "Prince Cupid at Home," *Washington Post,* May 24, 1903, E10. Prince Kalanianaole had an account at Bergstrom Music Co. "Local and General News," the *Independent,* July 31, 1903, 3.

93. "Likes Hawaiian Princess," *The [Berea, KY] Citizen,* July 7, 1910, 7. The princess is identified as "an especially fine musician."

94. Emerson, *Unwritten Literature,* 250–253; Elizabeth Tatar, "Q&A by Betty Tatar," *Ha'ilono Mele* 3 (February 1977), 7; Stillman, personal communication, May 7, 2005. *"Hula kui"* was the term used in the coronation program of February 12, 1883.

95. Amy K. Stillman, "History Reinterpreted in Song: The Case of the Hawaiian Counterrevolution," *Hawaiian Journal of History* 23 (1989): 20–21.

96. Reproduced in *Finding Paradise,* 241, and in Kuykendall, *Hawaiian Kingdom,* 3:614. Jubilee performances included a wide variety of styles; one eyewitness account of the hula performance on November 23, 1886, mentions *ipu* and *uliuli* as the only accompaniment. Wilma James, "Hawaii's Last King," *Pacific Historian* 24 (fall 1980): 314–315.

97. Meriwether, *Tramp*, 277. See also, "Played Poker with a Real King," *Chicago Daily Tribune*, November 2, 1896, 5.

98. Jonah Kumalae may have been the first 'ukulele maker to use the royal coat of arms on the headstocks of his instruments. Nunes advertised that his 'ukuleles were "Patronized by the Royal Hawaiian Family" in the 1916 *Polk-Husted Directory of Honolulu* (131); his ads competed with those of the Hawaiian Ukulele Co., which claimed its "Royal Ukuleles Have no Superior in Tone or Popularity" (121).

99. Kuykendall, *Hawaiian Kingdom*, 3:401.

100. "There is apparently much truth in the belief that the wonderful progress of the United States, as well as the character of the people, are the results of natural selection. . . . When civilized nations come into contact with barbarians the struggle is short . . . the decrease of the native population of the Sandwich Islands is as notorious as that of New Zealand." Charles Darwin, *On the Origin of Species* (New York: Modern Library, n.d. [1871]), 508, 543–544.

101. Pratt, *Expansionists of 1898*, 35; Bartholomew H. Sparrow, *The Insular Cases and the Emergence of American Empire* (Lawrence: University Press of Kansas, 2006), 71.

102. A.E.L., "Paradise in the Pacific," *New York Times*, November 6, 1892, 14; *Foreign Relations*, Appendix 2, 169.

103. Merze Tate, *The United States and the Hawaiian Kingdom: A Political History* (New Haven, CT: Yale University Press, 1965), 44; Hubert Howe Bancroft, *The New Pacific* (New York: Bancroft Co., 1899), 381.

104. *Foreign Relations*, Appendix 2, 90, 153.

105. For examples of this view, see Sereno Bishop interview, April 11, 1893, *Foreign Relations*, 2:699; Caspar Whitney, *Hawaiian America: Something of Its History, Resources, and Prospects* (New York: Harper & Brothers, 1899), 51; John W. Foster, *American Diplomacy in the Orient* (Boston: Houghton, Mifflin and Co., 1904), 385.

106. Carl Schurz, "Manifest Destiny," *Harpers New Monthly Magazine* 87 (October 1893), 741.

107. Jonathan Kay Kamakawiwoole Osorio, *Dismembering Lahui: A History of the Hawaiian Nation to 1887* (Honolulu: University of Hawaii Press, 2002), 146–157. See also Stacy L. Kamehiro, *The Arts of Kingship: Hawaiian Art and National Culture of the Kalakaua Era* (Honolulu: University of Hawaii Press, 2009), 2.

108. *Foreign Relations* 2, Appendix 2, 658.

109. Ibid., 658, 669.

110. Osorio, *Dismembering Lahui*, 223; Pratt, *Expansionists*, 128–129.

111. Smith, *Queen's Songbook*, 7.

112. Noenoe K. Silva, *Aloha Betrayed: Native Hawaiian Resistance to American Colonialism* (Durham, NC: Duke University Press, 2004), 5, 8. "The Hawaiians have, moreover, a different dialect for poetry. . . . Its metaphors and allusions, which give enjoyment to the native race, elude the comprehension of residents who are well acquainted with the Hawaiian language used in prose," Gerard Manley Hopkins observed in 1866. "An informant, who knew the prose language so perfectly that he could report in shorthand the speeches made in the houses of legislature, was entirely baffled in his attempts to comprehend the poetry, which by turns melted and inflamed its native hearers." Gerard Manley Hopkins, *Hawaii: The Past, Present, and Future of Its Island Kingdom* (London: Kegan Paul, 2003 [1868]), 353.

113. Silva, *Aloha Betrayed*, 182.

114. Stillman, "History Reinterpreted," 1–30.

115. "One thing that, more than anything else, will appease the natives and bring them around will be the band. . . . Seeing their boys taking the oath they will be influenced very much by their actions." "Will Follow The Band," *Boston Daily Globe*, February 25, 1893, 10.

116. The song was listed by its alternate title, "Aloha Aina," in a program published prior to the event. "First Public Concert at the Hotel This Evening," *Daily Bulletin*, March 22, 1893, 3. The *Bulletin* estimated the crowd at 5,000. "Rousing Ovation," *Daily Bulletin*, March 23, 1893, 2.

117. "Blount Is There," *Daily Inter Ocean,* April 6, 1893, 1; see also Krout, *Hawaii and a Revolution,* 141–142. "Kaulana na Pua o Hawaii" was first published on March 25, 1893, in the *Hawaii Holomua* as "He Inoa no na Keiki o ka Bana Lahui." Amy K. Stillman, "'Aloha Aina': New Perspectives on 'Kaulana Na Pua,'" *Hawaiian Journal of History* 33 (1999), 86. The song also was known as "Mele Ai Pohaku" (Stone-Eating Song). "To this day, a certain air that [the band plays] is called 'Go, Eat Stones,' and it is recorded that, although life has been very hard for some of the musicians since then, not one of them has ever applied to be reinstated." "At Liliuokalani's Hookupu," *Hartford Courant,* September 1, 1898, 12. A version in rhyming English verse was published in the *Daily Bulletin:* "What They Sing," November 27, 1893, 4.

118. Bernice Piilani Irwin, *I Knew Queen Liliuokalani* (Honolulu: Native Press, 2000 [1960]), 46. Newspaper correspondent Mabel Clare Craft noted in 1898 that "the Natives are royalist to a man—they love their Queen and their old institutions, and they are grief-stricken at the thought of annexation." "Poor Kaiulani," *Los Angeles Times* August 4, 1898, 5. For the political significance of flag quilts, see Joyce D. Hammond, "Hawaiian Flag Quilts: Multivalent Symbols of a Hawaiian Quilt Tradition," *Hawaiian Journal of History* 27 (1993): 5–11; and Robert Shaw, *Hawaiian Quilt Masterpieces* (Westport, CT: Hugh Lauter Levin Associates, 1996), 44, 46, 60.

119. Archibald Menzies, Vancouver's botanist, noted that koa is "very hard and close grained, and takes a very fine polish as may be seen by their canoes." Quoted in Jenkins, *Hawaiian Furniture,* 3.

120. A plan to include samples at the 1862 London International Exhibition was unsuccessful, and there is evidence that they may have been exhibited in Paris in 1867 and Vienna in 1873, but koa was certainly on display at the Philadelphia Centennial International Exhibition in 1876, at the World's Industrial and Cotton Centennial Exhibition in New Orleans in 1884–1885, at the Southern Exposition in Louisville, KY, and at the Exposition Universelle in Paris in 1889. "The names of our cabinet woods, koa and kou, are daily spelled out for the great multitude with untiring patience," commissioner H. R. Hitchcock reported from Philadelphia in 1876. Hopkins, *Hawaii,* 412; *Hawaiian Gazette,* February 24, 1875, quoted in *Papers Relating to the Foreign Relations of the United States* (Washington, D.C.: GPO, 1875), 1:676; James D. McCabe, *The Illustrated History of the Centennial Exhibition . . .* (Philadelphia: National Publishing Co., 1876), 460; *Hawaii: The Hawaiian Exhibit at the World's Exposition New Orleans . . .* (New Orleans: Hyman Smith, 1885), 10; "The Hawaiian Exhibit at Louisville," *Hawaiian Gazette,* October 7, 1885, 3; John A. Hassinger, *Catalogue of the Hawaiian Exhibits at the Exposition Universelle . . .* (Honolulu: Hawaiian Gazette Co., 1889), 16; "Letter From Philadelphia," *The Friend,* December 4, 1876, 102.

121. William Hillebrand, M.D., *Flora of the Hawaiian Islands: A Description of Their Phanerogams and Vascular Crytogams* (London: Williams and Norgate, 1888), 113.

122. "Honolulu and other growing Hawaiian towns were built very largely with lumber brought from the Columbia River and Puget Sound. From that period to the present day, Hawaii has drawn the bulk of its lumber from that region." Kuykendall, *Hawaiian Kingdom,* 1:301.

123. Thomas R. Cox, *Mills and Markets: A History of the Pacific Coast Lumber Industry to 1900* (Seattle: University of Washington Press, 1974), 118–119; Jenkins, *Hawaiian Furniture,* 6–11, 225–227. Japanese sawyers on the island of Hawaii were still cutting koa boards by hand as late as the 1930s. Jenkins, *Hawaiian Furniture,* 297.

124. In 1835, for example, Northwest lumber and California cedar were selling in Honolulu for 5 cents a foot; locally produced koa boards were selling for 6 cents per foot. Jenkins, *Hawaiian Furniture,* 9; *Foreign Relations* 2, Appendix 2, 165. "While furniture manufactured by [Hopp & Co.] may be more expensive than factory goods, imported from the States, it is manifestly superior in quality," the *Hawaiian Gazette* insisted in 1897. "Hopp & Co.," March 12, 1897, 9.

125. Cox, *Mills and Markets,* 299; Jenkins, *Hawaiian Furniture,* 106; Kim M. Wilkinson and Craig R. Elevitch, *Growing Koa: A Hawaiian Legacy Tree* (Holualoa, HI: Permanent Agricultural Resources, 2003), 3–5. As early as 1866, it was reported that "these monarchs of the wild are fast disappearing." "Local News," *Hawaiian Gazette,* October 13, 1866.

126. "At Kawaihau," *Hawaiian Gazette,* June 16, 1891, 7.

127. For Kamehameha III's throne, see Jenkins, *Hawaiian Furniture,* 105–106; for the heir apparent's cradle, see Jenkins, 115, 122–123; for royal coffins for Kamehameha III and IV, Lunalilo, Ruth Keelikolani, Queen Emma, Kalakaua, Liliuokalani, Bernice Pauahi Bishop, and Kaiulani, see Jenkins, 116–118, 146; Irwin, *I Knew Queen Liliuokalani,* 108; Briggs, *Experiences of a Medical Student,* 204; "Local and General News," *Daily Bulletin,* June 21, 1883, 2; "At Rest," *Hawaiian Gazette,* February 17, 1891, 4; and "The Casket Is Finished," *Hawaiian Gazette,* May 19, 1889. For royal bedsteads, see Jenkins, 78, 121, 159, 174–175 and Irwin, 107. Mark Twain was impressed by the coffin of koa and kou made for Princess Victoria in 1866, saying "nothing in the shape of wood can be more brilliant, more lustrous, more beautiful. It produces a sort of ecstasy in me to look at it, and holds me like a mesmeric fascination." Day, *Mark Twain,* 128.

128. Hopkins, *Hawaii,* 41; Jenkins, *Hawaiian Furniture,* 171.

129. Irwin, *I Knew Queen Liliuokalani,* 32; "At Kawaiahao," *Hawaiian Gazette,* June 16, 1891, 7. By contrast, a piano custom made for President Sanford B. Dole in 1896 was made of rosewood. "Piano for Hawaii," *Washington Post,* February 1, 1896, 12. Prince Cupid also ordered a koa piano from Chickering of Boston in 1901. "Local and General News," the *Independent,* February 1, 1901, 4.

130. Jenkins, *Hawaiian Furniture,* 146–47, 150–51.

131. This can be seen in Severson et al., *Finding Paradise,* 254; in a Dias shown in Smith et al., *Inventing Paradise,* 21; and in a Dias in the collection of Jack Ford of Oakland.

132. Husted, *Husted's Directory,* 65; Advertisement, *Evening Bulletin,* July 18, 1895, 3.

133. Santo signed (by mark) his oath on September 3, 1894; Dias signed his eight days later. Oath 44, Oath Book 24, and Oath 20, Oath Book 28, Hawaii State Archives. Most Portuguese did not support the monarchy. See *Foreign Relations* 2, 791, 1137. "The Portuguese are the only race which is undivided on this question," J. M. Vivas claimed in 1893. "They favor annexation because they know it will benefit every one of them. . . . They support [the provisional government] enthusiastically." "Vivas Talks," *Hawaiian Gazette,* April 25, 1893, 4.

134. Michael Myers Shoemaker, *Islands of the Southern Seas: Hawaii, Samoa, New Zealand, Tasmania, Australia, and Java* (New York: G.P. Putnam's Sons, 1897), 3.

135. Charles Warren Stoddard, "Lazy Letters From Low Latitudes," *Overland Monthly* 2 (October 1883): 340.

136. Burnett, *Land of the O-O,* 99.

Chapter 4: Have You Seen the Bouncing Flea?

1. Kuykendall, *Hawaiian Kingdom,* 3:115; 281–282; 289; 347; 360; George Chaplin, *Presstime in Paradise: The Life and Times of the Honolulu Advertiser, 1856–1995* (Honolulu: University of Hawaii Press, 1998), 111, 113.

2. Kuykendall, *Hawaiian Kingdom,* 3:534–535; Julius W. Pratt, "The 'Large Policy' of 1898," *Mississippi Valley Historical Review* 19 (September 1932): 227. Thurston was an enthusiastic proponent of Hawaii's involvement in the fair. He "thought it was the best opportunity we have ever had to advertise the Hawaiian Islands, and perhaps another chance would never occur again. . . . He thought every dollar expended in regard to the exhibit would be of great benefit to these islands." "Hawaii's Exhibit," *Hawaiian Gazette,* December 1, 1891, 1.

3. Thurston and his investors spent a reported $80,000 on the panorama. "The Story of the Midway Plaisance," Chicago *Daily Inter Ocean,* November 1, 1893, 25.

4. "12 Reasons Why . . . You Should See the Great Hawaiian Volcano on Midway Plaisance," handbill, Jeff Carr collection; Thurston, *Writings,* 82. A photograph of the cyclorama shows a signboard propped against the bandstand promising "Natives of Hawaii/Sing Their Beautiful Songs." *The Dream City, A Portfolio of Photographic Views of the World's Columbia Exposition . . .* (St. Louis, MO: N.D. Thompson Pub. Co., 1893), plate 142.

5. James Revell Carr, "Ethnomimesis and Authenticity on the American Popular Stage: Performing

Hawaiians and Musical Exotica in the 19th Century," working draft of paper presented at 2005 Pop Conference, 6–7.

6. Thurston later proudly took credit for bringing the Volcano Singers to the mainland: "I also took the first Hawaiian singers to the mainland—four of them; and their number was increased to eight in the course of the fair. One of the original four was Ben Jones, son of an American lawyer, married to a Hawaiian woman. He had the best bass voice ever developed in the islands. . . . A member of the second quartet that joined the cyclorama company was Duke K. Kahanamoku, the father of the boy of the same name who became the leading swimmer of Hawaii." Thurston, *Writings*, 82–83. The second group of musicians hired by George Beckley of the Cyclorama Co. were Joseph K. Kanepau, Duke Kahana Moku [*sic*], John Moses, William Olepau, and Dibble K. Eli. "Cylorama Company," *Hawaiian Gazette*, September 19, 1893, 2.

7. "World's Fair Music," *Chicago Daily Tribune*, August 22, 1893, 4. "The audience was satisfied with no less than four encores" from the quartet, reported the *Daily Inter Ocean*. "Knowing ones pronounced the singing perfect." August 22, 1893, 7.

8. Thurston, *Writings*, 83. Although Thurston lost money, he met his future wife in Chicago—Hattie Potter, the cashier and secretary of the Cyclorama. "Mr. Thurston and His Bride," *Hawaiian Gazette*, April 17, 1894, 1.

9. Clara Louise Burnham, *Sweet Clover: A Romance of the White City* (Boston: Houghton, Mifflin and Co., 1895), 166; David F. Berg, *Chicago's White City of 1893* (Lexington: University Press of Kentucky, 1976), 172; Suisman, *Selling Sounds*, 30.

10. Carr, *Ethnomimesis*, 2–3, 8–10; W. Kaye Lamb, ed., *A Voyage of Discovery to the North Pacific Ocean and Round the World 1791–1795* (London: Hakluyt Society, 1984), 2:732–33.

11. "Natives of Hawaiian Islands Are Gifted With Musical Talent," San Jose (CA) *Evening News*, March 10, 1909, 3.

12. "Some members of the band have formed a glee club among themselves and sing the native songs in a very entertaining manner," the San Francisco *Bulletin* reported. August 16, 1883, 3. See also "Music and Musicians," *Los Angeles Times*, August 1, 1897, 26; "Berger, Hawaiian Bandmaster, Honored by His Islanders," *New York Times*, August 3, 1924, X14; and Kanahele, *Hawaiian Music*, 337.

13. L. Vernon Briggs, *Around Cape Horn to Honolulu on the Bark "Amy Turner"* (Boston: Charles E. Lauriat Co., 1926), 156. Charles Warren Stoddard also praised the band's singing: "Wonderfully pleasing are these self-taught singers, and quite without the affectations of the more cultivated," and Isobel Field remembered the band best for its unforgettable singing at royal dances at Iolani Palace. Charles Warren Stoddard, "Lazy Letters From Low Latitudes," *Overland Monthly* 2 (October 1883): 340; Field, *This Life I've Loved*, 166.

14. Charles M. Taylor, *Vacation Days in Hawaii and Japan* (Philadelphia: George W. Jacobs & Co., 1898), 70.

15. Charles Chipman, *Honolulu: The Greatest Pilgrimage of the Mystic Shrine* (Charles Chipman, 1901), 237–238. Although Hiram's group at a Waipio luau for a visiting congressional delegation in 1897 was described only as "a quintette of native boys render[ing] Hawaiian songs," a photograph shows at least one 'ukulele among their instruments. Watson H. Wyman, "Hawaiian Hospitality," *Los Angeles Times*, October 5, 1897, 6; the photograph can be seen in Trumbull White, *Our New Possessions* (Chicago: A.B. Kuhlman Co., 1898), 672. Hiram, a former member of Prince Leleiohoku's Hui Kawaihau, was one of the leading orchestra leaders of the period and helped Sonny Cunha compile his 1902 music collection, *Songs of Hawaii*. Emerson C. Smith, "Hawaii's Royal Composers," in *The Hawaii Book* (Chicago: J.G. Ferguson Publishing Co., 1961), 302.

16. Charles Philip Trevelyan, *The Great New People: Letters From North America and the Pacific, 1898* (Garden City, NY: Doubleday & Co., 1971), 171.

17. For example, see "Music of the Kanakas," *Washington Post*, April 25, 1897, 26: "The Kanaka is an inspired musician, in that music is the mainspring of his being."

18. "Fairest Isles With Foulest Stain," *Minneapolis Journal*, June 3, 1899, 1.

19. Stoddard, "Lazy Letters," 340. See also "Island Locals," *Hawaiian Gazette,* July 4, 1880; *Daily Bulletin,* April 4, 1882, 1.

20. Leveritt H. Mesick, "In Hawaii," *Los Angeles Times,* January 17, 1898, 8. For example, see M. Forsyth Grant, *Scenes in Hawaii or Life in the Sandwich Islands* (Toronto: Hart & Co., 1888), 145; "A Hawaiian Christmas," *Portland Morning Oregonian,* January 13, 1895, 12; Briggs, *Experiences of a Medical Student,* 23; and John Scott Boyd Pratt, *The Hawaii I Remember* (Honolulu: Tongg Pub. Co., 1965), 23. "String bands paraded the town, delighting some and disturbing others with their Hawaiian melodies," the *Daily Bulletin* said of Christmas Eve 1883. "Local and General News," *Daily Bulletin,* December 27, 1883, 3.

21. "Hawaii Notes," *Saturday Press,* July 15, 1882, 4.

22. James D. Houston and Eddie Kamae, *Hawaiian Son: The Life and Music of Eddie Kamae* (Honolulu: 'Ai Pohaku Press, 2004), 108. Serenading continued well into the twentieth century: David Makapi of Waipio reported playing the 'ukulele with Sam Lia as a New Year's serenader through the early 1920s, and Harry A. Franck was serenaded by a group of New Year's Eve musicians on Molokai in the mid-1930s. Davianna Pomaikoi McGregor, *Nā Kua'āina: Living Hawaiian Culture* (Honolulu: University of Hawaii Press, 2007), 77–78; Harry A. Franck, *Roaming in Hawaii.* (New York: Frederick A. Stokes, 1937), 180

23. Lilian Whiting, *Kate Field: A Record* (Boston: Little, Brown and Co., 1900), 552.

24. "In Hawaii's Garden Spot," *New York Times,* February 25, 1894, 21.

25. Shoemaker, *Islands of the Southern Seas,* 24.

26. John La Farge, *An American Artist in the South Seas* (London: KPI Ltd., 1987 [1914]), 65.

27. "We children were not permitted to learn any of the native tongue until later years. The reason of this was to prevent mental contamination." Sereno Edwards Bishop, *Reminiscences of Old Hawaii* (Honolulu: Hawaiian Gazette Co., 1916), 20. See also Lucy G. Thurston, *Life and Times of Mrs. Lucy G. Thurston, Wife of Rev. Asa Thurston, Pioneer Missionary to the Sandwich Islands* (Ann Arbor, MI: S.C. Andrews, 1882), 128, and Lyman, *Hawaiian Yesterdays,* 14. This attitude persisted well into the twentieth century; see "Intermarrying in Honolulu," *Washington Post,* May 10, 1916, 6.

28. Nance O'Neil, "Nance O'Neil in Honolulu," *Los Angeles Times,* January 8, 1899, B4. Charles Hiroshi Garrett aptly summarized Hawaiian music's appeal as "a compelling blend of both the exotic and the familiar as well as a paradoxical combination of escapism tinged with melancholy." Charles Hiroshi Garrett, *Struggling to Define a Nation: American Music and the Twentieth Century* (Berkeley: University of California Press, 2008), 201.

29. "Robert J. Burdette's Comments," *Los Angeles Times,* March 6, 1910, 2:1.

30. Katherine Fullerton Gerould, *Hawaii: Scenes and Impressions* (New York: Charles Scribner's Sons, 1916), 103.

31. Andre Millard, *America on Record: A History of Recorded Sound* (Cambridge: Cambridge University Press, 1995), 80–83. The human ear can distinguish frequencies between 20 and 20,000 cycles per second; the range of acoustic recordings was between 168 and 2,000 cycles per second. Timothy Day, *A Century of Recorded Music: Listening to Musical History* (New Haven, CT: Yale University Press, 2000), 9.

32. Siddall, *Men of Hawaii,* 157–158.

33. Kanahele, *Hawaiian Music,* 193. Ernest Kaai, a twenty-year-old music teacher, is listed as living with his mother, Becky, on School Street in Honolulu in the 1900 census. Dwelling 16, Family 18, ED 18, Sheet 2, Honolulu District, Island of Oahu, June 1, 1900. He attended Oahu College, as Punahou was then known, from 1890 to 1893. *Oahu College: List of Trustees, Presidents, Instructors, Matrons, Librarians, Superintendents of Grounds, and Students 1841–1906* (Honolulu: Hawaiian Gazette Co., 1907), 54. For details on his father's career, see Kuykendall, *Hawaiian Kingdom,* 3:143, 195, 200, 210–211, 219, 247, 254, 267. For Ellis, see "John Ellis Has a Monopoly on Hawaiian Music," *Pacific Commercial Advertiser,* March 17, 1904, 9.

34. Gurre Ploner Noble, *Hula Blues: The Story of Johnny Noble, Hawaii, Its Music and Musicians* (Honolulu: Tongg Publishing Co., 1948), 23.

35. *Honolulu City Directory,* 1907, 81.

36. Kaai, *The Ukulele,* 3. Tablature, rather than standard notation, emerged as a standard teaching method because it could better accommodate the reentrantly tuned 'ukulele. A subject for further research would be to explore the relationship between early 'ukulele tablature and the chord diagrams now commonly used by guitarists. Are there examples of chord diagrams for guitar earlier than ca. 1917?

37. Kanahele, *Hawaiian Music,* 209–210; "David Nape," http://www.hawaiianmusicmuseum .org/honorees/nape.html; Bob Krauss, *Johnny Wilson: First Hawaiian Democrat* (Honolulu: University of Hawaii Press, 1994), 18. Nape, "quite a musical prodigy," was conducting the Reformatory School Band as early as 1881, when he was 12 or 13. "Local & General News," *Daily Bulletin,* June 12, 1882, 2. As a member of the Royal Hawaiian Band, he was not only a musician but a featured solo vocalist. "Local and General News," the *Independent,* July 16, 1896, 3; "At Emma Square," the *Independent,* August 25, 1896, 2.

38. Information on George Kia and the Nahaolelua family has been published by Kia great-granddaughter Vicki DeLeo on her Banyan Tree Web site, http://members.cox.net/banyan_tree/ index.html. A 1901 obituary of George's father notes that he left a widow and eight children, including one son at the Buffalo exposition. "Death of Nahaolelua," the *Independent,* June 14, 1901, 2. For Elizabeth Nahaolelua's role in Liluokalani's 1896–1897 mainland trip, see "Deposed Queen," *Boston Daily Globe,* December 26, 1896, 1; "Queen of Hawaii," *Washington Post,* January 24, 1897, 1.

39. *Ha'ilono Mele* 2 (March 1978): 3–4; "Called Caruso of the Islands, dies after long illness," *Honolulu Star-Bulletin,* February 25, 1914, 1.

40. "'Sonny' Cunha, Bard of Hawaii, Taken by Death," *Honolulu Advertiser,* January 24, 1933, 1; Richard A. Greer, "Cunha's Alley: The Anatomy of a Landmark," *Hawaiian Journal of History* 2 (1968): 144, 147–148; Rev. Henry P. Judd, *Henry Judd, The Third Generation in Hawaii: Memoirs of Rev. Henry P. Judd, Hawaii* (North Charleston, SC: BookSurge LLP, 2005), 15–16.

41. "Sousa would have been thrilled," one audience member wrote afterward. "It was a standing ovation for this unknown marvel who played the ukulele to sound as if he had an invisible trio accompaniment. That thrill of 61 years ago still lingers with me!" Manuel G. Jardim, *Commentary on Emigration to the Terra Nova* (Honolulu: n.p., 1971), 29–31. Antonio Abreu Santos may be the A. A. Santos who collaborated with Angeline Nunes on the 1915 method, *Original Method and Self-Instructor on the Ukulele.*

42. The number of articles on Hawaii cataloged in *Poole's Index to Periodical Literature* increased more than fivefold from the 1887–1892 volume (fourteen items) to the 1892–1896 period (seventy-two items).

43. *New York Times Book Review,* July 16, 1898, BR478. Among the books published that year was Mabel Loomis Todd's *Corona and Coronet,* in which she noted that "at a moment's notice any chance group [of Native Hawaiians] can take up guitars or the little 'ukulele,' playing and singing together in delightful harmony the half plaintive and wholly sweet Hawaiian airs." "Among the New Books," *Chicago Daily Tribune,* December 1, 1898, 8.

44. "New Books on Hawaii and the Philippines," *New York Times Book Review,* July 23, 1898, 1.

45. Richard Hamilton Potts, "Kulamea: A Romance of Honolulu," *Atlanta Constitution,* April 2, 1893, 3; *Daily* [Chicago] *Inter Ocean,* April 8, 1893, 10; *Omaha World Herald,* April 16, 1893, 10; *Philadelphia Inquirer,* August 6, 1893, 23. In Jessie Kaufman's January 1900 short story, "A Hawaiian Expedient," a Honolulu hostess relies on her 'ukulele to avoid embarrassing questions from visiting friends. Among the illustrations is a drawing of a lei-bedecked tourist couple standing on the deck of a steamer and displaying a 'ukulele, which the caption identifies as "a typical memento from Hawaii." Jessie Kaufman, "A Hawaiian Expedient," *Overland Monthly* 25 (January 1900): 16–17.

46. Elias Savada, comp., *The American Film Institute Catalog of Motion Pictures Produced in the United States: Film Beginnings, 1893–1910* (Lanham, MD: Scarecrow Press, 1995), 341, 480, 561, 1173.

47. Judd, *Henry Judd,* 51.

48. "Pronouncing Hawaii," *New York Times,* March 4, 1900, 6.

49. The first regular steamship service began in August 1883, when Claus Spreckel's Oceanic Steamship Co. began twice-monthly trips between Honolulu and San Francisco. By 1888, an estimated 500 to 750 tourists were visiting each year. Honolulu photographer James J. Williams launched *Paradise of the Pacific,* "a monthly journal devoted to Hawaiian tourist travel interests," in 1888. The first Raymond & Whitcomb vacation excursion arrived the following year. Kuykendall, *Hawaiian Kingdom,* 3:103–104, 110–111.

50. David Farber and Beth Bailey, "The Fighting Man as Tourist: The Politics of Tourist Culture in Hawaii during World War II," *Pacific Historical Review* 65 (November 1996): 642; "Promotion Committee Now Has Coast Agent," *Hawaiian Gazette,* December 4, 1903, 5; "Hawaii Wants Our Tourists," *Los Angeles Times,* March 1, 1904, A6. Small advertisements for "Hawaii, the Island Wonderland" began to appear in the *Times* in February 1904.

51. Bryan H. Farrell, *Hawaii: The Legend That Sells* (Honolulu: University Press of Hawaii 1982), 13.

52. The 1898 Honolulu directory identified four guitar manufacturers: A. Dias ("Guitar-maker and Repairer, Instruments Made of Hawaiian Wood"); M. "Munez"; J. Santos ("Manufacturer of guitars, ukuleles, and taropatch fiddles"); and Naapohou, the first known *kanaka maoli* 'ukulele maker. *Husted's Directory,* 1898, 65, 208, 251, 510. Little is known about Naapohou; he apparently was working from his Queen Street home in 1898. This is the only year he is listed as a guitar maker.

53. Advertisement, *Honolulu Evening Bulletin,* May 13, 1897, 2; advertisement, *Husted's Directory,* 1898, xv; advertisement, *San Francisco Chronicle,* September 23, 1898, 17. As early as 1895, the Hawaiian News Co. was advertising "Hawaiian Songs, Set to Music . . . Ukuleles, or Taro Patch Guitars. . . . In fact, anything as a Hawaiian Souvenir." Henry M. Whitney, *Tourists' Guide Through the Hawaiian Islands,* advertisement opposite p. 65. An August 10, 1905, invoice from the Hawaiian News Co. to Virginia Santos, widow of 'ukulele maker Jose do Espirito Santo, records the sale of eighteen 'ukuleles for a total of $104.50. 1905, No. 3781, Probate Div., First Circuit Court, T.H., In re Estate of Jose do Espirito Santo, reproduced in John King, *The Hawaiian Ukulele & Guitar Makers* (Saint Petersburg, FL: NALU Music, 2001), 56.

54. "Australia Departs," *Hawaiian Gazette,* June 5, 1896, 6. One of the earliest examples of the 'ukulele as souvenir was recorded in 1886, when a taro patch fiddle was included in two boxes of Hawaiian curios shipped to New York. "Curios Going Abroad," *Daily Bulletin,* October 1, 1886, 3.

55. Wray Taylor, "Musical Status of Hawaii," *Hawaiian Almanac & Annual, 1899* (Honolulu: Thos. G. Thrum, 1898): 166. Two such souvenirs, a "zaopatch [*sic*] Hawaiian guitar" and "Ukulele Guitar, Hawaiian" were placed on display at the April 1902 exhibition of antique musical instruments mounted by the Worcester (MA) Society of Antiquity. "Report of the Exhibition of Antique Musical Instruments . . . ," in *Proceedings of the Worcester Society of Antiquity,* vol. 18 (Worcester: Published by the Society, 1902), 110.

56. "On to Washington," *Chicago Daily Tribune,* February 3, 1893, 1. In 1901, Chicago native Mary Sprague returned from Honolulu after working there as a teacher and began giving "recitals of Hawaiian songs to the accompaniment of the ukulele, an instrument resembling a guitar, but much smaller, with four strings." "Matters Concerning Women," *Springfield* [MA] *Daily Republican,* March 21, 1901, 11.

57. *Pacific Commercial Advertiser,* December 29, 1909, 11. See also Gerould, *Hawaii,* 40: "Hawaiian curios consist chiefly of ukuleles, bead and shell necklaces, and tapa cloth." However, retail marketing left much to be desired, according to one contemporary critic: "A tour of the local curio and art shops discloses many choice articles typically Hawaiian . . . but in so heterogeneous a mass and so mixed with other things that their appeal is apt to miscarry. Tourists find it difficult to select mementoes to carry away with them, and so much valuable patronage is lost." Frances Blascoer, *The Industrial Condition of Women and Girls in Honolulu: A Social Study* (Honolulu: Paradise of the Pacific Printing, 1912), 21.

58. Mather, *One Summer,* iii.

59. "The Long Pilgrimage," *Daily Alta California,* August 14, 1883, 1; "Island Musicians," *Los Angeles Times,* August 15, 1883, 1. The belief that band members were lepers may have originated

from a report published in the *Advertiser* the year before, quoting Dr. George L. Fitch of the Honolulu Free Dispensary that leprosy was present everywhere, including among members of the band. *Pacific Commercial Advertiser,* April 8, 1882, quoted in Tate, *Hawaiian Kingdom,* 46–47. San Francisco's quarantine officer received an anonymous letter claiming two band members were lepers prior to their arrival at the conclave. "Board of Health," *San Francisco Daily Evening Bulletin,* August 9, 1883, 1. Tragically, ten years later, the wife of Mekia Kealakai—then a member of Ka Bana Lahui—was committed to Molokai as a leper. "Local and General News," *Daily Bulletin,* October 10, 1893, 3; "Local and General News," *Daily Bulletin,* October 12, 1893, 3.

60. The band played every evening on the trip to San Francisco, at the grand master's reception at the Palace Hotel, at the California Theater, the Templar's drill competition, and at Woodward's Gardens, the six-acre resort on Mission Street. "A Flying Trip," *Daily Alta California,* August 15, 1883, 1; "The Templar Pageant," *Sacramento Daily Record-Union,* August 21, 1883, 3; advertisement, *Daily Alta California,* August 19, 1883, 4; "The Knights," *Sacramento Daily Record-Union,* August 27, 1883, 1; advertisement, *Daily Evening Bulletin,* August 24, 1883, 4; Ira G. Hoitt, *Pacific Coast Guide and Programme of the Knights Templar Triennial Conclave . . .* (San Francisco: Ira G. Hoitt, 1883), 75, 77. The band's appearance cost the California Commandery $3,000. "Knights Templar," *San Francisco Daily Evening Bulletin,* October 22, 1893.

61. Patrick Hennessey, "Launching a Classic: Aloha 'Oe and the Royal Hawaiian Band Tour of 1883," *Journal of Band Research* 37 (September 2001): 33–34.

62. Phil Weaver Jr., "Going With the Swim," *Overland Monthly* 23 (April 1894): 417.

63. "At the Grandstand," *San Francisco Chronicle,* April 1, 1894, 2. This was probably "Midway Plaisance" by Dennis Mackin, a comic song published the year before by Chicago's Lyon & Healy that celebrated the original Midway in seven verses. The quartet also performed at a variety of other events, including the funeral of animal tamer Carlo Thieman and at a California Press Assn. reception. "From the Lion's Den," *San Francisco Chronicle,* February 17, 1894, 16; "Editors at the Fair," *San Francisco Chronicle,* April 5, 1894, 7.

64. "The Hawaiian Village at the Midwinter Fair," *Paradise of the Pacific* 7 (July 1894): 7. Not all the reviews of the Hawaiian Village were so positive. Honolulu businessman Theo Davies, whose sons had introduced the taro patch to England, denounced the "indecent spectacle" of the hula performances and the display of Queen Liliuokalani's throne and other royal items as a "disgraceful violation of the feelings and instincts of the poor and hounded Hawaiians." "The Hawaii Exhibit," *Daily Bulletin,* April 13, 1894, 1.

65. "Hawaiian Volcano Exhibit," *Boston Daily Globe,* April 30, 1895, 7. The story identifies the quartet by name: Maipine first tenor, Eluene second tenor, Kahuna baritone, and Aeko basso. The quartet was out of a job by the end of August; three members then joined the Hawaiian National Band, which was playing in Chicago. "Unfortunate Hula Girls," *Hawaiian Gazette,* September 6, 1895, 3.

66. "Hawaii's Ex-Queen's Concert," *New York Times,* February 5, 1897, 1; "Lil's Musicale," *Boston Daily Globe,* February 6, 1897, 12; "Still Exclusive," *Hawaiian Gazette,* February 12, 1897, 1; "The Hawaiian Queen," the *Independent,* February 20, 1897, 2. The Queen's aide, Joseph Heleluhe, played guitar. With her 'ukulele, Grace Hilborn became a regular performer at society events in Washington. See "Entertained with Hawaiian Songs," *Washington Post,* April 4, 1897, 14; "In Aid of the Blind," *Washington Post,* January 21, 1900, 7; "Among the Clubs," *Washington Post,* May 20, 1900, 16; and "Last Current Topics Talk for This Season," *Washington Post,* May 27, 1900, A4.

67. "National Band," *Hawaiian Gazette,* May 7, 1895. Spreckels was the recipient of a stringed serenade outside his home after the band's arrival in San Francisco. "Sweet Music of Hawaii," *San Francisco Call,* May 17, 1895, 7.

68. "Texas State Fair," *Dallas Morning News,* October 28, 1895, 6. In 1893, Lorrin Thurston had refused to take charge of the band in Chicago and the band later rejected an offer from George C. Beckley of Thurston's Cyclorama Co. as too late and financially insufficient. *Foreign Relations of the United States,* 477; "The Band Won't Go," *Hawaiian Gazette,* September 12, 1893, 9. The band was later reported as planning to appear at the Midwinter Exposition in San Francisco, but nothing came

of the plan. "Midwinter Fair to Have a Midway," *Chicago Daily Tribune*, September 21, 1893, 3; "Thurston Too Previous," *Daily Bulletin*, September 8, 1893, 2; "Musical Boys of Hawaii," *Daily Bulletin*, February 2, 1894, 3.

69. "Sweet Music of Hawaii," *San Francisco Call*, May 17, 1895, 7; Stillman, "History Reinterpreted," 3–6; Silva, *Aloha Betrayed*, 138–139.

70. Krauss, *Johnny Wilson*, 48. The band arrived in San Francisco on May 15, 1895, where it played at the Metropolitan Hall, in San Jose, and possibly other Bay Area venues before traveling to Los Angeles at the end of June. "Marine News," *San Francisco Chronicle*, May 16, 1895, 14; "Hawaiian Band Concert," *San Francisco Chronicle*, May 22, 1895, 8; "Amusements," *San Jose Evening News*, May 28, 1895; "News and Gossip of Plays and Players," *San Francisco Chronicle*, June 2, 1895, 5.

71. "The Music in the Park," *San Francisco Call*, June 3, 1895, 12.

72. "Redondo," *Los Angeles Times*, July 1, 1895, 9.

73. The band ended up stranded in Cleveland, Ohio, in December 1895, penniless and hungry, but refused help from the Provisional Government and managed to get back on its feet and continue its tour, playing in Chicago, Minneapolis, Kansas City, Denver, and San Francisco before returning to Honolulu in October 1896. "Woes of Band Boys," *Hawaiian Gazette*, January 7, 1896; "Spurn President Dole's Offer," *Chicago Daily Tribune*, January 17, 1896, 1; "Music Notes," *Chicago Daily Tribune*, April 19, 1896, 35; "To 'Open' Saturday," *Minneapolis Journal*, June 18, 1896, 5; "The Hawaiians Make a Hit," *Kansas City Star*, August 3, 1896, 2; "Farewell Concerts," *Rocky Mountain News*, September 20, 1896, 8; "News About the Passing Show," *San Francisco Chronicle*, September 29, 1896, 14; "The National Band," *Hawaiian Gazette*, October 23, 1896, 5. The amateurish management of the band was typical for Hawaiian organizations of the era; for insight into a more successful approach, see Margaret C. Brown, "David Blakely, Manager of Sousa's Band," in *Perspectives on John Philip Sousa*, ed. Jon Newson (Washington, D.C.: Library of Congress, 1983), 121–131.

74. "A Musical Treat," the *Daily Inter Ocean*, July 21, 1895.

75. "Texas State Fair," *Dallas Morning News*, October 28, 1895, 6.

76. "Twenty Thousand There," *Rocky Mountain News*, September 7, 1896, 1.

77. "Royal Hawaiians Visit Mr. Foster," *San Francisco Call*, October 27, 1896, 9. An estimated four thousand people turned out to welcome the band home at a gala concert at the Hawaiian Hotel in Honolulu. The band members all doffed their hats for "Hawaii Ponoi," the national anthem they sang "with a depth of feeling that gave to it an interpretation that no alien can ever hope to approach." "Our Boys," the *Independent*, December 12, 1896, 2.

78. See advertisements in the *Los Angeles Times*, July 18, 1897, II:18; July 23, 1899, III:1; July 17, 1900, I:16; January 11, 1901, II:5; April 5, 1907, 1:15. The first commercial shipment of poi flour to the mainland arrived early in 1897. "Poi by the Carload," *Chicago Daily Tribune*, February 5, 1897, 9.

79. "Society," *Los Angeles Times*, October 13, 1895, 14; "Santa Monica," *Los Angeles Times*, October 27, 1895, 22; "Society," *Los Angeles Times*, February 12, 1897, 6; "Events in Society," *Los Angeles Times*, May 30, 1897, 7.

80. "Musical Treasures," *Los Angeles Times*, April 5, 1897, 8.

81. "Society," *Sunday Oregonian*, November 29, 1896, 1; "In Hawaiian Isles," *Morning Oregonian*, May 7, 1893, 12.

82. "The California Club Gives an Interesting Hawaiian Day," *San Francisco Chronicle*, November 16, 1898, 12.

83. "Santa Catalina Island," *Los Angeles Times*, August 22, 1899, 13.

84. "Women's Club Holds Interesting Session," *San Jose Mercury*, November 16, 1902, 2; "Picturesque Salon of an Accomplished Oakland Woman Popular with the Exclusive Set," *San Francisco Call*, August 2, 1903, 14; "Afternoon with 'Hawaiians,'" *Bellingham Herald*, March 11, 1905, 3; Nancy Lee, "Society," *Morning Oregonian*, April 26, 1908, 2; "Federal Court Notes," *Daily Alaska Dispatch*, May 24, 1905, 1; "Program for Lawn Fete Friday Evening," *Idaho Daily Statesman*, June 27, 1907, 2. The "eukalele" even made an appearance at a meeting of the Bohemian Scribblers Club in San Antonio, Texas, in 1907. Among the Clubs," *Dallas Morning News*, January 28, 1907, 10.

85. Beth Abelson McLeod, "'Whence Comes the Lady Tympanist?' Gender and Instrumental Musicians in America, 1853–1990," *Journal of Social History* 27 (winter 1993): 291–292.

86. Russell Sanjek, *American Popular Music and Its Business: The First Four Hundred Years* (New York: Oxford University Press, 1988), 3:32; William Howland Kenney, *Recorded Music in American Life: The Phonograph and Popular Memory, 1890-1945* (New York: Oxford University Press, 1999), 90.

87. *Sherman, Clay & Co. 1912 Catalogue of Musical Merchandise* (San Francisco: n.p.), 12 (Jim Tranquada collection).

88. Susan Porter Benson, *Saleswomen, Managers and Customers in American Department Stores, 1890-1940* (Urbana, IL: University of Illinois Press, 1986), 76.

89. James H. Collins, "The Eternal Feminine," *Printers Ink* 35 (June 26, 1901): 3, quoted in Charles McGovern, "Consumption and Citizenship in the United States, 1900–1940," in Susan Strasser et al., eds., *Getting and Spending: European and American Consumer Societies in the Twentieth Century* (Washington, D.C.: German Historical Institute/Cambridge University Press, 1998), 45. See also Paul D. Converse, *Marketing Methods and Policies*, 2nd ed. (New York: Prentice Hall, 1924), 268–269.

90. "Mrs. Leland Stanford's Reception Entertained Faculty of Stanford Yesterday," *San Francisco Bulletin,* January 21, 1900; "University Men as the Guests; Mrs. Stanford Gives a Brilliant Reception to Faculty and Trustees," *San Francisco Examiner,* January 21, 1900. Both articles are found in Stanford University Clippings, SC 015, vol. 12, p. 181, Stanford University Special Collections. See also "Society," *San Francisco Chronicle,* January 21, 1900, 14.

91. "Mrs. Stanford Hostess to University Students," *San Francisco Call,* May 2, 1900, 2; "Mrs. Hearst Entertains the Graduating Class," *San Francisco Call,* May 15, 1900, 8.

92. "The City in Brief," *San Francisco Chronicle,* December 8, 1900, 9; "Events in Society," *San Francisco Call,* March 10, 1904, 6. For the Hawaiian background of the founders of Mills College, see Elias Olan James, *The Story of Cyrus and Susan Mills* (Stanford, CA: Stanford University Press, 1953), 133–163.

93. "American Concert in Berlin," *New York Times,* July 23, 1911, C2. A 1912 performance by the glee club featured "some beautiful Hawaiian songs by a native singer with a sweet voice who accompanied himself on the ukulele." "U. of C. Glee Club Entertains at Victory," San Jose *Sunday Mercury & Herald,* April 21, 1912, 28.

94. "Life's Gentler Side—Society, Music, Song and the Dance—The Theaters," *Los Angeles Times,* November 7, 1913, 2:7; Julian Johnson, "June Uplifts Frail April," *Los Angeles Times,* December 16, 1911, 1:7; Sydney Ford, "Women's Work, Women's Clubs," *Los Angeles Times,* June 18, 1914, 2:7. In October 1914, the Hawaiian Ukulele School advertised in Occidental's student newspaper, offering a free 'ukulele to the first ten pupils to enroll in its fifteen-lesson ukulele course. "We teach you all the strokes, solo work and accompaniments to popular songs," the ad promised. The *Occidental,* October 13, 1914, 3.

95. Sydney Ford, "Women's Work, Women's Clubs," *Los Angeles Times,* January 26, 1913, 3:6.

96. Ellen Blackmer Maxwell's 1896 novel, *Three Old Maids in Hawaii,* makes passing mention of the 'ukulele (New York: Eaton & Mains, 1896), 180, 193; Jessie Kaufman's 1912 novel, *A Jewel of the Seas,* is set in Honolulu, and references to the 'ukulele are sprinkled throughout. Jessie Kaufman, *A Jewel of the Seas* (Philadelphia: J.B. Lippincott Co., 1912), 66, 94, 242, 247, 252, 274.

97. Jack London, *The Valley of the Moon* (New York: Macmillan Co., 1913), 150, 391.

98. Kevin Starr, *Americans and the California Dream 1850–1915* (New York: Oxford University Press, 1973), 175–77.

99. "Southern Yachting Notes," *Los Angeles Times,* August 15, 1911, 3:3.

100. Arthur C. Verge, "George Freeth: King of the Surfers and California's Forgotten Hero," *California History* 80 (summer/fall 2001): 83, 86–88; "George Freeth," in Matt Warshaw, *The Encyclopedia of Surfing* (Orlando, FL: Harcourt, 2003), 214–215.

101. Hawaiian sextets and quintets began to appear at private dinners and benefits as early as 1896. "Ladies' Night at the Union League," *San Francisco Chronicle,* February 13, 1896, 11; "Benefit of

Miss A.J. Wolter," *San Francisco Chronicle,* April 19, 1896, 29; "Alameda's Showing at the Exposition," *San Francisco Chronicle,* July 30, 1896, 10.

102. "Society," *San Francisco Call,* March 4, 1910, 26; "Society," *San Francisco Call,* April 8, 1900, 24. It's possible that the quintet became a quartet in November 1900 when Hennessey was arrested by San Francisco police on suspicion of stealing $205 from an acquaintance. "Robbed His Companions," *San Francisco Chronicle,* November 6, 1900, 5.

103. "Fun Furnished at the Alcazar," *San Francisco Call,* February 21, 1900, 9; Emporium advertisement, *San Francisco Chronicle,* December 8, 1899, 5; "Will Dance After Dinner," *San Francisco Call,* February 13, 1900, 6; "Honored Guests," *San Francisco Call,* April 20, 1900, 5; "The City in Brief," *San Francisco Chronicle,* February 7, 1899, 12; "Fete Champetre at Arbor Villa a Brilliant Affair," *San Francisco Call,* May 6, 1900, 25; "Insurance Men and Their Wives Feasted," *San Francisco Call,* April 27, 1900, 9; "Liliuokalani and Suite Are in This City," *San Francisco Call,* May 20, 1900, 3. They also serenaded Prince David Kawananakoa two months later. "Ocean and Water Front," *San Francisco Chronicle,* July 26, 1900, 10.

104. "With the Players and the Music Folk," *San Francisco Call,* October 1, 1905, 19; "Hawaiian Musicians Heard in Excellent Programme," *San Francisco Call,* October 7, 1905, 16; "Hawaiian Music at Techau's," September 5, 1905, 2; advertisement, Neptune Casino, *San Francisco Call,* May 28, 1905, 41. The instrumentation for Kealakai's band was listed as violin, violoncello, double bass, flute, saxophone, two guitars, "ukelele and taro-patch, the last two being native string instruments." His lineup was impressive: David Nape, W. B. Jones, James Shaw, John Edwards, James Kulolia, Solomon Hiram, Charles Palikapu, John Aea, and Henry Kalani. "Musicians to Tour World," *Hawaiian Gazette,* September 19, 1905, 3. For Santa Cruz, see "Musician Begins Engagement at Santa Cruz," *Pacific Commercial Advertiser,* June 30, 1905, 5; and "Pianist, Leader of Sextette, Begins Engagement at Santa Cruz," *Pacific Commercial Advertiser,* June 30, 1905, 5.

105. "Excellent Bill at the Bell Theater," *Oakland Tribune,* August 7, 1905, 4.

106. "Theaters—Amusements—Entertainments," *Los Angeles Times,* October 30, 1907, 12; May 12, 1907, 12; April 13, 1907, 12; May 3, 1907, 2:9; "'Show' for Bilicke," June 24, 1907, 2:5.

107. "Romped Just Like Children," *Los Angeles Times,* July 19, 1907, 2:3.

108. Advertisement, *Los Angeles Times,* July 13, 1907, 2:1, and *Los Angeles Herald,* July 13, 1907, 5.

109. "Some Notable Festivities Incident to Society During the Past Week," *Los Angeles Times,* May 2, 1909, 3:3. Previously, a Hawaiian Quintet performed at a Hotel Alexandria reception put on by the Dohenys for the Mexican ambassador in 1907. "Senor Creel Is Honored," *Los Angeles Herald,* August 30, 1907, 3.

110. Quoted in the *Hawaiian Gazette,* September 8, 1905, and cited in David W. Bandy, "Bandmaster Henry Berger and the Royal Hawaiian Band," *Hawaiian Journal of History* 24 (1990): 76.

111. T.M.C., "Six Weeks More of the Big Show," *Ft. Wayne* [Indiana] *Journal Gazette,* September 3, 1905, 22.

112. Blanche Partington, "Island Music at Alhambra," *San Francisco Call,* August 18, 1905, 6.

113. This photograph, with its handwritten notations on the back, is in the Rosa Portell collection.

114. See "Ye Oregon Grille," *Morning Oregonian,* December 27, 1908, 6; advertisement, January 1, 1910, 5; "Hawaiians Honor Dead," May 3, 1910, 20; advertisement, March 22, 1911, 6.

115. "The Vaudeville Theaters," *Morning Oregonian,* February 18, 1908, 9.

116. Advertisement, Wigwam Theater, *Nevada State Journal,* July 9, 1908, 4; "Dances Next Week," *Salt Lake Herald,* March 22, 1908, 7; "Hawaiian Club," *Deseret Evening News,* April 14, 1908, 2; "Musicians Directory," *Deseret Evening News,* December 12, 1908, 21. Hawaiian Mormons first moved to Utah in 1889. Fred E. Woods, "A Most Influential Mormon Islander: Jonathan Hawaii Napela," *Hawaiian Journal of History* 42 (2008): 155.

117. "Hawaiian Exhibit," in *Participation in the Alaska-Yukon-Pacific Exposition,* Senate Docs. 61st Congress, 3rd Session, Vol. 29 (Doc. No. 671) (Washington, D.C.: GPO, 1911), 86–89.

118. "Exposition Programme," *Seattle Post-Intelligencer,* August 25, 1909, 1; "Gov. Hays Likes Hawaiian Pines," August 6, 1909, 1; "Hawaiian Dance Brilliant Function," August 27, 1909, 12.

119. "Royal Hawaiians Make Hit," *Idaho Daily Statesman,* November 7, 1910, 7. Pukui and Elbert define "wela ka hao" as "the iron is hot," i.e., "Whoopee!" or "Hurray!"

120. "Quintet Club with Polo Men," *Hawaiian Gazette,* September 22, 1903, 7.

121. "Promotion Work Brings Results," *Hawaiian Gazette,* September 24, 1909, 5.

122. Adria Imada, "Hawaiians on Tour: Hula Circuits through the American Empire," *American Quarterly* 56 (March 2004): 130.

123. "Death of John Ailau," *Daily Bulletin,* January 27, 1894, 3.

124. "To License Quintet Clubs," *Hawaiian Gazette,* February 2, 1909, 2.

125. "Local Brevities," *Pacific Commercial Advertiser,* June 11, 1905, 12. The 'ukulele did not make Santo a rich man: He left an estate valued at $1,575. "Old Way and New," *Hawaiian Gazette,* August 4, 1905, 6.

126. Vierra is listed as a guitar maker and cabinet maker in the 1900–1901 city directory; Fernandez as a guitar maker in the 1903–1904 edition.

127. *Husted's Directory of Honolulu and Territory of Hawaii 1908* (Honolulu: Polk Hustead, 1908): Advertisements are unpaginated.

128. *Pacific Commercial Advertiser,* December 29, 1909, 11.

129. *Polk-Husted Directory Co.'s Directory of Honolulu and the Territory of Hawaii, 1911* (Honolulu: Polk-Husted, 1911), 124, 608, 1057.

130. John William Siddall, ed., *Men of Hawaii: A Biographical Reference Library,* vol. 2 (Honolulu: Star-Bulletin, 1921), 241; Karen S. Drozd, "The Hawaiian 'Ukulele: Its Players, Makers, Teachers and Continuity in Traditional Transmission Processes," MA thesis, University of Hawaii, 1998 (Ann Arbor, MI: UMI Dissertation Services, 1999), 99.

131. John Hutchens, "'The Bird of Paradise' on an Eighteen-Year Front," *New York Times,* April 6, 1930, 120.

Chapter 5: A Landscape Set to Music

1. Helen M. Morosco and Leonard Paul Dugger, *The Oracle of Broadway: Life of Oliver Morosco* (Caldwell, ID: Caxton Printers, 1944), 182–184; Julian Johnson, "'Bird' Sheds a Few Feathers," *Los Angeles Times,* September 13, 1911, 2:5.

2. Morosco and Dugger, *Oracle of Broadway,* 185–186, 190–192; "Woman Wins Suit on Bird of Paradise," *New York Times,* May 30, 1924, 13. The original backers of the play were sugar mogul Claus Spreckels and San Francisco mayor James D. Phelan. Morosco and Dugger, *Oracle of Broadway,* 194. Phelan earned an estimated $200,000 for his initial investment of $10,000. "The Story of a Play," *Washington Post,* April 30, 1922, 53. Morosco formed his own movie company in 1914, when it was reported that "Bird of Paradise" was among his plays "certain to be filmed," but nothing came of it. "Oliver Morosco Enters Motion Picture Field," *Los Angeles Times,* November 6, 1914, 3:4.

3. "Morosco's Pet at the Majestic," *Los Angeles Times,* October 9, 1913, 2:7; "'Red Widow' at Morosco," *Los Angeles Times,* October 25, 1914, 3:1; "Popular Play Opens Tonight," *Los Angeles Times,* December 19, 1915, 3:1; "Our Latest Luana," *Los Angeles Times,* January 6, 1918, 3:19; "Laughter Is the Keynote," *Los Angeles Times,* January 4, 1920; "Native Hula Dancers with Exotic Drama," *Los Angeles Times,* December 18, 1921, 3:33.

4. "Vivid Romance of the South Seas Is This Week's Theatrical Novelty," *Washington Post,* April 30, 1916, MT2.

5. "Belasco—'The Bird of Paradise,'" *Washington Post,* December 24, 1912, 5.

6. "What Press Agents Say," *Duluth* [MN] *News Tribune,* February 28, 1918, 6; "Author of Bird of Paradise Honored," San Jose [CA] *Evening News,* April 10, 1916, 5. The Hawaii Promotion Committee was quick to recognize the value of Tully's play: It assisted him "in every way possible" during his 1910 visit to the Islands and provided grass skirts and other stage properties for the play's Los

Angeles debut, estimating the play would provide more than $100,000 in publicity for Hawaii. "'Bird of Paradise' Fine Advertisement," *Hawaiian Gazette,* October 17, 1911, 7. For Tully's 1910 trip, see "Local Brevities," *Hawaiian Gazette,* June 28, 1910, 8.

7. Harry Owens, *Sweet Leilani: The Story Behind the Song* (Pacific Palisades, CA: Hula House, 1970), c; Lee Shippey, "The Lee Side O' L.A.," *Los Angeles Times,* May 28, 1933, 8; Ronn Ronck, *Celebration: A Portrait of Hawaii through the Songs of the Brothers Cazimero* (Honolulu: Mutual Publishing, 1984), 30, 34. An Akron, Ohio, performance of the *Bird* reportedly inspired Clark Gable to become an actor. John C. Moffitt, "The Story of Clark Gable's Climb to Fame in Filmland," *Hartford Courant,* October 30, 1932, B5.

8. *Los Angeles Times,* September 22, 1911, 1:2; September 25, 1911, 1:5. For a list of the original musicians, see "'Bird of Paradise Has Scenic Beauty," *New York Times,* January 9, 1912. The *Los Angeles Times* reported that the New York cast included the original quintet that debuted with the play in Los Angeles. "Paradise Bird Gets Plumage," November 24, 1911, 2:5. A photo of the quintet and their instruments appeared in the *New York Times'* January 21, 1912, pictorial section.

9. This sales claim can be found on later editions of "Native Hawaiian Songs from Oliver Morosco's Production of The Bird of Paradise," sheet music published by the John Franklin Music Co. of New York. For the Victor sides, see the "July Victor Records" advertisement, *Los Angeles Times,* June 28, 1913, 2:1. The quintette made at least one New York record store appearance in support of their release. "Demand for Hawaiian Records," *Music Trade Review* (November 15, 1913): 52.

10. "Hawaiian Music Universally Popular," *Edison Phonograph Monthly* 14 (September 1916): 3, cited in Tim Gracyk and Frank Hoffman, *Popular American Recording Pioneers 1895–1925* (New York: Haworth Press 2002), 119.

11. For the rise of vaudeville, see Robert W. Snyder, *The Voice of the City: Vaudeville and Popular Culture in New York* (New York: Oxford University Press, 1989), 26–27; Sanjek, *American Popular Music,* 2:338. For the rise of Tin Pan Alley, see Sanjek, *American Popular Music,* 2:401, and David A. Jasen, *Tin Pan Alley: The Composers, the Songs, the Performers and Their Times* (New York: Donald I. Fine, 1988), 6–9. For the first phonograph record, see Andre Millard, *America on Record: A History of Recorded Sound* (Cambridge: Cambridge University Press, 1995), 46.

12. Michael Kammen, *American Culture, American Tastes: Social Change and the 20th Century* (New York: Alfred A. Knopf, 1999), 70–71, 77–80; Robert W. Rydell and Rob Kroes, *Buffalo Bill in Bologna: The Americanization of the World, 1869–1922* (Chicago: University of Chicago Press, 2005), 4; Nicholas E. Tawa, *The Way to Tin Pan Alley: American Popular Song, 1866–1910* (New York: Schirmer Books, 1990), 3; Janet M. Davis, *The Circus Age: Culture and Society Under the Big Top* (Chapel Hill: University of North Carolina Press, 2002), 34; Snyder, *Voice of the City,* xiv–xv.

13. Desmond, *Staging Tourism,* 17. Similarly, it was sound recordings that introduced John Philip Sousa and his band to a national audience. Patrick Warfield, "Making the Band: The Formation of John Philip Sousa's Ensemble," *American Music* 24 (spring 2006): 33–34.

14. Orvar Lofgren, *On Holiday: A History of Vacationing* (Berkeley: University of California Press, 1999), 216. For example, consider this passage from a 1930 guidebook: "Waikiki by moonlight is something that must be experienced and not read about. The golden glow of a tropical moon, silhouetting the bathers enjoying the softly langorous [sic] night, the faint strumming of ukuleles and guitars in the hands of expert players, accompanied by the falsetto and slurring voices of native singers, all help to make the beach a sentiment and not a locality." Townsend Griffis, *When You Go to Hawaii* (Boston: Houghton Mifflin, 1930), 56.

15. J. C. Furnas, *Anatomy of Paradise: Hawaii and the Islands of the South Seas* (London: Victor Gollancz, 1950), 194. "I think the Hawaiian Islands have received more first-class advertising through Hawaiian music than any other organized effort for publicity," Honolulu music publisher W. D. Adams said in 1916. "How Melody Is Sweeping Nation," *Daily* [Juneau] *Alaska Dispatch,* October 25, 1916, 8. Even the federal government recognized music's importance: A 1937 pamphlet issued by the Department of the Interior noted that "no small factor in the islands' appeal is the native music which is heard with all of the richness and melody of the olden days when an island monarchy

added to the glamour of everyday life." U.S. Department of the Interior, *General Information Regarding the Territory of Hawaii* (Washington, D.C.: Government Printing Office, 1937), 39.

16. Tully's play popularized the fallacious idea that Hawaiians practiced human sacrifice in volcanoes, a canard that lingered for decades. See "Suitor Leaps into Kilauea's Fiery Pit with Girl," *Los Angeles Times,* June 3, 1932, 1; "Fiery Sacrifice Tale Exploded," *Los Angeles Times,* June 16, 1932, 8.

17. Arthur Hobson Quinn, *A History of American Drama from the Civil War to the Present Day* (New York: Appleton-Century-Crofts, 1936), 130. A reviewer for *Munsey's Magazine* in its March 1912 issue noted that Tully's setting "is new to the stage, so far as I can recall, except possibly in comic opera."

18. Richard C. Norton, *A Chronology of American Musical Theater* (Oxford: Oxford University Press, 2002), 1:983.

19. Carr, *Ethnomimesis,* 4–5; George C. D. Dell, *Annals of the New York Stage* (New York: Columbia University Press, 1927), 1:328–329, 442, 446; 2:156, 375.

20. Cecil Smith and Glenn Litton, *Musical Comedy in America* (New York: Theater Arts Books, 1981), 39–42. It was this same comic opera fad that inspired Kalakaua vice chamberlain Edward Purvis to pen his *Grand Duke of Gynbergdrinkenstein* in 1886.

21. Norton, *American Musical Theater,* 1:518, 526, 562, 568, 576, 581, 582, 590.

22. Norton, *American Musical Theater,* 1:505; Forbes, *Hawaiian Bibliography,* 4:424.

23. "Lillee Walkee Lanny" originally appeared in the *Boston Courier* and was reprinted in the *Los Angeles Times,* January 31, 1894, 8. The cover art for "Queen Lily Ouki-Ouk-Alani" can be found at www.hulapages.com/00434b.jpg. For "Queen Lil," see Palace Theater advertisement, *Boston Daily Globe,* June 30, 1895, 19. It also was staged in Washington, D.C., in 1898. "Columbian Vaudeville Club Burlesque," *Washington Post,* May 22, 1898, 24. One unnamed but enterprising theatrical manager invited Liliuokalani to appear on stage. She declined. "Offer to Liliuokalani," *San Francisco Chronicle,* July 8, 1897, 9.

24. For Fields and Sousa, see "Queen Lil in Opera," *San Francisco Chronicle,* April 28, 1894, 1; "Ex-Queen Liliuokalani," *New York Times,* July 13, 1897, 4. The following day the *Times* reported Liliuokalani had settled down "into a sort of literary retirement" in a Manhattan hotel, devoting herself in part to "composing Hawaiian melodies and songs." "Liliuokalani Rests," July 14, 1897, 10.

25. Norton, *American Musical Theater,* 1:605; "Mr. Noblette's Losing Venture," *New York Times,* July 28, 1897, 3. *Captain Cook,* music by Noah Brandt, libretto by Sands W. Forman, was first staged in San Francisco in September 1895. "The Latest Amateur Opera," *San Francisco Chronicle,* August 30, 1895, 16; "At the Theaters," *San Francisco Chronicle,* June 27, 1897, 5.

26. "Keith's Theater," *Philadelphia Inquirer,* July 30, 1899, 8; "The Week's Attractions," *Los Angeles Times,* October 22, 1899, D1; "Vaudeville at the Arch," *Philadelphia Inquirer,* January 9, 1900, 7. The trio was identified as Oriska Worden, Adele Archer, and Vira Rial.

27. Advertisement, *Sunday Oregonian,* February 26, 1911, 2. In 1895, Portland audiences were regaled with an amateur burlesque, *The Hawaiian King, Pro Tem.* "Island Life in Burlesque," *Hawaiian Gazette,* June 4, 1895, 5.

28. Amy Kaplan, *The Anarchy of Empire in the Making of U.S. Culture* (Cambridge, MA: Harvard University Press, 2002), 10. For an early example of such a caricature, see the cover of the January 4, 1875, edition of the (New York) *Daily Graphic,* which treats King Kalakaua's visit to New York. See also Silva, *Aloha Betrayed,* 174–178.

29. Adler, *Liholiho,* 108; King, *American Diplomat,* 110, 141, 468, 492. "I know there were some about town, especially Americans, who were in the habit of indulging in disparaging reflections to His Majesty's disadvantage, calling him a d-n-d nigger and other epithets of a like character," Gregg noted on November 14, 1857. Members of the Royal Hawaiian Band were referred to as "niggers" during their 1883 visit to San Francisco, and a member of the National Band was refused service in a Leavenworth, Kansas, barbershop in 1895 by a barber who insisted he was black. "The Hawaiian Band," *Boston Daily Advertiser,* June 23, 1887, 1; *Atchison Daily Globe,* November 22, 1895, 8. When newly elected territorial delegate Jonah Kuhio Kalanianaole arrived in Washington, D.C., in 1903, it

was widely reported that on an earlier trip to Canada he had punched a man who called him "nigger." "Prince Cupid," *Boston Daily Globe,* February 1, 1903, 21.

30. Samuel C. Armstrong, "Lessons from the Hawaiian Islands," *Journal of Christian Philosophy,* January 1884: 213, cited in Gary Y. Okihiro, *A History of Hawaii and the United States* (Berkeley: University of California Press, 2008), 114.

31. "Pa Was a Barber," *Atlanta Constitution,* November 16, 1893, 1; Lucien Young, *The Boston at Hawaii, or the Observations and Impressions of a Naval Officer during a Stay of Fourteen Months in Those Islands on a Man-of-War* (Washington, D.C.: Gibson Brothers, 1898), 10, 22, 52; Armstrong, *Around the World,* 15. Hawaiians were not unaware of such racist attitudes: In the fall of 1897, *Ke Aloha Aina* published an editorial titled, "Are Hawaiians Going to Be Like Blacks?" noting that haole hatred and fear of blacks and Native Americans were well understood, and asking how Hawaiians could escape from "the bottles of poison they desire to feed to us." Silva, *Aloha Betrayed,* 148. Liliuokalani's 1896 trip to Washington, D.C., was reported in the *Atlanta Constitution* as an item under the heading, "What the Negro Is Doing" (December 27, 1896, B24).

32. Other examples include "The Belle of Honolulu" (San Francisco: Sherman, Clay & Co., 1898); "My Gal from Honolulu" (Boston: Evans Music Co., 1899); "The Honolulu Cakewalk" (New York: N. Weinstein, 1899); and "Honolulu Pranks" (St. Louis: Stark Music Co., 1902). Johnson's "Belle of Honolulu" and "Honolulu Lady" were performed at a benefit concert in Honolulu's Orpheum Theater in 1898. Advertisement, the *Independent,* December 29, 1898, 2. Banjoist Vess Ossman recorded "Honolulu Cakewalk" for Berliner in 1899. Rockwell, *Hawaiian Records,* 907.

33. Eric Ledell Smith, *Bert Williams: A Biography of the Pioneer Black Comedian* (Jefferson, NC: McFarland & Co., 1992), 8.

34. Smith, *Bert Williams,* 42.

35. Desmond, *Staging Tourism,* 68; Garrett, *Struggling to Define a Nation,* 194.

36. Karen Linn, *That Half-Barbaric Twang: The Banjo in American Popular Culture* (Urbana: University of Illinois Press, 1991), 7, 98–99.

37. Jeffrey J. Noonan, *The Guitar in America: Victorian Era to Jazz Age* (Jackson: University Press of Mississippi, 2008), 19, 27, 42, 44, 100–101.

38. Snyder, *Vaudeville,* xii, xv, 43.

39. Ibid., 37, 126.

40. At least two books credit Toots Paka as the "chief exponent" of the Hawaiian craze, beginning in 1910. See Joe Laurie Jr., *Vaudeville: From the Honky Tonks to the Palace* (New York: Henry Holt and Co., 1953), 323 (which cites "Toots Papka"), and Abel Green and Joe Laurie Jr., *Show Biz from Vaude to Video* (New York: Henry Holt & Co., 1981), 36.

41. Kanahele, *Hawaiian Music,* 388–389. The death record for Hannah Paka, dated March 4, 1942, gives a birthdate of January 18, 1871, and a birthplace of Michigan. California Death Index, 1940–1997, California Department of Health Services, Center for Health Statistics. Her birthdate was given as January 18, 1879, and her birthplace as Port Huron, Michigan, when she and July returned from a 1926 trip to Honolulu. List of United States Citizens, "City of Los Angeles," March 19, 1926, Passenger Lists of Vessels Arriving at San Francisco, 1893–1953, Micropublication M1410 RG085, National Archives. According to the 1930 Census, they were married ca. 1903, when July was twenty-eight and Toots was twenty-six. Dwelling 118, Family 118, Saugus Precinct #2, Soledad Twp., Los Angeles County, ED 1515, Sheet 4B, Roll 172, 1930 Census.

42. Advertisement, *Bellingham Herald,* December 14, 1906, 6.

43. Paka and her trio performed at Keith's Philadelphia the first week of January 1909, the Poli in Wilkes-Barre, Pennsylvania, the week of January 16, possibly at the Majestic in Lexington, Kentucky, in April, Keith's Boston the week of May 17, at Keith & Proctor's Fifth Avenue Theater in New York the week of June 6, and at a "Roman Feast" at the Hotel Knickerbocker in Manhattan on December 15. Advertisement, *Philadelphia Inquirer,* January 3, 1909, 13; "At the Theaters," Wilkes-Barre *Times Leader,* January 16, 1909, 8; advertisement, *Lexington Herald,* April 25, 1909, 8; Snyder, *Voice of the City,* 71–72; "At the Theaters This Week," *New York Times,* June 6, 1909, 10:9; "Hotel Men

Dine in Sunken Garden," *New York Times,* December 16, 1909, 9. For Paka's Edison recordings, see L. E. Andersen and T. Malcolm Rockwell, "Hawaiian Recordings: The Early Years," *Victrola and 78 Journal* (winter 1996): 3. Although Kekuku, a seminal figure in the development of the steel guitar, is not named in any of these accounts, a subsequent advertisement for a personal appearance at a Los Angeles music store noted that "many will doubtless remember Mr. Kekuku as soloist with 'Toots Paka' while on the Orpheum Circuit." Advertisement for Southern California Music Co., *Los Angeles Times,* September 3, 1914, 1:3. Kekuku's first documented appearance on the mainland was with a quintet in San Francisco in 1904. "Preparations Complete for Great Pageant Scheduled for To-Day," *San Francisco Call,* September 6, 1904, 5. In July 1904, it was reported that "Joseph E. Kekuku, the copyist in the Registry of Conveyances who doubly assigned a month's salary warrant and then disappeared, is in San Francisco making a precarious subsistence through his musical talents." "Local Brevities," *Hawaiian Gazette,* July 19, 1904, 4. For Kekuku's role in the development of the steel guitar, see Lorene Ruymar, *The Hawaiian Steel Guitar and its Great Hawaiian Musicians* (Anaheim Hills, CA: Centerstream Publishing, 1996), 1–26.

44. For Paka's role in *The Young Turk,* see "Tropical Dancing in The Young Turk," *Hartford Courant,* March 5, 1910, 15; for *The Echo,* see "Rehearsing 'The Echo,'" *New York Times,* March 23, 1910, 11; "Dillingham's 'Echo' Heard," *Philadelphia Inquirer,* August 11, 1910; "Musical Comedy Poised on Dancers' Toes," *New York Times,* August 21, 1910, 10:5; "Offerings at the Theaters This Week," *Washington Post,* October 4, 1910, 5; "Bessie McCoy, the Star of 'The Echo,' at the Colonial," *Boston Daily Globe,* December 25, 1910, 52.

45. "Paka Wiggles at Orpheum," *Los Angeles Times,* May 21, 1912, 2:5. Hawaiians were unimpressed by such acts. "Your American version of it is not correct," Liliuokalani's private secretary was quoted as saying during a visit to Boston. "Your theater people have exaggerated it. They have tried to improve it and have made it worse." "Red Roses for Liliuokalani," *Kansas City Star,* February 6, 1910, 3.

46. Judd, *Henry Judd,* 59. According to the show's 1899 *Route Book,* the seven Hawaiians were David Kipi, J. Kulia, G. Makalina, K. Natsia, W. Hopili, Isabella Pary, and Ribaka Natsia. The 1899 season was the show's biggest and most profitable, with performances in 132 locations during a two hundred–day season. Henry Blackman Sell and Victor Weybright, *Buffalo Bill and the Wild West* (New York: Oxford University Press, 1955), 206, 210. Advertisements for the New York show at Madison Square Garden also promised Hawaiian dancers; an opening night review mentioned only "the plaintive melody of the Hawaiian." "Wild West Show Opens," *New York Times,* March 30, 1899, 4; advertisement, *New York Times,* April 3, 1899, 10.

47. Kanahele, *Hawaiian Music,* 275.

48. Krauss, *Johnny Wilson,* 81–82; "The Music of Hawaii," *Fort Worth Register,* January 22, 1902; advertisement, Omaha *Sunday World-Herald,* January 26, 1902; "The Drama—Plays, Players and Playhouses: Music and Musicians," *Los Angeles Times,* March 9, 1902, C2. The musicians in Wilson's troupe were Kealakai, Paka, Nape, Tony Zablan, June Kuleila, Charles Baker, W. Alohikea, W. Macomber, and Richard Reuter. "Notes from the Coast," *Hawaiian Gazette,* March 7, 1902, 1. Vaudeville yodeler Mat Keefe, who had spent time in Hawaii as a boy, claimed to have introduced the 'ukulele to vaudeville in San Francisco in 1898. "Pioneer on Ukulele," *Philadelphia Evening Public Ledger,* January 11, 1919, 10.

49. "Is Leading a Hawaiian Troupe on the Keith Empire Vaudeville Circuit," *Pacific Commercial Advertiser,* December 5, 1901, 3; "Long for Island Home," *Washington Post,* December 8, 1902, 9, and "The World of Amusement," *Washington Post,* December 7, 1902, 40. A performance by "the Hawaiian band of musicians and vocalists" on Georgia's Jekyl Island was reported in the *Atlanta Constitution* of February 16, 1902, 23. The December 7 *Post* article identifies the members of the group as Kai, Mahoe, Holoua, Nahaolelua, Heleluhe, and Nawahine. Kai is called "Hawaii's most noted musician"; Mahoe is identified as the son of U.S. Circuit Court judge Mahoe of Molokai; Nahaolelua as the son (actually grandson) of the governor of Maui; Heleluhe as the son of Liliuokalani's private secretary; and Nawahine as a Maui native and son of a minister. The act also included Kamuela Kamakee, a traditional chanter, and his son Keoki, who danced the hula.

50. Advertisement, *Los Angeles Times,* June 9, 1902, 1; "Days at Woodside Park," *Philadelphia Inquirer,* July 24, 1902; advertisement, *Chicago Daily Tribune,* November 23, 1902, 64.

51. "Gossip of the Theaters," *New York Times,* April 11, 1903, 9; "Vaudeville," *New York Times,* October 18, 1903, 21; "Notes of the Theaters," *New York Times,* June 22, 1904, 9; advertisement, *New York Times,* August 17, 1904, 5; "In the Limelight at the Theaters," *Philadelphia Inquirer,* September 27, 1904; "The Theatres Last Night," *New York Times,* January 17, 1905, 5; "Forest Park's Opening," *Kansas City Star,* April 28, 1907, 4; advertisement, *Chicago Daily Tribune,* January 6, 1907, A8; "Haley's Restaurant Reopens Tonight," *Duluth News Tribune,* January 29, 1908, 12; "Thrillers of Coney Island Turned Inside Out," *New York Times,* August 23, 1908, SM8; "Theaters," *Atlanta Constitution,* July 7, 1910, 9; "Princess from Honolula 'Pinched' by the Police," *Atlanta Constitution,* August 27, 1910, 7; "Land Show Is On; Wilson Opens It to All Chicago," *Chicago Daily Tribune,* November 20, 1910, 1; "Visitors Come from Afar to Enjoy the Atlantic City Boardwalk and Bathing," *New York Times,* June 19, 1910, 10:3; "Hot Wave Defied by Ocean Breezes at Asbury Park," *New York Times,* July 9, 1911, 10:3. Some of these early appearances in New York likely were booked through Joe Puni, who landed there after the disastrous 1901–1902 tour with Kia, Heleluhe, et al. "Proposed Hawaii Agency in State of New York," *Hawaiian Gazette,* November 10, 1905, 3.

52. Mary Wood, "Kalikai of Hilo," *Boston Daily Globe,* February 15, 1906, 12.

53. "Hawaiian Music on the Mainland," *San Antonio* [Texas] *Light,* November 1, 1908, 25.

54. Lafayette Young, "At Sea with Taft Party," *Los Angeles Times,* August 31, 1905, 2:7; Elise K. Kirk, *Music at the White House: A History of the American Spirit* (Urbana: University of Illinois Press, 1986), 190; "Hawaiians Sing for Taft," *Washington Post,* April 29, 1910, 13. Quintet members were David Manuku, H. Smith, John Peterson, Harry Clark, and James Crowell. The group played in Atlantic City that summer. "Boardwalk Won't Give Up Singers," *Hawaiian Gazette,* August 5, 1910, 7.

55. The glee club included John and William Ellis, bass Ben Jones, Solomon Hiram, and James Shaw. "Sixty-One in the Band," *Hawaiian Gazette,* May 15, 1906, 5. Cunha had a disagreement with Berger and broke away from the band with a group of musicians that attempted their own tour. "Juanita Beckley Given Divorce from Husband," *San Francisco Call,* November 14, 1907, 5.

56. Bandy, "Royal Hawaiian Band," 78, 80. "Immediately after the conclusion of this number, the brass band disappeared and the stage was occupied by the Hawaiian Glee Club, which played dance music on guitars and native instruments, accompanying the music with singing characteristic of the islands." "The Hawaiians are Popular," *Kansas City Star,* July 31, 1906, 11. It was the same in St. Louis: "The Glee Club with its quaint native instruments, the ukulele and the taropatch, its beautifully blended voices and superb tenor, John H. Ellis, caught the popular fancy at once and received encore after encore." "Hawaiian Band at St. Louis," *St. Louis Republic,* quoted in *Hawaiian Gazette,* September 11, 1906, 3.

57. "Royal Hawaiian Band Is Also a Glee Club," *San Francisco Call,* May 23, 1906, 2.

58. *The Honolulu Students from the Hawaiian Islands* (Rochester, NY: Central Printing and Engraving Co., ca. 1909, Redpath Chautauqua Collection, Special Collections, University of Iowa).

59. Ibid.; "Lecture Course Presented by Church One of Splendid Merit," *Logansport* [Indiana] *Journal,* November 28, 1909, 1; "The College Lecture Course," *Emporia* [Kansas] *Daily Gazette,* September 5, 1908; "The Teachers Institute," *Wellsboro* [Pennsylvania] *Agitator,* October 28, 1908, 1; "Honolulu Students," *Gettysburg* [Pennsylvania] *Compiler,* November 11, 1908, 8.

60. "Saturday's Matinee," *Hawaiian Gazette,* March 17, 1891, 7. The Hawaiian National Band was recorded at the Queen Street Armory, the *Daily Bulletin* reported on April 5, 1893 (Local and General News, 3). An 1899 cylinder recording by William Ellis, July Paka, and others in San Francisco has generally been regarded as the first music recording. Andersen and Rockwell, "Hawaiian Recording," 1–2; Rockwell, *Hawaiian Records,* ix. Kalakaua recorded a ten-minute speech in Hawaiian on his San Francisco deathbed in 1891. "Kalakaua's Last Words Preserved by Phonograph," *Hawaiian Gazette,* February 10, 1891, 3. Liliuokalani recorded a brief message in Hawaiian in Honolulu in November 1891. "The Phonograph," *Hawaiian Gazette,* November 24, 1891, 3. Although the identity

of the Royal Hawaiian Troubadours has been the subject of much speculation, the spoken introductions to the recordings make the identity of the artists clear.

61. "Hawaiian Recordings," 3–4. Victor took out an ad in 1911 that listed records in nineteen different languages, including Hawaiian. *Christian Science Monitor,* March 25, 1911, 13; *Boston Daily Globe,* March 26, 1911, 52. The Columbia sides were recorded in Honolulu in July 1911 by Harry Marker at Sonny Cunha's Honolulu Music Co. on Alakea St. and were released in January 1912. "Making Records of Local Music," *Pacific Commercial Advertiser,* July 29, 1911; "Records of Hawaiian Music," *Music Trade Review* (January 20, 1912): 50.

62. Norton, *American Musical Theater,* 1:854–855, 939–940; Garrett, *Struggling to Define a Nation,* 165–166; "Dramatic and Musical," *New York Times,* November 14, 1899, 5. The *Grand Mogul* featured Luder's arrangement of "Aloha Oe," rendered by a male octet in the last act. Harlowe W. Hoyt, "Two Popular 'Come-Backs' and a Bang-Up Hipp Bill Here This Week," *Cleveland Plain Dealer,* September 22, 1918, 51. By 1914, "Aloha Oe" had appeared in at least eight different editions published in San Francisco, New York, Philadelphia, and Chicago.

63. "Theatrical," *Lexington* [Kentucky] *Herald,* February 2, 1907, 4. Librettist Frank Pixley and composer Gustav Luders reportedly spent nine months in Hawaii and the Philippines while writing the musical. "Footlight Flashes," *Philadelphia Inquirer,* September 8, 1907, 11.

64. Kanahele 308; *Queen's Songbook,* 43–44. The words and music to "He Mele Lahui Hawaii" were printed by the Boston-based Hawaiian Club in 1868. *Hawaiian Club Papers* (Boston: Press of Abner Kingman, 1868), 116–117.

65. Forbes, *Hawaiian National Bibliography,* 4:98–99.

66. A. R. Cunha, *Songs of Hawaii* (Honolulu: Bergstrom Music Co., 1902), 3.

67. Kanahele, *Hawaiian Music,* 69; Biographical Information Sheet, Albert R. Cunha file, Records of Yale Alumni (RU 830, Box 957), Special Collections, Yale University Library.

68. Kanahele, *Hawaiian Music,* 69, 106; Elizabeth Tatar, *Strains of Change: The Impact of Tourism on Hawaiian Music,* Bishop Museum Special Publication 78 (Honolulu: Bishop Museum Press, 1987), 11. Cunha's first-known compositions, "Our Bloomer Girls" (1895) and "Bay City March (Two Step)" (1898), were published in San Francisco. They are both ragtime, written for piano; copies of the sheet music are in the personal collection of Rick Cunha of Van Nuys, California. "Our Bloomer Girls" was performed by the Royal Hawaiian Band at the Hawaiian Hotel on October 25, 1895. "Band Concert," *Hawaiian Gazette,* October 25, 1895, 5. Cunha's "Bay City Wheelmen's March" debuted in San Francisco in April 1898. "The Annual Relay Race," *San Francisco Chronicle,* April 16, 1898, 8.

69. Arthur Loesser, *Men, Women and Pianos: A Social History* (New York: Simon & Schuster, 1954), 521.

70. James Parakilas et. al., *Piano Roles: Three Hundred Years of Life with the Piano* (New Haven, CT: Yale University Press, 1999), 316–317.

71. Young, "At Sea," *Los Angeles Times,* August 31, 1905, B7.

72. Martin Archives, sales ledger entry of December 10, 1907, cited in John King and Tom Walsh, "Pilgrimage to Nazareth: Reflections on Mike Longworth, Vintage Ukes, and Other Martinalia," 2007, unpublished MS. According to Martin historian Mike Longworth, these first 'ukuleles were guitarlike, spruce-topped instruments that "did not produce the light bouncy tone" for which the 'ukulele was known and were thus a commercial failure. Mike Longworth, *Martin Guitars: A History* (Minisink Hills, PA: Four Maples Press, 1988). The original source of this information may have been an interview Longworth had with C. F. Martin III, according to Martin archivist Dick Boak. Unfortunately, no Martin correspondence from this period is known to have survived, so it's not clear how the original 1907 order came about or how the Martin 'ukuleles fared after they reached Honolulu.

73. *New York Times,* March 19, 1910, 2. The window display in Ditson's East 34th Street store was placarded, "Musical Instruments You Don't See Every Day." "Clever Window Display," *Music Trade Review* (May 14, 1910): 51.

74. Rollinson, *Method for the Ukulele,* 3, 5. For background on Rollinson, see *Crescendo* 2 (June 1910): 25. "He is almost entirely responsible for the large and excellent mandolin orchestra catalog

published by Ditson. He is especially liked . . . because of his extreme progressiveness in matters connected with this industry." See also "T. H. Rollinson Dies," *Music Trade Review* (July 14, 1928): 33.

75. There is no evidence that Rollinson had any experience with Hawaii or its music. Why Ditson did not simply reprint the Kaai method is a matter for speculation, as there had been a working relationship between Ditson and Wall, Nichols—Kaai's publisher—since 1901, when both published Charles Hopkins' *Aloha Collection of Hawaiian Songs*.

76. Chicago's Lyon & Healy, the self-proclaimed "World's Largest Music House" and manufacturer of Washburn guitars, mandolins, and other stringed instruments, began advertising 'ukuleles in 1913. Advertisement, *Chicago Daily Tribune,* November 9, 1913, G2.

77. Advertisements, *Washington Post,* November 12, 1911, 3, and *Washington Herald,* December 14, 1911, 3; advertisement, *Idaho Daily Statesman,* November 26, 1911, 12. Both Oliver Ditson in Boston and Chas. H. Ditson in New York advertised "The Ukulele, $10 to $15," among other instruments in the May 29, 1912, edition of the *Christian Science Monitor* (p. 18) and beginning in the July 1912 issue of *Crescendo* magazine. The joint ad appeared on the back cover and ran for more than a year.

78. "For Gifts Musical," *Los Angeles Times,* December 13, 1911, 2:1.

79. "Vacation Music Ukulele Special," *Los Angeles Times,* June 29, 1912, 2:1.

80. *Sherman, Clay & Co., 1912 Catalogue of Musical Merchandise,* 159. Jim Tranquada collection. The maker is not identified. In 1915, Sherman, Clay had the exclusive agency for Kumalae 'ukulele. "Greatly Improved Conditions on Pacific Coast," *Music Trade Review* (September 25, 1915): 53.

81. *Polk-Husted Directory Co.'s Directory of Honolulu and the Territory of Hawaii 1912* (Honolulu: Polk-Husted Directory Co., 1912), 124, 344, 545, 618, 1112.

82. Birkel's *Los Angeles Times* advertisement of July 31 advertised "Nunes Hawaiian Ukuleles at $8 to $35": on December 1, Birkel asked *Times* readers, "Why not give a Ukulele, the little instrument that is so easy to 'pick up,' and whose sweet chords blend so beautifully with the singing voice? We can supply the genuine Neunes [*sic*] Hawaiian Ukuleles made of Coa [*sic*] wood, priced at $8 upward. Let us show them to you."

83. Leonardo was born March 24, 1874, and baptized on June 5, 1874, in Santa Maria Maior, Funchal (record 121, Baptism Book 2091, ARM). He is listed in Honolulu directories from 1902 on with a variety of occupations—real estate, hack driver, blacksmith—until 1908, when he is first listed as a guitar maker with his father. He is listed with the family firm of M. Nunes & Sons from 1910 to 1913, when he disappears from the Honolulu directory. He first appears in the Los Angeles city directory in 1914. Birkel first advertised "the famous L. Nunes Native Hawaiian Instruments" for its half-price sale in October 1913. *Los Angeles Times,* October 25, 1913, 2:1.

84. Advertisement, *Los Angeles Times,* July 3, 1914, 1:3. Southern California Music Co. was the exclusive national distributor of M. Nunes & Sons. "Los Angeles Dealers Report Fluctuating Trade," *Music Trade Review* (March 10, 1917): 25a.

85. According to Los Angeles city directories, Leonardo and his family lived at 5012 Sunset Boulevard from 1917 to 1929. In January 1920 Emanuel Costa, Leonardo's brother-in-law—identified as an instrument maker—was living with the family at that address. Dwelling 79, family 82, ED 155, Supervisory District 8, City of Los Angeles, 1920 Federal Census, Series T625, Roll 106, p. 205. Some sixteen workers are pictured in a photo of the Nunes ukulele factory at 1444 S. San Pedro St., Los Angeles. "Leonardo Nunes Sketches the History of the Origin of the Hawaiian Ukulele," *Music Trades,* January 17, 1920, 39.

86. Los Angeles city directories show that Raymond W. Heffelfinger was a salesman at Fitzgerald Music Co. before opening his own sheet music business around 1904. He appears to have opened the sheet music department at Birkel in 1909; the following year, he is also listed as an attorney. Heffelfinger was one of the movers behind the creation of the National Association of Sheet Music Dealers in 1915. He died in the 1918–1919 flu pandemic. "Death of R. W. Heffelfinger," *Music Trade Review* (January 18, 1919): 44.

87. "Ukeleles," *Los Angeles Times,* October 18, 1913, 2:1.

88. *Cadenza* 21 (December 1914): 39. The visitor, James H. Johnston, "'fell' for the ukulele craze and took some lessons himself."

89. Sears, Roebuck and Co., *Catalogue #129* (fall 1914), 1130; Boris Emmet and John E. Jeuck, *Catalogues and Counters: A History of Sears, Roebuck and Company* (Chicago: University of Chicago Press, 1950), 79, 112, 173, 191–195, 263. In 1910, Sears was described as "the largest single distributing dealers in musical merchandise in the country . . . who have brought to grief hundreds of regular dealers in musical merchandise throughout the country." "Sears, Roebuck & Co.'s Big Trade," *Music Trade Review* (November 19, 1910): 45.

90. "Many Hawaiian Ukuleles Now Used in States," *Popular Mechanics* (October 1915): 569.

91. "Ukuleles Special Offer!" *Los Angeles Times,* September 6, 1913, 2:1.

92. Ads touting Kia's services ran in the *Los Angeles Times* throughout August and September of 1913. See, for example, "Ukeleles: The Famous Instruments of the Hawaiians," *Los Angeles Times,* August 2, 1913, 2:1. Kia continued to work for Birkel the following year; he is listed in the 1914–1916 Los Angeles directories as a music teacher.

93. "Ernest Kaai," *Los Angeles Times,* July 31, 1914, 1:3; "Joseph Kekuku," *Los Angeles Times,* September 3, 1914, 1:3. Kaai spent several weeks traveling the West Coast from San Diego to Vancouver, where he met "quite a number of native musicians who are filling engagements with circuses and playing in cafes, etc." "Ernest Kaai Back from Coast Trip," *Honolulu Star-Bulletin,* September 16, 1914.

94. "Ukulele Concert Proves Popular," *Los Angeles Times,* September 18, 1914, 2:3.

95. Hector Alliot, "Hawaiian Songs and Ukuleles," *Los Angeles Times,* May 1, 1914, 2:6.

96. Graves Music Co. advertisement, *Morning Oregonian,* June 24, 1914, 13; The Music Store advertisement, *Tucson Daily Citizen,* December 1, 1914, 5; Rhodes Music Shop advertisement, *Des Moines Capitol,* December 11, 1914, 17; Christiansen Bros. Co. advertisement, *Racine Journal News,* August 20, 1914, 20; H. E. McMillin & Son advertisement, *Cleveland Plain Dealer,* December 13, 1914, 83.

97. *An Illustrated History of Los Angeles County, California* (Chicago: Lewis Publishing Co., 1889), 286–287. De Lano advertised "Lessons on the guitar, by competent instructor," in the *Los Angeles Times,* February 23, 1887, 6.

98. *Los Angeles and Southern California Blue Book . . . 1894–95* (Los Angeles: A. A. Thompson, 1894), 85; Swan, *Music in the Southwest,* 175; "Prominent Guild Members," *Crescendo* 3 (November 1910): 9. De Lano was one of the original members of the American Guild of Banjoists, Mandolinists and Guitarists in 1902.

99. "The Hawaiian Instruments: A Paper by C. S. Delano," *Cadenza* 24 (October 1917): 3.

100. De Lano is listed as a "teacher of Guitar, Banjo, Mandolin and Ukulele" in the 1912 *Los Angeles Directory* (464). Muntz took out a long-running classified ad; see the San Jose *Sunday Mercury & Herald,* May 19, 1912, 30. A Prof. Palmer in Oakland advertised ukulele lessons the same year. Classified ad, *Oakland Tribune,* September 17, 1912, 16.

101. De Lano's 1914 performances included an appearance by the Delano Steel Guitar Sextette at Temple Auditorium, steel guitar duets with his wife at a De Chauvenet Conservatory recital, and selections on the 'ukulele and Hawaiian steel guitar at a Stilwell Hotel musicale. Advertisement, *Los Angeles Times,* May 9, 1914, 1:5; "The City and Environs," *Los Angeles Times,* June 27, 1914, 2:2; "Musical Notes and Comment," *Los Angeles Times,* July 5, 1914, 3:2.

102. Display ad, *Cadenza* 20 (January 1914): 45. De Lano ran a similar ad in the December 1914 issue of the magazine, with an endorsement from a Seattle teacher calling his courses "a great success."

103. The methods were offered by music teacher James F. Roach of Cincinnati, who noted he was a pupil of D. Kaleikoa (one of the Honolulu Students); Lowell B. Shook of Riverside; Frank L. Littig of Los Angeles; and Mrs. Mae Muntz of San Jose.

104. F. L. Littig, "The Steel Guitar and Ukulele," *Cadenza* 22 (October 1915): 38–39.

105. "Monstrous Thunder Drum," *Music Trade Review* (October 26, 1912): 61.

106. "Dartmouth Clubs In Concert Tonight," *Hartford Courant,* April 15, 1912, 7.

107. "Barnard Girls Give Bazaar and Circus," *New York Times,* May 10, 1914, C7.

108. "By Musical Clubs of Tech," *Boston Daily Globe,* December 13, 1914, 38. The Tonaharp was a Hawaiian autoharp, played like a steel guitar but fitted with a pushbutton chording device. Noonan, *Guitar in America,* 206.

109. "Old Nassau Rings Out," *Washington Post,* April 6, 1915, 11.

110. "Plans for Early Spring Season Well Under Way," *New York Times,* March 15, 1914, 10:9; "Ukuleles Now a Fad," *Music Trade Review* (February 21, 1914): 50. Ditson's 'ukuleles were manufactured "by one of the best makers in Honolulu. . . . Our call for this type of instrument is so heavy that we have guaranteed to take care of the entire output of this manufacturer."

111. Frank Morton Todd, *The Story of the Exposition* (New York: G. P. Putnam's Sons, 1921), 1:35–36.

112. The quote is from attorney Gavin McNab in a December 7, 1909, speech. Todd, *Story of the Exposition,* 1:54.

113. Todd, *Story of the Exposition,* 1:113, 2:56–58.

Chapter 6: A Craze of the Frisco Exposition

1. Jenkins, *Hawaiian Furniture,* 106. The "extra fancy" table was made by Johann LaFrenz of Honolulu.

2. "The World Going to School," *The Friend,* January 1, 1876, 6.

3. The fairs were Paris in 1855, London 1862, Paris 1867, Philadelphia 1876, Louisville 1883, New Orleans 1884–1885, Louisville 1885, Sydney and Melbourne 1888, and Paris 1889. For Paris 1855, see Hawaiian Foreign Office and Executive Minute Books 7:261, 271; 8:251, 321; Circular, Department of Foreign Relations, Honolulu, August 2, 1854, "To Agriculturalists, Artists, Manufacturers, and Mechanics . . ." (Forbes, *Bibliography,* 3:96). In London in 1862, Lady Franklin exhibited her feather cape, Niihau mats, *kahili,* lava specimens, and other items from her personal collection; no official exhibit was submitted by the Hawaiian government. Korns, *Victorian Visitors,* 158; Hopkins, *Hawaii,* 412. For Paris 1867, see "Hawaiian Products in Paris," *Hawaiian Gazette,* August 14, 1867; "Hawaiian Pavilion," *Hawaiian Gazette,* September 25, 1867; and "Hawaiian Produce in France," *Hawaiian Gazette,* October 30, 1867. For Philadelphia 1876, see "Centennial Exhibitors," *Philadelphia Inquirer,* September 15, 1874, 3; McCabe, *Centennial Exhibition,* 400; and "A Trip to the Centennial, No. 7," *the Friend,* September 1, 1876, 9. For New Orleans 1884–1885, see *Hawaiian Exhibit,* 1885. For Louisville, see "Hawaii on Exhibition," *Daily Bulletin,* June 26, 1885, 3, and "The Hawaiian Exhibit at Louisville," *Hawaiian Gazette,* October 7, 1885, 3. For Sydney and Melbourne 1888, see Silva, *Hale Naua Society,* 79, 83–85, 102–103; "Hawaii in Australia," *Hawaiian Gazette,* November 20, 1888, 1; and "Hawaiian Exhibits in Sydney," *Hawaiian Gazette,* December 25, 1888, 6. For Paris 1889, see Hassinger, *Exposition Universelle,* 1889. Hawaii was invited to participate in the 1873 Vienna fair, but it is not clear if it sent any exhibits. *Hawaiian Gazette,* October 18, 1871, 2.

4. Detailed lists of Hawaiian displays can be found in *Hawaiian Club Papers* (Boston: Abner A. Kingman, 1868), 18–27 (Paris, 1867); McCabe, *History of the Centennial,* 460; *Hawaiian Exhibit . . . New Orleans;* and Hassinger, *Exposition Universelle.*

5. *Hawaiian Exhibit . . . New Orleans,* 14–15. The music on display in New Orleans was "Aloha Oe" and "Hooheno" by Liliuokalani and an early edition of Berger's *Mele Hawaii* containing nine songs. The same items were on display in Paris in 1889, with the addition of Liliuokalani's "Nani na Pua Koolau." The guitar was made by a Mr. Coleman of Honolulu in 1870 "to test not only his own mechanical ingenuity, but the adaptability of our native woods for the manufacture of musical instruments." "Guitar made of Hawaiian woods by Mr. Coleman as hobby," *Pacific Commercial Advertiser,* March 5, 1870, 3; *Hawaiian Gazette,* March 2, 1870. This may have been the blacksmith C. C. Coleman who advertised his services in 1885. *Saturday Press,* May 9, 1885, 1. A new concert guitar, "inlaid with over 2,000 pieces of Native woods," was advertised for sale in Honolulu in 1885. Advertisement, *Daily Bulletin,* December 30, 1885, 2.

6. Among the plans was an open-air theater for stereopticon views projected onto a forty-foot

screen. Lynn Ann Davis and Nelson Foster, *A Photographer in the Kingdom: Christian J. Hedemann's Early Images of Hawaii* (Honolulu: Bishop Museum Press, 1988), 120–122.

7. Rydell and Kroes, *Buffalo Bill,* 64; Robert Rydell, John E. Findling, and Kimberly D. Pelle, *Fair America: World's Fairs in the United States* (Washington, D.C.: Smithsonian Institution Press, 2000), 38.

8. "Through the Looking Glass," *Chicago Tribune,* November 1, 1893, 9, quoted in Rydell and Kroes, *Buffalo Bill,* 64. A photograph of William Aeko, one of the Volcano Singers, was included in a book of Midway portraits compiled by Harvard professor Frederic Ward Putnam, who headed the fair's Ethnology Department, as "a fair type of the middle class Hawaiians." F. W. Putnam, *Oriental and Occidental Northern and Southern Portrait Types of the Midway Plaisance . . .* (St. Louis: N. D. Thompson Publishing Co., 1894), no page numbers.

9. Robert W. Rydell, *All the World's a Fair: Visions of Empire at American International Expositions, 1876–1916* (Chicago: University of Chicago Press, 1984), 235–236.

10. Interview with Aunt Jennie Wilson, February 4, 1961, Charlot Tape 008, Special Collections, Hamilton Library, University of Hawaii, and interview with Jennie Kapahukulaokamamalu Wilson, January 1, 1962, Archives, HAW 59.3.1, Bishop Museum, Honolulu, cited in Okihiro, *Island World,* 194. The hula troupe that left Honolulu for Chicago on May 24, 1893, included Kini Kapahu, Nakai, Pauahi Pinao, Annie Kalupa, and two male chanters, Kanuku and Kamuku. They were first noted in Chicago in late July. Krauss, *Johnny Wilson,* 41–42; "That Hula Troupe," *Daily Bulletin,* May 28, 1893, 3; "As They Like It," *Chicago Daily Tribune,* July 30, 1893, 30. Wilson did not perform at Thurston's Kilauea cyclorama but at the nearby South Seas Islander (Samoan) concession. Sereno, *Images of the Hula Dancer,* 165–167, 181; "Return of Natives," *Daily Bulletin,* December 16, 1893, 2; "The Story of the Midway Plaisance," *Daily Inter Ocean,* November 1, 1893, 25; Benjamin C. Truman, *History of the World's Fair . . .* (Philadelphia: Mammoth Publishing Co., 1893), 571, 573.

11. "Madison Street Opera-House," *Daily Inter Ocean,* August 13, 1893, 21. For other accounts of Wilson's troupe, see "Calls the Hula Dancers Beautiful," *Chicago Daily Tribune,* March 3, 1893, 10; "Is Dance Gone Crazy," *Chicago Daily Tribune,* August 6, 1893, 28; "Amusements," *Daily Inter Ocean,* July 30, 1893, 25. Three of the original troupe returned to Honolulu aboard the schooner *Vine* in December 1893. "Return of Natives," *Daily Bulletin,* December 16, 1893, 2.

12. The troupe went on to perform at Doris's Museum for three weeks before appearing in Boston. Krauss, *Johnny Wilson,* 41–44; George C. D. Odell, *Annals of the New York Stage,* vol. 15: *1891–1894* (New York: Columbia University Press, 1949), 739; "Drama and Music," *Boston Daily Globe,* March 11, 1894, 18; advertisement, Howard Atheneum, *Boston Daily Globe,* March 25, 1894; Joann Wheeler Kealiinohomoku, "A Court Dancer Disagrees with Emerson's Classic Book on the Hula," *Ethnomusicology* 8 (May 1964): 161. It's possible that the hula troupe's European tour was made in connection with the Creole Company, which announced such a tour in August 1893. "Amusements," *Daily Inter Ocean,* August 20, 1893, 7.

13. "A Merger That Ought to Go," *Los Angeles Times,* July 19, 1903, A4. "We have shown the world that the main feature in the character of Hawaiians is their ability to tinkle-tinkle on an 'ukulele' and to twist and twirl," the *Independent* noted sarcastically in 1899. "Tourist Traveling," the *Independent,* July 12, 1899, 2.

14. "Umstead Writes of Hawaii," Omaha *Morning World-Herald,* May 27, 1899, 6; "Jolly Hawaiians Arrive," *Morning World-Herald,* July 19, 1899, 2; "Three Weeks of the Show," *Morning World-Herald,* July 23, 1899, 3. Wilson's musicians were identified as the famous Kawaihau Quartette, each being paid $50 a month plus room and board. "Off for Omaha," *Hawaiian Gazette,* August 31, 1898, 5.

15. "Midway Gleanings," *Morning World-Herald,* July 27, 1899, 8.

16. "In the Hawaiian Village," *New York Times,* August 11, 1901, SM2. Musicians performed at two separate Midway attractions: the Hawaiian Village, which featured a troupe of hula dancers, and the Kilauea cyclorama, where they appeared "in the crater and voice their tremulous sweet melodies, appealing to Pele, the Goddess, for divine protection." Richard H. Barry, *Snap Shots on the Midway*

Pan Am Expo (Buffalo: Robert Allen Reid, 1901), 52, 80, 82. See also "To Show Hawaii at Buffalo," *Honolulu Republican,* February 10, 1901, 3, and "Will Go to Buffalo," the *Independent,* March 29, 1901, 3.

17. Krauss, *Johnny Wilson,* 80–82, 85–86.

18. Mark Bennitt, Frank Parker Stockbridge, et al., *History of the Louisiana Purchase Exposition* (St. Louis: Universal Exposition Publishing Co., 1905), 481.

19. John E. Findling and Kimberly Pelle, eds., *Historical Dictionary of World's Fairs and Exposi- tions, 1851–1988* (New York: Greenwood Press, 1990), 189, 206.

20. Todd, *Story of the Exposition,* 3:325.

21. H. P. Wood, *Annual Report of the Honolulu Chamber of Commerce for the Year Ending August 16th, 1911* (Honolulu: Hawaiian Gazette Co., 1912), 11.

22. Ben Macomber, *The Jewel City: Its Planning and Achievement, Its Architecture, Sculpture, Symbolism and Music; Its Gardens, Palaces and Exhibits* (San Francisco: John H. Williams, 1915), 29–31, 177.

23. "Quintet Employed for World's Fair," *Pacific Commercial Advertiser,* February 16, 1915. The group embarked for San Francisco on the *Lurline* that day. "Passenger Lists of Vessels Arriving at San Francisco 1893–1953," Micropublication M1410 RG085.429, National Archives, Washington, D.C. For the contest between Kumalae and Kaai, see "Musicians Sound Discordant Note to Commission," *Honolulu Star-Bulletin,* January 1, 1915, 2, and "Fair Orchestra Still Puzzling Commissioners," *Hono- lulu Star-Bulletin,* January 8, 1915, 7. Keoki Awai of Awaialua, an experienced hotel entertainer and multi-instrumentalist, headed a second ensemble with Ben Zablan, Bill Kaina, and Henry Komo- mua that also performed at the fair. "George E. K. Awai Fueled the Hawaiian Music Craze in 1915," *Haʻilono Mele* 3 (September 1977): 5–6.

24. Todd, *Story of the Exposition,* 3:322–323. In *Billy Whiskers at the Exposition,* a volume in Frances Trego Montgomery's popular children's series, "some very quaint, plaintive music" is men- tioned, but it is the fish—"fish of every conceivable color"—that were deemed the main attraction at the Hawaiian Building. Francis Trego Montgomery, *Billy Whiskers at the Exposition* (Chicago: Saalfield Publishing Co., 1915), 156–57.

25. Todd, *Story of the Exposition,* 3:323.

26. Ibid., 3:313.

27. Roger Lea McBride, ed. *West from Home: Letters of Laura Ingalls Wilder to Almanzo Wilder, San Francisco 1915* (New York: Harper & Row, 1974), 82–83. There was a Hawaiian Village on the Joy Zone, the Panama-Pacific International Exposition's midway, but it "was hardly representative and executed a meager program. . . . Without the really beautiful and interesting things of island life it had no drawing power." Todd, *Story of the Exposition,* 2:352. For a photo of the village, see *The Red Book of Views of the Panama-Pacific International Exposition* (San Francisco: Robert A. Reid, 1915), unpaginated.

28. "Taxpayers, Attention," *Los Angeles Times,* April 11, 1915, 5:16; Jeanne Redman, "The Gor- geous Lord Nevill," *Los Angeles Times,* August 1, 1915, 2:12. A Hawaiian orchestra also played at the ball marking the formal opening of the New York Building. "New York Opens Exposition Gayety," *Washington Post,* March 4, 1915, 3.

29. Quoted in Burton Benedict, ed., *The Anthropology of World's Fairs: San Francisco's Panama Pacific International Exposition of 1915* (Berkeley, CA: Scolar Press, 1983), x.

30. Allan Nevins and Frank Ernest Hill, *Ford: Expansion and Challenge 1915–1933* (New York: Charles Scribner's Sons, 1957), 1–2.

31. "Hawaiian Singers for Henry Ford," *Los Angeles Times,* November 24, 1915, 2:9. In 1920, Kailimai was listed as an auto factory clerk living in the Detroit suburb of Highland Park with his family of seven. 1920 Census, Dwelling 142, Family 179, Highland Park, Wayne Co., Michigan, Sheet 9B, Precinct 6, ED 717, Roll 801, Series T625.

32. "Detroit Dealers Planning for Summer Business," *Music Trade Review* (June 10, 1916): 19; Rockwell, *Hawaiian Records,* 345–346.

33. Kumalae's gold medal was apparently awarded in the fair's Group 37, Musical Instruments, Class 176, for stringed instruments without a keyboard. On a scale of 1 to 150, 150 representing "perfection," exhibitors scoring between 85 and 94 were awarded a gold medal. The highest score in each class received the Grand Prize. Morton, *Story of the Exposition,* 5:131. For the stock Kumalae offered, see Morton 4:97.

34. Advertisements, *San Francisco Chronicle,* October 20, 1914, 9, and January 2, 1915, 8.

35. A. P. Taylor, "The Ukulele of the Hawaiian Islands," in *Commerce Reports* (Washington, D.C.: Bureau of Foreign and Domestic Commerce, Department of Commerce, September 18, 1915), 1357. By one estimate, some thirty thousand 'ukuleles were sold in California by October 1915. "September Business Breaks Record in Los Angeles," *Music Trade Review* (October 9, 1915): 66.

36. Advertisement, *Music Trade Review* (August 28, 1915): 27.

37. Lyon & Healy display ad, *Cadenza* 22 (November 1915): 41. See also "Hawaiian Music Is Hit of Exposition," *Duluth News-Tribune,* October 17, 1915, 7; "Ukuleles to Be Fashionable," *Anaconda* [Montana] *Standard,* November 15, 1915, 9; and "The Ukulele Is Becoming Popular," *Tucson Citizen,* December 11, 1915, 7.

38. J. E. Chinnery advertised as a teacher of piano, violin, guitar, mandolin, and 'ukulele in the *Kansas City Star,* September 5, 1915, 4c; "Conditions in Detroit Point to Fine Piano Trade," *Music Trade Review* (June 19, 1915): 62; J. W. Jenkins Sons Music Co. of Kansas City advertised Hawaiian and American-made 'ukuleles in the *Weekly Kansas City Star,* December 15, 1915, 4. Hirschfeld Piano Co. advertisement, *Fort Worth Star-Telegram,* November 28, 1915, 15; Boston Music Co. ad, *Duluth News-Tribune,* December 21, 1915, 11; Hanes Music Co. ad, *Columbus Ledger,* December 3, 1915, 11; Philip Werlein Ltd. ad, New Orleans *Times Picayune,* October 17, 1915, 11; *Anaconda* [Montana] *Standard,* November 28, 1915, 3.

39. *Columbia Records for October* (New York: Columbia Graphophone Co., 1917), 15.

40. Linn, *Half-Barbaric Twang,* 7, 10, 89–90. Lewis Erenberg incorrectly asserts that the fad for "Hawaiian dances and ukulele orchestras" originated in New York and subsequently was adopted on the West Coast in his *Steppin' Out: New York Nightlife and the Transformation of American Culture, 1890–1930* (Chicago: University of Chicago Press, 1984), 224–225.

41. "Society on the Threshold of a Gay Season," *New York Times,* October 29, 1916, 10:3. "Styles in songs change as quickly as those in ladies millinery," songwriter and publisher Charles K. Harris once wrote. "The fancy of the public is always capricious in these matters, whatever it may be in others." Charles K. Harris, *How to Write a Popular Song* (New York, 1906), quoted in Ian Whitcomb, *Irving Berlin and Ragtime America* (London: Century-Hutchinson, 1987), 59–60.

42. In August 1915, music teacher W. R. Jackson of Toronto reported the arrival of Hawaiian music there. *Cadenza* 22 (August 1915): 13.

43. Norton, *American Musical Theater,* xxx; Gerald Bordman, *Jerome Kern His Life and Music* (New York: Oxford University Press, 1980), 116. Fifteen years later, one of the stars of "Very Good Eddie," Ann Orr, claimed that "she sang the song called 'Waikiki,' and the song started the rage for strumming ukuleles on a national scale." "In the Spotlight Glare," *New York Times,* March 23, 1930, 10:3. E. H. Stover, the song's lyricist, was an "x-ray expert" who died in Denver in 1918. "Ashes of Writer to be Strewn on Waikiki Beach," *San Francisco Chronicle,* May 1, 1918, 3.

44. "The 1916 Follies Full of Splendor," *New York Times,* June 13, 1916, 2:9.

45. Grace Kingsley, "A Bit of Waikiki," *Los Angeles Times,* September 19, 1916, 2:3.

46. "Coming to the Theaters," *Washington Post,* October 12, 1916, 4; "The Garden of Aloha," *Los Angeles Times,* May 13, 1917, 3:3; "Honolulu Girl Opens Tonight at Salt Lake," *Salt Lake Telegram,* December 22, 1919, 20; "Miss Irma Gage, Clever Singing Ingenue with Ukulele Girl Co.," *San Jose Mercury Herald,* December 16, 1917, 32.

47. "Nailing a Few Lies about Waikiki Beach," *Washington Post,* December 3, 1916, MT4.

48. Al Dubin (1891–1945) was a lyricist whose hits included "42nd Street," "We're in the Money," and "I Only Have Eyes for You"; Harry Von Tilzer (1872–1946) gave Berlin his first job in the music

business and wrote "A Bird in a Gilded Cage" and "Wait till the Sun Shines, Nellie"; Bert Kalmar, lyricist for such hits as "Who's Sorry Now?" and "I Wanna Be Loved by You," was portrayed by Fred Astaire in the 1950 MGM biopic, *Three Little Words.* Berlin wrote "I'm Down in Honolulu"; Dubin cowrote "O'Brien Is Tryin' to Learn to Talk Hawaiian"; Von Tilzer wrote "On the South Sea Isle"; and Kalmar cowrote "Since Maggie Dooley Learned the Hooley Hooley." As music editor and critic Sigmund Spaeth observed, "Nearly every songwriter tried his hand at something Hawaiian." Spaeth, *A History of Popular Music in America* (New York: Random House, 1948), 400.

49. "How Melody Is Sweeping Nation," *Daily* [Juneau] *Alaska Dispatch,* October 25, 1916, 8. For details on Adams, a former piano salesman and actor from Massachusetts who arrived in Honolulu in 1899, see Siddall, *Men of Hawaii,* 1:13.

50. "Representative Programs," *The Dominant* 24 (February 1917): 30–73. Of the fifty orchestras and bands listed, thirty-seven list one or more "Hawaiian" tunes. While the majority of bands listed are from New York, New Jersey, and Pennsylvania, also included are playlists from St. Louis; Toledo, Ohio; Madison, Wisconsin; Baltimore; Austin, Texas; Detroit; San Diego; Kansas City; Winnipeg; and Montreal.

51. Display ad, *Boston Daily Globe,* August 13, 1916, 40.

52. Adams, *Hawaiian Almanac and Annual for 1917,* 143. This anecdotal account appears to be the source of the oft-repeated assertion that Hawaiian music outsold all other genres in the wake of the Panama-Pacific International Exposition.

53. Advertisement, *Music Trade Review* (December 11, 1920): 102.

54. Jonathan Bellman, *The Style Hongrois in the Music of Western Europe* (Boston: Northeastern University Press, 1993), 13–14, 22. As Gilbert Seldes wrote in 1924, "'On the Beach at Wai-ki-ki' is a rag in every respect, using material which is foreign only in appearance." Seldes, *The 7 Lively Arts* (New York: Sagamore Press, 1957 [1924]), 64.

55. Suisman, *Selling Sounds,* 44.

56. Victor Records advertisements, *Los Angeles Times,* March 28, 1917, 2:6, and June 28, 1917, 15; Victor advertisement, *New York Times,* September 1, 1917, 4. Despite all the new competition, "Aloha Oe" remained the country's most popular Hawaiian song, with at least a dozen editions published between 1908 and 1915 in six different cities.

57. Herbert G. Goldman, *Jolson: The Legend Comes to Life* (New York: Oxford University Press, 1988), 86–89; Larry F. Kiner, comp., *The Al Jolson Discography* (Westport, CT: Greenwood Press, 1983), 7. Jolson recorded a second Hawaiian-themed song, Irving Berlin's "I'm Down in Honolulu Looking Them Over," in September 1916, but it apparently was not released. So popular was "Yaaka Hula Hickey Dula" that eight other versions were recorded in 1916. Garrett, *Struggling to Define a Nation,* 192.

58. "Song Faking," *Los Angeles Times,* March 25, 1917, 3:3. W. D. Adams was appalled by "Oh How She Could Yacki Hacki Wicki Wacki Woo (That's Love in Honolulu)" by von Tilzer, Stanley Murphy, and Charles McCann: "Can any of our true citizens read these words without a feeling of disgust for the concern which would go so far to make a few dollars?" Adams, *Hawaiian Almanac and Annual for 1917,* 144.

59. Irving Berlin, *My Bird of Paradise* (New York: Waterson, Berlin & Snyder, 1915), 4; *Cadenza* 24 (February 1917): 46; "Few Know of Hawaii," *Kansas City Star,* June 15, 1919, 5. A 1915 edition of "Aloha Oe" published in Chicago defined the "tara fiddle" (taro patch fiddle) as being "very similar to our violin, except that it is in a very crude form and is played with fewer strings." *Aloha Oe* (Chicago: Artists Music House, 1915).

60. "Mrs. E. B. Close, Hostess," *New York Times,* February 1, 1916, 1:11; *Cadenza* 23 (July 1916): 47; "Miss Mason Makes Debut," *New York Times,* December 22, 1916, 9; "Mrs. C. Vanderbilt Hostess at Home," *New York Times,* February 6, 1917, 8; "Entertain at Newport," *New York Times,* August 17, 1916, 11.

61. Advertisement, *New York Times,* March 16, 1917.

62. "Ukulele Square, the Hawaiian Quarter of New York," *New York Tribune,* November 5, 1916, 5:5.

63. Stephen Leacock, *Frenzied Fiction* (London: John Lane, the Bodley Head, 1918), 25.

64. "Ukuleles Face Ban at Atlantic City," *Salt Lake Telegram,* October 7, 1917, 8.

65. "News Notes of the Stage," *Washington Post,* March 21, 1915, 67.

66. "At the Theaters," *Atlanta Constitution,* December 17, 1915, 7.

67. Britt Craig, "Hawaiian Music Intoxicates Britt, but Mabel Brings Him Back to Earth," *Atlanta Constitution,* November 26, 1916, 4; "Second of a Series of Musicales Is Held at White House," *Washington Post,* March 15, 1916, 7.

68. Classified ad, *Charlotte Observer,* March 19, 1916, 22; advertisement, *Lexington Herald,* June 1, 1916, 9; advertisement, *Miami Herald,* July 23, 1916, 7.

69. "Field's Minstrels Draw Big Houses," *Charlotte Observer,* September 14, 1916, 6; "Minstrelry at Crescent," *Times Picayune,* October 30, 1916, 2.

70. Advertisement, *Dallas Morning News,* February 18, 1917, 12. However, according to the *Wise County Messenger,* the "ukelele fad" did not strike in the small town of Decatur, northwest of Dallas, until 1917. "The State Press," *Dallas Morning Press,* October 15, 1917, 8.

71. "To Miss Margaret Pratt," *Atlanta Constitution,* March 26, 1916, C7; "Class Night Exercises," *Washington Post,* January 27, 1916, 3; "Impressive Exercises at Terrill School," *Dallas Morning News,* May 26, 1916, 5; "Unusual Musical Service," *Boston Daily Globe,* February 22, 1916, 4; "Jazz Series No. 6," *Duluth News Tribune,* September 14, 1919, 8.

72. Quoted in "The Day of the Ukulele," *Columbus* [Georgia] *Enquirer Sun,* February 12, 1917, 11.

73. "Seniors Ready for Show Friday Night," *Nevada State Journal,* April 13, 1916, 8; "Glee Club to Sing Here," *Dallas Morning News,* March 30, 1916, 4; "Miss Kyburg Ivy Day Orator at Mount Holyoke," *Christian Science Monitor,* June 13, 1916, 7; "Clubs of Cornell to Play Here," *Duluth News Tribune,* December 17, 1916, 9.

74. "Lafayette Clubs to Give Concert," *Wilkes Barre* [Pennsylvania] *Times Leader,* April 19, 1916, 17.

75. "That Honest Plunking," *Kansas City Star,* June 12, 1920, 12.

76. Kanahele, *Hawaiian Music,* 249–250.

77. Ibid., 48–49. Hokea began recording for HMV in Montreal in 1919. Rockwell, *Hawaiian Records,* 486.

78. "Strand," *Winnipeg Free Press,* June 30, 1917, 16. Prince Jack Heleluhe and his Hawaiian Serenaders appeared at the Imperial in May. "Hawaiians at the Imperial," *Manitoba Free Press,* May 12, 1917, 29.

79. Advertisement, *Winnipeg Free Press,* June 8, 1917, 10; advertisement, *Winnipeg Free Press,* February 10, 1917, 9.

80. Advertisement, *Winnipeg Free Press,* December 1, 1917, 26; classified ad, *Winnipeg Free Press,* December 3, 1917, 19.

81. Parham Werlein, head of Philip Werlein Ltd. of New Orleans and Jackson, Mississippi, also regarded the saxophone as a freak. "Ukulele Puts Pep in Business," *Music Trade Review* (April 10, 1920): 46. The value of non-keyboard instruments rose from $3.6 million in 1914 to $12.5 million in 1919, an increase of 245 percent, in sharp contrast to the previous fifteen years, when sales and production remained flat. *Fourteenth Census of the United States,* vol. 10: *Manufactures 1919* (Washington, D.C.: Government Printing Office, 1923), 984–985. During World War I, wartime shortages of materials made it impossible to meet the growing demand, Lyon & Healy reported. James F. Bowers, "Short Supply Cuts Trade of Music Houses," *Chicago Daily Tribune,* December 31, 1918, A9.

82. Robert Lewis, *Chicago Made: Factory Networks in the Industrial Metropolis* (Chicago: University of Chicago Press, 2008), 21, 24, 217; Nancy Groce, *Musical Instrument Makers of New York* (Stuyvestant, NY: Pendragon Press, 1991), vii, xiv; "Chicago Leads in Manufacturing Ukuleles," *Music Trade Review* (August 4, 1928): 14. Lyon & Healy was advertising "Chicago-made ukuleles" for $5 and up in November 1915. *Cadenza* 23 (November 1915): 41.

83. Bruno first advertised 'ukuleles in its fall 1915 Supplement B catalog. "Latest Bruno Literature," *Music Trade Review* (November 27, 1915): 75. B & J announced its first S. S. Stewart 'ukulele in

September 1916. "The S. S. Stewart Ukulele Soon Ready for Market," *Music Trade Review* (September 23, 1916): 59. S. S. Stewart, originally of Philadelphia, was best known for its banjos.

84. Advertisement for Mele Ukulele Strings, *San Jose Evening News,* January 2, 1917, 2. Well into the 1920s, musicians continued to use violin strings for 'ukuleles. See J. Kalani Peterson, *Peterson Ukulele Method* (New York: Irving Berlin Inc., 1924), 10.

85. Advertisements, *Chicago Daily Tribune,* October 8, 1916, E6; *Los Angeles Times,* August 12, 1917, 2:10; *Philadelphia Inquirer,* November 4, 1916, 6, and November 20, 1916, 11. In December 1916, Lit Brothers advertised for the "services of a man who can play, demonstrate, and sell ukuleles": classified ad, *Philadelphia Evening Public Ledger,* Night Extra, December 22, 1916, 14.

86. Advertisement, Klein's Sporting Goods Store, *Montgomery* [Alabama] *Advertiser,* October 15, 1917, 6; advertisement, Foster's, *Pawtucket* [Rhode Island] *Evening Times,* March 15, 1918, 22; advertisement, Rick Furniture Co., *Dallas Morning News,* January 5, 1919, 4.

87. *Los Angeles City Directory 1918* (Los Angeles: LA Directory Co. 1918), 1233; classified ad, *Los Angeles Times,* October 10, 1915, 4:12; "Rule by Commission Ruins His Business," *Los Angeles Times,* April 12, 1919, 2:1. The Hawaiian Ukulele and Violin Manufacturing Co. was organized in 1917 to expand the existing business of G. A. Wettlin. "To Take Over Ukulele Plant," *Music Trade Review* (November 3, 1917): 51.

88. "Canny Nipponese Flood the Market with Cheap Pianos," *Duluth News Tribune,* April 28, 1918, 3.

89. Entry of October 29, 1915, "Sales 1914–1922," Martin Archives, cited in King and Walsh, "Pilgrimage to Nazareth," 2. Martin guitars were sold in Hawaii as early as 1881. Advertisement, George F. Wells, *Hawaiian Gazette Supplement,* December 21, 1881, 7.

90. Jim Washburn and Richard Johnston, *Martin Guitars: An Illustrated Celebration of America's Premier Guitarmaker* (Emmaus, PA: Rodale Press, 1997), 95, 102; Richard Johnston and Dick Boak, *Martin Guitars: A History* (New York: Hal Leonard Books, 2008), 60–61.

91. *Cadenza* 24 (April 1917): 37.

92. "Why 'Cheap' Musical Instruments Are Dearest in the Final Analysis," *Music Trade Review* (June 5, 1920): 30; advertisement, *Los Angeles Times,* July 3, 1914, 1:3; advertisement, *Los Angeles Times,* December 16, 1915, 2:1; advertisement, *Los Angeles Times,* September 23, 1917, 2:1.

93. C. S. Delano, "The Hawaiian Instruments," *Cadenza* 24 (October 1917): 3.

94. Sales brochure, *Ukuleles* (Philadelphia: Fred C. Meyer & Co., n.d.), John King collection. J. W. Jenkins Sons of Kansas City offered similar advice: "We have them at $3.00, $4.00, $5.00, $6.50 etc. But we especially recommend the beautiful, genuine native Kumalae ukuleles at $8.00, $12.00, $14.00, and $17.00. . . . They are beauties." Advertisement, *Kansas City Star,* July 7, 1917, 3.

95. "Industry Enriches Hawaii," *New York Times,* October 15, 1916, 8:6. M. Nunes & Sons' monthly output was reported to be one thousand in March 1917. *Music Trade Review* (March 10, 1917): 25a.

96. Based on an analysis of the 1917 *Honolulu City Directory* listings by John King.

97. Kamaka (d. 1953), a friend of Jonah Kumalae, began making 'ukuleles ca. 1914 in the basement of his Kaimuki home in Honolulu, but he didn't launch the business until 1916. The Kamaka factory on South King Street wasn't opened until 1920–1921. Interview (1993) with Sam Kamaka Jr., in *An Era of Change: Oral Histories of Civilians in World War II Hawaii* (Honolulu: University of Hawaii Social Science Research Center, Center for Oral History, 1994), 2:540–541. Kamaka 'ukuleles appeared in mainland stores as early as 1919. Advertisement, William Krull Music House, *Idaho Statesman,* March 24, 1919, 3.

98. Lyon & Healy was advertising "genuine Hawaiian Ukuleles made by Leandro [*sic*] Nunes and M. Nunes and Sons" for $8 to $20 as early as November 1915. *Cadenza* 22 (November 1915): 41. Newspaper ads show that M. Nunes and Kumalae ukuleles received wide distribution on the mainland, sold by retailers in such places as St. Albans, Vermont; Salt Lake City; New Orleans; Boise, Idaho; and Detroit. Advertisements in the *St. Albans Daily Messenger,* October 24, 1917, 8; *Salt Lake Telegram,* January 4, 1917, 7; *Idaho Daily Statesman,* November 14, 1915, 16;

Times Picayune, October 24, 1915, 16; "Demonstrating the Ukulele," *Music Trade Review* (May 22, 1915): 98.

99. Advertisement, *Music Trade Review* (May 10, 1919): 45; "Doings in the Small Goods Trade," *Music Trade Review* (January 1, 1921): 30. Churchill was the Pacific Coast agent for the Poole Piano Co., Schaff Bros. pianos, and the Charles Parker Co. "H. C. Churchill Dies on Coast," *Music Trade Review* (April 16, 1921): 11.

100. *Hawaiian Almanac and Annual for 1917* (Honolulu: Thos. G. Thrum, 1916), 145–146.

101. *Cadenza* 23 (December 1916): 7. The ad ran for four months.

102. "Hawaiians Are Angry," *New York Times,* September 19, 1915, 2:10. As early as the summer of 1915, Hawaiian makers were making plans for a special "Made in Hawaii USA" mark to be placed on each of their instruments to distinguish the real article. Taylor, *Commerce Reports,* 1357.

103. U.S. trademark registration mark No. 118,524, U.S. Patent Office, 1917. For the significance of the *hoaka,* see Kamehiro, *Arts of Kingship,* 51, 72.

104. Advertisement, *Los Angeles Times,* November 20, 1916, 2:1.

105. King, *Ukulele & Guitar Makers,* lxxiii.

106. Ralph S. Kuykendall, *Hawaii in the World War* (Honolulu: Historical Commission of the Territory of Hawaii, 1928), 388, 390; "Hawaiians Get Ready to Greet Tourist Influx," *San Francisco Chronicle,* July 31, 1919, 3.

107. Kuykendall, *Hawaii in the World War,* 91; "Why Ukuleles Wail at Waikiki," *Grand Forks* (North Dakota) *Herald,* April 9, 1918, 6; Frank J. Taylor, Earl M. Welty, and Daniel W. Eyre, *From Land and Sea: The Story of Castle and Cooke of Hawaii* (San Francisco: Chronicle Books, 1976), 143.

108. "The Effect of the War on the Small Goods Trade," *Music Trade Review* (July 14, 1917): 55.

109. Kuykendall, *Hawaii in the World War,* 21–22, 81–85, 87, 90.

110. Brian McAllister Linn, *Guardians of Empire: The U.S. Army and the Pacific, 1902–1940* (Chapel Hill: University of North Carolina Press, 1997), 253; "Hawaii Regular Army Unit at Camp Kearny," *Los Angeles Times,* July 29, 1918, 2:2; "Soldiers from Hawaii Pass Through Dallas," *Dallas Morning News,* October 21, 1918, 5.

111. John Dos Passos, *One Man's Initiation: 1917* (London: Allen & Unwin, 1920), 1; Dos Passos, *Travel Books and Other Writings 1916–1941* (New York: Library of America, 2003), 664. Dos Passos was the grandson of a Madeiran emigrant who arrived in Baltimore in 1830.

112. "The value of music in preserving morale among troops is so universally recognized that the military officers in the instruction camps offer every encouragement to any of their men who show a proclivity for music." "Effect of the War," *Music Trade Review* (July 14, 1917): 55.

113. "Starts Drive for Ukulele in Every Tent in Camps," *Lexington* [Kentucky] *Herald,* February 17, 1918, 6. At Camp Funston outside San Antonio, Texas, "Every night after mess the men gather with fiddles and ukuleles under a big scrub oak tree in front of the barracks and sing in the twilight." George Wythe, "Training Camp Holds Memorial Services," *Dallas Morning News,* June 2, 1917, 4. See also "Preparation for War Has Its Lighter Sides," *San Francisco Chronicle,* June 27, 1916, 2, and "Duluth Boys Enjoy the Cool Evenings in Camp," *Duluth News-Tribune,* November 15, 1917, 12.

114. James W. Evans and Capt. Gardner L. Harding, *Entertaining the American Army: The American Stage and Lyceum in the World War* (New York: Association Press, 1921), 4, 22, 52, 173. See also "Have You a Ukulele? Would You Mind Loaning It to Sammy, Please?" *Fort Worth Star-Telegram,* April 21, 1918, 33; "Musical Instruments for Soldiers Wanted," *San Jose Mercury News,* April 21, 1918, 6; "Army Wants More Musical Instruments," *San Francisco Chronicle,* April 15, 1918, 9; "Musical Instruments Wanted for Soldiers," *Salt Lake Telegram-Herald-Republican,* August 12, 1918, 6; "Public Asked to Give Old Musical Instruments to Navy," *New York Tribune,* August 29, 1918, 7.

115. Suisman, *Selling Sounds,* 198.

116. Advertisement, *Trenton Sunday Times Advertiser,* December 16, 1917, 23; advertisement, *Miami Herald,* December 15, 1918, 22; advertisement, *Los Angeles Times,* November 28, 1917, 2:1. Southern California Music Co. had a large window display with the same theme. "Annual Fashion Show Week in Los Angeles Gives Dealers Opportunities for Fine Displays," *Music Trades* (September

28, 1918): 11. Oscar Schmidt of Jersey City donated a dozen of his 'ukuleles to the New Jersey National Guard. "Praise for Oscar Schmidt," *Music Trade Review* (December 8, 1917): 131.

117. Evans and Harding, *Entertaining*, 4, 9. The Knights of Columbus mounted a similar effort. "Knights of Columbus 'Circuit' in France," *San Jose* [California] *Mercury Herald*, July 16, 1919, 15. Even after the war, the Red Cross solicited the donation of 'ukuleles and other instruments for the wounded in hospitals. "'Food for Souls' of Wounded Men," *Cadenza* 26 (May 1919): 3; "Wounded Men Need Music," *Washington Post*, July 13, 1919, E16; "Ukuleles for Fox Hill Men," *Music Trade Review* (November 22, 1919): 44.

118. Kenneth Stever, *Pursuit of an "Unparalleled Opportunity": The American YMCA and Prisoner-of-War Diplomacy among the Central Power Nations During World War I, 1914–1923* (New York: Columbia University Press, 2009), 174.

119. Evans and Harding, *Entertaining*, 257; "The Liberty Belles," Affiliated Lyceum Bureaus of America brochure, ca. 1918, Redpath Chautauqua Collection, Special Collections, University of Iowa; "Music and Musicians," *Washington Post*, May 11, 1919, ES2.

120. Kanui (1890–1960) and Puni (b. 1868, a veteran of the 1901 Pan-American Exposition in Buffalo) were both from Honolulu. William K. Kanui, "Affidavit to Explain Protracted Foreign Residence and to Overcome Presumption of Expatriation," Paris, France, May 11, 1920; Passport Applications, January 2, 1906–March 31, 1925, ARC Identifier 583830/MCR No. A1 534, NARA Series M1490, Roll 482, National Archives and Records Administration, Washington, D.C.; Joseph Puni, "Affidavit to Explain Protracted Foreign Residence," Paris, December 23, 1922, Passport Applications, Roll 2165. See also Cyril LeFebvre, "Bill Kanui (1890–1960)," www.ukulele.fr/dc/index.php/2010/12/29/924-billy-Kanui.

121. *The Stars and Stripes* (Paris), February 22, 1918, 2. At a 1908 reception at the U.S. ambassador's residence in Paris, twenty-three-year-old Mary Adele Case "sang to her own accompaniment on a native Hawaiian instrument some Hawaiian songs which she had known in Honolulu, where she spent her youth." "Oregon Girl Wins," *Morning Oregonian*, October 16, 1908, 6.

122. William H. Taft et al., *Service with Fighting Men: An Account of the American Young Men's Christian Associations in the World War* (New York: Association Press, 1922), 2:192.

123. Cpl. Paul Warwick, "A Little Music Now and Then," *Atlanta Constitution*, March 23, 1919, 17.

124. "Merrymakers All," *New York Times*, September 4, 1927, 5:2.

125. "Philadelphia Lieutenant Unhurt in 10 Months War," *Philadelphia Inquirer*, July 7, 1918, 4.

126. Consuelo Kanaga, "Ukelele Now Popular in All Sections of the Country," *San Francisco Chronicle*, December 3, 1916, 7.

127. "Like Old Bill Bailey, Everybody Plays the Ukulele," *Kansas City Star*, November 19, 1916, 1.

128. *Grand Rapids Press*, October 31, 1917, 6.

129. As the *Colorado Springs Gazette* noted in 1919, with "all the fellows . . . home from France" at Colorado College, "the soothing whine of the fraternity ukulele will wreathe its way across campus again." "Affairs in Society," *Colorado Springs Gazette*, September 21, 1919, 22.

130. "War-Weariness and Jazz," *New York Times*, July 24, 1919, 8. See also "Hula-Hula Dance and Hawaii Music Catching London," *Atlanta Constitution*, July 24, 1919, 6. One of the earliest 'ukulele players in England was Lady Chetwynd, an American native, who took lessons from steel guitarist Sergis Luvaun in the summer of 1917. "London Society by Lady Mary," *Chicago Daily Tribune*, August 5, 1917, D2. Luvaun had recorded some of the earliest "Hawaiian" music in England the year before and in 1917 recorded several songs with Lady Chetwynd for the Winner label. Rockwell, *Hawaiian Records*, 745–751. Lady Nancy Astor, a Virginia native and the first woman elected to Parliament, also was reported to play the 'ukulele. Fred B. Pitney, "'American Personality' Won for Lady Astor," *New York Tribune*, December 7, 1919, 7:1; "David Lloyd George Likes Negro Songs of the South," New Orleans *Times Picayune*, March 21, 1920, 67.

131. Joseph Kekuku passport application, dated June 6, 1919, and Mekia Kealakai passport application, dated June 2, 1919; U.S. Passport Applications January 2, 1906–March 31, 1925, M1490,

Roll 0796, National Archives and Records Administration, Washington, D.C. Kealakai returned to the United States in October 1920 in response to a plea from Honolulu Mayor Johnny Wilson to head the Royal Hawaiian Band. Krauss, *Johnny Wilson,* 176; "List of U.S. Citizens," SS *Imperator,* arriving New York October 2, 1920, Microfilm Serial T715, Roll T715-2845, New York Passenger Lists, Records of the U.S. Customs Service, National Archives. Kekuku's passport applications show he remained in Europe through at least October 1924 on "theatrical business" in England, France, Belgium, and Spain.

132. "Hawaiian Band at the Savoy," *London Times,* July 4, 1919, 16.

133. "The Bird of Paradise," *London Times,* September 12, 1919, 5; J. P. Wearing, *The London Stage 1920–1929: A Calendar of Plays and Players,* vol. 1: *1920–1924* (Metuchen, NJ: Scarecrow Press, 1984), 241. By September 1921, three productions of the play had visited Manchester. "'The Bird of Paradise' at the Opera House," *Manchester Guardian,* September 20, 1921, 12. Tully had originally hoped to mount a London production as early as 1914 but was thwarted by the outbreak of World War I. "J. D. Phelan in Theatricals," *New York Times,* November 14, 1913, 5.

134. *Punch,* October 26, 1921, 327.

135. Because they introduced the instrument, the Keeches are often given credit for inventing it, and Alvin was not shy about taking credit for it. See "Commodore Corridor Chat," *Music Trade Review,* Section 2 (June 9, 1928): 13; David Bret, *George Formby: A Troubled Genius* (London: Robson Books, 1999), 286; and Alan Randall and Ray Seaton, *George Formby: A Biography* (London: W. H. Allen, 1974), 45. For Alvin's birthdate, see "Born," *Hawaiian Gazette,* April 15, 1890, 10. Kelvin's is given on the passenger list of the SS *Majestic,* New York, May 29, 1928. New York Passenger Lists 1820–1897, National Archives Microfilm Publication M237, Roll T715-5692, Record Group 36. For Kelvin's death, see Social Security Death Index, SSN 130-09-4191.

136. Advertisement, "May Outrun Ukulele's Popularity," *Music Trades,* October 28, 1916, 51. Thanks to Tom Walsh for this reference.

137. Bolander filed his application on December 3, 1917; it was registered June 29, 1920, Reg. No. 132,630, cited in King, ed., *Selected U.S. Trademarks and Patents for Ukuleles, Banjo Ukuleles and Accessories* (St. Petersburg, FL: NALU Music, 2003), xiv–xv. John Bolander, a fifty-nine-year-old Swedish immigrant and music store proprietor, was living with his family at 1605 Beverly Place in Berkeley in January 1920 (1920 Census, City of Berkeley, Oakland Twp., Alameda Co., Supervisor's Dist. 5, ED 198, Precinct 69, Sheet 2A, dwelling house 28, family 28). Advertisement, *San Francisco Chronicle,* November 19, 1916, 33; advertisement, *Los Angeles Times,* June 5, 1917, 2:1; advertisement, *San Francisco Chronicle,* June 7, 1917, 2; advertisement, *Cadenza* 24 (July 1917): 43; advertisement, *Los Angeles Times,* February 10, 1918, 3:4. For the Nortons as manufacturers, see "Rain at Pacific Grove Helps Garden Plots," *San Jose Mercury Herald,* December 28, 1917, 5, and "Coast Ukulele Factory Enlarges," *Music Trade Review* (August 23, 1919): 38. Buegeleisen & Jacobson introduced its No. 3S ukulele banjo in September 1917. "Introduce Ukulele Banjo," *Music Trade Review* (September 22, 1917): 51.

138. *San Francisco Chronicle,* November 7, 1915, 20; "Thanksgiving Feast to Be a Joyous One," *San Francisco Chronicle,* November 24, 1915, 3. The earliest evidence of the Keeches in San Francisco is their participation in the staging of a benefit play, *The South Sea Idol,* in June 1914. "Funds from Play to Benefit Blind," *San Francisco Chronicle,* June 11, 1914, 14. Both are listed in the 1915 and 1916 San Francisco City Directories. *Crocker-Langley San Francisco Directory 1915* (San Francisco: Crocker-Langley, 1915), 1051, and 1916 edition, 1041. Kelvin was a mandolin soloist and a member of a mandolin quartet that included Kaai at a 1907 recital at the Alexander Young Hotel in Honolulu. "The Kaai Music School," *Hawaiian Star,* April 19, 1907. Their father, Alvin W. Keech, was a Pennsylvania native and engineer who worked for the Inter-Island Steam Navigation Co. and later the Honolulu Iron Works and Honomu Plantation. "Timely Topics," *Hawaiian Gazette,* January 21, 1898, 2; *Hawaiian Gazette,* October 18, 1904, 4. Both Alvin and Kelvin attended Oahu College and St. Louis College in Honolulu. *Oahu College: List of Trustees,* 55. Catalogues of Franklin & Marshall College in Lancaster, Pennsylvania, list Kelvin as a student there from 1909 to 1913, but apparently he did not

graduate. (He is not listed as a member of the 1913–1914 senior class and is not listed as a graduate in the 1914–1915 catalogue.)

139. *Los Angeles City Directory,* 1916 (Los Angeles: Los Angeles Directory Co., 1916), 1138; advertisement, *Los Angeles Times,* March 16, 1917, 1:18.

140. Kelvin K. Keech emergency passport application No. 146310, Paris, France, October 13, 1919; U.S. Passport Applications January 2, 1906–March 31, 1925, M1490, Roll 0796, National Archives. When Kelvin registered for the draft in 1917, he was working as a musician at Maxim's Café in New York City. Draft Registration, Draft Board 158, New York City, FHL Roll 1786820. Kelvin returned to the United States in 1928 and became an announcer for NBC. Ray Poindexter, *Golden Throats and Silver Tongues: The Radio Announcers* (Conway, AR: River Road Press, 1978), 76.

141. "Change Wrought in Los Angeles Amazes Visitor," *Los Angeles Times,* November 5, 1926, A1. Birkel was advertising Keech ukulele banjos as late as November 1920. *Los Angeles Times,* November 17, 1920, 1:3. Alvin Keech was in Salt Lake City in May 1919 demonstrating his instruments at Daynes-Bebee Music Co. Advertisement, *Salt Lake Telegram,* May 27, 1919, 8. He left New York for Antwerp on February 20, 1920. Alvin D. Keech passport application No. 63853, Antwerp, Belgium, April 6, 1920; U.S. Passport Applications January 2, 1906–March 31, 1925, M1490, Roll 0796, National Archives.

142. Kelvin Keech passport application No. 27846, dated London, April 6, 1921; *Los Angeles Times,* November 5, 1926. The Keeches had two factories that made ukuleles and guitars in London and Birmingham. "Trade Winds and Idle Zephyrs," *Gramophone,* April 1926, 15. In 1926, Alvin Keech released a well-received two-sided instructional record on the HMV label, "Banjulele Banjo and Ukulele Instruction." M. W. W., "Dance Notes," *Gramophone,* November 1926, 47.

143. Carter, *Gibson Guitars,* 228.

144. L. A. Wilholt, "Soldier Boy Ousts Maiden of Hawaii from Ragtime Realms," *Atlanta Constitution,* August 19, 1917, C10; "Former Fads," *Boston Daily Globe,* June 23, 1918, SM19.

145. Advertisement, *New York Times,* February 22, 1920, 20:10; advertisement, *Los Angeles Times,* June 2, 1921, 1:2; advertisement, *World Almanac and Encyclopedia 1921* (New York: Press Publishing Co., 1921), 153.

146. Sinclair Lewis, *Babbitt* (New York: Harcourt, Brace & World, 1922), 83; advertisement, *New York Times,* December 8, 1921, 1:4; "President Wilson Must Remain in Bed for 'Extended Period,'" *Wilkes Barre Times Leader,* October 11, 1919, 1.

147. "May Singhi Breen, Ukulele Lady of Radio in 20's and 30's, Dead," *New York Times,* December 20, 1970, 65.

148. "Oceans of Empathy," *Time* magazine, February 27, 1950, 73–74.

Chapter 7: The Height of Its Popularity

1. Susan J. Douglas, *Inventing American Broadcasting 1899–1922* (Baltimore: Johns Hopkins University Press, 1987), 303; Gleason L. Archer, *History of Radio to 1926* (New York: American Historical Society, 1938), 241, 248.

2. Archer, *History of Radio,* 203, 280.

3. Douglas, *Inventing American Broadcasting,* 303.

4. Susan Smulyan, *Selling Radio: The Commercialization of American Broadcasting 1920–1934* (Washington, D.C.: Smithsonian Institution Press, 1984), 94.

5. "Today's Radio Program," *New York Times,* April 18, 1922, 39; "Today's Radio Program," *New York Times,* May 17, 1922, 14; "Today's Radio Program," *New York Times,* June 14, 1922, 29; "Life and Its Meaning Told," *Los Angeles Times,* June 5, 1922, 2:10; "Today's Radio Program," *New York Times,* June 19, 1922, 15; "Today's Radio Program," *New York Times,* May 17, 1921, 14. Hawaiian music retained its popularity throughout the decade; a 1929 survey of radio listeners found that "Hawaiian music after the Aloha pattern is a three-to-one favorite over the best offerings of Tin Pan Alley." "Like Good Music," *Los Angeles Times,* November 9, 1929, A4.

6. "Ukes and the Summer Months' Trade," *Music Trade Review* (August 1, 1925): 35.

7. "Melody of Hawaiian Isles Broadcast," *Los Angeles Times,* June 6, 1923, 2:10. The *New York Times* came to a similar conclusion: "Since the growth of broadcasting, the kindness with which the microphone treats them [the saxophone, banjo, and ukulele] has carried the three to a prominence they could never have attained in the same period of time through any other medium." "Microphone Has Popularized Obscure Musical Instruments," *New York Times,* March 6, 1927, 10:19.

8. Charles Merz, *The Great American Band Wagon* (New York: Literary Guild of America, 1928), 47.

9. Advertisement, Martin Ukuleles, "Noted for Broadcasting Qualities," *Music Trade Review* (March 12, 1927): 10; "Play Washburn Ukes," *Music Trade Review* (February 26, 1927): 33: "The scientific construction of the Shrine model . . . is particularly adopted for radio broadcasting." Nine radio artists are listed as using Washburns. Leonardo Nunes trademarked the name "Radio Tenor" in 1926, claiming he first used the name in 1925. Reg. No. 212,946, in King, *Trademarks and Patents,* 16.

10. "Ukulele No Longer Favored by Public," *Hartford Courant,* August 1, 1921, 6; "Ukulele's Whine Is Still Popular," *Hartford Courant,* August 11, 1921, 7. "The whole face of the earth has bloomed with ukuleles this summer, is the report of Lyon & Healy," the *Music Trade Review* reported. "Chicago Dealers Busy," *Music Trade Review* (September 3, 1921): 30. See also J. H. Reed, "Shades of Chopin! Flapper Still Buys Ukulele in Atlanta," *Atlanta Constitution,* September 24, 1922, 11; "Modern 'Jazz' Music Has Caused Death of Ukulele's Popularity," *Columbia* [Missouri] *Evening Missourian,* December 18, 1922, 6. In 1926, the *Courant* reported that several music dealers said that "all of the younger set at one time or another obtain a ukulele and learn to play it." "Ukulele Lessons Broadcast from WTIC Tonight," May 26, 1926, 12.

11. In their classic study of Muncie, Indiana, in 1924–1925, Robert and Helen Lynd speculated, "When great artists or dance orchestras are in the cabinet in the corner of one's living room, or 'on the air,' the ability to 'play a little' may be in increasingly less demand." Robert S. Lynd and Helen Merrell Lynd, *Middletown: A Study in Contemporary American Culture* (New York: Harcourt, Brace & Co., 1929), 247. For a different contemporary view, see "Radio Music Aids Music Sale, Chicago Dealers Find," *Washington Post,* May 23, 1926, M16. "Radio was thought by many to sound the death knell of the musical instrument business," said Phil Nash of Fred Gretsch Manufacturing Co. "In point of actual fact this notion was far from the truth." "Ukulele Leads Music Instruments in Its Gross Volume of Sales at Present," *Music Trade Review* (September 19, 1925): 49.

12. Hans Michaelis, "America Unvisited: Some Premature Impressions," *New York Times,* July 7, 1929, 69.

13. Aaron Copland and Vivian Perlis, *Copland 1900 through 1942* (New York: St. Martin's/Marek, 1984), 119, 125–126.

14. "Buddy De Sylva, 54, Film Leader, Dead," *New York Times,* July 12, 1950, 29; Lee Shippey, "The Lee Side O' L.A.," *Los Angeles Times,* July 23, 1933, I:16; "Child Musical Prodigy Grows Up to Win Fame as Composer of Catchy Air," *Los Angeles Times,* May 7, 1916, 3:3; "Buddy De Sylva," *Life* Magazine (December 30, 1940): 50. After suffering a stroke in 1945, De Sylva used a ukulele as a form of physical therapy. Leonard Lyons, "Bud De Sylva, A Show Great, Whipped His Paralysis with a Ukulele," Santa Fe *New Mexican,* July 27, 1950, 4.

15. "Sirens of the Sea Dance on the Sands," *Baltimore American,* December 16, 1917, 22C.

16. Sydney Greenbie, *The Pacific Triangle* (New York: Century Co., 1921), 23.

17. "Reviews of Wednesday's Pictures," *Ft. Worth Star-Telegram,* October 31, 1916, 4.

18. James L. Neibaur, *Arbuckle and Keaton: Their 14 Film Collaborations* (Jefferson, NC: McFarland & Co., 2007), 141. *Backstage* can be seen at http://www.youtube.com/watch?v=jmAZy06IrRm. This may be the first example of the fat man with a tiny 'ukulele scenario, as seen in subsequent films such as *Shallow Hal* (2001), which featured Joshua "Lil' Boy" Shintani.

19. "Majestic Theater," *Hartford Courant,* June 14, 1917, 7; the Ford film, which shows Manuel Nunes and a performer who may be Henry Kailimai, can be seen at http://www.ukulele.org/?videos.

Newsreel footage also was shot at Leonardo Nunes' Los Angeles factory in 1917. "Unsettled Conditions Prevail in Los Angeles Trade," *Music Trade Review* (March 24, 1917): 25.

20. *Los Angeles Times* society columns contain numerous examples of Hawaiian orchestras at Hollywood parties; for example, see "Society of Cinemaland," October 18, 1925, C11; "Whooping Up the Hula," April 4, 1926, 1:4; and "Ah! Christmas," January 16, 1927, J5. For D. W. Giffith, see "'Real Inspiration,'" *New York Times,* June 24, 1923, 10:2, and Kevin Brownlow, *The Parade's Gone By . . .* (Berkeley, CA: University of California Press, 1968), 339–341. For the Ince funeral, see "Film World Mourns Ince," *Los Angeles Times,* November 22, 1924, A1.

21. "Bessie Love Has Ukuleles from Many Countries," *Los Angeles Times,* September 17, 1929, A9.

22. For Normand, see "News and Comment on the Stage," *Anaconda* [Montana] *Standard,* May 19, 1918, 13. For Keaton, see "Buster Gives Account of Self," *Los Angeles Times,* July 6, 1919, 3:13, and "Movie Facts and Fancies," *Boston Daily Globe,* February 20, 1922, 12. For Velez, see "The New Pictures," *Time,* March 11, 1929, and Mollie Herrick, "Rare Antique Is Enameled by Oil Folks," *Hartford Courant,* April 18, 1934, 11. For Cooper, see "Ritz Scene of Benefit for Clinic," *Los Angeles Times,* April 30, 1929, A11, and "Westlake's Big Event," *Los Angeles Times,* May 6, 1929, A7. For Gibson, see "Scope of Radio Rights at Issue," *Los Angeles Times,* February 4, 1928, A6, and "'The Tigress' Turning Point in Two Careers," *Los Angeles Times,* February 12, 1928, C26.

23. "The New Week's Bills," *Washington Post,* June 3, 1929, 16; Nelson B. Bell, "Who Is Singing for Whom—and a Chance to Win Fame," *Washington Post,* June 16, 1929, A2. One possible candidate for Novarro's 'ukulele player is Mike Hanapi (1898–1959). See "Mike Hanapi's Life Story Like Joe Cook Yarn," *Hartford Courant,* October 12, 1930, 9E.

24. Swanson's beach photo can be seen at http://www.catfish1952.com/album42.html. She hated posing for this photo: "In those days, I was rather a prissy young lady." Brownlow, *Parade's Gone By,* 372. For other examples, see "No Need Here of Ukulele to Cheer Cameraman," *Cleveland Plain Dealer,* June 11, 1917, 4; *Los Angeles Times,* April 18, 1926, H8, and November 14, 1926, 1:1; the cover of the March 1926 issue of *California Pictorial* magazine, pictured in Jim Beloff, *The Ukulele: A Visual History,* 2nd ed. (San Francisco: Backbeat Books, 2003), 113; and "A Picture Journey to Atlantic City, Where the Surf Beckons to Philadelphians," Philadelphia *Evening Public Ledger,* July 19, 1917, Pictorial section, 16. For Clara Bow, see *Life* Magazine (October 8, 1965): 106B. For Garbo, see *Life* Magazine (January 10, 1955): 88.

25. "Uke-Strummers, Attention!" *Los Angeles Times,* March 28, 1927, A7; "Ukulele Contest Offers Nice Prizes in Addition to Chance for Stage Fame," San Jose *Evening News,* September 3, 1927. For other examples, see "Photoplay News," *Atlanta Constitution,* March 13, 1927, B4; "Grand to Stage Ukulele Contest," *Atlanta Constitution,* February 19, 1928, C5; and "Ukulele Tilt is Attractive to Musicians," *Pittsburgh Post-Gazette*, April 18, 1929, 11.

26. *Saturday Evening Post,* June 14, 1930. It was not the last time the 'ukulele appeared on the magazine's cover in the hands of college students; for example, see the March 16, 1940, and November 30, 1940, issues.

27. Max McConn, "A Super-Kindergarten for College Men," *New York Times,* February 23, 1930, 83; "Voice of the People," *Chicago Daily Tribune,* December 27, 1930, 6. See also "Says Few Collegians Pass Summer Playing Ukuleles," *Colorado Springs Gazette,* February 25, 1922, 3.

28. In his 1919 novel, *A Damsel in Distress,* Wodehouse refers to "the handsome sophomore from Yale sitting beside her on the porch, playing the ukulele"; in *Elmer Gantry* (1927), Lewis mentions "a ukulele solo by the champion uke player from the University of Winnemac." Ukuleles also figure in Fitzgerald's 1920 *Smart Set* story, "May Day," and in Booth Tarkington's 1921 story, "Girl, Girl, Girl." *Washington Post,* November 16, 1919, SM1.

29. Gordon Barker, *Pursued by Furies: A Life of Malcolm Lowry* (New York: St. Martin's Press, 1995), 38, 49, 53, 57, 103, 135, 306.

30. Lynn Dumenil, *The Modern Temper: American Culture and Society in the 1920s* (New York: Hill and Wang, 1995), 3–4, 10.

31. Jon Savage, *Teenage: The Creation of Youth Culture* (New York: Viking Penguin, 2007), 66, 200, 208; Roger M. Olien and Diana Davids Olien, *Easy Money: Oil Promoters and Investors in the Jazz Age* (Chapel Hill: University of North Carolina Press, 1990), 3–7; Dumenil, *Modern Temper,* 12, 57.

32. Mark Sullivan, *Our Times: The United States 1900–1925,* vol. 6: *The Twenties* (New York: Charles Scribner's Sons, 1935), 384.

33. See "The Fable of the Two Mandolin Players and the Willing Performer" in George Ade's *Fables in Slang* (Chicago: Herbert S. Stone & Co., 1900), 181.

34. Viña Delmar, *Bad Girl* (New York: Literary Guild of America, 1928), 3.

35. "Ukes and the Summer Months' Trade," *Music Trade Review* (August 1, 1925): 35.

36. "May Singhi Breen, Ukulele Lady of Radio in 20's and 30's, Dead." *New York Times,* December 20, 1970, 65.

37. Breen arranged music for collections by Remnick, Witmark, and Berlin and self-published her own *Peter Pan* method with Peter De Rose in 1925; Edwards' name appeared on at least two comic songbooks published by Robbins-Engel in 1925–1926 and on a 1927 method published by Robbins Music Corp. Other well-known performers whose names appeared on methods and song collections include Wendell Hall, Roy Smeck, Frank Crumit, W. C. Handy, and Frank Ferera and Anthony Franchini. The Milwaukee method was K. Killianus' *Practical Method for the Ukulele* (1925); Teresita De Harport's method of the same name was published in Denver that same year; the *Modern Method for Ukulele, Ukulele-Banjo and Tenor Banjo* by Lloyd Loar, Gibson's famed acoustical engineer, was published in Altoona, also in 1925.

38. *EZ Method for Ukulele and Ukulele Banjo* (New York: William J. Smith Music Co., 1924); Frank L. Littig, *Littig's New Practical Method for Hawaiian Ukulele, Banjuke & Taro Patch Fiddle* (Chicago: Chart Music Publishing House, 1921); *15-Minute Guaranteed Ukulele Course for Hawaiian Ukulele and Banjo Ukulele* (Chicago: M. M. Cole, 1925); *"Uke" Hughes' Simplified Instructor for Ukulele* (New York: H. Stadlmair Co., 1924); Will D. Moyer, *Conservatory Method for Ukulele* (Chicago: Chart Music Publishing House, 1926); Art King, *Symphonic Ukulele Arrangements* (San Francisco: Sherman, Clay, & Co., 1928?).

39. "Robbins-Engel Opens Ukulele Department," *Music Trade Review* (April 4, 1925): 51.

40. Noonan, *Guitar in America,* 128. Her method, *The Bickford Method for the Ukulele* (Boston: Oliver Ditson Co., 1920) was coauthored with her husband Myron.

41. For campgrounds, see Anne O'Hare McCormick, "Tenting on the New Campground," *New York Times,* August 13, 1922, 45, and "His Camping Trip," *Washington Post,* July 29, 1922, 5. For the battleship Arizona, see Eddie Boyden, "Arizona Has Music Record for Navy," *San Francisco Chronicle,* January 24, 1922, 13. For Folsom Prison, see "New Folsom Riot Near," *Los Angeles Times,* November 28, 1927, 1. For the "Ukulele Slayer," see "Slayer of Musician Convicted," *Los Angeles Times,* September 22, 1926, 5.

42. For Bentley, see Harry Cross, "New Cards Await Weakened Giants," *New York Times,* June 4, 1925, 16, and John Kieran, "Sports of the Times," *New York Times,* January 10, 1931, 19. For Grimm, see Ring Lardner, "Ring Lardner Thinks Yankees Will Win Series If Cubs Don't," *Hartford Courant,* September 28, 1932, 25. For the term "ukulele umpire," see Westbrook Pegler, "Nobody's Business," *Chicago Daily Tribune,* April 5, 1931, A4. Dodger shortstop Maury Wills learned to play the ukulele while in the minors in Spokane, Washington. Bob Thomas, "Signing Autographs Is Art to Baseballers, Says Wills," Fredericksburg, VA, *FreeLance Star,* October 3, 1963, 31.

43. "Ukulele Leads Music Instruments in Gross Volume of Sales at Present," *Music Trade Review* (September 19, 1925): 49.

44. Edwin Schallert, "Cinema's New Art Revealed," *Los Angeles Times,* October 29, 1926, A9. Schallert reported that Smeck's "tricks . . . in switching ukulele around as he played on it brought a mirthful response from the audience." Smeck remembered being paid $350 for his performance, which was filmed in a Manhattan theater. James Sallis, *The Guitar Players: One Instrument and Its Masters in American Music* (New York: William Morrow and Co., 1982), 89. The first public demonstration of

Vitaphone was at the Warner Theater in New York City on August 5, 1926. Mordaunt Hall, "Vitaphone Stirs as Talking Movie," *New York Times,* August 7, 1926, 6. For the first television broadcast, see "Radio Television to Home Receivers Is Shown in Tests," *New York Times,* January 14, 1928, 1.

45. Anthony Slide, *The Encyclopedia of Vaudeville* (Westport, CT: Greenwood Press, 1994,) 471; "How to Be Amos 'n' Andy Is Simple—One Thing Just Led to Another," *Christian Science Monitor,* January 14, 1930, 3.

46. Sallis, *The Guitar Players,* 77–96.

47. "Wendell Hall, a Pioneer of Radio, Is Dead," *Chicago Tribune,* April 3, 1969, W14; "Vows to Be Aired," *Chicago Daily Tribune,* June 1, 1924, E11. Released by Victor in November 1923, "It Ain't Gonna Rain No Mo" was marketed as the "first Victor record by this nationally-known singer, comedian, and composer of popular songs. He gives two of his own compositions [the other was "Red-Headed Music Maker"] and is a 'whole show' in himself." Advertisement, *Los Angeles Times,* November 23, 1923, 12. Smeck, whose recording career took off in the mid-twenties and continued largely uninterrupted during the Depression, usually soloed on guitar or steel guitar on his records, many of which were released under a variety of pseudonyms. Rockwell, *Hawaiian Records,* 1066–1103.

48. Elmer Douglass, "Marriage of Friends Stirs Elmer's Soul," *Chicago Daily Tribune,* June 5, 1924, 10.

49. Pitts and Hoffman, *Crooners,* 160.

50. Ibid., 162.

51. Ibid., 167, 169; "Harmony Makes Ukulele for the Prince of Wales," *Music Trade Review* (May 26, 1928): 71. The koa and mahogany instrument with gold-plated trimmings made by Harmony of Chicago became a production model known as the Prince of Wales that retailed at $25. Advertisement, *Music Trade Review,* Musical Merchandise Section (June 9, 1928): 14.

52. "Ohio State Alumnus Proves Bright Star on Vaudeville Bill," *Atlanta Constitution,* January 10, 1917, 9; "At the Local Theaters," *Washington Post,* May 7, 1918, 11. For Crumit's use of ukulele, see "Big Orpheum Bill Pleases First Nighters," *Salt Lake Telegram,* February 7, 1916, 6; "The Theaters," *Grand Rapids* [Michigan] *Press,* September 26, 1916, 6; "Orpheum Bill Bolstered by Grattan Play," *Duluth News-Tribune,* December 3, 1917, 6.

53. "Ukulele Music Scores at Poli's," *Hartford Courant,* November 15, 1918, 18; "Betty Be Good at the Wilbur," *Boston Daily Globe,* December 9, 1919, 4.

54. Pitts and Hoffman, *Crooners,* 118. Irving Berlin published *Strum It with Crumit* in 1925. "New Crumit Song Book," *Music Trade Review* (June 6, 1925): 46.

55. Durkee's birthdate is recorded as December 1877 in the 1900 Census, which lists her as a music teacher living at 664 Washington Blvd., Chicago. Dwelling 15, Family 15, 12th Ward, Supervisorial District 1, ED 331, Sheet 1, June 2, 1900. George B. Durkee, Jennie's father, was "for many years superintendent of the Lyon & Healy factory, and inventor of many appliances for musical instruments." "Obituary," *Chicago Daily Tribune,* April 13, 1913, 2. Durkee was a student of noted guitarist William Foden. Noonan, *Guitar in America,* 67. Later editions of Durkee's method were published by Lyon & Healy. Jennie Durkee, *The American Way of Playing Ukulele Solos* (Chicago: Jennie Durkee, 1917). For her death, see "Deaths," *Los Angeles Times,* November 2, 1941, 16.

56. For examples of Durkee's Lyon & Healy performances, see advertisements in the *Chicago Daily Tribune,* December 9, 1917, 9; April 8, 1919, 11; November 20, 1920, 3; March 17, 1923, 3. Durkee's first-known Los Angeles radio appearance was on October 5 of that year, in a performance sponsored by Southern California Music Co. "Uncle Remus, Howdy! Bring On Your Entertainers," *Los Angeles Times,* October 5, 1923, 2:8. Durkee made almost 130 radio appearances in Los Angeles, the last known of which was December 25, 1931. She is listed as a music teacher in the 1930 Census living at 618 Vendome, Los Angeles, Dwelling 186, Family 289, Assembly District 64, ED 19–393, Sheet 13A, April 16, 1930.

57. "May Singhi Breen, Staunch Defender of the Ukulele," *Hartford Courant,* February 16, 1930, E12. For family details, see the 1900 Census, Dwelling 130, Family 137, Bronx Borough Dist. 1, ED 1030, Sheet 8, p. 198A, Roll T623 1126.

58. "Today's Radio Program," *New York Times,* September 17, 1923, 27; "Anniversary Program on Air Tonight," *Washington Post,* June 13, 1929, 9; "May and Peter at Work," *Hartford Courant,* May 18, 1930, E8.

59. Breen's ukulele arrangements began to appear regularly in 1923–1924 in sheet music published by such major firms as Irving Berlin (for whom she became an arranger in 1924) and Leo Feist. For Harris' role, see "Sheet Music with Ukulele Arrangement Planned," *Music Trade Review,* Musical Merchandise Section (August 5, 1922): 25. For Breen as arranger, see "May Singhi Breen Will Arrange for Irving Berlin," *Music Trade Review* (February 16, 1924), 58. Ukulele arrangements were widespread by early 1925. See "Will Inclusion of Saxophone Arrangements in Popular Sheet Music Create New Market?" *Music Trade Review* (February 21, 1925): 42.

60. Daniel I. McNamara, *The ASCAP Biographical Dictionary of Composers, Authors and Publishers* (New York: Thomas Y. Crowell, 1952), 52.

61. Advertisement, *Popular Mechanics* (May 1926): 78.

62. Breen ultimately achieved some success; in 1941, Cliff Edwards was required to join the musicians' union in Los Angeles, "which has decided that the uke is a musical instrument." "Jimmie Fidler in Hollywood," *Los Angeles Times,* May 8, 1941, 17. New York Local 802 did not require membership for ukulele players until 1950. Ross Parmenter, "World of Music: Ukulele Players," *New York Times,* October 22, 1950, 10:7; "The Professional Uke," *Time* Magazine, October 30, 1950. By 1954, Breen was a member of Local 802. "Pianists Cover 111 Pages, But What's a Bouzouki?" *Billboard* (May 1, 1954): 18.

63. "The Microphone Will Present—" *New York Times,* June 26, 1932, 20:5. The performance was broadcast on WJZ.

64. Edwards registered for the draft in Chicago on June 5, 1917, reporting that he was born June 14, 1895, in Hannibal, a single white male employed as a theatrical entertainer, living at 1000 Dakin Street. U.S. Selective Service System, World War I Draft Registration Cards 1917–1918, M1509, Roll 1613575, Draft Board 54, Chicago, Cook County, Ill. Gary Giddins, *Bing Crosby: A Pocketful of Dreams, The Early Years 1903–1940* (Boston: Little, Brown and Co., 2001), 91; Pitts and Hoffman, *Crooners,* 162; advertisement, *Los Angeles Times,* June 10, 1933, 3; "Margaret Mann and James Hall Greet Patrons," *Los Angeles Times,* September 13, 1928, A9; "'Ukulele Ike' Well Received," *Hartford Courant,* March 18, 1926, 2.

65. *Los Angeles Times,* March 7, 1930, A11.

66. Larry F. Kiner, *The Cliff Edwards Discography* (New York: Greenwood Press, 1987), x; "Buffaloes Attacked Truck," *Los Angeles Times,* July 14, 1929, 24; "Ukulele Player Undergoes Hard Training Course," *Los Angeles Times,* March 7, 1930, A11; "Town Fosters Crooners," *Los Angeles Times,* June 30, 1935, 8. Edwards once quipped that he first took up the 'ukulele because "it's more easily pawned." "Ukulele Ike's Story," *Washington Post,* September 25, 1949, 2E.

67. Kiner, *Cliff Edwards,* x; Stanley Levey, "Purveyor of Nostalgic Tunes," *New York Times,* July 28, 1946, 10:7. For the Arsonia Café, see Charles A. Sengstock, *That Toddlin' Town: Chicago's White Dance Bands and Orchestras, 1900–1950* (Urbana: University of Illinois Press, 2004), 115. Edwards appeared in Mack's Musical Revue in Miami, Florida, in July 1918. "Mack's Musical Revue at Airdrome Next Week," *Miami Herald Record,* July 7, 1918, 6.

68. Ed Lowrey with Charlie Foy, *Joe Frisco: Comic, Jazz Dancer, and Railbird* (Carbondale: Southern Illinois University Press, 1999), 52; "The Theatre," *Wall Street Journal,* May 5, 1928, 4; "Cracked Voice Wins Fame," *Los Angeles Times,* June 30, 1929, 21; Kiner, *Cliff Edwards,* xi.

69. David Bakish, *Jimmy Durante: His Show Business Career* (Jefferson, NC: McFarland & Co., 1995), 21; Norton, *Musical Theater,* 2:257–259. Clayton and Edwards were billed as "colored comedians" or "blackface comedians"; see "Theaters in Boston," *Christian Science Monitor,* October 16, 1923, 4, and "Russian Nightingale and Prima Danseuse on Bill at Keith's," *Washington Post,* December 9, 1923, 64. As late as March 1925, Edwards was depicted in blackface in newspaper advertising, and the same image appeared on the peghead of his eponymous 'ukulele. *Washington Post,* March 8, 1925, 63. Blackface and minstrel shows remained popular through the Depression, as the success of *Amos*

'n' Andy demonstrates; during the same period, the Federal Theater Project produced minstrel shows and distributed such productions as "The Darktown Follies." John Springhall, *The Genesis of Mass Culture: Show Business Live in America 1840 to 1940* (New York: Palgrave Macmillan, 2008), 76–77.

70. Kiner, *Cliff Edwards*, xii, 4–14; William G. Hyland, *George Gershwin: A New Biography* (Westport, CT: Praeger, 2003), 82, 87–88; Astaire, *Steps in Time*, 128, 134; Robert Wyatt and John Andrew Johnson, eds., *The George Gershwin Reader* (New York: Oxford University Press, 2007), 73–74.

71. Will Friedwald, *Jazz Singing: America's Great Voices from Bessie Smith to Bebop and Beyond* (New York: Collier Books, 1992), 16, 18; Scott Yanow, *The Jazz Singers: The Ultimate Guide* (New York: Backbeat Books, 2008), 70. Contemporary critics were not always impressed with Edwards. "He has only the ukulele and his voice, and sometimes they are quite separate instruments of harmony; but curiously enough, one does not mind," Philip Scheuer wrote in 1929. "Singer of Blues at Orpheum," *Los Angeles Times,* January 8, 1929, A11.

72. Kiner, *Cliff Edwards*, 4–65; Norton, *Musical Theater,* 2: 417–418, 502–503. On Edwards' death, it was claimed he was credited with selling more than 74 million records; by 1929, he was said to have sold 15 million. "Cliff Edwards, 76, 'Ukulele Ike' of Stage and Film, Dies on Coast," *New York Times,* July 22, 1971, 36; "Cracked Voice Wins Fame," *Los Angeles Times,* June 30, 1929, 21. However, as Tim Gracyk has pointed out, no reliable sales figures exist for this early period. Gracyk and Hoffman, *Popular American Recording Pioneers,* 8–11.

73. Kiner, *Cliff Edwards*, 155–178.

74. Bill C. Malone, *Country Music U.S.A.,* 2nd rev. ed. (Austin: University of Texas Press, 2002), 43–44; Elijah Wald, *Escaping the Delta: Robert Johnson and the Invention of the Blues* (New York: Amistad, 2004), 43–69; Bob Carlin, *String Bands in the North Carolina Piedmont* (Jefferson, NC: McFarland & Co., 2004), 130–141.

75. Malone, *Country Music,* 33; Victor advertisement, *Los Angeles Times,* November 7, 1924, 2; "'Hill Billies' at Church," *Washington Post,* January 25, 1926, 16; Walter Carter, *Gibson Guitars: 100 Years of an American Icon* (Los Angeles: General Publishing Group, 1994), 119.

76. Nolan Porterfield, *Jimmie Rodgers: The Life and Times of America's Blue Yodeler* (Urbana: University of Illinois Press, 1992), 58, 70–71, 206–209, 235–236, 251. Even Rodgers' songbooks were provided with ukulele chords; see, for example, *Jimmie Rodgers (America's Blue Yodeler) Album of Songs Number 5* (New York: Southern Music Co., n.d.).

77. Carlin, *String Bands,* 18. A group called the North Carolina Hawaiians recorded several sides for OKeh in Atlanta in 1928. Rockwell, *Hawaiian Records,* 888.

78. James R. Goff, Jr., *Close Harmony: A History of Southern Gospel* (Chapel Hill: University of North Carolina Press, 2002), 102, 127. A 1927 portrait of the well-known Frank Stamps Quartet shows pianist Dwight Brock fingering a 'ukulele (100).

79. "Iowans on Vessel Named After State," *Philadelphia Inquirer,* June 23, 1919, 5.

80. Prof. A. B. Hughes advertisement, *Baltimore Afro-American,* August 22, 1919, 7; "To Open Ukulele School," *Baltimore Afro-American,* October 13, 1928, 24; Eugene Dutton classified ad, *Philadelphia Tribune,* March 22, 1919, 8; W. Franklin Hoxter, "Music Hath Its Charms," *Philadelphia Tribune,* January 9, 1925, 5; "Social News," *Baltimore Afro-American,* April 19, 1927, 13; "Cleveland News," *Pittsburgh Courier,* October 18, 1924, 14; "McKeesport, Pa.," *Pittsburgh Courier,* January 23, 1926, 11; "Ukulele Club to Be Organized," *Norfolk [Virginia] Journal & Gazette,* September 2, 1922, 6; "Whistling Chorus Feature of Public School Music Here," *Baltimore Afro-American,* December 20, 1924, 11.

81. "Our Students' Conduct," *Chicago Defender,* November 1, 1924, 12.

82. Advertisement, the Coloured Music Shoppe, *Pittsburgh Courier,* December 25, 1926, A2; "Who's Who in Business," *Pittsburgh Courier,* May 14, 1927, A1; Dorsey Bros. ad, *Pittsburgh Courier,* December 17, 1927, A3.

83. For Small and Mays, see "Two Headliners Share Honors on Orpheum Bill," *Los Angeles Times,* September 19, 1926, C23; "Capitol," *Hartford Courant,* June 13, 1927, 11; and "Theaters," *Christian*

Science Monitor, July 12, 1927, 5B. For Ukulele Bob Williams, see "Jubilee Is Billed to Head List," *Los Angeles Times,* April 24, 1927, 17, and advertisement, *Baltimore Afro-American,* January 31, 1925, A4. For Grant, see advertisement, *Baltimore Afro-American,* May 30, 1924, A2. For Clarence Williams, see advertisement, *Chicago Defender,* August 15, 1925, 6, and Jasen, *Tin Pan Alley,* 69–70. For Brown, see Tom Reed, *The Black Music History of Los Angeles—Its Roots* (Los Angeles: Black Accent on LA Press, 1996), 14. For Lewis, see Ralph Berrier Jr., "Remembering Rabbit," *Roanoke* [Virginia] *Times,* February 27, 2007.

84. Lynne Heffley, "A Big Reputation for Entertaining Little Listeners," *Los Angeles Times,* February 2, 2004, E6.

85. "New Lyon & Healy Plant Doubles Capacity," *Music Trade Review* (February 19, 1927): 31.

86. King and Walsh, "Pilgrimage to Nazareth," 3–6.

87. "New Banjo and Ukulele," *Presto* (March 10, 1923): 20.

88. "Announces Special Ukulele," *Music Trade Review* (September 26, 1925): 21. Advertisements for tenor and concert 'ukuleles are scarce; dealers usually advertised instruments by price.

89. "Adopts Standard String Length for Ukuleles," *Music Trade Review* (October 9, 1926): 30; "Standardization Principal Topic at Musical Instrument and Accessories Meet," *Music Trade Review* (October 15, 1927), 27.

90. "Luck Eludes Song Writer," *New York Times,* September 7, 1924, 20:2.

91. King and Walsh, "Pilgrimage to Nazareth," 4–6.

92. John Teagle, *Washburn: Over One Hundred Years of Fine Stringed Instruments* (New York: Music Sales Corp., 1996), 32, 77, 101, 108–109; Beloff, *The Ukulele,* 91, 96. For Gretsch, see advertisement featuring ten different models, *Music Trade Review* (July 2, 1921): 22.

93. "Gibson, Inc. Adds Ukulele Banjo to Its Catalog," *Music Trade Review* (May 17, 1924): 38. George Gruhn and Walter Carter, *Gruhn's Guide to Vintage Guitars* (San Francisco: GPI Books, 1991), 156, do not mention this instrument.

94. "Merchandising the Ukulele at Retail," *Music Trade Review* Musical Merchandise Section (May 26, 1923): 1.

95. Advertisement, *Los Angeles Times,* December 15, 1926, 8.

96. Advertisements, *Los Angeles Times,* December 6, 1925, and November 28, 1926, 14.

97. King, *Selected U.S. Trademarks,* xix–xxi.

98. "'Aero Uke' Introduced by Stromberg-Voisinet Co.," *Musical Trade Review* (December 1930), 31. The unique design was patented by Emil Starke of Oak Park, Illinois, in 1929. King, *Selected U.S. Trademarks,* 48–49.

99. Advertisement, *Los Angeles Times,* September 6, 1928, 3.

100. "Hawaii Cannot Supply Demand for Ukuleles," *Christian Science Monitor,* August 26, 1916, 6.

101. "Ukulele Crop Greatest Ever," *Los Angeles Times,* July 22, 1920, 2:3.

102. *Hawaiian Annual for 1922* (Honolulu: Thomas G. Thrum, 1921), 23–24. Musical instrument shipments to the mainland declined from $35,382 in 1920 to $15,415 in 1921, as compared to imports from the mainland, which rose from $135,345 to $254,341.

103. "Kumalae's Ukulele Factory Burned," *Honolulu Advertiser,* October 16, 1922, 1; "4000 Ukuleles Go Up in Smoke But No Jazz Records," *San Francisco Chronicle,* October 17, 1922, 1.

104. "Hawaiian Makes New Instrument Out of Coconut," *Los Angeles Times,* December 18, 1925, 7; "Hawaiian Poi King Reaches Here," *Los Angeles Times,* July 11, 1926, 7; King, *Selected U.S. Trademarks,* 40–41; "New Ukulele of More Volume and Sweeter Tone Invented by Honolulu Maker of Bell Tone," *Honolulu Advertiser,* January 15, 1928, 5; "Powerful 'Uke,'" *Los Angeles Times,* February 13, 1928, 4. Rudolph Duncan of Honolulu trademarked "Niu Kani" on December 7, 1926, claiming it was first used on October 28, 1925. King, *Selected U.S. Trademarks,* 23.

105. Charles Phillips, *Paderewski: The Story of a Modern Immortal* (New York: Macmillan Co., 1934), 489. Mossman's marketing also earned him a brief mention in *Time* Magazine: see "Music," March 12, 1928, 25.

106. "Makers of Ukuleles in Merger," *Los Angeles Times,* April 24, 1927, 16; "More and More Ukuleles to Go Forth from Hawaii," *Christian Science Monitor,* April 26, 1927, 3.

107. The $12 million figure is cited in *Los Angeles Times,* April 24, 1927, 16.

108. Noble, *Hula Blues,* 51.

109. Burnet Hershey, "Jazz Latitude," *New York Times,* June 25, 1922, SM5.

110. *Honolulu Tourist Guide and Handbook* (Honolulu: Mid-Pacific Folder Distributing, 1925), 41, cited in Desmond, *Staging Tourism,* 82.

111. "Jazz Is Replacing Old Native Tunes of Hawaii Islands," *Washington Post,* September 13, 1925, 40. "It is jazz and other modern syncopated music that is fast dragging our ancient hula into something disgraceful, rather than preserving it as one of the most beautiful dances of any people," complained Helen Desha Beamer in 1929. "Little Girl Devoted to Hula Study," *Los Angeles Times,* June 8, 1929, A3.

112. "Miscellany," *Manchester Guardian,* June 8, 1921, 5.

113. "Wales Playing Jazz at Palace," *Hartford Courant,* December 7, 1924, A8. For Keech's claim, see "2 Chains Agog Over Report of Wales U.S. Trip," *Chicago Daily Tribune,* March 6, 1932, F6, and Poindexter, *Golden Throats,* 76.

114. "British Prince Kills Wildebeest and Then Plays the Uke," *Chicago Daily Tribune,* July 6, 1925, 23; "The Prince's 25,000 Miles' Tour," *Manchester Guardian,* October 16, 1925, 13; Sophie Tucker, *Some of These Days: The Autobiography of Sophie Tucker* (Garden City, NY: Doubleday, Doran & Co., 1949), 219–220.

115. "Ad Libitum," *Musical Times* 67 (August 1, 1926): 697.

116. "Ukulele Craze Hits England," *Presto* (August 22, 1925): 23.

117. For example, see "To-Day's Wireless Programmes," *Manchester Guardian,* May 30, 1927, 10; June 20, 1927, 10; July 2, 1927, 14; August 31, 1927, 10. For Fowler, see "Art Fowler," *New York Times,* April 10, 1953, 21, and "Art Fowler, TV Singer, Dies at Oklahoma City," *Ada* [Oklahoma] *Evening News,* April 8, 1953, 12. In 1961, Nesbit released "Let Me Teach You to Play the Ukulele" on the Music Minus One label. "Reviews of New Albums," *Billboard Music Week* (July 24, 1961): 38.

118. "Berlin Now Vibrating to Home-Made Ukuleles," *Hartford Courant,* July 27, 1924, 10. At least one method was published in Berlin: Domingo Gregorio's *Hawaiian-Ukulele-Method, for Self Instruction* (1928).

119. See http://www.brueko.com/en/company.html.

120. "Kaai Will Make Tour of Antipodes," *Pacific Commercial Advertiser* (January 5, 1911); "Music and Pictures for Sydney Public," *Hawaiian Gazette,* March 10, 1911, 1; "Talked Hawaiian with the Maoris," *Hawaiian Gazette,* June 27, 1911, 2. Kaai and the Royal Hawaiians opened at Sydney's YMCA Concert Hall on April 18. Advertisement, *Sydney Morning Herald,* April 8, 1911, 3. The 'ukulele had made its way to Australia prior to Kaai's arrival: A February 1910 production of the musical comedy *Sergeant Brue* featured the song "Rose of Honolulu," "sung artistically by Harold Thurley . . . assisted by a specially selected chorus, to the accompaniment of Genuine Hawaiian Ukuleles." Advertisement, *Sydney Morning Herald,* February 2, 1910, 2.

121. "The Royal Hawaiians," *Sydney Morning Herald,* April 10, 1911, 4; "Music and Drama," *Sydney Morning Herald,* April 15, 1911, 11.

122. John King, *The Hawaiian Ukulele and Guitar Makers . . . 1884 to 1930* (St. Petersburg, FL: NALU Music, 2001), lxx; Henry A. Peelua Bishaw, *The Albert Ukulele Hawaiian Guitar: Complete Instructions for Accompaniment & Solo Work* (Sydney: J. Albert & Son, 1919), no page number. "Mr. Bishaw" is listed as a performer in an April 14, 1911, performance at Sydney's Palace Theater, and "H. Bishaw" is listed among the passengers returning with Kaai aboard the *Zealandia* that July. Advertisement, *Sydney Morning Herald,* April 14, 1911, 2; "Port of Honolulu," *Hawaiian Gazette,* July 21, 1911, 8.

123. Mr. Henry A. Bishaw, head of the "Company of Hawaiians . . . now performing in 'The Bird of Paradise' at the Theatre Royal," was advertised by Allen's, Ltd., as giving 'ukulele lessons in Adelaide in March 1918. Advertisement, *Adelaide Advertiser,* March 27, 1918, 2. By April 20, Bishaw was in

Sydney, offering ʻukulele lessons at the "Albert" College of Music. Advertisement, *Sydney Morning Herald*, April 20, 1918, 2. J. Albert & Son, founded in Sydney in 1885 as a clock, watch, and violin repair shop, was well on its way to becoming Australia's largest music publishing house. http://www .albertmusic.com/company. For the later history of Hawaiian music in Australia, see Jackey Coyle and Rebecca Coyle, "Aloha Australia: Hawaiian Music in Australia (1920–55)." *Perfect Beat* 2 (January 1995): 31–63.

124. Ernest Kaai passport application, December 10, 1920, Passport Applications January 2, 1906–March 31, 1925, NARA Microfilm Publication M1490; *Hawaiian Songs* (Soerabaia, Java: Compliments of the Simpang Hotel, n.d.), songs copyright 1917 by Ernest Kaai; "Kaai Returns after Long Stay in Orient," *Honolulu Star-Bulletin*, October 19, 1922, 4. The ʻukulele appeared in Tonga as early as 1898 in the hands of Elona Alapai, assistant to the government medical officer, who reportedly was "a great favorite with the chiefs, to whom he sings the sweet Hawaiian melodies accompanied by the ʻukulele' or guitar." "Our Tonga Letter," the *Independent*, November 11, 1898, 1.

125. "Ernest Kaai, now in Columbo, sends aloha to friends," unidentified Honolulu newspaper, July 31, 1937. Clipping from morgue file, Hamilton Library, University of Hawaii; "Pioneer Isle Musician Mourns Decline of Art," *Honolulu Advertiser*, October 9, 1937. Kaai is likely the reason why J. H. Seeling & Zoon of Semarang, Java, contacted a Chicago firm to inquire about importing Hawaiian instruments in 1923. "Where Doubts Are Dispelled," *Presto* (September 22, 1923): 11. As leader of the Ernest Kaai Jazz Band, Kaai recorded with Japanese singers in Tokyo in 1928 and again in 1930–1931, including a song titled "Ukulele no Oto" ("The Sound of the Ukulele"). Rockwell, *Hawaiian Records*, 559–560.

126. "A One Man Vaudeville Show: A Comedy Sketch Written by Joe Cook," Library of Congress, Rare Book and Special Collections Division, online at American Memory (http://memory.loc. gov, digital ID (h) varsep s42725).

127. For the complete routine, see Douglas Gilbert, *American Vaudeville: Its Life and Times* (New York: Whittlesey House, 1940), 255–257. Cook's book, published by Simon and Schuster, was advertised in the *Los Angeles Times*, April 22, 1930, 11.

128. Thomas R. Ybarra, "Hawaii," *New York Times*, November 2, 1916, 6. The reference to the "whining ukelali" can be found under "Theatrical Notes," *New York Times*, June 26, 1916, 11.

129. Edith Knight Holmes, "Politics Arouse Women's Session," *Morning Oregonian*, October 12, 1916, 6.

130. *Ft. Wayne* [Indiana] *News and Sentinel*, May 22, 1918, 9.

131. "Mutt and Jeff—Mutt's Ukulele Must Have a Swiss Movement," *Los Angeles Times*, January 28, 1917, 1:5. A second Mutt and Jeff ukulele strip ran on March 30 of that year. It's not surprising that Bud Fisher (1884–1954) was one of the first to make fun of the ʻukulele: He worked for the *San Francisco Examiner*. Ron Goulart, ed., *The Encyclopedia of American Comics* (New York: Facts on File, 1990), 130, 270. Other slighting ukulele references in the comics can be found in "Dicky Dippy's Diary," April 29, 1920 (*Boston Daily Globe*) and Ella Cinders, June 3 and July 18, 1931 (*Los Angeles Times*). Modern comics continue the tradition: See, for example, Jerry Scott and Jim Borgman's "Zits," *Los Angeles Times*, September 22, 2003, E19, and February 24, 2006.

132. "A Musical Outlaw," *Los Angeles Times*, October 2, 1921, 2:4; "Brightening Up," *Los Angeles Times*, July 23, 1923, 2:4; "Jazz No Joy to Desert Despot," *Los Angeles Times*, March 12, 1928, 8. "Ukuleles have vicious functions," said Lincoln Park superintendent William H. Wesley. "They are among the reasons why—er, people leave home and that sort of thing." "Ukuleles Banished as Vicious Home Wreckers," *San Francisco Chronicle*, September 29, 1921, 1.

133. "Supreme Court Okehs Zone Act," *Los Angeles Times*, May 8, 1927, D10.

134. "Talley on Ukuleles," *New York Times*, May 5, 1923, 13; "Jail Ukulele Thief? Court Prefers Not," *Los Angeles Times*, May 13, 1923, 2:2.

135. John Steven McGroarty, "Seen from the Green Verdugo Hills," *Los Angeles Times*, November 27, 1927, L3.

136. "Laugh at the Ukulele," *New York Times*, January 20, 1923, 12.

137. Keaton, who also featured a ʻukulele in his 1923 feature, *The Balloonatic,* enjoyed the ʻukulele and played it all his life. Eleanor Keaton and Jeffrey Vance, *Buster Keaton Remembered* (New York: Harry N. Abrams, 2001), 39.

138. Sam Kamaka Sr. was proud of his 1931 sale of a ukulele to Oliver Hardy. Al Goldfarb, "Ukulele: Sweetest Sounds in Hawaii," *Los Angeles Times,* April 26, 1987, G21.

139. P. G. Wodehouse, *Thank You, Jeeves* (Woodstock, NY: Overlook Press, 2003 [1934]), 15. Perhaps the low point in ʻukulele literature came in Agatha Christie's 1930 story, "The Bird with the Broken Wing," in which a ʻukulele string is used to strangle a beautiful young woman. Agatha Christie, *The Mysterious Mr. Quin* (New York: Dell, 1972 [1930]), 183–203.

140. In his 1914 method, George Kia claimed that "the ukulele is a native Hawaiian instrument." Kia, *Self Instructor,* 4. In one 1916 record ad, Victor claimed that "Even when discovered by Captain Cook, the native instruments were the ukulele and ʻtaropatch.'" Advertisement, *Montgomery* [Alabama] *Advertiser,* November 29, 1916, 7. E. N. Guckert also asserted that it "originated among the natives of Hawaii" in *Guckert's Chords for the Ukulele at Sight* (Chicago: Lyon & Healy, 1917), 2.

141. Virgil Jordan, "The Yarn of the Ukulele," *Everybody's Magazine* (March 1917): 336.

142. "Not to Blame for the Ukulele," *Kansas City Star,* September 9, 1917, 1; "Not to Blame for the Ukulele," *Los Angeles Times,* September 16, 1917, 3:18; "The Ukulele Culprit," *Charlotte Observer,* November 7, 1917, 4; "Origin of the Ukulele," *Aberdeen* [South Dakota] *Daily News,* February 26, 1918, 6.

143. "Grass Skirts and Ukuleles All Made Here," *Los Angeles Times,* May 17, 1922, 11; "Hawaiian Floral Leis All Made in America," *Washington Post,* June 24, 1927, 13.

144. Gene Ahern, "Ain't Nature Wonderful?" *Charlotte Observer,* June 8, 1917, 12; "Bessie Love Has Ukuleles from Many Countries," *Los Angeles Times,* September 17, 1929, A9; "Old Legends of Hawaii to Be Told Anew," *Los Angeles Times,* April 13, 1930, A8.

145. *The Playground* 21 (May 1927): 73; (July 1927): 184; (September 1927): 298; (January 1928): 529; (February 1928): 586; "Craft Classes for Winnipeg's Children," *Christian Science Monitor,* July 9, 1928, 3.

146. "Lomb Heads the Musical Instrument and Accessories Manufacturers," *Music Trade Review* (June 9, 1928): 11.

147. Augustus Delafield Zanzig, *Music in American Life, Present and Future* (London: Oxford University Press, 1932), 81.

148. Giddins, *Bing Crosby,* 368.

149. Sanjek, *American Popular Music,* 3:117.

150. Norton, *Musical Theater,* 2:622.

151. "The Show Window," *Hartford Courant,* October 29, 1930, 10.

152. "Behind the Microphone," *Christian Science Monitor,* February 28, 1936, 10.

Chapter 8: Made of a New Gleaming Plastic Material

1. Display advertisement, *Abilene* [Kansas] *Reporter-News,* March 14, 1946, 9.

2. "Popularity of Uke Wanes on Mainland," *Honolulu Advertiser,* November 14, 1948, 8.

3. "Ukuleles Offered in Stores," *Long Beach Press Telegram,* November 21, 1948, 72.

4. Edward Moore, "Music Powwow Leaves Topics of Discussion," *Chicago Daily Tribune,* April 6, 1930, G1.

5. Teagle, *Washburn,* 32–35; "Lyon & Healy Reports 1930 Loss of $351,102," *Chicago Daily Tribune,* May 10, 1931, A7.

6. Carter, *Gibson Guitars,* 132. Gibson manufactured toys from August 1931 through February 1934.

7. Beloff, *The Ukulele,* 20; Washburn and Johnson, *Martin Guitars,* 136. For ʻukulele sales in 1930, see "Fretted Instrument Trade Reports Improved Business," *Music Trade Review,* Section 2 (April 1930): 39.

8. Donaldson B. Thorburn, "By-Products Aid Hawaiian Trade," *Wall Street Journal,* October 21, 1932, 8.

9. "Opera and Concert Asides," *New York Times,* August 1, 1937, 10:5.

10. *Metropolitan Music Co. Catalog,* 1935, 173; "Fall in Banjo Output Laid to 'Jitterbugs,'" *Christian Science Monitor,* October 10, 1938, 6.

11. Giddins, *Bing Crosby,* 368, 373.

12. Sanjek, *American Popular Music,* 3:54–55; Suisman, *Selling Sounds,* 262.

13. "Radio Song Hits for 1935 Listed," *New York Times,* September 2, 1936, 18.

14. Suisman, *Selling Sounds,* 263.

15. Giddins, *Bing Crosby,* 480. Bluesman B. B. King was among those caught up in the new enthusiasm for Hawaiian music: "I was crazy about, believe it or not, the Hawaiian style of music," he said in a 2005 interview. "The Hawaiians have a different sound, the ukulele and the guitar, and so does country music with that steel guitar. To me, man, that's the greatest sound of a guitar ever." Gary Graff, "Q&A: B.B. King marks his 80th birthday," Reuters, September 25, 2005.

16. "National Ukulele Week Set for August 1st to 8th," *Presto Times* (June-July 1937): 12.

17. M. H. Berlin, "Cooperation—A Challenge," *Presto* (December 1939): 26. A 1938 Zenith ad for its latest line of easy-to-use radios showed how far the 'ukulele had fallen: "I'm no musician," an attractive woman is quoted as saying. "Strumming a ukulele is my only accomplishment. I don't know one note from another. But when I can pull a button [on my new Zenith] . . ." Advertisement, *Los Angeles Times,* August 7, 1938, 4.

18. H. Allen Smith, *Waikiki Beachnik* (Boston: Little, Brown and Co., 1960), 4. In 1955, among the most requested numbers on the weekly "Hawaii Calls" radio broadcast were "Sweet Leilani" and "Blue Hawaii," both from *Waikiki Wedding.* Kanahele, *Hawaiian Music,* 112.

19. Wayne Curtis, "Tiki," *American Heritage* (August/September 2006): 39–40; Kevin Starr, *Golden Dreams: California in an Age of Abundance 1950–1963* (New York: Oxford University Press, 2009), 49–50. For King's Tropical Inn, see the grand opening advertisement, *Los Angeles Times,* April 26, 1930, 5; for Clifton's, see official opening advertisement, *Los Angeles Times,* September 16, 1931, 5; for the South Seas, see "Hollywood's No. 1 'Hawaiian' Club Open for 43 Years," *Ha'ilono Mele* 5 (April 1979): 8–9, and Roger Vincent, "A New Hollywood Revival," *Los Angeles Times,* February 6, 2007, D-1.

20. Kanahele, *Hawaiian Music,* 120, 254–255; Imada, "Hawaiians on Tour," 133–134.

21. Kenneth Crist, "Hawaiian Music Came from—Where?" *Los Angeles Times,* May 16, 1937, H13. Almost twenty years later, *Life* echoed this assessment: "Americans think of Hawaii in terms of scenery, pineapple plantations, and Pearl Harbor, but mostly in terms of its familiar music. . . . Hawaiian tunes have probably had a greater influence on the mainland than any other import from the islands." "Decision Approaches for Hawaii," *Life* (February 22, 1954): 24.

22. Kanahele, *Hawaiian Music,* 109–111; Owens, *Sweet Leilani,* 73.

23. Tony Todaro, *The Golden Years of Hawaiian Entertainment 1874–1974* (Honolulu: Tony Todaro Publishing Co., 1974), 110; Kanahele, *Hawaiian Music,* 111–112.

24. Imada, "Hawaiians on Tour," 120–121; Michi Kodama-Nishimoto et al., eds., *Talking Hawaii's Story: Oral Histories of an Island People* (Honolulu: University of Hawaii Press, 2009), 114. Two of Mossman's daughters, Pualani and Piilani, were later dancers at the Lexington Hotel's Hawaiian Room in New York.

25. Sigmund Spaeth, "Hawaii Likes Music," *Harpers Magazine* 176 (March 1938): 424.

26. Noble, *Hula Blues,* 106.

27. Randall and Seaton, *Formby,* 45; Bret, *George Formby,* 13; John Fisher, *George Formby* (London: Woburn-Futura, 1975), 8, 19.

28. Bret, *George Formby,* 26, 246.

29. Fisher, *Formby,* 8, 47; Bret, *George Formby,* 125.

30. Fisher, *Formby,* 76.

31. "Spies Cavort in Comedy," *Los Angeles Times,* October 26, 1940, A7; Fisher, *Formby,* 49.

Formby has been "acclaimed by experts as the finest rhythm banjulele player this country has ever known." Fisher, *Formby*, 47.

32. Randall and Seaton, *Formby*, 7.

33. Interview with Samuel K. Kamaka, April 2, 1993, in *Era of Change*, 2:548. In the late 1930s, Kamaka launched a short-lived joint venture with John Lai of Metronome Music, Ka-Lai String Instrument Co. *Era of Change*, 2:570–571; "News and Notes of the Advertising Field," *New York Times*, August 26, 1939, 30.

34. Kenneth G. Kramer, "Singing Soldiers Are Good Soldiers; Morale Officers Stress Music and More Music," *Wall Street Journal*, December 26, 1942, 1; Lloyd Shearer, "Brightening the Corners Where They Are," *New York Times*, November 1, 1942, SM19.

35. "Navy Criticized for Handing 2 Jobs to Admiral," *Ogden* [Utah] *Standard-Examiner*, May 25, 1946, 1. As part of a postwar investigation, the Senate War Investigating Committee discovered that 'ukuleles shipped to Pearl Harbor later ended up in a civilian store's anniversary sale.

36. Advertisement, *Los Angeles Times*, January 31, 1943, 5.

37. Carter, *Gibson Guitars*, 170. Only 10 percent of Gibson's production capacity was devoted to musical instruments during the war.

38. "Servicemen Need 200 Harmonicas," *Los Angeles Times*, August 31, 1944, 9; "Musical Instruments Going to U.S. Captives," *New York Times*, August 20, 1942, 23; "Musical Instruments Sent by Corps to Alaska Posts," *Los Angeles Times*, August 16, 1943, A5; "Music for War Fronts," *New York Times*, January 28, 1944, 11; "Opera Guild's Latest Drive," *New York Times*, December 31, 1944, 10:5.

39. "Music for War Fronts," *New York Times*, January 28, 1944, 11.

40. Denis Crowdy, "The Guitar Cultures of Papua New Guinea: Regional, Social and Stylistic Diversity," in Andy Bennett and Kevin Dawe, eds., *Guitar Cultures* (Oxford: Berg, 2001), 135–142.

41. Advertisement, *Chicago Tribune*, December 16, 1945, 6. 'Ukuleles of unspecified make were offered at $2.50, $5.50, $6, and $12.

42. Advertisement, *Chicago Tribune*, November 11, 1945, 2. An early form of plastic manufactured by Bakelite was used in the molded rims of Gretsch banjo-ukuleles in 1928. Advertisement, *Music Trade Review*, Section 2 (February 11, 1928): 22.

43. "Plastics Show Opens Today," *Los Angeles Times*, March 26, 1946, A1.

44. David A. Hounshell and John Kenly Smith Jr., *Science and Corporate Strategy: DuPont R&D, 1902–1980* (Cambridge: Cambridge University Press, 1988), 327; Jeffrey Meikle, *American Plastic: A Cultural History* (New Brunswick, NJ: Rutgers University Press, 1995), 1–2, 89, 125.

45. Arthur J. Singer, *Arthur Godfrey: The Adventures of an American Broadcaster* (Jefferson, NC: McFarland & Co., 2000), 17, 25.

46. Arthur Godfrey, "This Is My Story," *Saturday Evening Post* 228 (November 19, 1955): 146.

47. Jack Gould, "Early Summer Crop," *New York Times*, July 1, 1945, 25. When Godfrey went in for major reconstructive hip surgery in 1953, he brought his 'ukulele. "Arthur Godfrey Brings Along Ukulele to Await Surgery," *Oakland Tribune*, May 14, 1953, 93.

48. Singer, *Arthur Godfrey*, 76, 83, 88, 90, 92; "Ukulele's Comeback Indicated by Its Use on Television Programs," Hagerstown, MD, *Daily Mail*, June 10, 1949, 20.

49. Gary R. Edgerton, *The Columbia History of American Television* (New York: Columbia University Press, 2007), 102, 118–119.

50. Singer, *Arthur Godfrey*, 1.

51. Singer, *Arthur Godfrey*, 131. "Arthur Godfrey and his Ukulele" debuted April 4 and ran through June 30, 1950. Vincent Terrace, *The Complete Encyclopedia of Television Programs 1947–1976* (S. Brunswick, NJ: A. S. Barnes & Co., 1976), 1:67. This was not the first time 'ukulele lessons were offered over the air: Dan Nolan, "widely known master of the popular art of playing the ukulele," offered once-a-week, prime-time lessons on Hartford's WTIC in the spring of 1926. "Ukulele Lessons Broadcast from WTIC Tonight," *Hartford Courant*, May 26, 1926, 12. Eddie Chapelle also offered over-the-air lessons on WIBA in Madison, Wisconsin, in 1926. "Cole & Dumas Publish Chapelle Ukulele Course," *Music Trade Review* (July 10, 1926): 29.

52. Ruth Handler with Jacqueline Shannon, *Dream Doll: The Ruth Handler Story* (Stamford, CT: Longmeadow Press, 1994), 67. The Uke-A-Doodle also came with pick, song sheet, and instructions.

53. Handler, *Dream Doll,* 69.

54. Ibid., 68.

55. APP's trademark registration for the Uke-a-Tune indicated a first use of the name on April 28, 1947. King, *U.S. Trademarks,* 2. A Pick-A-Tune ukulele also was on the market in September 1948 for 49 cents. Shirlington Drug Store advertisement, *Washington Post,* September 17, 1948, 19.

56. Mattel wholesalers in Los Angeles and San Francisco originally advertised the Uke-A-Doodle at $86 to $90 per gross; rival firms in New York quickly offered a gross of "two tone plastic ukuleles" for $75. By September, the New York price had dropped to $69. Advertisement, Pico Novelty Co., *Billboard* (March 29, 1947): 125; advertisement, West Coast Novelty Co., *Billboard* (June 7, 1947): 92; advertisement, Mills Sales Co., *Billboard* (June 28, 1947): 85, and (September 27, 1947): 82. Among those advertising toy plastic 'ukuleles were Western Auto Supply (advertisement, *Council Bluffs* [Iowa] *Nonpareil,* December 4, 1947, 10; *Joplin* [Missouri] *Globe,* December 5, 1947, 15); the B. W. Reeder Hardware Co. (*Huntington* [Pennsylvania] *Daily News,* December 4, 1947, 15); and Montgomery Ward (*Portland* [Maine] *Press Herald,* November 13, 1947, 11). Plastic 'ukuleles of an unknown make also were on sale at the Los Angeles Farmers Market in May 1947. Advertisement, *Los Angeles Times,* May 14, 1947, 4.

57. Advertisement, *Indiana Evening Gazette,* November 28, 1947, 11.

58. Handler, *Dream Doll,* 69.

59. "Merchandise Topics," *Billboard,* December 9, 1950, 60.

60. Advertisement, Seagull Drug, *Salt Lake Tribune,* February 1, 1951, 7.

61. S. N. Duncan, "War Buying Rush Hits a Strictly Civilian Industry: Musical Instruments," *Wall Street Journal,* July 15, 1950, 1.

62. Robert C. Ruark, "No Ukeleles," *Charleston* [West Virginia] *Daily Mail,* December 18, 1948, 4.

63. Both stores were selling plastic 'ukuleles that Christmas season. See advertisements in the (Jefferson City, Missouri) *Daily Capital News,* December 18, 1948, 8, and the *Modesto* [California] *Bee and News-Herald,* November 25, 1948, B4.

64. "Ukulele's Comeback," Hagerstown, MD, *Daily Mail,* June 10, 1949, 20; "Return of the Uke," *Lebanon* [PA] *Daily News,* July 1, 1949, 6. *South Pacific* was based on James Michener's 1948 Pulitzer Prize–winning novel, *Tales of the South Pacific;* both take place thousands of miles away from Hawaii. Even so, it's no coincidence that *Bird of Paradise* was remade in 1951, starring Debra Paget.

65. "Music Industry Sees Sales Drop," *New York Times,* July 26, 1949, 37; Sam Dawson, "Ukuleles Are Booming and Zithers Sell Well," *Los Angeles Times,* July 27, 1949, A5.

66. "Ukulele Stages Strong Comeback," *Middletown* [NY] *Times Herald,* July 29, 1949, 5.

67. "Guitar and Uke Sheets Sought," *Billboard* (October 1, 1948): 18.

68. "Guest Editorial—What Other Papers Say," *Portsmouth* [NH] *Herald,* August 4, 1949, 4. "Now take the banjo, or better yet, the mandolin. Both of these were capable of furnishing real music."

69. Jeremy M. Tubbs, "From Maestro to Mastro: The Life, Music and Instruments of Mario Maccaferri," Ph.D. dissertation, University of Memphis, 2008, iv.

70. Tubbs, "Maestro to Mastro," 8–16.

71. Tubbs, "Maestro to Mastro," 150, 289; Editors of Fortune, *100 Stories of Business Success: Case Histories of American Enterprise* (New York: Simon and Schuster, 1954), 12.

72. Tubbs, "Maestro to Mastro," 154.

73. Galperin's advertisement, *Charleston* [West Virginia] *Daily Mail,* May 28, 1950, 11; King, *U.S. Trademarks,* 155–160.

74. King, *U.S. Trademarks,* 6; Andrew R. Boone, "They Make Fortunes by Mail," *Popular Science* (January 1953): 124–125; Happy Tunes advertisement, *Life* (November 27, 1950): 70. Happy Tunes' celebrity endorsers included Gene Krupa, Cab Calloway, Tex Beinecke, Rosemary Clooney, and Morey Amsterdam.

75. King, *U.S. Trademarks,* 161–196.

76. "Arthur Godfrey, Styron Spark Ukulele Comeback," *Wall Street Journal,* March 15, 1950, 1. Godfrey's television plug came on one of his regular CBS shows; his fifteen-minute 'ukulele lesson, *Arthur Godfrey and His Ukulele,* did not air until April 4, three weeks after the first report of Maccaferri being overwhelmed with orders. In June 1950, Mastro was marketing the Islander as "The Sensation of 1950! The Uke That's Used by Arthur Godfrey on his TV Show!" Advertisement, *San Antonio* [Texas] *Express,* June 2, 1950, 3.

77. Editors of Fortune, *100 Stories,* 12; Tubbs, "Maestro to Mastro," 176–177. Maccaferri's Islander Deluxe model, at $7.95, was designed to be the Arthur Godfrey signature model, but a libel suit against Godfrey filed by a firm whose instrument he disparaged on the air convinced Maccaferri it wasn't worth the risk. Tubbs, "Maestro to Mastro," 173. For information on the lawsuit, see "Godfrey Faces Libel Suit by Ukulele Firm," *Billboard* 62 (September 9, 1950): 6. Vega eventually produced a Godfrey signature uke. Beloff, *The Ukulele,* 65. Godfrey was unapologetic about speaking out on what he called "cheap, poorly made instruments nobody can play." "Godfrey Bewails Lack of Uke Tuning Standards on Sheets," *Billboard* (July 8, 1950): 4.

78. Bob Stevens, "Strumming the 'Uke' Craze Hits This Area," *Lowell* [MA] *Sun,* May 14, 1950, 43.

79. Bert Wise, "Mystic Strings of Ukulele Bring Harmony to Harlingen," *Valley Morning Star,* April 30, 1950, 19. See also Elfreeda Kolsch, "Stand by for the 'Plunks' Folks, Ukulele Makes a Comeback in Iowa City," *Iowa City Press-Citizen,* February 4, 1950, 10.

80. "Big Change in Television Predicted," *Chicago Tribune,* July 11, 1950, B7.

81. *Wall Street Journal,* July 15, 1950, 1.

82. Jack O'Brian, "Ukelele Sales Skyrocket to Records Following 'The Great Godfrey's' Plugs," *Cumberland* [MD] *Evening Times,* August 2, 1950, 14. For the origins of the baritone ukulele, see "Tower Tucker," *Chicago Tribune,* July 17, 1950, 26; Ross Parmenter, "World of Music: Ukulele Players," *New York Times,* October 22, 1950, 10:7. Favilla reportedly was the first to bring out a production model of the baritone uke. Tom Favilla, "Origin of the Baritone Uke," Uke Yak, February 8, 2005, http://www.fleamarketmusic.com/bulletin/default.asp?view=classic.

83. "Hawaii Shares in Ukulele 'Boom,'" *Paradise of the Pacific* 62 (September 1, 1950): 14–15.

84. Lynn B. Krantz, Nick Krantz, and Mary T. Fobian, *To Honolulu in Five Days: Cruising Aboard Matson's S.S. Lurline* (Berkeley: Ten Speed Press, 2001), 50–51.

85. The Wendell Hall TV Concert 'ukulele was offered in 1953 for $10.95. Advertisement, *Valparaiso* [IN] *Vidette-Messenger,* November 6, 1953, 2. Hall's method was available at Lyon & Healy in Chicago. Advertisement, *Chicago Tribune,* May 14, 1950, 3. Hall's method, as well as Guckert's, Ukulele Ike's, and the 5-Minute Method, were all sold at Glen Brothers Music Co. in Ogden, Utah. Advertisement, *Standard-Examiner,* June 29, 1950, 17. At Sherman, Clay's Oakland, California, store, customers could buy the EZ Method and Wolff's as well as the 5-Minute Method. Advertisement, *Oakland Tribune,* May 28, 1950, 2.

86. Sidney Lohman, "News and Notes on Television," *New York Times,* May 22, 1949, 10:9; Larry Wolters, "Wendell Hall's Debut in Video Promises Well," *Chicago Tribune,* August 1, 1951, A6; Val Adams, "Format: A Ukulele and a Memory," *New York Times,* September 9, 1951, 10:11.

87. "Ukulele Star to Play Here with Troupe," *Galveston Daily News,* July 16, 1950, 22; "Uke Contest Climaxed in a Shower of Prizes," *Amarillo Daily News,* February 9, 1951, 6; "Art Fowler, TV Singer, Dies at Oklahoma City," *Ada* [OK] *Evening News,* April 8, 1953, 12; "The Final Curtain," *Billboard* (April 18, 1953): 53; Macy's advertisement, *New York Times,* February 11, 1958, 14. Smeck was slow to capitalize on the revival in one respect; his first-ever LP, *The Magic of the Ukulele,* didn't appear until 1959. "Reviews and Ratings of New Popular Albums," *Billboard* (May 18, 1959): 36.

88. "You Have No Talent? You're Made for TV," *Washington Post,* March 28, 1952, B15.

89. David Halberstam, *The Fifties* (New York: Villard Books, 1993), 9–10, 25–26, 52, 68–69.

90. Terry Teachout, *Pops: A Life of Louis Armstrong* (Boston: Houghton Mifflin, 2009), 259.

91. "Dealers Write Good Music in Ukulele Sales," *Chicago Tribune,* May 7, 1950, 3A; "Older

Women Are Demanding Return of 1920 Hair Style," Traverse City, Michigan, *Record-Eagle,* August 29, 1949, 9; Bob Thomas, "Here's Hollywood!" St. Joseph, Michigan, *Herald-Press,* December 13, 1949, 4; Milt Gabler, "Hot Renaissance of Dixieland Jazz," *New York Times,* September 24, 1950, SM14; "300 to Attend Gay 12th Night Masque," *Chicago Tribune,* January 4, 1950, A5; "Here's Young Hollywood," *Oakland Tribune,* May 14, 1950, 53; "1950 Debutante Roster, Listing Only 51 Names, Is Smallest Since 1947," *Chicago Tribune,* September 6, 1950, 2:3. Nostalgia remains comforting in troubled times; see Stuart Elliott, "Like Comfort Food, Warm and Fuzzy Makes a Comeback," *New York Times,* April 7, 2009.

92. George Cable Wright, "Army Tidies Up Kilmer for 5,000 Refugee Hungarians," *New York Times,* November 16, 1956, 1.

93. T. P. Giddings, "Stringless? Why?" *Music Educators Journal* 35 (May-June 1949): 38–39.

94. "Ukulele Getting Refresher Course to Aid Youngsters," *Mason City* [Iowa] *Globe-Gazette,* July 24, 1953, 4. One speaker at the 1950 Music Educators National Conference noted an increased interest in "the so-called recreation instruments, such as the ukulele and harmonica." "5,000 Music Teachers Convene in St. Louis," *New York Times,* March 20, 1950, 17.

95. "Ukulele Band Plays at PHS," *Paris News,* February 29, 1952, 9.

96. Marjorie Pulley, "The Ukulele Goes to College," *Music Educators Journal* 40 (September-October 1953): 81.

97. For Hendrix, see Harry Shapiro and Caesar Glebbeck, *Jimi Hendrix: Electric Gypsy* (New York: St. Martin's Press, 1990), 36; Steven Roby, *Black Gold: The Lost Archives of Jimi Hendrix* (New York: Billboard Books, 2002), 8; and Sharon Lawrence, *Jimi Hendrix: The Man, the Magic, the Truth* (New York: Harper Entertainment, 2005), 14. For Winter, see Nick Krewen, "He's Got the Winter Blues," *Toronto Star,* February 12, 2004. For Benson, see David Yonke, "All That Jazz," *Toledo Blade,* June 12, 2005. For Seger, see Dave Hoekstra, "Seeger: Save the 'Spirit of Voices,'" *Chicago Sun-Times,* June 13, 2006. For Jones, see Gordon Thompson, *Please Please Me: Sixties British Pop, Inside Out* (New York: Oxford University Press, 2008), 159–160. For Anderson, see Aidan Smith, "Pomp and Circumstance," *Scotsman,* January 16, 2005. For Frampton, see Michelle Mills, "'Frampton Comes Alive'—Again!" *Pasadena* [California] *Star-News,* November 3, 2006, 23.

98. Jimmy McDonough, *Shakey: Neil Young's Biography* (New York: Random House, 2002), 58.

99. Joan Baez, *And a Voice to Sing With: A Memoir* (New York: Summit Books, 1987), 31–32. The 'ukulele also was the first instrument of Frank Sinatra and Pete Seeger, the seminal American folk artist. George Frazier, "Frank Sinatra," *Life* (May 3, 1943): 58; David King Dunaway, *How Can I Keep from Singing: Peter Seeger* (New York: McGraw-Hill Book Co., 1981), 37.

100. Dave Van Ronk, *The Mayor of MacDougal Street: A Memoir* (Cambridge, MA: Da Capo Press, 2005), 6.

101. Lyle Ritz interview by Jim Tranquada, April 24, 2004, Santa Cruz, California.

102. Ibid. For Niehaus, see Ted Gioia, *West Coast Jazz: Modern Jazz in California 1945–1960* (New York: Oxford University Press, 1992), 162.

103. Ritz interview. On a visit to Los Angeles while on leave from Fort Ord, Ritz went back to Southern California Music to see Tom O'Connor, his old boss. "He said, 'Hey man,' and he grabbed a uke, a tenor, and he gave it to me and said, 'Play something'. OK, so I played this song, that song, and I wasn't paying attention, but here comes Barney Kessel over to the counter. And he had heard me playing. . . . So my friend Tom had set this up. He knew Barney was there, and got me to play. . . . Barney said, 'Gee, that sounds good man, here's my card, call me, maybe we can do something.' So I said, 'Oh man, yeah, but I'm in the Army, I've got another year to go.' He says, 'Call me when you get out.'"

104. Verve MG VS 6007, reissued on CD in 2004.

105. Heidi Chang, "Bassist Lyle Ritz: Father of the Jazz Ukulele," National Public Radio, July 30, 2007, http://www.npr.org/, viewed July 30, 2007.

106. Houston, *Hawaiian Son,* 5, 7.

107. Ibid., xiii, 10.

108. Harry B. Soria, Jr., liner notes, "Vintage Hawaiian Legends, Vol. 1. The Kalima Brothers &

the Richard Kauhi Quartette," Cord International, HOCD 27000, 2003; Bob Krauss, "Hawaii Plays a 100-Year-Old Love Song for the Uke," *Honolulu Advertiser,* August 24, 1979; Kanahele, *Hawaiian Music,* 405. "Some day [I want] to become the greatest ukulele player in the world," Kalima said in a 1953 interview. "I still practice two or three hours a day in addition to playing every night. I play every kind of music on this instrument." *Chicago Tribune,* February 12, 1953, C9.

109. Houston, *Hawaiian Son,* 9–13.

110. Ibid., 15, 19–23.

111. Penny Sparke, ed., *The Plastics Age: From Modernity to Post-Modernity* (London: Victoria & Albert Museum, 1990), 8.

112. Advertisement, *Washington Post,* December 20, 1956, D8.

113. Meikle, *American Plastic,* 169.

114. Jack O'Brien, "Godfrey Plunks; Home Entertainment Booms," *Washington Post,* July 18, 1950, B9. As Jeffrey Noonan points out, "Studies of American popular music regularly emphasize the transgressive character of the guitar, celebrating its role in breaking down musical and social barriers, emphasizing the iconic and the mythological." Noonan, *Guitar in America,* 4.

115. "Business World," *New York Times,* June 30, 1951, 19.

116. O'Shea had been appearing on Broadway in *The Girl Who Came to Supper,* the musical comedy set in London starring Florence Henderson and Jose Ferrer. It opened in December 1963 and closed in March 1964. Norton, *American Musical Theater,* 3:152. Among the other performers that night on the Sullivan show was the English actor Davy Jones, appearing with part of the Broadway cast of the musical *Oliver,* who two years later was cast as a member of the Monkees.

117. Jack Paar had played a BBC film on the Beatles on his television show on January 3, 1964, and claimed he introduced the group to America. "Yes, I Remember It Well," *Rolling Stone* 415 (February 16, 1984): 22.

118. Bob Spitz, *The Beatles: The Biography* (New York: Little, Brown and Co., 2005), 473. Emerson Strong would have been delighted to see George Harrison playing a Gretsch on national television.

119. At Gibson, for example, guitar sales doubled between 1964 and 1966, the greatest period of growth in the company's history. Carter, *Gibson Guitars,* 226.

Chapter 9: The Growing Underground Movement

1. Video of this performance can be found at http://www.youtube.com/watch?v=R_bljeflsBc (accessed January 9, 2010). Tiny Tim was born Herbert Khaury in New York City's Washington Heights. Harry Stein, *Tiny Tim* (Chicago: Playboy Books, 1976), 14. Although introduced on *Laugh-In* as appearing for the first time anywhere, Tiny Tim actually made his television debut on the *Merv Griffin Show* on March 7, 1966 (Stein, *Tiny Tim,* 97).

2. Walt Dutton, "Rowan and Martin Begin Their Laugh-In," *Los Angeles Times,* January 23, 1968, C12.

3. Tiny Tim appeared on *Laugh-In* on January 22, February 5, and April 29, 1968, and on the *Tonight Show* on April 4, May 27, and July 10. "God Bless Tiny Tim" reached No. 9 on the *Cashbox Magazine* chart in June 1968. "Tops in Pops," *Los Angeles Times,* June 14, 1968, H14. For *You Are What You Eat,* see William Kloman, "A Grotesque Mirror of Our Times," *New York Times,* March 2, 1969, D19. Tiny Tim met his first wife, Vicki Budinger, at a signing of *Beautiful Thoughts.* See Margaret Harford, "Tiny Tiptoeing to Altar on TV Show," *Los Angeles Times,* November 8, 1969, A6. For his Fillmore and Albert Hall performances, see "The Last Innocent," *Newsweek* (May 20, 1968): 113, and Ken Michaels, "Just Plain Tiny Tim," *Chicago Tribune,* March 2, 1969, 54.

4. Albert Goldman, "And He Keeps His Ukulele in a Shopping Bag," *New York Times,* April 28, 1968, D25; Alfred G. Aronowitz, "It's High Time Fame Came to Tiny Tim," *Life* (June 14, 1968): 10; "The Purity of Madness," *Time* (May 17, 1968): 66; William Leonard, "Hairy Hoax Exposed at Sherman House," *Chicago Tribune,* May 18, 1969, A8.

5. For Godfrey's influence, see Stein, *Tiny Tim,* 48–49.

6. A review of more than forty major stories on the 'ukulele published or aired in major outlets since 1998, including the *New York Times, Los Angeles Times, USA Today, Boston Globe, San Francisco Chronicle, St. Louis Post Dispatch, Philadelphia Inquirer,* London *Times,* and the *National Post,* found only three that did not mention Tiny Tim. One of the most recent examples: a story headlined "No Tiptoeing through the Tulips," on the front page of the September 30, 2009, edition of the *New York Times,* a feature on the Ukulele Orchestra of Great Britain. Journalists in the UK are similarly challenged; stories there inevitably make reference to George Formby.

7. "Tiny Tim Weds His Miss Vicki on Carson TV Show," *New York Times,* December 18, 1969, 95; "Tiny Tim Weds Vicki," *Washington Post,* December 18, 1969, B1; "Tiny Tim's TV Wedding Caused Surge of Viewing," *Wall Street Journal,* December 19, 1969, 20.

8. Ian Whitcomb, *Rock Odyssey: A Musician's Chronicle of the Sixties* (Garden City, NY: Dolphin Books, 1983), 211, 267. "This purchase was to turn out to be a fatal mistake for my career," Whitcomb lamented.

9. John L. Scott, "Whitcomb Rocks, Rolls in History," *Los Angeles Times,* September 8, 1966, D16.

10. Ian Whitcomb interview by Jim Tranquada, Altadena, California, December 27, 2003. Whitcomb's "Where the Action Is" performance can be seen on YouTube at http://www.youtube.com /watch?v=9DJDpM1JxMo.

11. Lillian Roxon, *Lillian Roxon's Rock Encyclopedia* (New York: Grosset & Dunlap, 1969), 282, 250, 356–357, 462, 609. "The Intro and the Outro" appears on the Bonzo Dog Band's 1967 debut album, *Gorilla* (Imperial Records LP-12370).

12. Beloff, *The Ukulele,* 21. In 1966, the *Los Angeles Times* incorrectly reported that Martin had stopped making ukuleles to focus solely on guitars. Eliot Tiegel, "Guitar Sales Pick a Pretty Tune— $100 Million a Year," *Los Angeles Times,* February 26, 1966, B8.

13. Leonard Feather, "Torme Has a Word for Singers: Arrange," *New York Times,* August 14, 1966, B24; John S. Wilson, "Torme Shows Versatility," *New York Times,* October 6, 1971, 38; Steven R. Weisman, "Going Out Guide," *New York Times,* September 13, 1974, 28.

14. John S. Wilson, "Moaning Sigh of Steel Guitar on Wane in Hawaii," *New York Times,* December 21, 1966, 47.

15. Burlingame and Kasher, *Da Kine Sound,* 131; Ronck, *Celebration,* 17.

16. Burlingame and Kasher, *Da Kine Sound,* 157. Lake, a Maui native whose step-grandmother was Nani Alapai, singer with the Royal Hawaiian Band, is credited with being the first Hawaiian 'ukulele player to adopt and popularize the baritone 'ukulele. John Berger, "Uncle K: Artist Kahauanu Lake Is a Pioneer in Hawaiian Music," *Honolulu Star-Bulletin,* September 28, 2003. Lake received the Hawaii Academy of Recording Arts Lifetime Achievement Award in 1995.

17. Elizabeth B. Buck, "A Brief History of Music Production in Hawaii," in Alison J. Ewbank and Fouli T. Papageorgiou, eds., *Whose Master's Voice? The Development of Popular Music in Thirteen Cultures* (Westport, CT: Greenwood Press, 1997), 94.

18. Michael Simmons, "Herb Ohta: A Ukulele Legend Plays from the Heart," *Ukulele Occasional* 2 (2003): 34.

19. *New York Times,* December 21, 1966, 47. John Kaaihue, better known as Johnny Ukulele, also worked steadily through the first half of the sixties, at Los Angeles restaurants and clubs, Disneyland, and in Las Vegas. Disneyland advertisement, *Los Angeles Times,* June 14, 1960, 14; Betty Martin, "Le Crazy Horse Real Long Shot," *Los Angeles Times,* October 7, 1961, B7; John L. Scott, "Stars Vie for Favor in Vegas," *Los Angeles Times,* March 21, 1963, C13. Kaaihue was the father of Mary Kaye (1924–2007), the jazz singer/songwriter/guitarist perhaps best known for her work with the Mary Kaye Trio, a popular Vegas lounge act.

20. Simmons, "Herb Ohta," 34.

21. George Kanahele, "Must We Bid Sad Aloha to Hawaiian Music?" *Honolulu Advertiser,* January 15, 1971, quoted in *Ha'ilono Mele* 1 (February 1975): 2.

22. Heather A. Diamond, *American Aloha: Cultural Tourism and the Negotiation of Tradition*

(Honolulu: University of Hawaii Press, 2008), 45–47; George H. Lewis, "Da Kine Sounds: Music as Social Protest," *American Music* 2 (summer 1984): 41; Amy Kuuleialoha Stillman, "Hawaiian Hula Competitions: Event, Repertoire, Performance, Tradition," *Journal of American Folklore* 106 (autumn 1996): 360.

23. Haunani-Kay Trask, *From a Native Daughter: Colonialism and Sovereignty in Hawaii* (Honolulu: University of Hawaii Press, 1999), 66–69.

24. Burlingame and Kasher, *Da Kine Sound,* 45.

25. Kanahele, *Hawaiian Music,* 120.

26. Houston, *Hawaiian Son,* 26–27, 327–238; Kanahele, *Hawaiian Music,* 363–364.

27. Kanahele, *Hawaiian Music,* 332.

28. Burlingame and Kasher, *Da Kine Sound,* 122, 128; Stillman, "Hula Competitions," 360.

29. Burlingame and Kasher, *Da Kine Sound,* 44.

30. Dawn Kaniaupio, "Four Strings: A History of the Ukulele," Pacific Resources for Education and Learning, aired on Hawaiian Public Television, December 2000.

31. Dawne Dawson, "Hawaii's Beloved Ukulele," *Spirit of Aloha* (July/August 2001): http://www.hawaii-products.com/ukulele01.html.

32. Buck, "Brief History," 94.

33. John Berger, "Ukulele Fest Strums Along," *Honolulu Star-Bulletin,* July 23, 2004; John Henry Felix, Leslie Nunes, and Peter F. Senecal, *The ʻUkulele: A Portuguese Gift to Hawaii* (Honolulu: Privately printed, 1980), 36–37; *A Tradition in Hawaiian Music: The ʻUkulele* (Honolulu: Bernice Pauahi Bishop Museum, 1980).

34. Dawson, "Hawaii's Beloved Ukulele."

35. Beverly Creamer, "Israel's Way: Activism beyond Politics," http://iz.honoluluadvertiser.com/story_activist.html.

36. Other major-media exposure included *American Idol* finalist Jason Castro's performance on the seventh season of the top-ranked show and the season-ending episode of *Glee,* aired June 8, 2010.

37. Jeff Chang, "A Big Man's Ukulele, Plucking Heartstrings," *Washington Post,* December 16, 2001, G2.

38. Dawson, "Hawaii's Beloved Ukulele."

39. Jim Beloff interview by Jim Tranquada, January 6, 2003, Studio City, California. Early on, the Beloffs contacted Maria Maccaferri to see if the original Maccaferri instrument molds were available. "But the uke molds were not to be," Beloff said. "They sold them to Carnival, but Carnival didn't do as good a job as they did, and that was the end of it. They probably were sold for scrap and melted down."

40. Ibid. "Timing is everything," Beloff said. "This was the time when Japan was going uke crazy, and we were swamped with orders. I think we got 300, 400 orders at that show."

41. George S. Kanahele and Toshihiko Hayatsu, "Hawaiian Music in Japan," in *Hawaiian Music,* 178–179.

42. Kanahele, *Hawaiian Music,* 186, 189.

43. Marie Woolf, "Ukulele Band Storms Japan," London *Independent,* March 5, 1995.

44. Yuko Naito, "Nothing Shocking in Ukulele Revival," *Japan Times,* August 26, 1999.

45. London *Independent,* March 5, 1995.

46. George Hinchliffe, "They're small but perfectly performed," London *Times,* May 12, 2006.

47. Laura Battle, "The Ukulele Isn't What It Used to Be," *Financial Times,* August 8, 2009; Sarah Lyall, "No Tiptoeing through the Tulips," *New York Times,* September 30, 2009, 1.

48. "Interview: J. Chalmers Doane (Part I)," *Ukulele Yes!* 7 (winter 2008): www.ukuleleyes.com/issues/vol7/no4/interview.htm. Doane patented his distinctive triangular teaching ukulele in the United States in 1977. King, *Trademarks & Patents,* 211.

49. See http://www.ukulelejames.com/bio.htm. Hill, one of the most talented of the modern ʻukulele virtuosos, who has been called "the Wayne Gretzky of the ukulele," has teamed up with Doane

to revive *Ukulele Yes!* as an online publication and to evangelize for the use of the 'ukulele in the classroom to promote musical literacy. See http://www.ukuleleintheclassroom.com.

50. Among the earliest well-trafficked 'ukulele Web sites were the Ukulele Diner (http://ukediner.ukulele.org) and Dan Scanlan's Cool Hand Uke's Lava Tube (http://www.coolhanduke.com).

51. A recent (August 21, 2011) keyword search for "ukulele" on YouTube yielded 58,900 results.

52. International 'ukulele Web sites include the Ukulele.Fr (France), Deutscher Ukulelenclub, Ukulelenurkka.arkku (Finland), De Ukulele Winkel (Netherlands), Ukulele Brasil, Ukulele Movement (Singapore), and Australele (Australia.)

53. "Me and My . . . Ukulele," *Bangkok Post,* July 10, 2010.

54. In 2008–2009, festivals were held in Denver (the Colorado Ukulele Fest); Seattle (Dusty Strings Ukefest); Hood River and Portland, Oregon (Gorge Ukulele Festival and Portland UkeFest); Reno, Nevada (Tahoe Area Ukulele Festival); St. Helena, Cerritos, and San Diego, California (Wine Country, Southern California, and San Diego Ukulele Festivals); Dallas (Lone Star Ukulele Festival); Milwaukee, Wisconsin; Des Plaines, Illinois (Windy City Ukulele Festival); Nokomis, Florida (Suncoast Ukulele Festival); Annapolis, Maryland (Mid-Atlantic Uke Fest); in New York; and in Halifax, Nova Scotia (International Ukulele Ceilidh). Further overseas, there were festivals in England, Ireland, France, Belgium, Germany, Italy, Sweden, Finland, and New Zealand.

55. David Mannweiler, "At this new festival, the musicians are expected to uke it out," *Indianapolis Star,* October 30, 2003.

56. Darrell R. Santschi, "'There's a lot of music in those four strings,'" *Riverside Press-Enterprise,* May 11, 2004.

57. Andy Newman, "Plunkers Seek Stringed Serenity with the Little Island Guitar," *New York Times,* April 10, 2000, B1; Kim Murphy, "Ukulele Strikes a New Chord," *Los Angeles Times,* October 1, 2002, 1; Anthony DeBarros, "After 125 years, the ukulele still keeps people smiling," *USA Today,* April 16, 2004, 7D; "Ukulele Could Be Making a Comeback," National Public Radio's *Morning Edition,* broadcast March 9, 1993; Charles Osgood, "Taking Note: Exhibition at the Stamford Museum Featuring the Ukulele," CBS *Sunday Morning,* broadcast April 28, 2002; Patrick Langston, "Forget Luaus and Tiny Tim, Ukuleles Are Hot," *Ottawa Citizen,* July 7, 2006; Dan Synge, "The Ukulele Comeback: Hawaii's Most Famous Musical Export Is in Vogue with Collectors," *Financial Times,* December 18, 2004, 11; Michael Dwyer, "The Joy of the Jumping Flea," the Melbourne, Australia *Age,* March 7, 2008; Carsten Volkery, "Abrocken mit der Bonsai-Axt," *Der Spiegel,* November 19, 2009; Susan Stamberg, "'The Mighty Uke': A Musical Underdog Makes a Comeback," NPR's *Morning Edition,* broadcast June 4, 2010.

58. Jason Verlinde, "Lumby, Kamloops, Honolulu . . . Peter Luongo and the Langley Ukulele Ensemble Hit the Road," *Ukulele Occasional* 1 (summer 2002): 90–98; www.langleyukes.com/LUE/history.htm.

59. Kris Ketonen, "Make Your Own Kind of Music," *Thunder Bay* [Ontario] *Chronicle Journal,* April 13, 2010.

60. Amber Smith, "Ukulele Program Spreads from Modest Start," *Lakeland* [Florida] *Ledger,* March 1, 2003; Edith Brady-Lunny, "Morton Students Soon to Be Strumming Away," Bloomington, IL, *Pantagraph,* January 7, 2005; "Little Ukulele Is Growing in Popularity," Portland, Oregon, *Asian Reporter,* January 7, 2003, 9; Lynn Saxberg, "A Gift with Strings Attached," *Ottawa Citizen,* June 16, 2009; Julie Middleton, "Plan to Set Little Fingers Plucking," *New Zealand Herald,* February 12, 2004.

61. Amelia Hill, "They'll Be Cleaning Windows Next," *Guardian,* November 25, 2006. More recent coverage includes David Wilkes, "Schools Ditch Unpopular Recorders for Trendy George Formby-Style Ukuleles," *Daily Mail,* July 1, 2009.

62. Matt Blackett, "Jake Shimabukuro," *Frets* 2 (fall 2005): 27.

63. Luanne J. Hunt, "Shimabukuro Makes the Ukulele Exciting," *Pasadena* [California] *Star-News,* November 20, 2009, 8.

64. Blackett, "Jake Shimabukuro," 29. Shimabukuro also took classes with Byron Yasui at the

University of Hawaii, Manoa. Wayne Harada, "'Ukulele: Four Men, One Instrument, Four Styles, One Basic Love," *Honolulu Advertiser,* September 27, 2002, 24.

65. Wade Tatangelo, "Ukulele Phenom Creates Cutting-Edge Sound," *Bradenton* [Florida] *Herald,* August 13, 2004.

66. Ibid.

67. For Shimabukuro's "Gently Weeps" video, see http://www.youtube.com/watch?v =puSkP3uym5k. His first appearance on national U.S. television was on *Late Night with Conan O'Brien* on December 13, 2005. For the Buffett tour, see Tim Ryan, "Buffett Sings High Praises for Uke Star Joining Tour," *Honolulu Star-Bulletin,* June 13, 2005.

68. Dave Dondondeau, "'Ukulele Phenom to Play for Queen," *Honolulu Advertiser,* November 26, 2009. Shimabukuro's December 7, 2009, performance does not make him the first 'ukulele player to appear at a Royal Variety Performance. George Formby and Formby biographer and impersonator Alan Randall both made appearances. Midler herself played the 'ukulele during her 2008–2009 *Showgirl* production at Caesar's Palace in Las Vegas. Mike Weatherford, "Bette Midler Looking Forward to Some Downtime as 'Showgirl Must Go On' Comes to a Close," *Las Vegas Review Journal,* January 8, 2010. Jim Beloff gave her lessons. Larry LeBlanc, "Industry Profile: Jim Beloff," www.celebritypress.com, accessed September 26, 2010. For the Playboy Jazz Festival appearance, see Chris Barton, "Playboy Jazz Festival has the Bowl Jumpin'," *Los Angeles Times,* June 14, 2010, D8.

69. For McCartney, see Robert Hilburn, "Steeped in Memories," *Los Angeles Times,* April 2, 2002, F1; Jon Pareles, "Memories Here, There and Everywhere," *New York Times,* April 19, 2002, B5; and Paul McCartney, *Each One Believing: Paul McCartney on Stage, off Stage, and Backstage* (San Francisco: Chronicle Books, 2004), 188. For Springsteen, see Jeff Spevak, "Springsteen Serenades 4,500 Fans," Rochester [NY] *Democrat and Chronicle,* October 7, 2005. For Costello, see Laura Emerick, "Costello and Nieve Score Political Points in Song," *Chicago Sun-Times,* March 18, 2004. For Daltrey, see Jim Sullivan, "Who's Still the Man? Roger Daltrey," *Boston Herald,* November 9, 2009. For Mann, see Bill White, "Sun Puts a Sizzling Spin on Mann's 'Spice,'" *Seattle Post-Intelligencer,* 2. McCartney has owned a 'ukulele for "quite a long time, since the early days of recording in New York in the early seventies." McCartney, *Each One Believing,* 188. For *Brainwashed,* see "Harrison Gently Weeps Again," *Toronto Star,* November 9, 2002. Harrison wrote the preface for Jim Beloff's sixth songbook, *Jumpin' Jim's '60s Uke-In* (2000). Multiple videos of Taylor Swift performing "Fearless" in concert on a 'ukulele are posted on YouTube.

70. Dan Murdoch, "Eddie Vedder: Less Strings, More Melody," *Ukulele Occasional* 1 (summer 2002): 109–111.

71. Karina Lopez, "For Train, It's Success with 'Hey, Soul Sister,'" *USA Today,* May 3, 2010.

72. Stephen Holden, "An Uptown Weekend for a Downtown Songwriter," *New York Times,* March 6, 2002, E5; Richard Cromelin, "A Man, 5 Bands and 100 Musicals," *Los Angeles Times,* July 20, 2004, E4. For Condon, who cites Merritt as an influence, see "Worldly Influences on a Young Artist," *New York Times,* July 24, 2011, AR15.

73. Interview with Stephen Swartz and Alan Drogin by Scott Simon, National Public Radio's *Weekend Edition,* broadcast May 28, 2005.

74. For Craig, see Byron Alexander, "Hollywood's Cowboys Bond over 'Aliens,'" *USA Today,* July 19, 2011, 10. For Macy, see Jason Verlinde, "William H. Macy: Losing Talent Shows, but Still Strumming," *Ukulele Occasional* 2 (2003): 22–23. For Deschanel, see "5 More Women We Love," *Esquire* (October 2002): 116–117. For Blunt, see "Emily Blunt's a Strum Pet," *Daily Express,* December 8, 2009. For Shepherd, see Alexis Petridis, "Cabaret: Cybill Does Dylan on the Ukulele," *Guardian,* March 15, 2002, 25. For Brosnan, see Jennifer V. Cole, "Fast Talk: Pierce Brosnan," *Travel & Leisure* (November 2005). For Blair, see Gordon Rayner, "By George, It's Tony Blair with a Little Ukulele in His Hand," *Daily Mail,* August 25, 2005, 9. For Buffett, see Alice Schroeder, *The Snowball: Warren Buffett and the Business of Life* (New York: Bantam Books, 2008), 123; "Preaching to the Converted," *Economist* (May 7, 2005): 68; Michael J. de la Merced, "Buffett Offers Firm Support of Goldman at Meeting," *New York Times,* May 2, 2010, A26.

75. For Rockettes, see Michael Sommers, "A Leg Up on Treasured Holiday Traditions," *Newark Star-Ledger,* November 10, 2004. For Sophocles, see Neil Genzlinger, "Sophocles Gets Truly Retro, Back to the Beginning of Time," *New York Times,* May 20, 2004. For Shi-Zeng, see Mark Swed, "A Fresh Breeze from the East," *Los Angeles Times,* April 12, 2004, E1.

76. Joe Hagan, "Uke Can Take It with You," *Civilization* (February/March 1999): 28.

77. "Ukulele Sales Continue to Soar," *Musical Merchandise Review* (October 2010).

78. Judy Fladmark, "Ukulele Send UK Crazy," BBC News, February 19, 2010.

79. http://www.ukuleleguild.org, accessed January 8, 2010.

80. Harvey Leonard Gotliffe, "Pride and Pineapples," *Fretboard Journal* 10 (summer 2008): 108, 110.

81. Longworth, *Martin Guitars,* 92–97. Gibson dropped out of ukulele production altogether in 1967. Gruhn and Carter, *Gruhn's Guide,* 156.

82. http://www.fender.com/products/search.php?section=acoustics&bodyshape=ukulele, accessed January 8, 2010.

83. For Hohner, see http://www.hohnerusa.com/index.php?326; for Oscar Schmidt, see http://oscarschmidt.com; for Takamine, see http://ukulelia.com/uploaded_images/migmnammflyer_709413.jpg, all accessed January 8, 2010.

84. http://www.candela.com/ukulele.php, accessed January 8, 2010.

85. Oahu-based Koolau Guitar and Ukulele Co. manufactures its affordable Pono line in Indonesia: http://www.koolauukulele.com; Lehua ukuleles are made in Portugal: http://lehuaukulele.com; one brand of Hilo ukuleles is made in China. Chinese production of a wide range of musical instruments has increased dramatically over the past decade. Tim Johnson, "China Making Noise with Music Instruments," *San Jose Mercury News,* May 4, 2005.

86. For SonnyD ukuleles, see http://sonnydukuleles.net; for David Gomes, http://www.gomesguitars.com/site/welcome_.html; for Palm Tree Ukuleles, http://www.palmtreeukuleles.com; for Kepasa, see http://kepasaukuleles.com, all accessed January 8, 2010. Dahlin (b. 1940), a Honolulu native, is self-taught; Gomes (b. 1951), a native of the Big Island, studied flamenco and classical guitar in Spain before turning to luthiery, opening his shop in 1977. Drozd, *Hawaiian Ukulele,* 89–92.

87. Beloff, *The Ukulele,* 47.

88. For example, in 2009 Kaneohe ʻukulele dealer Michael Aritani offered a ca. 1890–1895 soprano ʻukulele by Jose de Espirito Santo for $13,850. In 2005, Martin reintroduced a modern version of its 5K model, in koa with abalone trim, which retails for $5,199.

89. *Antiques Roadshow,* San Jose, aired May 9, 2010.

90. Toni Logan, "Fountain of Uke," *San Francisco Examiner,* April 25, 2002.

91. For examples, see Beloff, *The Ukulele,* 92–100.

92. For Ukebrand, see http://www.ukebrand.com; for Dave Means, see http://www.glyphukulele.com; for Michael DeSilva, see http://www.ukemaker.com, all accessed January 8, 2010.

93. "Ukulele Fever: The Craze That Swept America," Stamford [CT] Museum & Nature Center, February 2–May 26, 2002; "History of the Ukulele," Huntington Beach [CA] International Surfing Museum, May 21–October 15, 2007; "Strings of Paradise: The Ukulele and Steel Guitar," Fullerton [CA] Museum Center, May 26–September 9, 2007; "Evolution of the ʻUkulele: The Story of Hawaiʻiʼs Jumping Flea," San Francisco Museum of Craft and Folk Art, August 2–October 21, 2007; "The Ukulele and You," Carlsbad [CA] Museum of Making Music, August 11, 2007–January 31, 2008. Probably the first ʻukulele museum exhibit was "A Tradition in Hawaiian Music: The Ukulele," at Honoluluʼs Bernice Pauahi Bishop Museum, March 1–September 30, 1980. The Tsumura collection from Japan was on exhibit at the Honolulu Academy of Arts September 8–October 3, 1993.

94. Gordon Markʼs "Oriental Fantasy" debuted in Honolulu on November 24, 1979, as part of the ʻukulele centennial observances [Felix et al., *The ʻUkulele,* 46]. Jim Beloffʼs "Uke Canʼt Be Serious" debuted with the Wallingford, Connecticut, Symphony on November 13, 1999. Robert Sherman, "Out of Hawaiian Pop, into the Classics," *New York Times,* November 7, 1999. For Varone, see Sarah Kaufman, "Fingers Outrace Feet in ʻUkelele,'" *Washington Post,* July 26, 2007, C13.

95. Wade Tatangelo, "Ukulele Phenom Creates Cutting-Edge Sound," *Bradenton* [Florida] *Herald,* August 13, 2004; Sandy Alexander, "Ukulele Strikes a Chord," *Baltimore Sun,* June 16, 2004; Daniel Durchholz, "Look Out, Tiny Tim: Ukulele Player Takes Novelty Instrument to an Art Form," *St. Louis Post-Dispatch,* September 22, 2005.

96. Don Heckman, "Bix and the Boys Showcased Properly," *Los Angeles Times,* December 16, 2001, Calendar section, 75. Vedder's 2011 tour in support of his 'ukulele album drew a similar response: "On paper, the ukulele is to Vedder's voice what a minibike is to an obese McCrary twin: a ridiculous proposal that might be entertaining to witness, but to what end?" critic Randall Roberts wrote. "In a mellow mood but going strong," *Los Angeles Times,* July 11, 2011, D1.

97. For the "F.U.N. Song," see http://spongebob.nick.com/music; cartoon characters have been playing the 'ukulele since Minnie Mouse strummed one in Disney's *Steamboat Willie* in 1928. For Selleck in *A Thousand Clowns,* see Bruce Weber, "Back When Oddballs Roamed the Earth," *New York Times,* July 12, 2001. For Jackson, see Tom Shales and James Andrew Miller, *Live from New York: An Uncensored History of Saturday Night Live* (Boston: Little, Brown and Co., 2002), 316–317, and John Rogers, "Rapper Li'l Romeo Expands with New Show," *Washington Post,* October 9, 2003.

98. Jerry Spinelli, *Stargirl* (New York: Alfred A. Knopf, 2000); Mark Peter Hughes, *Lemonade Mouth* (New York: Delacorte Press, 2007), 210.

99. Lex Van Den Berghe, "Strung Out on a Strange, New Addition for Ukuleles," *Santa Cruz Sentinel,* January 30, 2005. English prime minister Tony Blair learned the same lesson when spotted strumming a ukulele on a 2005 Caribbean vacation: "Blair has been treated in the press as an essentially comic figure . . . [in part because of] the ukulele that seems ill-advisedly to have replaced the electric guitar that once testified to his youthful coolness." Mark Lawson, "Blair's Big Holiday Boob," the *Guardian,* August 27, 2005.

100. *Pleasant Holidays 2006 Travel Guide Hawaii/Mexico,* 4; Fairmont Kea Lani Hotel advertisement, *Los Angeles Magazine* (March 2009): 87; "Ukuleles and Evening Wear All the Way to Sydney," Cunard ad, *Los Angeles Times,* November 3, 2002; "Bishop Museum: Preserving, Exploring, Sharing," tri-fold brochure, ca. 2004; Jill Engledow, "Explore Paradise Imi Loa," special section in *Oahu Drive Guide,* 2004, 16; "The Ukulele: Hawaii's Little Musical Giant," *Maui Gold Coast* 13 (summer 2001): 30. Kamaka Hawaii, which will celebrate its centennial in 2016, is even listed in some guidebooks. See Stacy Pope, *Honolulu and O'ahu: Great Destinations Hawai'i, Including Waikiki* (Woodstock, VT: Countryman Press, 2008), 249.

101. "Explore Paradise Imi Loa," 15.

102. "Hawaii Thrilled by New Marketing Effort in Japan," *Japan Times,* February 6, 2004; Trask, *From a Native Daughter,* 136–147.

103. Jason Verlinde, "Uke Lust: An Interview with Stephin Merritt of the Magnetic Fields," *Ukulele Occasional* (summer 2002): 67.

Bibliography

Adams, Henry. *The Letters of Henry Adams,* vol. 3: *1886–1892.* Ed. J. C. Levenson. Cambridge, MA: Belknap Press, 1982.

Adams, John. *The Works of John Adams, Second President of the United States . . .* Ed. Charles Francis Adams. Vol. 8. Boston: Little, Brown and Co., 1853.

Ade, George. *Fables in Slang.* Chicago: Herbert S. Stone & Co., 1900.

Alcafarado, Francisco. *An Historical Relation of the First Discovery of the Isle of Madera.* London: William Cademan, 1675.

Alexander, Mary C., and Charlotte P. Dodge. *Punahou 1841–1941.* Berkeley, CA: University of California Press, 1941.

Andersen, L. E., and T. Malcolm Rockwell. "Hawaiian Recordings: The Early Years." *Victrola and 78 Journal* (winter 1996): 1–4.

Anderson, Charles Roberts. *Melville in the South Seas.* New York: Columbia University Press, 1939.

Anderson, Isabel. *The Spell of the Hawaiian Islands and the Philippines.* Boston: Page Co., 1916.

Anderson, Mary E. *Scenes in the Hawaiian Islands and California.* New York: American Tract Society, 1865.

Anderson, Rufus. *The Hawaiian Islands: Their Progress and Condition under Missionary Labors,* 2nd ed. Boston: Gould & Lincoln, 1864.

Andrews, Lorrin. *A Dictionary of the Hawaiian Language.* Waipahu, HI: Island Heritage Publishing, 2003. Reprint of 1865 ed.

Archer, Gleason L. *History of Radio to 1926.* New York: American Historical Society, 1938.

Armstrong, William N. *Around the World with a King.* Honolulu: Mutual Publishing, 1995. Reprint of 1904 ed.

Astaire, Fred. *Steps in Time.* New York: Harper and Brothers, 1959.

Baez, Joan. *And a Voice to Sing With: A Memoir.* New York: Summit Books, 1987.

Baines, Anthony. *European and American Musical Instruments.* New York: Viking Press, 1966.

———. *Victoria and Albert Museum: Catalogue of Musical Instruments.* London: Her Majesty's Stationery Office, 1968.

Bakish, David. *Jimmy Durante: His Show Business Career.* Jefferson, NC: McFarland & Co., 1995.

Balbi, Adrien. *Essai Statistique sur le Royaume de Portugal et d'Algarve.* Paris: Rey & Gravier, 1822.

Bancroft, Hubert Howe. *The New Pacific.* New York: Bancroft Co., 1899.

Bandy, David W. "Bandmaster Henry Berger and the Royal Hawaiian Band." *Hawaiian Journal of History* 24 (1990): 69–90.

Banks, Joseph. *The Endeavour Journal of Joseph Banks 1768–1771.* Ed. J. C. Beaglehole. Sydney: Angus and Robertson, 1962.

Barker, Gordon. *Pursued by Furies: A Life of Malcolm Lowry.* New York: St. Martin's Press, 1995.

Barrow, John. *A Voyage to Cochinchina in the Years 1792 and 1793.* London: T. Caddell and W. Davies, 1806.

Barry, Richard H. *Snap Shots on the Midway Pan Am Expo.* Buffalo: Robert Allen Reid, 1901.

Beechey, Capt. F. W. *Narrative of a Voyage to the Pacific and Beering's Strait . . .* London: Henry Colburn and Richard Bentley, 1831.

Bellman, Jonathan. *The Style Hongrois in the Music of Western Europe.* Boston: Northeastern University Press, 1993.

Beloff, Jim. *The Ukulele: A Visual History,* rev. ed. San Francisco: Backbeat Books, 2003.

Benedict, Burton, ed. *The Anthropology of World's Fairs: San Francisco's Panama Pacific International Exposition of 1915.* Berkeley, CA: Scolar Press, 1983.

Benjamin, S. G. W. *The Atlantic Islands as Resorts of Health and Pleasure.* New York: Harper and Brothers, 1878.

Bennitt, Mark, Frank Parker Stockbridge, et al. *History of the Louisiana Purchase Exposition.* St. Louis: Universal Exposition Publishing Co., 1905.

Benson, Susan Porter. *Saleswomen, Managers and Customers in American Department Stores, 1890–1940.* Urbana: University of Illinois Press, 1986.

Berg, David F. *Chicago's White City of 1893.* Lexington: University Press of Kentucky, 1976.

Berger, H[enry]. *Mele Hawaii.* Honolulu: Hawaiian News Co., n.d.

Bergin, Billy. *Loyal to the Land: The Legendary Parker Ranch 750–1950.* Honolulu: University of Hawaii Press, 2004.

Bernice Pauahi Bishop Museum. *A Tradition in Hawaiian Music: The 'Ukulele.* Exhibition publication. Honolulu: Bernice Pauahi Bishop Museum, 1980.

Bickford, Vadah Olcott, and Zarh Myron Bickford. *The Bickford Method for the Ukulele.* Boston: Oliver Ditson Co., 1920.

Biddle, A. Drexel. *The Land of Wine: Being an Account of the Madeira Islands at the Beginning of the Twentieth Century, and from a New Point of View.* Philadelphia: Drexel Biddle, 1901.

Bingham, Hiram. *A Residence of Twenty-One Years in the Sandwich Islands . . . ,* 3rd ed. Canandaigua, NY: H. D. Goodwin, 1855.

Birkett, Mary Ellen. "The French Perspective on the Laplace Affair." *Hawaiian Journal of History* 32 (1998): 67–99.

Bishaw, Henry A. Peelua. *The Albert Ukulele Hawaiian Guitar: Complete Instructions for Accompaniment & Solo Work.* Sydney: J. Albert & Son, 1919.

Bishop, Isabella Bird. *Six Months among the Palm Groves, Coral Reefs, and Volcanoes of the Sandwich Islands.* New York: G. P. Putnam's Sons, 1894.

Bishop, Sereno Edwards. *Reminiscences of Old Hawaii.* Honolulu: Hawaiian Gazette Co., 1916.

Blackburn, Robin. *The Making of New World Slavery: From the Baroque to the Modern, 1492–1800.* London: Verso, 1997.

Blascoer, Frances. *The Industrial Condition of Women and Girls in Honolulu: A Social Study.* Honolulu: Paradise of the Pacific Printing, 1912.

Bluteau, Raphael. *Vocabulario Portuguez e Latino,* tome 5. Coimbra, Portugal: Collegio das Artes da Companhia de Jesus, 1716.

Bolt, Rodney. *Madeira & Porto Santo.* London: Cadogan Guides, 1999.

Bordman, Gerald. *Jerome Kern: His Life and Music.* New York: Oxford University Press, 1980.

Bradley, Harold Whitman. *The American Frontier in Hawaii: The Pioneers 1789–1843.* Stanford, CA: Stanford University Press, 1942.

Bret, David. *George Formby: A Troubled Genius.* London: Robson Books, 1999.

Brettell, Caroline. *Anthropology and Migration: Essays on Transnationalism, Ethnicity and Identity.* Walnut Creek, CA: Altamira Press, 2003.

Breve Noticia Àcerca das Ilhas de Sandwich e das vantagens que ellas offerecem á emigração que as procure. Funchal, Madeira: Typographia Liberal, 1878.

Briggs, L. Vernon. *Around Cape Horn to Honolulu on the Bark "Amy Turner."* Boston: Charles E. Lauriat Co., 1926.

———. *Experiences of a Medical Student in Honolulu, and on the Island of Oahu 1881.* Boston: David D. Nickerson Co., 1926.

Brown, Margaret C. "David Blakely, Manager of Sousa's Band." In Jon Newson, ed., *Perspectives on John Philip Sousa.* Washington, D.C.: Library of Congress, 1983, 121–131.

Browne, J. Ross. *Etchings of a Whaling Cruise . . .* New York: Harper & Bros., 1846.

Brownlow, Kevin. *The Parade's Gone By . . .* Berkeley: University of California Press, 1968.

Buck, Elizabeth. "A Brief History of Music Production in Hawaii." In Alison J. Ewbank and Fouli T. Papageorgiou, eds., *Whose Master's Voice? The Development of Popular Music in Thirteen Cultures.* Westport, CT: Greenwood Press, 1997.

———. *Paradise Remade: The Politics of Culture and History in Hawai'i.* Philadelphia: Temple University Press, 1993.

Burlingame, Burl, and Robert Kamohalu Kasher. *Da Kine Sound: Conversations with the People Who Create Hawaiian Music,* vol. 1. Kailua, HI: Press Pacifica, 1978.

Burnett, Charles C. *The Land of the O-O: Figures, Fables, and Fancies.* Cleveland, OH: Cleveland Printing & Publishing Co., 1892.

Burney, Fanny Anne. *A Great-Niece's Journals: Being Extracts from the Journals of Fanny Anne Burney (Mrs. Wood), from 1830–1842.* Ed. Margaret S. Rolt. Boston: Houghton Mifflin, 1926.

Burnham, Clara Louise. *Sweet Clover: A Romance of the White City.* Boston: Houghton, Mifflin and Co., 1895.

Burton, Richard Francis. *Wanderings in West Africa from Liverpool to Fernando Po.* London: Tinsley Brothers, 1863.

Canario, Lucille da Silva. "Destination, Hawaiian Islands." *Hawaiian Journal of History* 4 (1970): 3–52.

Carlin, Bob. *String Bands in the North Carolina Piedmont.* Jefferson, NC: McFarland & Co., 2004.

Carr, James Revell. "Ethnomimesis and Authenticity on the American Popular Stage: Performing Hawaiians and Musical Exotica in the 19th Century." Working draft of paper presented at 2005 Pop Conference.

Carter, Walter. *Gibson Guitars: 100 Years of an American Icon.* Los Angeles: General Publishing Group, 1994.

Center for Oral History. *An Era of Change: Oral Histories of Civilians in World War II Hawaii.* Honolulu: University of Hawaii, Social Science Research Institute, Center for Oral History, 1994.

Chaney, George Leonard. *"Alóha!" A Hawaiian Salutation.* Boston: Roberts Bros., 1888.

Chapin, Helen Geracimos. *Shaping History: The Role of Newspapers in Hawai'i.* Honolulu: University of Hawaii Press, 1996.

Chaplin, George. *Presstime in Paradise: The Life and Times of the Honolulu Advertiser, 1856–1995.* Honolulu: University of Hawaii Press, 1998.

Chipman, Charles. *Honolulu: The Greatest Pilgrimage of the Mystic Shrine.* Published by author, 1901.

Choules, Rev. John Overton. *The Cruise of the Steam Yacht North Star: A Narrative of the Excursion of Mr. Vanderbilt's Party to England, Russia, Denmark, France, Spain.* Boston: Gould and Lincoln, 1854.

Christie, Agatha. *The Mysterious Mr. Quin.* New York: Dell Publishing Co., 1972.

Cole, M. M. *15-Minute Guaranteed Ukulele Course for Hawaiian Ukulele and Banjo Ukulele.* Chicago: M. M. Cole, 1925.

Coleridge, Henry Nelson. *Six Months in the West Indies in 1825.* London: John Murray, 1825.

Colton, Rev. Walter. *Deck and Port: Or, Incidents of a Cruise in the United States Frigate Congress to California.* New York: A. S. Barnes & Co., 1850.

———. *Three Years in California.* New York: A. S. Barnes & Co., 1850.

Columbia Records for October. New York: Columbia Graphophone Co., 1917.

Coman, Katharine. "The History of Contract Labor in the Hawaiian Islands." *Publications of the American Economic Association*, 3rd Series (August 1903): 1–61.

Combe, William. *A History of Madeira, with a Series of Twenty-Seven Coloured Engravings, Illustrative of the Costumes, Manners, and Occupations of the Inhabitants of that Island.* London: Ackermann, 1821.

Commerce Reports. Bureau of Foreign and Domestic Commerce, Department of Commerce. Washington, D.C.: Government Publishing Office, September 18, 1915.

Conroy, Hilary. *The Japanese Frontier in Hawaii, 1868–1898.* Berkeley: University of California Press, 1953.

Converse, Paul D. *Marketing Methods and Policies*, 2nd ed. New York: Prentice-Hall, 1924.

Copland, Aaron, and Vivian Perlis. *Copland 1900 through 1942.* New York: St. Martin's/Marek, 1984.

Cox, Thomas R. *Mills and Markets: A History of the Pacific Coast Lumber Industry to 1900.* Seattle: University of Washington Press, 1974.

Coyle, Jackey, and Rebecca Coyle. "Aloha Australia: Hawaiian Music in Australia (1920–55)." *Perfect Beat* 2 (January 1995): 31–63.

Crowdy, Denis. "The Guitar Cultures of Papua New Guinea: Regional, Social and Stylistic Diversity." In Andy Bennett and Kevin Dawe, eds., *Guitar Cultures*. Oxford: Berg, 2001: 135–155.

Cunha, A. R. *Songs of Hawaii.* Honolulu: Bergstrom Music Co., 1902.

Dalton, Henry. *The History of British Guiana.* London: Longman, Brown, Green and Longmans, 1855.

Dana, Richard Henry, Jr. *Two Years before the Mast: A Personal Narrative.* Boston: Houghton Mifflin Co., 1912.

d'Anglade, M. G. Bosseront. *A Tree in Bud: The Hawaiian Kingdom 1889–1893.* Trans. Alfons L. Korn. Honolulu: University of Hawaii Press, 1987.

Darwin, Charles. *On the Origin of Species.* New York: Modern Library, n.d.

da Silva, Fernando Augusto, and Carlos Acevedo de Menezes. *Elucidario Madeirense.* 2 vols. Funchal: Tipografia "Esperança," 1921.

Davis, Janet M. *The Circus Age: Culture and Society under the Big Top.* Chapel Hill: University of North Carolina Press, 2002.

Davis, Lance E., Robert E. Gallman, and Karin Gleiter. *In Pursuit of Leviathan: Technology, Institutions, Productivity and Profits in American Whaling, 1816–1906.* Chicago: University of Chicago Press, 1997.

Davis, Lynn. *Na Pa'i Ki'i: Photographers in the Hawaiian Islands 1845–1910.* Honolulu: Bishop Museum Press, 1980.

Davis, Lynn, and Nelson Foster. *A Photographer in the Kingdom: Christian J. Hedemann's Early Images of Hawai'i.* Honolulu: Bishop Museum Press, 1988.

Davis, William Heath. *Seventy-Five Years in California.* San Francisco: John Howell Books, 1967.

Daws, Gavan. *Honolulu the First Century: The Story of the Town to 1876.* Honolulu: University of Hawaii Press, 2006.

Day, Timothy. *A Century of Recorded Music: Listening to Musical History.* New Haven, CT: Yale University Press, 2000.

de França, Isabella. *Journal of a Visit to Madeira and Portugal (1853–1854).* Funchal: Junta Geral do Distrito Autónomo do Funchal, 1969.

De Harport, Teresita. *Practical Method for the Ukulele.* Denver: Chas. E. Wells Music Co., 1925.

Dell, George C. D. *Annals of the New York Stage.* Vols. 1, 2, 15. New York: Columbia University Press, 1927.

Delmar, Viña. *Bad Girl.* New York: Literary Guild of America, 1928.

de Oliveira, Ernesto Veiga. *Instrumentos Musicais Populares Portugueses.* Lisbon: Fundação Calouste Gulbenkian, 1966.

Desmond, Jane C. *Staging Tourism: Bodies on Display from Waikiki to Sea World.* Chicago: University of Chicago Press, 1999.

de Soto, Andres. *Arte Para Aprender, Con Facilidad, y sin Maestro, a templar a taner rasgado La Guitarra . . . y tambien el Tiple.* Madrid: Lopez y compañia, 1760.

de Varigny, Charles. *Fourteen Years in the Sandwich Islands 1855–1868.* Honolulu: University Press of Hawaii, 1981.

Dewar, J. Cumming Dewar. *Voyage of the Nyanza R.N.Y.C. . . .* Edinburgh: William Blackwood and Sons, 1892.

Diamond, Heather A. *American Aloha: Cultural Tourism and the Negotiation of Tradition.* Honolulu: University of Hawaii Press, 2008.

Dibble, Sheldon. *History and General Views of the Sandwich Islands' Mission.* New York: Taylor & Dodd, 1839.

Dix, John A. *A Winter in Madeira; and a Summer in Spain and Florence,* 2nd ed. New York: William Holdredge, 1851.

D'Orsey, Rev. Alexander J. D. *Colloquial Portuguese; or, the Words and Phrases of Every-Day Life.* London: Trubner & Co., 1860.

Dos Passos, John. *One Man's Initiation: 1917.* London: Allen & Unwin, 1920.

———. *Travel Books and Other Writings 1916–1941.* New York: Library of America, 2003.

Douglas, Susan J. *Inventing American Broadcasting 1899–1922.* Baltimore: Johns Hopkins University Press, 1987.

Driver, John. *Letters from Madeira in 1834.* London: Longman & Co., 1838.

Drozd, Karen S. "The Hawaiian 'Ukulele: Its Players, Makers, Teachers and Continuity in Traditional Transmission Processes." MA thesis, University of Hawaii, 1998. Ann Arbor, MI: UMI Dissertation Services, 1999.

Dumenil, Lynn. *The Modern Temper: American Culture and Society in the 1920s.* New York: Hill and Wang, 1995.

Dunaway, David King. *How Can I Keep From Singing: Peter Seeger.* New York: McGraw-Hill Book Co., 1981.

Duncan, T. Bentley. *Atlantic Islands: Madeira, the Azores and the Cape Verdes in Seventeenth Century Commerce and Navigation.* Chicago: University of Chicago Press, 1972.

Dunn, Barbara E. "William Little Lee and Catherine Lee, Letters from Hawai'i 1848–1855." *Hawaiian Journal of History* 38 (2004): 59–88.

Durkee, Jennie. *The American Way of Playing Ukulele Solos.* Chicago: Jennie Durkee, 1917.

Eannes de Azurama, Gomes. *The Chronicle of the Discovery and Conquest of Guinea.* Trans. Charles R. Beazley and Edgar Prestage. New York: Burt Franklin, n.d.

Edgerton, Gary R. *The Columbia History of American Television.* New York: Columbia University Press, 2007.

Editors of Fortune. *100 Stories of Business Success: Case Histories of American Enterprise.* New York: Simon and Schuster, 1954.

Emerson, Nathaniel. *Unwritten Literature of Hawaii: The Sacred Songs of the Hula.* Washington, D.C.: Government Printing Office, 1909.

Emerson, Oliver Pomeroy. *Pioneer Days in Hawaii.* Garden City, NY: Doubleday, Doran & Co., 1928.

Emmet, Boris, and John E. Jeuck. *Catalogues and Counters: A History of Sears, Roebuck and Company.* Chicago: University of Chicago Press, 1950.

Erenberg, Lewis. *Steppin' Out: New York Nightlife and the Transformation of American Culture, 1890–1930.* Chicago: University of Chicago Press, 1984.

Evans, James W., and Capt. Gardner L. Harding. *Entertaining the American Army: The American Stage and Lyceum in the World War.* New York: Association Press, 1921.

Farber, David, and Beth Bailey. "The Fighting Man as Tourist: The Politics of Tourist Culture in Hawaii during World War II." *Pacific Historical Review* 65 (November 1996): 641–660.

Farrell, Andrew, ed. *John Cameron's Odyssey.* New York: Macmillan Co., 1928.

Farrell, Bryan H. *Hawaii: The Legend that Sells.* Honolulu: University Press of Hawaii, 1982.

Felix, John Henry, Leslie Nunes, and Peter F. Senecal. *The 'Ukulele: A Portuguese Gift to Hawai'i.* Honolulu: Privately printed, 1980.

Felix, John Henry, and Peter F. Senecal. *The Portuguese in Hawaii.* Honolulu: Privately printed, 1978.

Ferreira, Jo-Anne. "Madeiran Portuguese Migration to Guyana, St. Vincent, Antigua and Trinidad: A Comparative Overview." *Portuguese Studies Review* 14 (2006/2007): 63–85.

——. *The Portuguese of Trinidad and Tobago.* St. Augustine, Trinidad and Tobago: Institute of Social and Economic Research, University of the West Indies, 1994.

Field, Isobel. *This Life I've Loved.* New York: Longmans, Green and Co., 1937.

Findling, John E., and Kimberly Pelle, eds. *Historical Dictionary of World's Fairs and Expositions, 1851–1988.* New York: Greenwood Press, 1990.

Fisher, John. *George Formby.* London: Woburn-Futura, 1975.

Fitzgerald, F. Scott. "May Day." In *F. Scott Fitzgerald Novels and Stories 1920–1922.* New York: Library of America, 2000.

Forbes, David W., comp. *Hawaiian National Bibliography 1780–1900.* 4 vols. Honolulu: University of Hawaii Press/Hordern House, 1999.

Forster, Johann Reinhold. *The Resolution Journal of Johann Reinhold Forster 1772–1775.* Ed. Michael E. Hoare. London: Hakluyt Society, 1982.

Forster, John. *A Voyage Round the World, in His Britannic Majesty's Sloop Resolution . . .* London: Printed for B. White, J. Robson, P. Elmsly, and G. Robinson, 1777.

Foster, John W. *American Diplomacy in the Orient.* Boston: Houghton Mifflin & Co., 1904.

Franchere, Gabriel. *A Voyage to the Northwest Coast of America.* New York: Citadel Press, 1968.

Franck, Harry A. *Roaming in Hawaii.* New York: Frederick A. Stokes Co., 1937.

Frear, Walter F. *Anti-Missionary Criticism with Reference to Hawaii.* Honolulu: Privately printed, 1935.

Freer, Mary Dillingham. *Lowell and Abigail: A Realistic Idyll.* New Haven, CT: Privately printed, 1934.

Friedwald, Will. *Jazz Singing: America's Great Voices from Bessie Smith to Bebop and Beyond.* New York: Collier Books, 1992.

Frisbie, Charlotte J. "Helen Heffron Roberts (1888–1985): A Tribute." *Ethnomusicology* 33 (winter 1989): 97–111.

Fuld, James J. *The Book of World-Famous Music: Classical, Popular and Folk.* New York: Crown Publishers, 1966.

Furnas, J. C. *Anatomy of Paradise: Hawaii and the Islands of the South Seas.* London: Victor Gollancz, 1950.

Garrett, Charles Hiroshi. *Struggling to Define a Nation: American Music and the Twentieth Century.* Berkeley: University of California Press, 2008.

Gatewood, William B., Jr. *Black Americans and the White Man's Burden 1898–1903.* Urbana: University of Illinois Press, 1975.

Gerould, Katherine Fullerton. *Hawaii: Scenes and Impressions.* New York: Charles Scribner's Sons, 1916.

Gessler, Clifford. *Hawaii: Islands of Enchantment.* New York: D. Appleton-Century Co., 1937.

Gibson, Walter Murray. *The Diaries of Walter Murray Gibson.* Ed. Jacob Adler and Gwynn Barrett. Honolulu: University Press of Hawaii, 1973.

Giddins, Gary. *Bing Crosby: A Pocketful of Dreams—the Early Years 1903–1940.* Boston: Little, Brown and Co., 2001.

Gilbert, Douglas. *American Vaudeville: Its Life and Times.* New York: Whittlesey House, 1940.

Gioia, Ted. *West Coast Jazz: Modern Jazz in California 1945–1960.* New York: Oxford University Press, 1992.

Gleason, Duncan and Dorothy. *Beloved Sister: The letters of James Henry Gleason 1841 to 1859 from Alta California and the Sandwich Islands.* Glendale, CA: Arthur H. Clark Co., 1978.

Glick, Clarence E. *Sojourners and Settlers: Chinese Migrants in Hawaii.* Honolulu: Hawaii Chinese History Center and University Press of Hawaii, 1980.

Goff, James R. *Close Harmony: A History of Southern Gospel.* Chapel Hill: University of North Carolina Press, 2002.

Goldman, Herbert G. *Jolson: The Legend Comes to Life*. New York: Oxford University Press, 1988.

Goulart, Ron, ed. *The Encyclopedia of American Comics*. New York: Facts on File, 1990.

Gracyk, Tim, and Frank Hoffman. *Popular American Recording Pioneers 1895–1925*. New York: Haworth Press, 2002.

Grant, M. Forsyth. *Scenes in Hawaii or Life in the Sandwich Islands*. Toronto: Hart & Co., 1888.

Green, Abel, and Joe Laurie Jr. *Show Biz from Vaude to Video*. New York: Henry Holt & Co., 1981.

Greenbie, Sydney. *The Pacific Triangle*. New York: Century Co., 1921.

Greer, Richard A. "Cunha's Alley: The Anatomy of a Landmark." *Hawaiian Journal of History* 2 (1968): 142–151.

———. *Downtown Profile: Honolulu a Century Ago*. Honolulu: Kamehameha Schools Press, 1966.

———. "The Founding of Queen's Hospital." *Hawaiian Journal of History* 3 (1969): 110–145.

———. "'Sweet and Clean': The Chinatown Fire of 1886." *Hawaiian Journal of History* 10 (1976): 33–51.

Gregg, David Lawrence. *The Diaries of David Lawrence Gregg: An American Diplomat in Hawaii 1853–1858*. Ed. Pauline King. Honolulu: Hawaiian Historical Society, 1982.

Gregorio, Domingo. *Hawaiian-Ukulele-Method, for Self Instruction*. Berlin, 1928.

Gregory, Desmond. *The Beneficient Usurpers: A History of the British in Madeira*. Rutherford, NJ: Farleigh Dickinson University Press, 1988.

Griffis, Townsend. *When You Go to Hawaii*. Boston: Houghton Mifflin Co., 1930.

Groce, Nancy. *Musical Instrument Makers of New York*. Stuyvestant, NY: Pendragon Press, 1991.

Gruhn, George, and Walter Carter. *Gruhn's Guide to Vintage Guitars*. San Francisco: GPI Books, 1991.

Guckert, E. N. *Guckert's Chords for the Ukulele at Sight*. Chicago: Lyon & Healy, 1917.

Gura, Philip F. *C. F. Martin and His Guitars 1796–1873*. Chapel Hill: University of North Carolina Press, 2003.

Gura, Philip F., and James F. Bollman. *America's Instrument: The Banjo in the Nineteenth Century*. Chapel Hill: University of North Carolina Press, 1999.

Haas, Glen E., P. Quentin Tomich, and Nixon Wilson. "The Flea in Early Hawaii." *Hawaiian Journal of History* 5 (1971): 59–74.

Halberstam, David. *The Fifties*. New York: Villard Books, 1993.

Hall, Dale E. "Opera and Operetta in Nineteenth Century Hawai'i." *Hawaiian Journal of History* 31 (1997): 71–96.

Hamilton, Alexander. *The Papers of Alexander Hamilton*. Vol. 7: *September 1790–January 1791*. Ed. Harold C. Syrett. New York: Columbia University Press, 1963.

Hammond, Joyce D. "Hawaiian Flag Quilts: Multivalent Symbols of a Hawaiian Quilt Tradition." *Hawaiian Journal of History* 27 (1993): 1–27.

Hancock, David. *Oceans of Wine: Madeira and the Emergence of American Trade and Taste*. New Haven, CT: Yale University Press, 2009.

Handler, Ruth, with Jacqueline Shannon. *Dream Doll: The Ruth Handler Story*. Stamford, CT: Longmeadow Press, 1994.

Hanson, Carl A. *Economy and Society in Baroque Portugal*. Minneapolis: University of Minnesota Press, 1981.

Harcourt, Edward William. *A Sketch of Madeira: Containing Information for the Traveller, or Invalid Visitor*. London: John Murray, 1851.

Harris, Marvin. *The Rise of Anthropological Theory: A History of the Theories of Culture*. New York: Thomas Y. Crowell Co., 1968.

Hassinger, John A. *Catalogue of the Hawaiian Exhibits at the Exposition Universelle . . .* Honolulu: Hawaiian Gazette Co., 1889.

Hawaiian Club Papers. Boston: Press of Abner Kingman, 1868.

Hawaiian Foreign Office and Executive Minute Books. Vols. 7–8, Hawaii State Archives.

Hedemann, Nancy Oakley. *A Scottish-Hawaiian Story: The Purvis Family in the Sandwich Islands*. Honolulu: Privately printed, 1994.

Heiman, Jim, ed. *Hula: Vintage Hawaiian Graphics*. Cologne, Germany: Taschen, 2003.

Hennessey, Patrick. "Launching a Classic: Aloha ʻOe and the Royal Hawaiian Band Tour of 1883." *Journal of Band Research* 37 (September 2001): 29–44.

Higgs, David, ed. *Portuguese Migration in Global Perspective*. Toronto: Multicultural History Society of Ontario, 1990.

Hillebrand, William M. D. *Flora of the Hawaiian Islands: A Description of Their Phanerogams and Vascular Crytogams*. London: Williams and Norgate, 1888.

Hitchcock, H. Wiley. *Music in the United States: A Historical Introduction*. 2nd ed. Englewood Cliffs, NJ: Prentice Hall, 1974.

Hoitt, Ira G. *Pacific Coast Guide and Programme of the Knights Templar Triennial Conclave . . .* San Francisco: Ira G. Hoitt, 1883.

Holden, E. D. "California's First Pianos." *California Historical Society Quarterly* 13 (March 1934): 34–37.

Holstein, Edward. *Chords of the Taro-Patch Guitar: A New System for Learning to Play the Chords of the Taro-Patch Guitar without a Teacher*. Honolulu: Hawaiian News Co., 1894.

———. *Ka Buke Mele o na Himeni Hawaii*. Honolulu: Bishop Museum Press, 2003. Reprint of 1897 ed.

Hopkins, Gerard Manley. *Hawaii: The Past, Present, and Future of Its Island Kingdom*. London: Keegan Paul, 2003. Reprint of 1868 ed.

Hounshell, David A., and John Kenly Smith Jr. *Science and Corporate Strategy: DuPont R&D, 1902–1980*. Cambridge: Cambridge University Press, 1988.

Houston, James D., and Eddie Kamae. *Hawaiian Son: The Life and Music of Eddie Kamae*. Honolulu: ʻAi Pohaku Press, 2004.

Hughes, E. S. *"Uke" Hughes' Simplified Instructor for Ukulele*. New York: H. Stadlmair Co., 1924.

Hughes, Mark Peter. *Lemonade Mouth*. New York: Delacorte Press, 2007.

Hulme, Peter. "Dominica and Tahiti: Tropical Islands Compared." In Felix Driver and Luciana Martins, eds., *Tropical Visions in an Age of Empire*. Chicago: University of Chicago Press, 2005.

Hustace, Frank Ward. *Victoria Ward and Her Family: Memories of Old Plantation*. Honolulu: Victoria Ward, 2000.

Hyland, William G. *George Gershwin: A New Biography*. Westport, CT: Praeger, 2003.

Hyman Smith. *Hawaii: The Hawaiian Exhibit at the World's Exposition New Orleans . . .* New Orleans: Hyman Smith, 1885.

Igler, David. "Diseased Goods: Global Exchanges in the Eastern Pacific Basin, 1770–1850." *American Historical Review* 109 (June 2004): 693–719.

Imada, Adria. "Hawaiians on Tour: Hula Circuits through the American Empire." *American Quarterly* 56 (March 2004): 111–149.

Irwin, Bernice Piilani. *I Knew Queen Liliuokalani*. Honolulu: Native Press, 2000. Reprint of 1960 ed.

James, Elias Olan. *The Story of Cyrus and Susan Mills*. Stanford, CA: Stanford University Press, 1953.

James, Wilma. "Hawaii's Last King." *Pacific Historian* 24 (fall 1980): 312–315.

Jardim, Manuel G. *Commentary on Emigration to the Terra Nova*. Honolulu: n.p., 1971.

Jarrett, Lorna H. *Hawaii and Its People*. Honolulu: Honolulu Star-Bulletin, 1933.

Jasen, David A. *Tin Pan Alley: The Composers, the Songs, the Performers and Their Times*. New York: Donald I. Fine, 1988.

Jefferson, Thomas. *The Papers of Thomas Jefferson*. Vol. 9: *1 November 1785 to 22 June 1786*. Ed. Julian P. Boyd. Princeton, NJ: Princeton University Press, 1954.

Jenkins, Irving. *Hawaiian Furniture and Hawaii's Cabinetmakers 1820–1940*. Honolulu: Daughters of Hawaii, 1983.

Johnson, Rubellite Kinney. *Kukini ʻAhaʻilono (Carry On the News)*. Honolulu: Topgallant Publishing Co., 1976.

Johnston, Richard, and Dick Boak. *Martin Guitars: A History*. New York: Hal Leonard Books, 2008.

Judd, Gerrit P., IV. *Dr. Judd, Hawaii's Friend: A Biography of Gerrit Parmale Judd (1803–1873)*. Honolulu: University of Hawaii Press, 1960.

Judd, Laura Fish. *Honolulu: Sketches of Life in the Hawaiian Islands from 1828 to 1861*. Chicago: Lakeside Press/R.R. Donnelly & Sons, 1966.

Judd, Rev. Henry P. *Henry Judd, the Third Generation in Hawaii: Memoirs of Rev. Henry P. Judd, Hawaii*. North Charleston, SC: BookSurge, 2005.

Kaai, Ernest K. *Hawaiian Songs*. Soerabaia, Java: Compliments of the Simpang Hotel, n.d. (ca. 1917).

———. *The Ukulele: A Hawaiian Guitar and How to Play It*. Honolulu: Wall Nichols Co., 1906.

Kamehiro, Stacy L. *The Arts of Kingship: Hawaiian Art and National Culture of the Kalakaua Era*. Honolulu: University of Hawaii Press, 2009.

Kammen, Michael. *American Culture, American Tastes: Social Change and the 20th Century*. New York: Alfred A. Knopf, 1999.

Kanahele, George H., ed. *Hawaiian Music and Musicians: An Illustrated History*. Honolulu: University Press of Hawaii, 1979.

Kaplan, Amy. *The Anarchy of Empire in the Making of U.S. Culture*. Cambridge, MA: Harvard University Press, 2002.

Kartomi, Margaret J. "The Processes and Results of Musical Culture Contact: A Discussion of Terminology and Concepts." *Ethnomusicology* 25 (May 1981): 227–249.

Kaufman, Jessie. "A Hawaiian Expedient." *Overland Monthly* 25 (January 1900): 10–18.

———. *A Jewel of the Seas*. Philadelphia: J. B. Lippincott Co., 1912.

Kealakai, Mekia. *The Ukulele and How to Play It*. Los Angeles: Southern California Music Co., 1914.

Kealiinohomoku, Joann Wheeler. "A Court Dancer Disagrees with Emerson's Classic Book on the Hula." *Ethnomusicology* 8 (May 1964): 161–164.

Keaton, Eleanor, and Jeffrey Vance. *Buster Keaton Remembered*. New York: Harry N. Abrams, 2001.

Kemble, John Haskell, ed. *Journal of a Cruise to California and the Sandwich Islands in the United States Sloop-of-War Cyane*. San Francisco: Book Club of California, 1955.

Kenney, William Howland. *Recorded Music in American Life: The Phonograph and Popular Memory, 1890–1945*. New York: Oxford University Press, 1999.

Kia, George. *Self Instructor for the Ukulele and Taro-Patch Fiddle*. Los Angeles: R. W. Heffelfinger, 1914.

Killianus, K. *Practical Method for the Ukulele*. Milwaukee: K. Kotty, 1925.

Kiner, Larry F., comp. *The Al Jolson Discography*. Westport, CT: Greenwood Press, 1983.

———. *The Cliff Edwards Discography*. New York: Greenwood Press, 1987.

King, Art. *Symphonic Ukulele Arrangements*. San Francisco: Sherman, Clay & Co., n.d. (ca. 1928).

King, John. *The Hawaiian Ukulele & Guitar Makers . . . for the Years 1884 to 1930*. Saint Petersburg, FL: Nalu Music, 2001.

———, ed. *Selected U.S. Trademarks and Patents for Ukuleles, Banjo Ukuleles and Acessories*. St. Petersburg, FL: Nalu Music, 2003.

King, John, and Jim Tranquada. "The Singular Case of Manuel Nunes and the Invention of the Bouncing Flea." *Galpin Society Journal* 60 (April 2007): 85–95.

King, John, and Tom Walsh. "Pilgrimage to Nazareth: Reflections on Mike Longworth, Vintage Ukes, and Other Martinalia." Unpublished manuscript, 2007.

Kipling, Rudyard. *Something of Myself for My Friends Known and Unknown*. Garden City, NY: Doubleday, Doran & Co., 1937.

Kirk, Elise K. *Music at the White House: A History of the American Spirit*. Urbana: University of Illinois Press, 1986.

Kodama-Nishimoto, Michi, Warren S. Nishimoto, and Cynthia A. Oshiro. *Talking Hawai'i's Story: Oral Histories of a Hawaiian People*. Honolulu: University of Hawaii Press, 2009.

Korn, Alfons L., ed. *News from Molokai: Letters between Peter Kaeo and Queen Emma, 1873–1876*. Honolulu: University Press of Hawaii, 1976.

———. *The Victorian Visitors*. Honolulu: University of Hawaii Press, 1958.

Krantz, Lynn B., Nick Krantz, and Mary T. Fobian. *To Honolulu in Five Days: Cruising Aboard Matson's S.S. Lurline*. Berkeley, CA: Ten Speed Press, 2001.

Krauss, Bob. *Johnny Wilson: First Hawaiian Democrat*. Honolulu: University of Hawaii Press, 1994.

Krauss, Bob, and William P. Alexander. *Grove Farm Plantation: The Biography of a Hawaiian Sugar Plantation.* 2nd ed. Palo Alto, CA: Pacific Books, 1984.

Krout, Mary H. *Hawaii and a Revolution: The Personal Experiences of a Correspondent in the Sandwich Islands during the Crisis of 1893 and Subsequently.* New York: Dodd, Mead & Co., 1898.

———. *The Memoirs of Hon. Bernice Pauahi Bishop.* New York: Knickerbocker Press, 1908.

Kupperman, Karen Ordahl. "Fear of Hot Climates in the Anglo-American Colonial Experience." *William and Mary Quarterly* 41 (April 1984): 213–240.

Kuykendall, Ralph S. *Hawaii in the World War.* Honolulu: Historical Commission of the Territory of Hawaii, 1928.

———. *The Hawaiian Kingdom 1778–1854: Foundation and Transformation.* Honolulu: University of Hawaii Press, 1947.

———. *The Hawaiian Kingdom 1854–1874: Twenty Critical Years.* Honolulu: University of Hawaii Press, 1953.

———. *The Hawaiian Kingdom 1874–1893: The Kalakaua Dynasty.* Honolulu: University of Hawaii Press, 1967.

La Farge, John. *An American Artist in the South Seas.* London: KPI, 1987. Reprint of 1914 ed.

Lamb, W. Kaye, ed. *A Voyage of Discovery to the North Pacific Ocean and Round the World 1791–1795.* London: Hakluyt Society, 1984.

Lambertini, Michael'angelo. "Portugal." In *Encyclopedie de la Musique.* Paris: Librairie Delagrave, 1920.

Larkin, Thomas Oliver. *The Larkin Papers: Personal, Business and Official Correspondence of Thomas Oliver Larkin . . .* Vol. 1: *1822–1842.* Ed. George P. Hammond. Berkeley: University of California Press, 1951.

Laurie, Joe, Jr. *Vaudeville: From the Honky Tonks to the Palace.* New York: Henry Holt and Co., 1953.

Lawrence, Sharon. *Jimi Hendrix: The Man, the Magic, the Truth.* New York: Harper Entertainment, 2005.

Leacock, Stephen. *Frenzied Fiction.* London: John Lane, Bodley Head, 1918.

Lewis Publishing Co. *An Illustrated History of Los Angeles County, California.* Chicago: Lewis Publishing Co., 1889.

Lewis, George H. "Da Kine Sounds: Music as Social Protest." *American Music* 2 (summer 1984): 38–52.

Lewis, Robert. *Chicago Made: Factory Networks in the Industrial Metropolis.* Chicago: University of Chicago Press, 2008.

Lewis, Sinclair. *Arrowsmith, Elmer Gantry, Dodsworth.* New York: Library of America, 2002.

———. *Babbitt.* New York: Harcourt, Brace & World, 1922.

Liholiho, Alexander. *The Journal of Prince Alexander Liholiho.* Ed. Jacob Adler. Honolulu: University of Hawaii Press, 1967.

Liliuokalani. *Hawaii's Story by Hawaii's Queen.* Rutland, VT: Charles E. Tuttle Co., 1964.

Linn, Brian McAllister. *Guardians of Empire: The U.S. Army and the Pacific, 1902–1940.* Chapel Hill: University of North Carolina Press, 1997.

Linn, Karen. *That Half-Barbaric Twang: The Banjo in American Popular Culture.* Urbana: University of Illinois Press, 1991.

Littig, Frank L. *Littig's New Practical Method for Hawaiian Ukulele, Banjuke & Taro Patch Fiddle.* Chicago: Chart Music Publishing House, 1921.

Livermore, H. V. *A History of Portugal.* Cambridge: Cambridge University Press, 1947.

Loar, Lloyd. *Modern Method for Ukulele, Ukulele-banjo and Tenor Banjo.* Altoona, PA: Nicomede Music Co., 1925.

Lochner, Louis P. *Fritz Kreisler.* New York: Macmillan Co., 1950.

Loesser, Arthur. *Men, Women and Pianos: A Social History.* New York: Simon & Schuster, 1954.

Lofgren, Orvar. *On Holiday: A History of Vacationing.* Berkeley: University of California Press, 1999.

London, Jack. *The Cruise of the Snark.* New York: MacMillan, 1932.

———. *The Valley of the Moon.* New York: Macmillan Co., 1913.

Longworth, Mike. *Martin Guitars: A History.* Cedar Knolls, NJ: Colonial Press, 1975.

———. *Martin Guitars: A History.* Rev. ed. Minisink Hills, PA: Four Maples Press, 1988.

Lowrey, Ed, with Charlie Foy. *Joe Frisco: Comic, Jazz Dancer, and Railbird.* Carbondale: Southern Illinois University Press, 1999.

Lyman, Chester S. *Around the Horn to the Sandwich Islands and California 1845–1850.* New Haven, CT: Yale University Press, 1924.

Lynd, Robert S., and Helen Merrell Lynd. *Middletown: A Study in Contemporary American Culture.* New York: Harcourt, Brace & Co., 1929.

Macomber, Ben. *The Jewel City: Its Planning and Achievement, Its Architecture, Sculpture, Symbolism and Music; Its Gardens, Palaces and Exhibits.* San Francisco: John H. Williams, 1915.

Macpherson, Ossian. *The Dreamer: A Poem in Three Cantos, with Other Poems; and an Introductory Epistle Upon the Island of Madeira.* London: Printed for the Author, 1848.

Malone, Bill C. *Country Music U.S.A.* 2nd rev. ed. Austin: University of Texas Press, 2002.

March, Charles W. *Sketches and Adventures in Madeira, Portugal, and the Andalusias of Spain.* New York: Harper and Brothers, 1856.

Mather, Helen. *One Summer in Hawaii.* New York: Cassell, 1891.

Maxwell, Ellen Blackmer. *Three Old Maids in Hawaii.* New York: Eaton & Mains, 1896.

McCabe, James D. *The Illustrated History of the Centennial Exhibition . . .* Philadelphia: National Publishing Co., 1876.

McCartney, Paul. *Each One Believing: Paul McCartney on Stage, off Stage, and Backstage.* San Francisco: Chronicle Books, 2004.

McDonough, Jimmy. *Shakey: Neil Young's Biography.* New York: Random House, 2002.

McGovern, Charles. "Consumption and Citizenship in the United States, 1900–1940." In Susan Strasser et al., eds., *Getting and Spending: European and American Consumer Societies in the Twentieth Century.* Washington, D.C.: German Historical Institute/Cambridge University Press, 1998.

McGregor, Davianna Pomaikoi. *Nā Kua'āina: Living Hawaiian Culture.* Honolulu: University of Hawaii Press, 2007.

McLeod, Beth Abelson. "'Whence Comes the Lady Tympanist?' Gender and Instrumental Musicians in America, 1853–1990." *Journal of Social History* 27 (winter 1993): 291–308.

McNamara, Daniel I. *The ASCAP Biographical Dictionary of Composers, Authors and Publishers.* New York: Thomas Y. Crowell, 1952.

Meikle, Jeffrey. *American Plastic: A Cultural History.* New Brunswick, NJ: Rutgers University Press, 1995.

Menezes, Mary Noel. *The Portuguese of Guyana: A Study in Culture and Conflict.* N.p., 1993.

Meriwether, Lee. *The Tramp at Home.* New York: Harper & Brothers, 1889.

Merz, Charles. *The Great American Band Wagon.* New York: Literary Guild of America, 1928.

Message of the President of the United States with the Accompanying Documents . . . Washington, D.C.: Government Publications Office, 1873.

Millard, Andre. *America on Record: A History of Recorded Sound.* Cambridge: Cambridge University Press, 1995.

Mohr, James C. *Plague and Fire: Battling Black Death and the 1900 Burning of Honolulu's Chinatown.* Oxford: Oxford University Press, 2005.

Montgomery, Francis Trego. *Billy Whiskers at the Exposition.* Chicago: Saalfield Publishing Co., 1915.

Morais, Manuel, ed. *Collecção de Peças para Machete por Cândido Drumond de Vasconcelos.* Casal de Cambra: Caleidoscópio, 2003.

———. *A Madeira e a Música: Estudos c. 1508–1974.* Funchal: Empresa Municipal "Funchal 500 Anos," 2008.

Morison, Samuel Eliot. *The Maritime History of Massachusetts 1783–1860.* Boston: Houghton Mifflin, 1921.

Morosco, Helen M., and Leonard Paul Dugger. *The Oracle of Broadway: Life of Oliver Morosco.* Caldwell, ID: Caxton Printers, 1944.

Moyer, Will D. *Conservatory Method for Ukulele.* Chicago: Chart Music Publishing House, 1926.

Neibaur, James L. *Arbuckle and Keaton: Their 14 Film Collaborations.* Jefferson, NC: McFarland & Co., 2007.

Nepomuceno, Rui. *As Crises de Subsistência na Historia da Madeira: Ensaio Histórico.* Lisbon: Caminho, 1994.

Nevins, Allan, and Frank Ernest Hill. *Ford: Expansion and Challenge 1915–1933.* New York: Charles Scribner's Sons, 1957.

The New York World. *World Almanac and Encyclopedia 1921.* New York: Press Publishing Co., 1921.

Ninde, Edward S. *The Story of the American Hymn.* New York: Abingdon Press, 1921.

Noble, Gurre Ploner. *Hula Blues: The Story of Johnny Noble, Hawaii, Its Music and Its Musicians.* Honolulu: Tongg Publishing Co., 1948.

Noonan, Jeffrey J. *The Guitar in America: Victorian Era to Jazz Age.* Jackson: University Press of Mississippi, 2008.

Nordhoff, Charles. *Northern California, Oregon, and the Sandwich Islands.* New York: Harper & Brothers, 1874.

Norton, Richard C. *A Chronology of American Musical Theater.* Oxford: Oxford University Press, 2002. Vols. 1–3.

Nowell, Charles E. *A History of Portugal.* New York: D. Van Nostrand Co., 1952.

Nunis, Doyce B., ed. *The California Diary of Faxon Dean Atherton.* San Francisco: California Historical Society, 1964.

Oahu College: List of Trustees, Presidents, Instructors, Matrons, Librarians, Superintendents of Grounds, and Students 1841–1906. Honolulu: Hawaiian Gazette Co., 1907.

Oberholtzer, Ellis Paxson. *A History of the United States since the Civil War.* Vol. 5: *1884–1901.* New York: Macmillan Co., 1937.

Okihiro, Gary Y. *A History of Hawaii and the United States.* Berkeley: University of California Press, 2008.

Olien, Roger M., and Diana Davids Olien. *Easy Money: Oil Promoters and Investors in the Jazz Age.* Chapel Hill: University of North Carolina Press, 1990.

Ortiz, Fernando. *Cuban Counterpoint: Tobacco and Sugar.* Durham, NC: Duke University Press, 1995.

Osorio, Jonathan Kay Kamakawiwoole. *Dismembering Lahui: A History of the Hawaiian Nation to 1887.* Honolulu: University of Hawaii Press, 2002.

Ovington, John. *A Voyage to Surat in the Year 1689.* Ed. H. G. Rawlinson. London: Oxford University Press, 1929.

Owen, Jean A. *The Story of Hawaii.* London: Harper & Bros., 1898.

Owens, Harry. *Sweet Leilani: The Story Behind the Song.* Pacific Palisades, CA: Hula House, 1970.

Panama-Pacific International Exposition. *The Red Book of Views of the Panama-Pacific International Exposition.* San Francisco: Robert A. Reid, 1915.

Parakilas, James, et. al. *Piano Roles: Three Hundred Years of Life with the Piano.* New Haven, CT: Yale University Press, 1999.

Perkins, Edward T. *Na Motu: Or, Reef-Rovings in the South Seas.* New York: Pudney & Russell, 1854.

Peterson, J. Kalani. *Peterson Ukulele Method.* New York: Irving Berlin Inc., 1924.

Phillips, Charles. *Paderewski: The Story of a Modern Immortal.* New York: Macmillan Co., 1934.

Pitta, N. C., M.D. *Account of the Island of Madeira.* London: Printed for Longman, Hurst, Rees, Orme & Brown, and for John Anderson, Edinburgh, 1812.

Pitts, Michael, and Frank Hoffman. *The Rise of the Crooners.* Lanham, MD: Scarecrow Press, 2002.

Poindexter, Ray. *Golden Throats and Silver Tongues: The Radio Announcers.* Conway, AR: River Road Press, 1978.

Pope, Stacy. *Honolulu and Oʻahu: Great Destinations Hawaiʻi Including Waikiki.* Woodstock, VT: Countryman Press, 2008.

Porterfield, Nolan. *Jimmie Rodgers: The Life and Times of America's Blue Yodeler.* Urbana: University of Illinois Press, 1992.

Potts, Richard Hamilton. "Kulamea: A Romance of Honolulu." *Atlanta Constitution,* April 2, 1893, 3.

Pratt, John Scott Boyd. *The Hawaii I Remember.* Honolulu: Tongg Publishing Co., 1965.

Pratt, Julius W. "The 'Large Policy' of 1898." *Mississippi Valley Historical Review* 19 (September 1932): 219–242.

Pukui, Mary Kawena, and Samuel H. Elbert. *Hawaiian Dictionary.* Honolulu: University Press of Hawaii, 1975.

Putnam, F. W. *Oriental and Occidental Northern and Southern Portrait Types of the Midway Plaisance* . . . St. Louis: N. D. Thompson Publishing Co., 1894.

Quinn, Arthur Hobson. *A History of American Drama from the Civil War to the Present Day.* New York: Appleton-Century-Crofts, 1936.

Randall, Alan, and Ray Seaton. *George Formby: A Biography.* London: W. H. Allen, 1971.

Randel, D. M. *The Harvard Concise Dictionary of Music and Musicians.* Cambridge, MA: Belknap Press, 1999.

Reed, Tom. *The Black Music History of Los Angeles—Its Roots: A Classical Pictorial History of Black Music in L.A. from 1920–1970.* Los Angeles: Black Accent on LA Press, 1996.

Riddell, Maria. *Voyages to the Madeira and Leeward Caribbean Isles.* Salem, MA: N. Coverly, 1802.

Roberts, Helen H. *Ancient Hawaiian Music.* Bulletin No. 29. Honolulu: Bernice P. Bishop Museum, 1926.

Roby, Steven. *Black Gold: The Lost Archives of Jimi Hendrix.* New York: Billboard Books, 2002.

Rockwell, T. Malcolm. *Hawaiian & Hawaiian Guitar Records 1891–1960.* Kula, HI: Mahina Piha Press, 2007, CD-ROM.

Rogers, Francis M. *Atlantic Islanders of the Azores and Madeira.* North Quincy, MA: Christopher Publishing House, 1979.

Rollinson, T. H. *Method for the Ukulele (Hawaiian Guitar).* Boston: Oliver Ditson Co., 1909.

Ronck, Ronn. *Celebration: A Portrait of Hawai'i through the Songs of the Brothers Cazimero.* Honolulu: Mutual Publishing, 1984.

Rose, Roger G. *Hawai'i: The Royal Isles.* Honolulu: Bernice P. Bishop Museum, 1980.

Roxon, Lillian. *Lillian Roxon's Rock Encyclopedia.* New York: Grosset & Dunlap, 1969.

Ruymar, Lorene. *The Hawaiian Steel Guitar and Its Great Hawaiian Musicians.* Anaheim Hills, CA: Centerstream Publishing, 1996.

Rydell, Robert W. *All the World's a Fair: Visions of Empire at American International Expositions, 1876–1916.* Chicago: University of Chicago Press, 1984.

Rydell, Robert W., John E. Findling, and Kimberly D. Pelle. *Fair America: World's Fairs in the United States.* Washington, D.C.: Smithsonian Institution Press, 2000.

Rydell, Robert W., and Rob Kroes. *Buffalo Bill in Bologna: The Americanization of the World, 1869–1922.* Chicago: University of Chicago Press, 2005.

Sallis, James. *The Guitar Players: One Instrument and Its Masters in American Music.* New York: William Morrow and Co., 1982.

Sanjek, Russell. *American Popular Music and Its Business: The First Four Hundred Years.* Vols. 1–3. New York: Oxford University Press, 1988.

Santos, A. A., and Angeline Nunes. *Original Method and Self-Instructor on the Ukulele.* Honolulu: Santos-Nunes Studios, 1915.

Santos, Carlos M. *Tocares e Cantares da Ilha: Estudo do Foclore da Madeira.* Funchal: Empreza Madeirense Editora Lda., 1937.

———. *Trovas e Bailados da Ilha: Estudo do Foclore Musical da Madeira.* Funchal: Edição da Delegação de Turismo da Madeira, 1939.

Savada, Elias, comp. *The American Film Institute Catalog of Motion Pictures Produced in the United States: Film Beginnings, 1893–1910.* Lanham, MD: Scarecrow Press, 1995.

Savage, Jon. *Teenage: The Creation of Youth Culture.* New York: Viking Penguin, 2007.

Schroeder, Alice. *The Snowball: Warren Buffett and the Business of Life.* New York: Bantam Books, 2008.

Scott, Edward B. *Saga of the Sandwich Islands.* Crystal Bay, NV: Sierra-Tahoe Publishing Co., 1968.

Sears, Roebuck and Co. *Catalogue #129,* fall 1914.

———. *Sears, Roebuck and Co. Consumer's Guide for 1894.* Sears reprint, n.d., ca. 1976.

Seldes, Gilbert. *The 7 Lively Arts.* New York: Sagamore Press, 1957 [1924].

Sell, Henry Blackman, and Victor Weybright. *Buffalo Bill and the Wild West.* New York: Oxford University Press, 1955.

Sengstock, Charles A. *That Toddlin' Town: Chicago's White Dance Bands and Orchestras, 1900–1950.* Urbana: University of Illinois Press, 2004.

Sereno, Aeko. "Images of the Hula Dancer and the 'Hula Girl': 1778–1960." Ph.D. diss., University of Hawaii, 1990.

Severson, Don R., Michael D. Horikawa, and Jennifer Saville, eds. *Finding Paradise: Island Art in Private Collections.* Honolulu: Hawaiian Academy of Arts/University of Hawaii Press, 2002.

Shales, Tom, and James Andrew Miller. *Live from New York: An Uncensored History of Saturday Night Live.* Boston: Little, Brown and Co., 2002.

Shapiro, Harry, and Caesar Glebbeck. *Jimi Hendrix: Electric Gypsy.* New York: St. Martin's Press, 1990.

Shaw, Arnold. *The Jazz Age: Popular Music in the 1920s.* New York: Oxford University Press, 1987.

Shaw, Robert. *Hawaiian Quilt Masterpieces.* Westport, CT: Hugh Lauter Levin Associates, 1996.

Shaw, William. *Golden Dreams and Waking Realities: Being the Adventures of a Gold-Seeker in California and the Pacific Islands.* London: Smith, Elder and Co., 1851.

Sherman, Clay & Co. *Sherman, Clay & Co. 1912 Catalogue of Musical Merchandise.* San Francisco: Sherman, Clay & Co., 1912.

Shoemaker, Michael Myers. *Islands of the Southern Seas: Hawaii, Samoa, New Zealand, Tasmania, Australia, and Java.* New York: G. P. Putnam's Sons, 1897.

Siddall, John William, ed. *Men of Hawaii.* Vol. 1. Honolulu: Honolulu Star-Bulletin, 1917.

———. *Men of Hawaii: A Biographical Reference Library.* Vol. 2. Honolulu: Honolulu Star-Bulletin, 1921.

Silva, Carol. *Hale Naua Society 1886–1891: Translation of Documents at the Hawai'i State Archives and Hawaiian Mission Children's Society Library.* Honolulu: Hawaiian Historical Society, 1999.

Silva, Noenoe K. *Aloha Betrayed: Native Hawaiian Resistance to American Colonialism.* Durham, NC: Duke University Press, 2004.

Simpson, Sir George. *An Overland Journey around the World, during the Years 1841 and 1842.* Philadelphia: Lea and Blanchard, 1842.

Singer, Arthur J. *Arthur Godfrey: The Adventures of an American Broadcaster.* Jefferson, NC: McFarland & Co., 2000.

Slide, Anthony. *The Encyclopedia of Vaudeville.* Westport, CT: Greenwood Press, 1994.

Smith, Barbara Bernard, ed. *The Queen's Songbook.* Honolulu: Hui Hanai, 1999.

Smith, Cecil, and Glenn Litton. *Musical Comedy in America.* New York: Theater Arts Books, 1981.

Smith, Emerson C. "Hawaii's Royal Composers." In *The Hawaii Book.* Chicago: J. G. Ferguson Publishing Co., 1961: 301–303.

Smith, Eric Ledell. *Bert Williams: A Biography of the Pioneer Black Comedian.* Jefferson, NC: McFarland & Co., 1992.

Smith, H. Allen. *Waikiki Beachnik.* Boston: Little, Brown and Co., 1960.

Smith, Richard R., et al. *Inventing Paradise: Hawaiian Image and Popular Culture.* Fullerton, CA: Fullerton Museum Center, 2001.

Smith Music Co. *EZ Method for Ukulele and Ukulele Banjo.* New York: William J. Smith Music Co., 1924.

Smulyan, Susan. *Selling Radio: The Commercialization of American Broadcasting 1920–1934.* Washington, D.C.: Smithsonian Institution Press, 1984.

Snyder, Robert W. *The Voice of the City: Vaudeville and Popular Culture in New York.* New York: Oxford University Press, 1989.

Sotheby's. *Lewis Carroll's Alice: The Photographs, Books, Papers and Personal Effects of Alice Liddell and Her Family.* London: Sotheby's, 2001.

Southern Music Co. *Jimmie Rodgers (America's Blue Yodeler) Album of Songs Number 5.* New York: Southern Music Co., n.d.

Spaeth, Sigmund. *A History of Popular Music in America.* New York: Random House, 1948.

Spalding, J. Willett. *The Japan Expedition: Japan and around the World: An Account of Three Visits to the Japanese Empire . . .* New York: Redfield, 1855.

Sparke, Penny, ed. *The Plastics Age: From Modernity to Post-Modernity.* London: Victoria & Albert Museum, 1990.

Sparrow, Bartholomew H. *The Insular Cases and the Emergence of American Empire.* Lawrence: University Press of Kansas, 2006.

Spinelli, Jerry. *Stargirl.* New York: Alfred A. Knopf, 2000.

Spitz, Bob. *The Beatles: The Biography.* New York: Little, Brown and Co., 2005.

Springhall, John. *The Genesis of Mass Culture: Show Business Live in America 1840 to 1940.* New York: Palgrave Macmillan, 2008.

Stanley, Albert A. *Catalogue of the Stearns Collection of Musical Instruments.* Ann Arbor: University of Michigan, 1918.

Starr, Kevin. *Americans and the California Dream 1850–1915.* New York: Oxford University Press, 1973.

———. *Golden Dreams: California in an Age of Abundance 1950–1963.* New York: Oxford University Press, 2009.

Stein, Harry. *Tiny Tim.* Chicago: Playboy Books, 1976.

Stevenson, Robert Louis. *The Letters of Robert Louis Stevenson.* Vol. 3. Ed. Sidney Colvin. New York: Scribner's, 1915.

Stever, Kenneth. *Pursuit of an "Unparalled Opportunity": The American YMCA and Prisoner-of-War Diplomacy among the Central Power Nations during World War I, 1914–1923.* New York: Columbia University Press, 2009.

Stewart, C. S. *Journal of a Residence in the Sandwich Islands during the Years 1823, 1824, and 1825 . . .* London: H. Fisher, Son, and P. Jackson, 1830.

Stillman, Amy K. "Access and Control: A Key to Reclaiming the Right to Construct Hawaiian History." In Andrew N. Weintraub and Bell Yung, *Music and Cultural Rights.* Chicago: University of Illinois Press, 2009.

———. "'Aloha Aina': New Perspectives on 'Kaulana Na Pua.'" *Hawaiian Journal of History* 33 (1999): 83–99.

———. "Beyond Bibliography: Interpreting Hawaiian Language Protestant Hymn Imprints." *Ethnomusicology* 40 (fall 1996): 469–488.

———. "Hawaiian Hula Competitions: Event, Repertoire, Performance, Tradition." *Journal of American Folklore* 106 (autumn 1996): 357–380.

———. "History Reinterpreted in Song: The Case of the Hawaiian Counterrevolution." *Hawaiian Journal of History* 23 (1989): 1–30.

Strong, Isobel. *The Girl from Home: A Story of Honolulu.* Honolulu: Crossroads Bookshop, 1912.

Suisman, David. *Selling Sounds: The Commercial Revolution in American Music.* Cambridge, MA: Harvard University Press, 2009.

Sullivan, Mark. *Our Times: The United States 1900–1925.* Vol. 6: *The Twenties.* New York: Charles Scribner's Sons, 1935.

Sunderman, Lloyd Frederick. "The Era of Beginnings in American Music Education (1830–1840)." *Journal of Research in Music Education* 4 (spring 1956): 33–39.

Swan, Howard. *Music in the Southwest 1825–1950.* San Marino, CA: Huntington Library, 1952.

Taft, William H., Frederick Harris, Frederic Houston Kent, and William J. Newlin. *Service with Fighting Men: An Account of the American Young Men's Christian Associations in the World War.* New York: Association Press, 1922.

Takaki, Ronald. *Pau Hana: Plantation Life and Labor in Hawaii 1835–1920.* Honolulu: University of Hawaii Press, 1983.

Tarkington, Booth. "Girl, Girl, Girl." *Washington Post,* November 16, 1919, SM1.

Tatar, Elizabeth. *Strains of the Change: The Impact of Tourism on Hawaiian Music.* Bishop Museum Special Publication 78. Honolulu: Bishop Museum Press, 1987.

Tate, Merze. *The United States and the Hawaiian Kingdom: A Political History.* New Haven, CT: Yale University Press, 1965.

Tawa, Nicholas E. *The Way to Tin Pan Alley: American Popular Song, 1866–1910.* New York: Schirmer Books, 1990.

Taylor, Charles M. *Vacation Days in Hawaii and Japan.* Philadelphia: George W. Jacobs & Co., 1898.

Taylor, Ellen M. *Madeira: Its Scenery, and How To See It.* London: Edward Standford, 1889.

Taylor, Frank J., Earl M. Welty, and David W. Eyre. *From Land and Sea: The Story of Castle & Cooke of Hawaii.* San Francisco: Chronicle Books, 1976.

Taylor, Roger, and Edward Wakeling. *Lewis Carroll Photographer: The Princeton University Library Albums.* Princeton, NJ: Princeton University Press, 2002.

Teachout, Terry. *Pops: A Life of Louis Armstrong.* Boston: Houghton Mifflin, 2009.

Teagle, John. *Washburn: Over One Hundred Years of Fine Stringed Instruments.* New York: Music Sales Corp., 1996.

Terrace, Vincent. *The Complete Encyclopedia of Television Programs 1947–1976.* New Brunswick, NJ: A. S. Barnes & Co., 1976.

Thomas, Hugh. *The Slave Trade: Story of the Atlantic Slave Trade 1440–1870.* New York: Simon and Schuster, 1997.

Thomas-Stanford, Charles. *Leaves from a Madeira Garden.* London: John Lane, 1910.

Thompson, A. A. *Los Angeles and Southern California Blue Book . . . 1894–95.* Los Angeles: A. A. Thompson, 1894.

Thompson, Gordon. *Please Please Me: Sixties British Pop, Inside Out.* New York: Oxford University Press, 2008.

Thompson Publishing Co. *The Dream City: A Portfolio of Photographic Views of the World's Columbian Exposition . . .* Intro. by Halsey C. Ives. St. Louis: N. D. Thompson Publishing Co., 1893.

Thurston, Lorrin A. *Writings of Lorrin A. Thurston.* Ed. Andrew Farrell. Honolulu: Advertiser Publishing Co., 1936.

Thurston, Lucy G. *Life and Times of Mrs. Lucy G. Thurston, Wife of Rev. Asa Thurston, Pioneer Missionary to the Sandwich Islands.* Ann Arbor, MI: S. C. Andrews, 1882.

Todaro, Tony. *The Golden Years of Hawaiian Entertainment, 1874–1974.* Honolulu: T. Todaro Publishing Co., 1974.

Todd, Frank Morton. *The Story of the Exposition.* Vols. 1–3. New York: G. P. Putnam's Sons, 1921.

Tracy, Joseph. *History of American Missions to the Heathen, from Their Commencement to the Present Time.* Worcester, MA: Spooner & Howland, 1840.

Trask, Haunani-Kay. *From a Native Daughter: Colonialism and Sovereignty in Hawai'i.* Honolulu: University of Hawaii Press, 1999.

Trevelyan, Charles Philip. *The Great New People: Letters from North America and the Pacific, 1898.* Garden City, NY: Doubleday & Co., 1971.

Truman, Benjamin C. *History of the World's Fair . . .* Philadelphia: Mammoth Publishing Co., 1893.

Tubbs, Jeremy M. "From Maestro to Mastro: The Life, Music and Instruments of Mario Maccaferri." Ph.D. diss., University of Memphis, 2008.

Tucker, Sophie. *Some of These Days: The Autobiography of Sophie Tucker.* Garden City, NY: Doubleday, Doran & Co., 1949.

Twain, Mark. *Mark Twain's Letters.* Vol. 1: *1853–1866.* Ed. Edgar Marquess Branch et al. Berkeley: University of California Press, 1988.

———. *Mark Twain's Letters from Hawaii.* Ed. A. Grove Day. London: Chatto & Windus, 1967.

———. *Roughing It.* Berkeley: University of California Press, 1995.

Tyler, James. *The Early Guitar.* London: Oxford University Press, 1980.

U.S. Bureau of the Census. *Fourteenth Census of the United States.* Vol. 10: *Manufactures 1919.* Washington, D.C.: Government Printing Office, 1923.

———. *Twelfth Census of the United States.* Vol. 2: *Population, Part 2.* Washington, D.C.: Government Printing Office, 1902.

U.S. Department of the Interior. *General Information Regarding the Territory of Hawaii.* Washington, D.C.: Government Printing Office, 1937.

U.S. Department of State. *Foreign Relations of the United States 1894: Affairs in Hawaii, Appendix 2.* Washington, D.C.: Government Printing Office, 1895.

———. *Papers Relating to the Foreign Relations of the United States.* Vol. 1. Washington, D.C.: Government Printing Office, 1875.

U.S. Senate. *Participation in the Alaska-Yukon-Pacific Exposition.* Senate Docs. 61st Congress, 3rd Session, Vol. 29 (Doc. No. 671). Washington, D.C.: Government Printing Office, 1911.

Vancouver, George. *A Voyage of Discovery to the North Pacific Ocean and Round the World 1791–1795.* Ed. W. Kaye Lamb. London: Hakluyt Society, 1984.

Vannes, Rene. *Dictionnaire universal des luthiers.* Brussels: Les Amis de la Musique, 1972.

Van Ronk, Dave. *The Mayor of MacDougal Street: A Memoir.* Cambridge, MA: Da Capo Press, 2005.

Verge, Arthur C. "George Freeth: King of the Surfers and California's Forgotten Hero." *California History* 80 (summer/fall 2001): 82–105.

Verlinde, Jason. "Uke Lust: An Interview with Stephin Merritt of the Magnetic Fields." *Ukulele Occasional* 1 (summer 2002): 62–67.

Vieira, Alberto. "Sugar Islands: The Sugar Economy of Madeira and the Canaries, 1450–1650." In Stuart B. Schwartz, ed., *Tropical Babylons: Sugar and the Making of the Atlantic World, 1450–1680.* Chapel Hill: University of North Carolina Press, 2004.

Vincent, Frank, Jr. *Through and Through the Tropics: Thirty Thousand Miles of Travel in Oceania, Australasia, and India.* New York: Harper and Brothers, 1876.

Wald, Elijah. *Escaping the Delta: Robert Johnson and the Invention of the Blues.* New York: Amistad, 2004.

Warfield, Patrick. "Making the Band: The Formation of John Philip Sousa's Ensemble." *American Music* 24 (spring 2006): 30–66.

Warrin, Donald, and Geoffrey L. Gomes. *Land, As Far As the Eye Can See: Portuguese in the Old West.* Spokane, WA: Arthur H. Clark Co., 2001.

Warshaw, Matt. "George Freeth." Entry in Matt Warshaw, *The Encyclopedia of Surfing.* Orlando, FL: Harcourt, 2003: 214–215.

Washburn, Jim, and Richard Johnston. *Martin Guitars: An Illustrated Celebration of America's Premier Guitarmaker.* Emmaus, PA: Rodale Press, 1997.

Washington, George. *The Writings of George Washington from the Original Manuscript Sources 1745–1799.* Vol. 2: *1757–1769.* Ed. John C. Fitzpatrick. Washington, D.C.: U.S. Government Printing Office, 1931.

Wearing, J. P. *The London Stage 1920–1929: A Calendar of Plays and Players.* Vol 1: *1920–1924.* Metuchen, NJ: Scarecrow Press, 1984.

Whitcomb, Ian. *Irving Berlin and Ragtime America.* London: Century-Hutchinson, 1987.

———. *Rock Odyssey: A Musician's Chronicle of the Sixties.* Garden City, NY: Dolphin Books, 1983.

White, Robert. *Madeira, Its Climate and Scenery.* London: Cradock & Co., 1851.

White, Robert, and James Yate Johnson. *Madeira: Its Climate and Scenery.* Edinburgh: Adam & Charles Black, 1856.

White, Trumbull. *Our New Possessions.* Chicago: A. B. Kuhlman Co., 1898.

Whiting, Lilian. *Kate Field: A Record.* Boston: Little, Brown and Co., 1900.

Whitney, Caspar. *Hawaiian America: Something of Its History, Resources, and Prospects.* New York: Harper & Brothers, 1899.

Whitney, Henry M. *The Tourists' Guide through the Hawaiian Islands.* 2nd ed. Honolulu: Hawaiian Gazette, 1895.

Wilde, W. R. *Narrative of a Voyage to Madeira, Teneriffe, and along the Shores of the Mediterranean.* Dublin: William Curry, Jr., 1840.

Wilder, Laura Ingalls. *West from Home: Letters of Laura Ingalls Wilder to Almanzo Wilder, San Francisco 1915.* Ed. Roger Lea McBride. New York: Harper & Row, 1974.

Wilkes, Charles. *Narrative of the United States Exploring Expedition during the Years 1838, 1839, 1840, 1841, 1842.* Philadelphia: C. Sherman, 1844.

Wilkinson, Kim M., and Craig R. Elevitch. *Growing Koa: A Hawaiian Legacy Tree.* Holualoa, HI: Permanent Agricultural Resources, 2003.

Withers, W. J. "Geography, Enlightenment, and the Paradise Question." In David N. Livingstone and Withers, eds., *Geography and Enlightenment.* Chicago: University of Chicago Press, 1999.

Wodehouse, P. G. *A Damsel in Distress.* London: Herbert Jenkins Ltd., 1919.

———. *Thank You, Jeeves.* Woodstock, NY: Overlook Press, 2003.

Wood, H. P. *Annual Report of the Honolulu Chamber of Commerce for the Year Ending Aug. 16th, 1911.* Honolulu: Hawaiian Gazette Co., 1912.

Woods, Fred E. "A Most Influential Mormon Islander: Jonathan Hawaii Napela." *Hawaiian Journal of History* 42 (2008): 135–157.

Worcester Society of Antiquity. "Report of the Exhibition of Antique Musical Instruments . . ." *Proceedings of the Worcester Society of Antiquity,* vol. 18. Worcester, MA: Published by the Society, 1902.

Wortley, Lady Emmeline Stuart. *A Visit to Portugal and Madeira.* London: Chapman and Hall, 1854.

Wyatt, Robert, and John Andrew Johnson, eds. *The George Gershwin Reader.* New York: Oxford University Press, 2007.

Yanow, Scott. *The Jazz Singers: The Ultimate Guide.* New York: Backbeat Books, 2008.

York, Ute, ed. *Insight Guides Madeira.* Singapore: APA Publications, 1992.

Young, Lucien. *The Boston at Hawaii, or the Observations and Impressions of a Naval Officer during a Stay of Fourteen Months in Those Islands on a Man-of-War.* Washington, D.C.: Gibson Brothers, 1898.

Zanzig, Augustus Delafield. *Music in American Life, Present and Future.* London: Oxford University Press, 1932.

Index

A

accordion, 27, 28, 135
Adams, W. D., 99
Aeko, Nulhama "William," 55, 76
Aiken, Conrad, 117
Ailau, John "Jack," 72
Akiyami, Tami, 162
Alapai, Nani, 59, 83
Albert College of Music, 131
aloha aina, 52, 53
Aloha Collection of Hawaiian Songs, 83
"Aloha Oe," 31, 32, 57, 59, 67, 68, 69, 72, 76,
    83, 99, 118
American Board of Commissioners for
    Foreign Missions, 21, 24
American Federation of Musicians, 121, 148
Anderson, Alex, 139
Anderson, Ian, 149
Andrews, Lorrin, 41
Andrews, Mabel, 62, 111
Anthony, Earle, 77
Arbuckle, Fatty, 116
Armstrong, Samuel Chapman, 78
Ash, Sammy, 164
Ashford, Volney, 51
Astaire, Fred and Adele, 6, 122–123
autoharp, 49, 64
Awai, Keoki, 97

B

Babbitt, 113
Bad Girl, 118

Baez, Joan, 149
Bailey, N. B., 87
Balfour, Francis, 61
bands: Reform School band, 32; ships'
    bands, 25. *See also* Hawaiian National
    Band; Royal Hawaiian Band
banjo, 28, 40, 45, 46, 50, 59, 67, 71, 83, 86,
    102, 110, 119, 121, 125, 132, 138, 144,
    149; confused with ʻukulele, 57
Banjo ukulele (banjo uke, banjuke,
    banjulele), 111–112, 139, 152
Beloff, Jim and Liz, 158, 159, 160, 165
Benson, George, 149
Bentley, Jack, 118
Berger, Henry, 31, 33, 57, 71, 83, 91, 134
Bergstrom Music Co., Honolulu, 62, 83–84,
    85, 99, 106
Berlin, Irving, 98, 101
Berliner, Emil, 76
Bingham, Rev. Hiram, 21, 23, 24, 41
Bird, Wiki, 114
Bird of Paradise, The, 6, 73, 74–76, 86;
    in Australia and New Zealand, 131;
    in England, 111
Bishaw, Henry A. Peelua, 131, 133
Bishop, Bernice Pauahi, 25
Blaine, James, 50
Blair, Tony, 164
Blanding, Don, 76
Blunt, Emily, 164
Bolander, John, 112
Bow, Clara, 116

Breen, May Singhi, 113, 118, 121, 146
Breve Noticia Àcerca das Ilhas de Sandwich,
    34–35, 38
Brigham, Helen, 67
Broadway, 74, 78, 79, 83, 98, 99, 115, 119,
    122, 135
Brown, Billie, 125
Buck, Gene, 122
Buegeleisen & Jacobson, 103–104, 105
Buffalo Bill's Wild West Show, 80
Buffett, Warren, 164
Burt, Virginia, 114
Bush, Eddie, 158

C

cabinetmaking: in Hawaii, 39; in Madeira,
    14–15
Cabral, Joaquim Monteiro, 13, 14
Captains Courageous, 18
Carlin, Bob, 123
Carr, James Revell, 55
Carroll, Lewis, 14
Cartwright, Daisy, 67, 111
cavaquinho, 11
Cazimero, Robert and Roland, 155, 157
C. Bruno & Son, 99, 103, 106, 121, 146
C.F. Martin & Co., 85, 104, 125, 126–127,
    137, 148, 155, 164
Chamberlain, Levi, 23
Chamberlin, Ron, 161
chautauqua, 5, 137
Churchill, H. C., 106, 169
Clay, Philip T., 91
Cleghorn, Annie, 49
Cleveland, Grover, 52
Collins, Earl, 130
Collins, James H., 67
Columbia Records, 83, 98, 99, 100, 123
comic opera, 77–78
Connors, Eddie, 148
Cook, Amos and Juliette, 24
Cook, Joe, 131
coon songs, 78
Cooper, Gary, 116
Cooper, Will J., 72
Copland, Aaron, 115
Correa, João Luis, 48
Correll, Charles, 119
Costa, Augusto M. da, 15–16

Costello, Elvis, 162
country music, 123
Cracroft, Sophia, 25, 31
Craig, Daniel, 164
Crawford, Joan, 116
Crosby, Bing, 114, 121, 138
Crumit, Frank, 5, 119
Cunha, Albert "Sonny," 61, 69, 81, 83, 84,
    129, 134

D

Daltrey, Roger, 162
Darwin, Charles, 50
da Silva, João Gomes, 37
Davies, Theophilus H., 46
Dean, Louis, 119
De Lano, Charles, 90, 104
Delima, Kelly Boy, 157
Delmar, Viña, 118
DeRose, Peter, 121
Deschanel, Zooey, 164
De Sylva, Buddy, 116
Dias, Augusto, 38–40, 43, 48, 50, 53–54, 62,
    73, 167
Dibble, Rev. Sheldon, 21
Dickey, C. W., 94
Dillingham, Charles, 79
Ditson, Charles H., 85, 90, 91
Ditson, Oliver, 83, 85, 106
Dix, John, 11, 12–13, 17
Doane, J. Chalmers, 160
Dole, Rev. Daniel, 24
Dorsey, George and Cornelius, 125
Dos Passos, John, 108
Downing, Mabel, 102
Drogin, Alan, 163
Drumond de Vasconcellos, Candido, 13–14
Dubin, Al, 98
Durkee, George B., 121
Durkee, Jennie, 121

E

Edison Co., 61, 79
Edwards, Cliff (Ukulele Ike), 6, 118,
    121–124, 135, 139, 148
Edwards, John, 93
Edwards, Webley E., 139
Elemeni, Keoui, 55
Elizabeth of Bavaria, 6–7

Ellis, John, 59, 61, 69, 83

Ellis, William, 61, 69, 79, 83

Estudos para Machete, 14

expositions: Alaska-Yukon-Pacific Exposition,
Seattle (1909), 72, 94; Centennial
International Exposition, Philadelphia
(1876), 93; Crystal Palace Exhibition,
London (1851), 92; Exposition
Universelle, Paris (1889), 92; Greater
America Exposition, Omaha (1899), 93;
Lewis & Clark Centennial and American
Pacific Exposition and Oriental Fair,
Portland, Ore. (1905), 70–71, 94;
Louisiana Purchase Exposition, St. Louis
(1904), 94; means of publicizing Hawaii,
55, 92; Panama Pacific International
Exposition (1915), 91, 94–96, 112;
Pan-American Exposition, Buffalo
(1901), 79, 80, 81, 93–94; San Francisco
Midwinter Fair (1894), 64, 78; South
Carolina Inter-State and West Indian
Exposition (1902), 80; World's
Columbian Exposition, Chicago (1893),
55–56, 92–93; World's Industrial and
Cotton Centennial Exposition, New
Orleans (1884), 92

F

Fayne, Chuck, 165

Ferera, Helen and Frank, 100

Fernandes, João, 37, 48

Fernandez, Troy, 157

Fisher, Bud, 131, 132

Fitzgerald, F. Scott, 117, 137

flute, 27, 57, 59, 70, 71, 82

Flying Karamazov Brothers, 164

Ford Motor Co., 96, 116

Formby, George, 139–140, 163

Fowler, Art, 130, 148

Frampton, Peter, 149

França, Isabella Hurst de, 9, 11–12, 17

Frank Pallma and Son (Chicago), 111

Freeth, George, 69

Friedwald, Will, 123

Funchal, Madeira, 8, 9, 32, 38, 39, 58

G

Galloway, Chick, 118

Garbo, Greta, 116

George J. Birkel Co. (Los Angeles), 70–71,
85, 86, 87, 88, 112, 128, 168

Gershwin, George and Ira, 5, 115, 122, 123

Gibson, Hoot, 116

Gibson Mandolin-Guitar Manufacturing
Co., 113, 118, 127, 137, 141

Giddings, T. P., 149

Giddins, Gary, 138

Gilbert and Sullivan, 77

Gilliland, Christina Dias, 49

Gilson, Lottie, 77

Glacken, L. M., 101

Gleason, James, 25

Gluck, Alma, 99

Godfrey, Arthur, 113, 136, 141–142, 143,
145–146, 148, 152, 154

Gosden, Freeman, 119

Grant, Sterling, 125

Great Depression, 135, 137

Griffith, D. W., 116

Grimm, Charlie, 118

guitar: 10, 11, 40, 41, 47, 55, 58, 59, 65, 69,
71, 76, 78, 80, 81, 82, 83, 84, 92, 108,
110, 119, 135, 152; introduction to
Hawaii, 27–28; royal family use of, 31,
49, 50. *See also* steel guitar

H

Haida, Yukihiko and Katsuhiko, 158

Hall, Wendell, 6, 119, 128, 135, 148

Hammerstein, Oscar, 123

Handler, Elliot and Ruth, 142–143

hapa haole songs, 84, 98, 155

Harold, Charles, 121

Harper, Lee Ann, 161

Harris, Charles K., 56

Harris, Jerome, 121

Harrison, George, 162, 163

Hawaii: American influence in, 22, 50;
annexation to U.S., 51; commerce,
21, 66–67; contract labor, 34, 35–36;
population decline, 33–34, 50–51;
public interest in, post-annexation,
61–62; racist attitudes toward native
Hawaiians, 78, 93; stereotypes of native
Hawaiians, 20, 22, 51, 77–78, 101; sugar
industry, 33, 40, 50; tourism, 32, 54,
57, 61–63, 108, 138–139, 166; whaling,
21–22

Hawaiian Board of Immigration, 34, 38
Hawaiian Guide Book for Travelers, The, 32
Hawaiian guitar. *See* steel guitar
Hawaiian Hotel, 28, 32, 52, 57
Hawaiian Legends and Folklore
    Commission, 5
Hawaiian music: in Australia and New
    Zealand, 130–131; in Canada, 102,
    160, 161; decline of, 155–156;
    described, 58; in England, 46, 111,
    158–159, 162; in France, 109, 110–111;
    as genre, 98–101, 138; Hawaiians
    as natural musicians, 54, 57; at
    international expositions, 55–56, 64,
    70–71, 72, 80, 92–96; and introduction
    of jazz, 129–130; introduction of
    western music, 22–24; as marketing
    tool, 57, 72, 76–77, 138–139, 166;
    popularized by *Bird of Paradise,* 74–76;
    popular music in Hawaii, 25–26;
    recordings, 59, 82–83, 99; revival of,
    156–158; royal composers' influence
    of, 28–32; in Southeast Asia, 131,
    158; in vaudeville, 69, 76, 79–81,
    98, 102; western instruments in,
    24–25, 27
Hawaiian Music Foundation, 156
Hawaiian National Band, 52, 64; mainland
    tour of 1895–1896, 64–66
Hawaiian News Co., 45, 62, 63
Hawaiian Room, Lexington Hotel, 138
Hawaiian Songs, 131
Hawaii Promotion Committee, 62, 72
Hawaii Territorial Exposition Committee, 94
Hay, M. E., 72
Hayes, Lucie May, 67
Hearst, Phoebe, 68
Heffelfinger, R. W., 87
Held, Anna, 83
Heleluhe, Jack, 80
Hendrix, Jimi, 149
Hennessey, Thomas, 69, 93
Henry, Edna, 90
Henshaw, Bobbie, 102, 148
Hickey, Janey, 114
Highet, Gilbert, 130
Hiianaia, Gordon, 94
Hilborn, Grace, 64, 111
Hill, James, 160, 161, 162

Hillebrand, Dr. William, 34, 53
himeni, 22, 23–24, 50
Hiram, Solomon, 57
Hokea, Ben, 102
Holstein, Edward, 41, 45, 59, 62
Honolulu Advertising Club, 106, 107
Honolulu Chamber of Commerce, 62, 76, 94
Hoopii, Sol, 138
Hopkins, Charles A. K., 83
Howe, Harriet E., 67
Hudson's Bay Co., 21, 53
hula, 23, 24, 45–46, 50, 51, 57, 61, 93, 111,
    139
hula kui, 50, 52, 56, 84
Hussey, Kimo, 161

I
Ikemi, Shoi, 151
Ince, Thomas, 116
Internet, 160
ipu, 50, 76
Irwin, Bernice Piilani, 52

J
Jackson, Elbert, 116
J. Albert & Son, 131
Jans, Harry, 110
jazz, 101, 111, 115, 118, 125, 129–130,
    149, 150
Jenkins, Ella, 125
Johnson, Julian, 74
Jolson, Al, 99, 116, 138
Jones, John Paul, 149
Jones, W. B., 93
Judd, Agnes, 80
Judd, Charles H., 43
Judd, Gerrit P., 24
Judd, Henry R., 62, 80
Judd, Laura Fish, 26, 28

K
Kaai, Ernest, 43, 59–61, 73, 86, 89, 94, 112,
    128, 158, 169; at Alaska-Yukon-Pacific
    Exposition, 72; in Australia and New
    Zealand, 130–131; in Southeast Asia,
    131
Kaawa, Robert, 99
Ka Bana Lahui. *See* Hawaiian National Band
Ka Buke Mele Lahui, 52

Kahanu, Elizabeth, 50
Kai, William, 69
Kaiawe, S. M., 76
Kaili, David, 99
Kailimai, Henry, 94, 95, 96, 97, 98
Kaiulani, Victoria, 49–50, 57
Kalainaina, Sam Kia, 58
Kalakaua, David, 28, 29, 30, 31, 33, 39, 43, 78; role in Hawaiian culture revival, 51; 'ukulele patron, 47–48, 49, 50
Kalanianaole, Jonah Kuhio, 50
Kalima, Jesse, 151
Kalmar, Bert, 98
Kamae, Eddie, 149, 151, 155, 156, 157
Kamaka, Samuel K., 106, 128, 140, 164, 171
Kamakaia, Samuel K., 66
Kamakawiwoole, Israel, 157–158, 166
Kamamalu, Victoria, 30
Kamehameha I, 51
Kamehameha II (Liholiho), 21, 23, 24
Kamehameha III, 30, 42, 53, 92
Kamehameha IV (Alexander Liholiho), 24, 30, 53, 78
Kamehameha V (Lot), 24, 32, 52
Kamualualii, A. O. East, 55
Kanahele, George, 156
Kanui, William, 109
Karloff, Boris, 6
Kaumakapili Church, 28
Kaumualii, George, 23
Kawaiahao Church, 28, 30, 32, 53
Kawaiahao Girls' Seminary, 32, 83
Kealakai, Mekia (Major), 33, 59, 69, 70, 71, 72, 79, 80, 87, 93, 94, 111
Keaton, Buster, 116, 134
Keech, Alvin, 111, 112
Keech, Kelvin, 111, 112, 130
Keegan, Pierce, 122
Kekuku, Joseph, 79, 89, 111
Kema, Frank, 94
Kern, Jerome, 98, 123
Kia, George. *See* Nahaolelua, George Kia
Kilauea volcano cyclorama, 55, 64
Kiliwa, Thomas, 69
King, Charles, 130
Kingsley, Grace, 98
Kipling, Rudyard, 18
Kiwala, A., 76
koa, 52–53, 86, 87, 92, 104

Kollitz, Franz and Josef, 130
Kolomoku, Walter, 76
Krout, Mary, 48, 52
Kumalae, Jonah, 73, 86, 94, 96, 106, 128, 169

L
Lake, Kahauanu, 155
Langley Ukulele Ensemble, 160, 161
Laurel and Hardy, 134
Lawrence, Gertrude, 130
Leacock, Stephen, 101
Leleiohoku, William Pitt, 28, 30, 31, 32
Lemonade Mouth, 166
Levi, Ray, 90
Lewis, Sinclair, 113, 117
Liberty Belles, 109, 110
Libornio, Jose S., 65
Liddell, Alice, 14, 15
Liholiho (Kamehameha II), 21, 23, 24
Liholiho, Alexander (Kamehameha IV), 24, 30, 53, 78
Likelike, Miriam Kekauluohi, 28, 30
Liliuokalani (Lydia Kamakaeha Paki), 23, 28, 45, 52, 53, 55, 61, 64, 65, 69; as composer, 31–32, 83; mocked on mainland, 77, 78, 101; as musician and singer, 29–30, 49
Lincoln, William, 94
Littig, Frank, 90
Lloyd, Harold, 117
London, Jack, 42, 68–69
Los Angeles, 62, 65, 66–67, 69–70, 74–75, 87, 89, 90, 104, 112, 121, 123, 134
Los Angeles Chamber of Commerce, 96
Los Angeles Playground and Recreation Department, 134
Love, Bessie, 116
Lowry, Malcolm, 117
Lua, Pale K., 99
Lyon, Rev. Lorenzo, 23
Lyon & Healy, 103, 106, 121, 125, 126, 127, 137, 141, 168

M
Maccaferri, Mario, 144–146, 151, 152
machete, 10–11, 16, 18, 20, 43; how played, 11; introduction to Hawaii, 37; makers of, 14; repertory and instruction, 12–14

Macy, William H., 164

Madeira: domination by England, 8; economy, 17; emigration from, 17–18, 34–35; famine in, 18; inhabitants of, 9; music in, 9–10, 17; similarities to Hawaii, 6; sugar industry, 7–8; tourism, 8–9; wine industry, 8, 17, 18–19

Maipinepine, Keoui, 55, 56

mandolin, 40, 48, 50, 59, 67, 69, 83, 86, 90, 102, 110, 113, 118, 141; mandolin technique adapted to 'ukulele, 86, 121; 'ukulele mistaken as, 48, 57, 93, 94

Mann, Aimee, 162

Manning, James, 121

Marks, Edward, 99

Marques, Augustus, 45

Marshall, Thomas Riley, 102

Marvin, Johnny, 5, 119–120, 121, 135, 160

Mather, Helen, 41, 63

Mattel, 142–143

May, Frank W., 114

May, Tom, 106

Mays, Harry, 125

McCartney, Paul, 162

McGiffert, Katherine, 90

McLane, Thomas, 108

mele, 5, 22, 52

Mele Hawaii, 32, 83

Menezes, Vicente de, 15

Merritt, Stephin, 163, 166

Merz, Charles, 115

Midler, Bette, 162

Midway Plaisance, Chicago, 55, 92

Miles, William, 102

Milhalyi, William, 149

Mills, E. C., 126

missionaries: arrival in Hawaii, 21; attitude toward Hawaiian culture, 21; musical culture, 22, 24

M. Nunes & Sons, 73, 87, 106, 167

Moon, Peter, 156–157

Morosco, Oliver, 74–75

Morris, Howard K., 148

movies: *A Mighty Wind,* 166; *Backstage,* 116; *Boots! Boots!,* 139; "Don Juan," 119; *Gold Diggers of 1935,* 138; *Hawaiian Buckaroo,* 138; *Hawaiian Nights,* 138; *Hawaii Calls,* 138; "His Pastimes," 119; *Honolulu,* 138; "Let George Do It," 140;

Moonlight in Hawaii, 138; *Pinocchio,* 123; *Sirens of the Seas,* 116; *Sons of the Desert,* 134; *Steamboat Bill Jr.,* 134; *Teddy at the Throttle,* 116; *The Beach Combers,* 116; *The Freshman,* 117; *The Pagan,* 116; *Top Hat,* 138; *Waikiki Wedding,* 138; *You Are What You Eat,* 153

Muntz, Mae, 90

Muse, Lewis "Rabbit," 125

musical groups: Al G. Fields Minstrels, 102; American Quartet, 99; Beatles, 152, 156; Beirut, 163; Bob Canfield's Hawaiian Beach Boys, 138; Bonzo Dog Band, 155; Boston Minstrels, 26; Clark's Royal Hawaiians, 102; Crockett's Kentucky Mountaineers, 123; De Lano Steel Guitar and Ukulele Sextette, 113; Fiddlin' Powers and Family, 123; Ford Hawaiians, 96; Frank Wagner's Hilo Five Hawaiian Orchestra, 123; Hawaiian Queens, 78; Hill Billies, 123; Honolulu Students, 82–83; Jim Kweskin & the Jug Band, 155; Kaau Crater Boys, 157; Kapena, 157; Kennelle's Iolani Hawaiian Orchestra, 115; King's Singing Boys, 47–48, 52; Lou Hemming and the Royal Hawaiians, 102; Magnetic Fields, 163; Makaha Sons of Niihau, 157; Mele Hawaiian Quartet, 114; New Vaudeville Band, 155; Nitty Gritty Dirt Band, 155; Olomana, 156; Original Dixieland Jazz Band, 101; Pearl Jam, 163; Pele Quartet, 64; Royal Hawaiian Troubadours, 83; Schenectady Hawaiian Trio, 114; Schrader and Lensner, 114; Songs From a Random House, 163; Sons of Hawaii, 156; Sopwith Camel, 155; South Sea Islanders, 93; South Sea Troubadours, 101; Spanish Students, 28; Speer Family, 123; Sunday Manoa, 156–157; Toots Paka's Hawaiians, 79–80, 100; Train, 163; Ukulele Orchestra of Great Britain, 158–159; Volcano Singers, 55–56, 57, 76, 92; Waikiki Hawaiians, 123; White Lyres, 113

Music Publishers Protective Association, 127

Mutt and Jeff, 131, 132

M. Witmark & Sons, 76, 138

N

Nahaolelua, George Kia, 61, 80, 87, 88–90
Nahienanea, 30
Na Himeni Hawaii, 23
Naonan, Pasapum, 160
Nape, David, 33, 59, 80, 94
National Association of Musical Instrument
    and Accessories Manufacturers, 126
National Association of Musical Merchandise
    Manufacturers, 146, 148, 152, 158
National Association of Musical Merchandise
    Wholesalers, 138
National Playground and Recreation
    Association, 135
National Recreation Association, 135
Nesbitt, Sydney, 130
New York, 80, 82, 83, 93, 108, 122, 132; as
    arbiter of popular culture, 76, 79, 85, 98,
    111; embrace of Hawaiian music, 101
Noble, Johnny, 59, 129, 139
Normand, Mabel, 116
Norton, Edward and F. A., 112
Novarro, Ramon, 116
Nunes, Angeline, 41
Nunes, João (Diabinho), 15, 39
Nunes, Julius, 73, 87
Nunes, Leonardo, 73, 87, 103, 106, 168
Nunes, Manuel, 38–40, 43, 62, 73, 86, 113, 167
Nunes, Octaviano João da Paixão, 15, 39

O

Ohta, Herb, 155–156, 157, 158, 166
Olcott-Bickford, Vahda, 118
Olsen, Esther, 68
Orpheum vaudeville circuit, 80
O'Shea, Tessie, 152
Owens, Harry, 76, 138, 139

P

Paehaole, A. P., 44
Paka, Iolai (July), 69, 79
paniolo, 27, 80
Philpitt, S. Ernest, 102, 108
piano, 10, 12, 24, 26, 27, 28, 50, 53, 84, 103, 113,
    118, 137, 140
Pickford, Mary, 6
plastics, 136–137, 141, 142–146, 151–152
plays, musicals, and reviews: *A Broadway
    Melody,* 116; *Antigone,* 164; *A Thousand*

Clowns, 166; *Betty Be Good,* 119;
    Captain Cook, 77; *Dillon and King
    in Honolulu,* 78; *El Capitan,* 77;
    Footlights Review, 117; *Girlies,* 83;
    Hello Honolulu, 98; *HMS Pinafore,* 77;
    Honeymoon Lane, 119; *Honolulu,* 77;
    King Kaliko, 77; *King Moo's Wedding
    Day,* 78; *Lady Be Good,* 6, 122–123;
    Luana, 135; *Madame Butterfly,* 77;
    My Honolulu Girl, 98; *No, No Nanette,*
    119; *Oh, Kay,* 119; *Papa's Wife,* 83;
    Peach Blossom Fan, 164; *Potluck
    Show,* 151; *Prince of Hawaii,* 130;
    Queen Lil, 77; *Robinson Crusoe, Jr.,* 99;
    South Pacific, 144; *Stop! Look! Listen!,*
    98; *Sunny,* 123; *Tangerine,* 119;
    The Death of Captain Cook, 77;
    The Echo, 79; *The Garden of Aloha,*
    98; *The Grand Mogul,* 83; *The Mikado,*
    77; *The Mimic World of 1921,* 122;
    The Pearl Maiden, 77; *The Policy
    Players,* 78; *The Ukulele Girl,* 98; *The
    Young Turk,* 79; *Very Good Eddie,* 98;
    Ziegfeld Follies, 98; *Ziegfeld Follies of
    1927,* 123; *Ziegfeld's Midnight Frolic,*
    122. See also *Bird of Paradise, The*
Pokipala, Dan, 129
Power, Tyrone, 6
*Primeiro Colecção de differentes Peças de
    Muzica,* 13–14
Prince of Wales (Edward Windsor), 6, 119,
    130
Puni, Joe, 80, 109
Purvis, Edward William, 43

Q

Quintal, Antonio dos Reis, 15

R

radio, 113, 114–115, 119, 121, 123, 130
radio shows: *Amos 'n' Andy,* 119; *Arthur
    Godfrey's Talent Scouts,* 142; *Arthur
    Godfrey Time,* 142; *Hawaii Calls,* 139
ragtime, 78, 79, 84, 116
rajão, 16, 40, 41
Ransom, Anita, 114
recorded music, 59, 76, 79, 82–83, 99–100,
    137, 138, 155, 157
Reform School (Honolulu), 32, 40, 61

retail stores: A.M. Rothschild & Co. (Chicago), 80; Barlow's Music (Trenton, N.J.), 108; Byron Mauzy Music (San Francisco), 96; Dart Drug, 151; E.C. Christian Music Co. (Lexington, Ky.), 102; E.F. Droop & Co. (Washington, D.C.), 86, 109; Elderly Instruments (Lansing, Mich.), 164; Fred C. Meyers & Co. (Philadelphia), 104; Gimbel's, 144; Golden Rule Bazaar (Honolulu), 72; Henry Paty & Co. (Honolulu), 27; Kohler & Chase (San Francisco), 112; Lit Brothers (Philadelphia), 104; Lycan & Co. (Honolulu), 28; Macy's, 148; May Co. (Los Angeles), 140; Mclean & Co. (Winnipeg), 102; Montgomery Ward, 143; Murphy's (Indiana, Penn.), 143; National Dollar Store, 144; Newberry's, 144; Sam Ash Music Stores, 164; Sampson Music Co. (Boise, Idaho), 86; Sears, Roebuck Co., 87, 103; Stieffer's Music House (Charlotte, N.C.), 102; The Broadway (Los Angeles), 104; The Fair (Chicago), 104; Wanamakers (Philadelphia), 104; West, Dow & Co. (Honolulu), 28; Western Automatic Music Co. (Dallas, Texas), 102; Whaley, Royce & Co. (Winnipeg), 102; Wurlitzer Music (Chicago), 141. *See also* Bergstrom Music Co.; Ditson, Charles H.; Ditson, Oliver; George J. Birkel Co.; Sherman, Clay & Co.; Southern California Music Co.

Reynolds, W. F., 72

Ribeiro, Jose Silvestre, 18

Ritz, Lyle, 149–150, 157, 166

Robbins-Engel, 118

Roberts, Helen, 5, 28, 41

Rodgers, Jimmie, 123

Roland, Edith, 90

Rollinson, Thomas, 85–86

Rooke, Emma, 30

Royal Hawaiian Band, 25, 32, 33, 52, 57, 59, 61, 64, 83, 91; 1906 mainland tour, 81–82; at Lewis & Clark Exposition, 70–71; in San Francisco (first mainland appearance), 63–64. *See also* Berger, Henry

Royal School, Honolulu, 24, 27, 28, 29

Rundgren, Todd, 162

S

Sakuma, Roy, 150, 157, 162

Sam T. Jack's Creole Co., 93

Sanderson, Julia, 121

San Francisco, 26, 62, 65, 67, 71, 91, 111, 112; as center of Hawaiian music, 57, 63–64, 69

San Francisco Merchants Association, 91

Santo, Jose do Espirito, 38–40, 43–44, 47, 53–54, 62, 73, 168

Santos, Antonio Abreu, 41, 61

Santos, Jerry, 156, 157

Sault, Robert E., 133, 134

saxophone, 99, 117, 119, 129, 130, 132, 135

Seger, Bob, 149

Shaw, Jim, 93

sheet music, 83–85, 92, 99, 109, 118, 121, 138

Shepherd, Cybill, 164

Sherman, Clay & Co. (San Francisco), 67, 86, 87, 90, 91, 96, 97, 106, 112

Shimabukuro, Jake, 157, 162, 163, 165

Shoemaker, Michael, 58

Small, Denny (or Danny), 125

Smeck, Roy, 119, 148, 160

Smith, Rev. Lowell, 23, 24

songs: "Adios Ke Aloha," 31; "After the Ball," 56; "Ahi Wela," 57, 76, 80, 84; "Ainahau," 57; "Ain't She Sweet?," 119; "A Lemon in the Garden of Love," 155; "America," 86; "Annie Laurie," 26; "A Tisket, A Tasket," 153; "Billy Boy," 26; "Blue Bells of Scotland," 86; "California, Here I Come," 115; "Come, Holy Spirit, Heavenly Dove," 23; "Cool Water," 149; "Crazy Words, Crazy Tune," 155; "Dark Eyes," 151; "Don't Get Around Much Anymore," 150; "E Ala E," 158; "Earth Angel," 149; "E Ola Ka Moi I Ke Aka," 30; "Fascinating Rhythm," 6, 123; "F.U.N. Song," 166; "God Save the Queen," 14; "Hawaii 78," 158; "Hawaiian Wedding Song," 155; "Hawaii Ponoi," 31, 32, 57, 59; "Hello Hello," 155; "He Mele Lahui Hawaii," 83; "Hey, Soul Sister," 163; "Home Sweet Home," 26; "Honolulu, America Loves You," 99;

"Honolulu Hicki Boola Boo," 99; "Honolulu Rag," 83; "Honolulu Tom Boy," 59, 69, 84; "Hula Blues," 129; "I Can Hear the Ukuleles Calling Me," 99; "Il Trovatore," 90; "I'm Shy, Mary Ellen," 155; "Iron Man," 163; "I Saw Her Standing There," 152; "It Ain't Gonna Rain No Mo," 6, 119, 125; "It Had To Be You," 123; "I Told My Baby With a Ukulele," 139; "I Wish I Could Shimmy Like My Sister Kate," 155; "Jalousie," 151; "John Brown's Soul is Marching On," 26; "Just Before the Battle, Mother," 26; "Ka Mele Lahui Hawaii," 31; "Kaulana na pua o Hawaii," 52; "Kuu Ipu i ka Hee Pue One," 31; "Leilehua," 57; "Liliuokalani March," 83; "Lilli Walkee Lanny," 77; "Little Jazz Bird," 123; "Lulu's Back in Town," 150; "Ma Honolulu Queen," 78; "Mai Poina Oe," 76; "Marching Through Georgia," 26; "Moani Ke Ala," 31; "My Bird of Paradise," 101; "My Flower of Hawaii," 113; "My Hawaiian Maid," 84; "My Honolulu Queen," 83; "My Hula Hula Girl," 83; "My Hula Lula Girl," 83; "My Waikiki Mermaid," 84; "Nani Na Pua," 83; "Nani Wale Kuu Home O Ainahau," 31; "Oh, Susannah," 26; "Old Folks At Home," 86; "Onipaa," 52; "On The Beach at Waikiki," 94, 98; "Over the Rainbow/What A Wonderful World," 159; "Paddlin' Madelin' Home," 123; "Pualilia," 157; "Queen Lily Ouki-Ouk-Alani," 77; "Rock of Ages," 24; "Rule Britannia," 14; "Say It With a Ukulele," 5; "She Loves You," 152; "She Was Poor But She Was Honest," 155; "Singing in the Rain," 123, 134; "Singing Pete," 123; "Sonny Boy," 115; "Soon Forget," 163; "Stardust," 151; "Stars and Stripes Forever," 61, 151; "Sushi," 155; "Swanee River," 59; "Sweet Leilani," 138, 158; "Sweet Lei Lehua," 31, 32, 48, 59, 69; "The Good Ship Lollipop," 153; "The Honolulu Pa-ki-ka," 116; "The Intro and the Outro," 155; "The Last Rose of Summer," 26; "The Midway Plaisance," 64; "The Pagan Love Song," 116;

"Tico Tico," 150; "Tomi Tomi," 59, 71; "Ukulele Lady," 130, 155; "Ukulele Lorelei," 115; "Under the Double Eagle," 61, 151; "Waikiki Mermaid," 59; "Wearing of the Green," 26; "What Are The Wild Waves Saying?" 26; "When Johnny Comes Marching Home," 26; "Where Does Robinson Crusoe Go With Friday on Saturday Night," 154; "While My Guitar Gently Weeps," 162; "Winchester Cathedral," 155; "Wind Song," 4; "Woodman, Spare That Tree," 26; "Yaaka Hula Hickey Dula (Hawaiian Love Song)," 99, 138; "You Turn Me On," 154; "You Won't See Me," 155. *See also* "Aloha Oe"

Songs of Hawaii, 83–84

Sousa, John Phillip, and band, 56, 59, 77, 81, 91

Southern California Music Co., 87, 88, 89, 104, 106, 107, 108, 112, 125, 127, 128, 150, 167

SpongeBob Squarepants, 166

Spreckels, John D., 64

Springsteen, Bruce, 162

Stanford, Jane, 68

Stannard, George, 104

Stargirl, 166

Stearns Collection, University of Michigan, 14

steel guitar, 59, 76, 79, 89, 90, 99, 101, 114, 119, 125, 142

Stevenson, Robert Louis, 41, 47, 48

Stoddard, Charles Warren, 58

Strauss Music Co., 78

Strong, Isobel, 47–48

Sumner, Nancy Wahinekapu, 61

Swanson, Gloria, 116

Swartz, Stephen, 163–164

Swift, Taylor, 163

T

Tabu trademark, 106, 107

Taft, William, 81, 85

Tarkington, Booth, 117

taro patch fiddle, 40–41, 43–44, 45, 46, 49, 50, 55, 56, 57, 59, 62, 64, 65, 67, 71, 82, 108, 128

Taua, Kelii, 157

Taylor, Charles, 57

television, 119, 136, 142, 153, 154

television shows: *Antiques Roadshow,* 165; *Arthur Godfrey and His Friends,* 142; *Arthur Godfrey and His Ukulele,* 142; *ER,* 159; *Late Night with Conan O'Brien,* 162; *Laugh-In,* 153; *Romeo,* 166; *Saturday Night Live,* 166; *Texaco Star Theater,* 149; *The Ed Sullivan Show,* 152; *Toast of the Town,* 148; *Tonight Show,* 119, 154, 162; *Where the Action Is,* 155

Telles, Rufino, 15

Templeton, Mrs. C. R., 67, 111

Thank You, Jeeves, 134

Thompson, Ernest, 123

Thurston, Asa, 23

Thurston, Lorrin, 31, 55–56, 62, 64, 72, 92

Thurston, Pauline, 102

Tin Pan Alley, 76, 98–99, 129, 138

Tiny Tim, 119, 153–154

Tolentino, Bryan, 161

Torme, Mel, 155

Townsend, H. S., 44

Tucker, Sophie, 130

Tully, Richard Walton, 6, 73, 74, 76, 77, 78

Twain, Mark, 20, 22, 26, 31, 44

"Two Pieces for Violin and Piano," 115

U

'ukulele: adoption by college students, 68, 90, 102, 116–118; adoption by Hawaiian royal family, 47–50; adoption of, in Hawaii, 45–46; in African-American community, 124; association with outdoors, 68–69; in Australia and New Zealand, 130–131; in Canada, 81, 102, 160, 161; in classroom, 133, 149, 160, 161–162; in country music, 123; design, 44–45, 53, 136; in England, 46, 111, 119, 130, 139–140, 158–159, 162; festivals, 157, 161; Fifties revival, 136–152; first appearance on mainland, 46; first instrument, 149; first makers, 39–40; in France, 109, 110–111; as Hawaiian nationalism symbol, 52; in Hollywood, 116, 117, 119, 134, 138, 164; in Japan, 104, 131, 158–159, 166; koa wood, 52–53; in literature, 61, 68–69, 81, 117, 118, 133, 134; machete introduced to Hawaii, 37–38; Madeiran origins, 5, 10–19; manufacture in Hawaii, 39–40, 53, 73, 104, 106, 128, 137; manufacture on mainland, 85, 87, 103, 125–126, 164–165; modern revival, 158–165; as native invention, 5, 133; origin of name, 40–43; playground programs, 134–135; popularity in 1920s, 5–6, 115–119, 123; PPIE triggers national craze, 94–98; pricing, 47, 87, 96, 104, 105, 125–128, 136; regarded as American, 115; sales and marketing on mainland, 70, 85–88, 104, 105, 115, 118, 125–127, 137, 140, 158, 164; sizes and styles, 126, 128, 148; in Southeast Asia, 131, 158; as souvenir, 62–63; tablature, 59, 121, 144; target of abuse, 131–134, 165–166; technological promotion, 82–83, 99–100, 114–115, 119, 136, 160; tuning, 41; viewed as toy, 137, 142–144, 151; vintage instruments, 165; women's role in popularizing on mainland, 67–68, 111; World War I's role in introducing, to Europe, 108–110

Ukulele Ike. *See* Edwards, Cliff

'ukulele makers: Aloha Ukulele Manufacturing Co. (Honolulu), 106, 128, 171; Brüko, 130; BW Photo Utilities, 146; Candelas, 164; Chang Lau Cheong, 172; Chris-Kraft Instrument Co., 146; Clarence Kinney, 170, 172; Dave Means, 165; David Gomes, 165; David W. Kaiwa, 171; Enos Kealoha, 172; Ernesto Machado, 170; Fender, 164; George Finder, 146; George Paele Mossman, 128, 139, 172; Gretsch Manufacturing Co., 127, 136, 148; Harmony Music Co., 103, 120, 127; Hawaiian Mahogany Co., 128, 129; Hawaiian Ukulele and Violin Manufacturing Co. (Los Angeles), 104; Hawaiian Ukulele Co. (Honolulu), 106, 170; Heilborn Manufacturing Co., 172; Hohner, 164; Ishiga Sakai, 73, 86, 169; James N. Anahu, 73, 86, 106, 169; João M. Soares, 169; John S. Perry, 148; Jonah P. Davis, 170; Jose Vierra, 73, 168; J.R. Stewart Co., 127, 137; Kepasa Ukuleles, 165; Kinney & Mossman, 106, 170; Lapin Products, 146, 147;

Lot K. Pelio, 171; Manuel Fernandez, 73, 168; Mastro Plastic Corp., 145–146; Metropolitan Music Co., 137; Michael Da Silva, 165; Naapohou, 168; Non-Slip Key Socket and Ukulele Manufacturing Co., 104; Nunes Ukulele Co., 168; Nuuanu Ukulele Co., 172; Pahu Ukulele Manufacturing Co., 170; Palm Tree Ukuleles, 165; Paradise Ukulele and Guitar Works, Ltd., 106, 171; P. F. Ungson, 172; Regal, 127; Schulz & Moenning, 126; Singers Ukulele Manufacturing Co., 106, 171; Slingerland, 127; Sonny Dahlins, 165; Stromberg-Voisinet Co., 128; Takamine, 164; Ukebrand, 165; Ukulele Co., Ltd., 170; U.S. Music Corp., 164; Wood Manufacturing Co. (Los Angeles), 104. *See also* Buegeleisen & Jacobson; C. Bruno & Son; C.F. Martin & Co.; Dias, Augusto; Gibson Mandolin-Guitar Manufacturing Co.; Kamaka, Samuel K.; Keech, Alvin; Keech, Kelvin; Kumalae, Jonah; Lyon & Healy; Maccaferri, Mario; Nunes, Leonardo; Nunes, Manuel; Santo, Jose do Espirito

Ukulele Manufacturing Association of Hawaii, 128

'ukulele methods and songbooks: *15-Minute Guaranteed Ukulele Course for Hawaiian Ukulele and Banjo Ukulele,* 118; *A Practical Method for Self Instruction on the Ukulele,* 87, 174; *A Standard Method and Self-Instructor on the Ukulele,* 175; *Bickford Method for the Ukulele,* 178; *California-Hawaiian Souvenir Collection of Songs and Views,* 177; *Chords of the Taro-Patch Guitar,* 41–42, 45, 173; *Chords of the Ukulele,* 174; *Conservatory Method for Ukulele,* 118; *Correspondence Course for the Ukulele,* 175; *EZ Method for Ukulele and Ukulele Banjo,* 118; *Famous Ukulele Solos,* 176; *Instructions for Playing the Ukulele,* 174; *Jumpin' Jim's Ukulele Favorites,* 158; *Littig's New Practical Method for Hawaiian Ukulele, Banjuke, and Taro Patch Fiddle,* 118; *Method For the Ukulele (Hawaiian Guitar),* 85, 174; *Modern Method for the Ukulele,* 177; *Moyer's Up-to-Date Collection of Solos for the Ukulele,* 178; *National Self Teacher for Hawaiian Ukulele,* 175; *Original Method and Self-Instructor on the Ukulele,* 175; *Self Instruction Book for the Ukulele or the Banjo-Uke,* 174; *Self Instructive Course of Twenty-Five Lessons for the Ukulele and Taro-Patch Fiddle,* 177; *Self Instructor for the Ukulele and Taro-Patch Fiddle,* 87, 174, 175; *Simplified Chords of All the Major and Minor Keys for the Ukulele, Guitar, Steel Guitar,* 176; *Simplified Course in Ukulele Playing,* 135; *Songs for the Ukulele,* 177; *Songs from Aloha Land,* 176; *Stumpf's Ukulele-Method and Solo Book,* 177; *Symphonic Ukulele Arrangements,* 118; *The Albert Ukulele Hawaiian Guitar Complete Instructions,* 133, 177; *The American Way of Playing Ukulele Solos,* 121, 177; *The Bridal School for the Hawaiian Ukulele,* 176; *The New Kamiki Ukulele Method,* 176; *The Original Guckert's Chords for the Ukulele At Sight Without Notes or Teacher,* 176; *The Ukulele: A Hawaiian Guitar, and How to Play It,* 59–60, 173, 174; *The Ukulele and How It's Played,* 176; *The Ukulele and How To Play It,* 177; *The Ukulele As a Solo Instrument,* 175; *"Uke" Hughes Simplified Instructor for Ukulele,* 118; *Ukulele Instructor,* 176; *Ukulele Method,* 173, 175; *Ukulele Solos and Hawaiian Songs with Ukulele Accompaniment,* 175; *Universal Ukulele Instructor,* 175

'ukulele models: Aero Uke, 128; Artist's Model, 126; Art Moderne, 137; Belltone, 128; Diamond Head Finder, 146; Flamingo, 146; Fluke, 158; Happy Tunes, 146–147; Islander, 146; Le Domino, 137; Mauna Loa, 146; Niu Kani, 128; Red Head, 6, 128; Sparkle Plenty Ukette, 146; Ukahola, 128; Uke-A-Doodle, 142; Uke-a-Tune, 142; Ukulele O Hawaii, 87; Venetian, 128

"Ukelele Serenade," 115

Unwritten Literature of Hawaii, 41

V

Valley of the Moon, The, 68–69

Van Ronk, Dave, 149

vaudeville, 5, 76, 78–79, 80, 98, 102, 110, 122, 125, 137, 149

Vedder, Eddie, 163

Vekey, Aladair de, 113

Velez, Lupe, 116

Victor Talking Machine Co., 76, 83, 99, 121, 123

Victrola, 67, 113

Vierra, Frank J., 81

violin, 10, 25, 27, 28, 41, 50, 57, 58, 59, 65, 67, 71, 81, 108, 130, 135

Von Elts, Eleanor, 90

Von Tilzer, Harry, 98

Vos, Hubert, 45

W

Waialeale, Robert, 94

Waiwaiole, B., 76

Wall, Nichols Co., 59, 62

Ward family, 46

Washburn instruments, 128, 137. *See also* Lyon & Healy

Weaver, Phil Jr., 64

Wells, C. B., 47

Wells, George F., 28

Werbin, Stan, 164

Whalen, Harold, 110

Whitcomb, Ian, 154

White House, 81, 113

Whiteman, Paul, 121

Whitney, Henry, 22, 32

Wichman & Sons, 45

Wilde, William, 12

Wilder, James, 46

Wilder, Laura Ingalls, 96

Williams, Bert, 78

Williams, C. E., 39

Williams, Clarence, 125, 126

Williams, J. J., 46

Williams, Ukulele Bob, 125

Wilson, Charles, 65

Wilson, Jennie (Kini Kapahu), 93

Wilson, Johnny, 65, 80, 93, 94, 128

Wilson, Woodrow, 108, 113

Winter, Johnny, 149

Wodehouse, P. G., 117, 134

Works, Isabelle, 108

World War I, 98, 106, 108–110, 113, 117, 125

World War II, 140–141

Wright, Irene, 109

Y

Young, Neil, 149

Young Men's Christian Association, 61, 108, 135

YouTube, 160

Z

Zither, 59, 67